Thus says the Lord:

Do justice and righteousness,
and deliver from the hand of the oppressor
the one who has been robbed.

Jeremiah 22:3

DATE DUE

BRODART   Cat. No. 23-221

DO JUSTICE!

The Social Teaching
of the Canadian Catholic Bishops

(1945-1986)

Edited by E.F. Sheridan, S.J.

Jesuit Centre for Social Faith and Justice

Éditions Paulines &
The Jesuit Centre for Social Faith and Justice

Phototypesetting: *Les Éditions Paulines*

Cover: *Antoine Pépin*

ISBN 2-89039-113-2

Dépôt légal — 1er trimestre 1987
Bibliothèque nationale du Québec
Bibliothèque nationale du Canada

© 1987 **Éditions Paulines**
     250 boul. St-François nord
     Sherbrooke, Qc, J1E 2B9

Jesuit Centre for Social Faith and Justice
947 Queen Street East
Toronto, Ont. M4M 1J9

CONTENTS

THE DOCUMENTS

12　　　　　　　　　　　　　*Contents*

ACKNOWLEDGEMENTS

So many acknowledgements are due for so much help in the realization of this volume that I am forced to be brief in my expressions of appreciation. The brevity is no measure of the sincerity of my gratitude.

First I must thank the Canadian Conference of Catholic Bishops in the person of its then president, Most Reverend John M. Sherlock, D.D., for permission to reproduce the fifty-three documents of the collection emanating from the Conference, and for a subsidy towards the expenses of production.

I am grateful too, for many services and courtesies of the Conference staff, especially of its General Secretary, Father William F. Ryan, S.J., and of the Assistant General Secretary, Mr. Bernard Daly, of Miss Bonnie Brennan, Public Information Officer, of Miss Patricia McKale, Documentation Secretary, and of Mrs. Pierrette Warwick of the Social Affairs Office, all of whom were patient and generous in response to many requests, often hurried and importunate, for documents, information and advice.

I thank Archbishop E.W. Scott, former Primate of the Anglican Church in Canada and president of the Canadian Council of Churches, for permission to reproduce joint statements or briefs of the Canadian Council of Churches with the Canadian Conference of Catholic Bishops (Documents 20, 23, 42, 54, 57). The same thanks are extended to Ms. Jeanne Moffat, National Coordinator of World Development Education (Toronto), for permission to reproduce the statement *Development Demands Justice* (Doc. 34), prepared by the sponsors of Ten Days for World Development, an educational programme of the Anglican, Lutheran, Presbyterian, Roman Catholic and United Churches.

Closer to home, I am greatly indebted to Father Michael Czerny, S.J., director of the Jesuit Centre for Social Faith and Justice, who conceived the idea of the collection and persuaded me to undertake the work. If I have had occasion to regret his powers of persuasion, he never failed in encouragement and help throughout the unconscionably long time it took me to finish. Further thanks are due to all the staff of the Centre for unflagging help and cooperation, and especially to Miss Anne Goodwill for careful and cheerful secretarial assistance and fine literary and editorial judgment; also to Mrs. Susan Lussier for emergency help in completing the Index.

Substantial financial help has been forthcoming from the Ontario Council of the Knights of Columbus through the good offices of its State Deputy, Mr. A.L. DeWitte, from the Canadian Jesuits through their Provincial Superior, Father William Addley, S.J., and from the Loyola Jesuits' University Fund (Montreal).

I thank all the above who have helped me so much and the many not mentioned by name. May they all share richly in any good the book may do in the cause of social justice.

Edward F. Sheridan, S.J.

INTRODUCTION

The purpose of this collection is to make available to those interested in social justice advocacy in Canada a corpus of the significant, representative social statements of the Canadian Conference of Catholic Bishops (CCCB) since its inception in 1943.

No collection, even of the more important texts, has ever been made in English,[1] though partial collections exist in French,[2] in which language they were already fairly accessible in the pages of Catholic reviews.[3] Some have been printed by the CCCB in pamphlet form and are still available, while others are out of print. Yet others were circulated only in mimeograph form.

The apparently endemic socio-economic difficulties of Canada and the developing sophistication of the Bishops' social commentary on the same, the urgency of their "preferential option for the poor," their appeals for more effective relief of regional and general poverty, of marginalized and disadvantaged groups, their critique of government policies for control of inflation, for future industrial development, for preservation of the environment, for justice to native peoples, their call for alternative models of socio-economic organization, all give some importance to this literature and suggest that it should be more easily accessible. The very widespread interest expressed by widely diverse groups in the Bishops' *Ethical Reflections on the Economic Crisis*[4] (Document 55) attests that the bishops are addressing vital issues and have something to say. They have in fact been doing so for years and with developing insight, relevance and force. This volume would like to be a useful reference or source book where one might readily find what the Bishops have said on a given subject over the last forty years, and where a student might trace the development of their ethical and social teaching.[5]

The purpose of this introduction is to provide some information which will help the reader to appreciate the texts: on the sources from which the bishops have drawn their teaching, their perspective and claim to speak to such issues, on the nature of the Conference of Bishops, the authorship and authority of different documents.

The texts presented are in great majority from the national Canadian Conference of Catholic Bishops (CCCB), its General Assembly, its Permanent Council (earlier called the Administrative Board), one of its responsible officers or delegated representatives. Five are joint briefs or statements of leaders of Canadian churches (Documents 23, 34, 42, 54, 57), the President of the CCCB being a signatory. One (Doc. 20) is the Report of the Ecumenical Strategy Committee of the Canadian Council of Churches and of the CCCB, later approved by both bodies. There is none of an individual bishop in his own name, or of a regional conference.

Some information on the origin, nature and structures of the CCCB will be found in Part III of this Introduction.

I — SOURCES AND INSPIRATION OF THE SOCIAL TEACHING OF THE CANADIAN BISHOPS

Before turning to some general comment on the justice advocacy of the CCCB, it would be useful and perhaps necessary for those less familiar with the social teaching of the Roman Catholic Church, to offer some pages on the recent evolution of that teaching, which is the source from which the Canadian bishops have drawn with great fidelity. This will serve for better interpretation and understanding of that teaching, and more importantly for an appreciation of the perspective of the bishops and of the new sense of their role and that of the church in such secular concerns. Failure in such appreciation is the cause of puzzlement and even resentment among some of their own constituents.

1 — The Social Teaching of the Church[6]

The social teaching of the Church has its roots in Scripture, in the teaching of the Fathers and in the political and social philosophy of the medieval scholastics. Under the name of ''social teaching'', however, it is generally reckoned to date from Pope Leo XIII (d. 1903) and more exactly from his encyclical *On the Condition of the Worker* (1891), or *Rerum Novarum*, from its initial words in the official Latin.[7]

This social teaching is a body of ethical principles deriving from Christian doctrine on the nature, dignity and destiny of the human person and family. It embraces the whole spectrum of human rights and duties as these concern the organization of a socio-economic-political order, corresponding to that nature, dignity, destiny, aiming at the optimum development of society on every level and of each individual member.

In its earlier exposition from Leo XIII to Piux XII this teaching was couched in scholastic language and categories, part of a highly developed philosophy of natural law. Social obligations, like much of Catholic moral teaching, were presented as obligations of natural law, consequent on the divine sanction of that law, rather than as part of a Gospel morality integral to the Good News. The meticulously detailed moral theology of Catholic moralists of the seventeenth, eighteenth and early nineteenth centuries was the moral division of a general catechesis which insisted strenuously on a very accurate proclamation of doctrine, moral and dogmatic. The tendency had been greatly favoured by the long period of doctrinal controversy with reforming theologians of other churches.

Beginning with the encyclicals of John XXIII (d. 1963) and notably in the Pastoral Constitution of the Second Vatican Council, *The Church in the Modern World* (1965), social teaching is based more immediately on revelation and the Gospel, is more biblical in the derivation and even enunciation of its precepts and obligations, while retaining some of the intellectual discipline of its scholastic origins. The thesis might be stated briefly: this social teaching at first presented as a moral catechesis of rights and duties relative to the socio-economic order, begins to be appreciated and presented increasingly as evangelization, a proclamation of the Good News of Jesus Christ. We can begin to trace this development in the Second Vatican Council (1962-1965).

2 — The Second Vatican Council

Many catalysts affected the course of the Council. An important one was the searing experience of the World War II, not only the bombing, slaughter and holocaust, but the awful fact that Christian nations had engaged in such inhumanity on both sides and that the churches had been rather passive. It seemed that Christians and churches had been educated to a righteousness of personal and private life, but to eschew responsibility for cultural currents, social institutions, political activity.

This guilty reflection stimulated the European theological currents known as theology of hope and political theology. As early as 1946, the tremendously influential Swiss Calvinist theologian, Karl Barth, had penned the powerful lines (quoted in Doc. 14, n. 7) which have such a contemporary ring:

> The Church is witness to the fact that the Son of Man came to seek and to save the lost. And this implies that casting all false impartiality aside, the Church must concentrate first on the lower and lowest levels of society. The poor, the socially and economically weak and threatened, will always be the object of its primary and particular concern, and it will always insist on the State's special responsibility for these weaker members of society. That it will bestow its love on them — within the framework of its own task (as part of its service) is one thing and the most important thing: but it must not concentrate on this and neglect the other thing to which it is committed by its political responsibility: the effort to achieve such a fashioning of law as will make it impossible for "equality before the law" to become a cloak under which strong and weak, independent and dependent, rich and poor, employers and employees, in fact receive different treatment at its hands: the weak being unduly restricted, the strong unduly protected.[8]

Theology of hope is associated with the name of the Reformed theologian Jurgen Moltmann. The church is the community of those who indeed await the coming of the Kingdom, but fully accept a responsibility for its inchoative realization, not only in the end times but in this world as a beginning of the new heaven and new earth. Among Catholic theologians the German, John-Baptist Metz, is probably the best known of political theologians. The Church, not itself the Kingdom, is in and part of the world, accepting from its Lord responsibility, both religious and secular, for society, culture, and the socio-economic order.

The Second Vatican Council opened Oct. 4, 1962, after nearly three years of preparation. The theology of the draft decrees as prepared under the direction of the Preparatory Commission was distinctly conservative and came under fire in discussion of the decrees on *Liturgy, Sources of Revelation,* and *Unity of the Church.* The decree on the Church was severely criticized by a series of influential speakers, among others, Julius Cardinal Doepfner (Munich), Achille

Cardinal Liénard (Lille), and Joseph Cardinal Frings speaking in the name of all the German bishops. On Dec. 4, the charismatic Jozef Cardinal Suenens (Brussels) proposed a radical revision of the draft on an entirely new plan, pleading that the Council turn its attention not to juridical questions, but to the world of men and women, all, inside and outside the Church, to the anxieties and even agonies of a world evidently in the throes of profound change. Giovanni Cardinal Montini (Milan) rallied strongly to this position and it was widely believed that he was expressing the mind of John XXIII. He was supported by Giacomo Cardinal Lercaro (Bologna), Augustin Cardinal Bea (Sarasota) and others, evidently representing a majority conviction.

On Dec. 6, the Secretary General of the Council, Archbishop Pericle Felici, announced in the name of the Pope, that all the draft decrees would be revised by new Commissions and sent to the bishops for comment. A new committee to be struck by the Holy Father would organize the work of the commissions. Significantly, the names Doepfner, Liénard and Suenens eventually appeared on the roster of seven.

It came as no surprise then that the Suenens position was adopted enthusiastically by the new Pope, Paul VI (Giovanni Montini) in the Council's Second Session of the following September. A new area of discussion was opened, eventually giving rise to the *Pastoral Constitution on the Church in the Modern World (Gaudium et Spes*, from its opening words, and GS in Roman Catholic shorthand).[9]

The late Karl Rahner proposed an illuminating interpretation of the Council, pointing out that though the Church was always *called* to be a world church, "Vatican II was the first major official event in which the Church actualized itself precisely as a world church".[10] During the Council, in the long interaction of the more than two thousand five hundred bishops — among them a sizeable, representative minority from new churches of non-Christian cultures — the church came, inchoatively and confusedly, to a recognition of its call not only to spread the Gospel among all peoples, but to become at home in the diverse cultures of the world, to become differentiated culturally.

In apostolic times the Church broke out of the Judaic chrysalis into the vastly expanded Greco-Roman world culture.

> (Since that break-out) the concrete activity of the Church in relation to the non-European world was the activity... of an

export firm which exported a European religion as a commodity it did not want to change, but sent throughout the world together with the rest of the culture and civilization it considered superior.[11]

And Rahner adds something very suggestive for our purpose.

> In *Gaudium et Spes*... the Church as a totality becomes conscious of its responsibility for the dawning history of humanity... This responsibility, our political theology, can no longer be excluded from the consciousness of a world Church.[12]

The Church then, to be a world church and act as such, to evangelize the world, inculturated in every culture, must also be a *worldly* church, a church of *this* world, vitally concerned for terrestrial values, while reverencing always a primary mission to preach Jesus Christ the Saviour of the world. His salvation is first liberation from sin and death, but also from all the sad sequelae of sin, oppression, poverty, hunger, war, as far as these can be reduced by unflagging human effort.

There is a beginning of this new self-consciousness of the Church in the opening words of *Gaudium et Spes* which have been such a clarion in the Roman Church.

> The joys and the hopes, the griefs and the anxieties of the men and women of our age, especially of those who are poor or in any way afflicted, these too are the joys and the hopes, the griefs and the anxieties of the followers of Christ. (n.1)

In these words the Council recognized the Church's "responsibility for the dawning history of humanity".

The Council's Constitution, *The Church in the Modern World*, is the best of its documents in which to verify this new openness to the world, the source of a new social teaching and new appreciation of the promotion of justice as integral to evangelization. It is this stance of the supreme ecclesial authority, the Council, which prepared the ground for the extraordinarily rapid spread of the theology of liberation in the Church and its influence on the Canadian (as on so many other) bishops' pastoral teaching and action. It merits some closer scrutiny before surveying more briefly another half dozen Church documents in the nearly two decades since the close of the Second Vatican Council.

3 — The Pastoral Constitution, *The Church in the Modern World*

The Constitution begins with a firm expression of faith in the presence, purpose and activity of God in His world, and wishes to discern authentic "signs of the times", in order to meet and further that activity, the Kingdom or Reign of God. The earnest desire is to learn God's will not only from the revelation of Scripture, which is never forgotten, but from an unfolding revelation in the world. (nn. 3 ff.)

The first chapter is a very positive appreciation of the dignity of the human person, fashioned in the image of God (n. 12):

— dignity of mind to know truth and to acquire wisdom (n. 15);

— dignity of moral conscience, to discern the loving will of God (n. 16);

— dignity of liberty, freely to choose that will (n. 17);

— dignity of immortality, "an endless sharing in divine life" (n. 18).

In a more traditional treatment of rights in terms of natural law, the person has rights because he/she has duties, ultimately the divinely sanctioned duty to observe the natural law. The correlation is obviously not unconnected with human dignity, but more explicitly and immediately the Council grounds human rights in the person's dignity, widening the area and enhancing the sanctity of those rights (nn. 26-29, 31 f.). The Canadian bishops have made this the linch-pin of their most comprehensive statement on social justice when they wrote: "In Catholic social teaching, the value and dignity of the human person lies at the centre of an economy based on justice."[13] The U.S. bishops do the same in their 1986 *Statement on the Economy*, now in process of final edition.

Persons are called to live in community, God having willed that they constitute one family, interacting on different levels and in different communities but always in a spirit of brother/sisterhood, absolutely demanded by the Gospel of love (nn. 23-32). "The person is the only creature on earth which God willed for itself and cannot fully find itself except in the sincere gift of self to others" (n. 24).

The ethos of openness, of turning to the world in concern and desire to serve is very evident in Chapter Four.

> Modern men and women are in process of fuller personality development and of discovery and vindication of their rights...

> The Gospel announces and proclaims the freedom of the children of God and repudiates every bondage which ultimately comes from sin... By virtue of the Gospel committed to her, the Church proclaims the rights of man... She acknowledges and greatly esteems the dynamic movements of today by which those rights are everywhere fostered. (n. 41)

This denunciation of repression as sinful anticipates the teaching which would be explicit at the Medellin Conference of the Latin American bishops (1968).

The specific mission of the Church is not political, economic or social, but religious.

> Out of this religious mission however, comes a function, a light and energy, serving to structure and consolidate the human community according to divine law so that the Church can at need initiate activities on behalf of all people... especially the needy, such as works of mercy and similar undertakings. (n. 42)

The immediate (nn. 41 & 43) and wider contexts preclude the interpretation that *any* legitimate promotion of *justice* is excluded by "works of mercy".

Of the Second Part of the Constitution *(Problems of Special Urgency)*, the third chapter, *Socio-Economic Life* is particularly relevant. Noting the vast potential of contemporary technology, the Council observes:

> The fundamental purpose of this increased productivity must not be the mere multiplication of products, not profits nor domination, but the service of persons, all persons, the whole person, and when we say persons, we mean every man and woman, every group, of whatever race, everywhere. (n. 64)

Thus a distribution of goods and services best conducive to the common good, rather than the Gross National Product, is the primary measure of a just socio-economic order.[14]

The Council's explicit aim is greater equality. "If the demands of justice are to be satisfied, vigorous efforts must be made... to remove as quickly as possible the immense economic inequalities which now exist (n. 66)." Following a biblically based tradition, it taught that "God intended the earth and all it contains for the use of every human being", adding by way of amendment, giving it greater emphasis, "every human being *and people*" (n. 69). And the Fathers of the Council courageously drew the inevitable conclusion:

> According to their ability, let all individuals and governments undertake a genuine sharing of their goods, especially to provide individuals and nations with the means to help and develop themselves. *(ibid.)*

It is here that the Council makes its case for a New International Economic Order, recognizing that economic injustice — especially the grinding poverty to which more and more of the world's majority are doomed — inevitably breeds wars. An international community should see to

> ... regulating economic procedures throughout the world so that these operate according to justice... Adequate organizations should be established for harmonizing international trade... to compensate for the structural defects which result from excessive disproportion in the power of different nations. (n. 96, c)

But enough has been said to substantiate Rahner's thesis that the Council, most notably in *Gaudium et Spes*, turns to the world, the whole world, in genuine concern and endeavour to be a world church. Proclaiming "the dignity of the human person, strengthening the seams of human society... the Church believes she can contribute greatly towards making humanity and its history more human" (n. 40). And this is in virtue of her mission to preach the Gospel, a Gospel of love, and hence of justice which is minimal love. For "By no human law can the personal dignity and liberty of man be so aptly safeguarded as by the Gospel of Christ which has been entrusted to the Church" (n. 41). Let us see how this developing insight into the full content of evangelization in our world reaches greater clarity and explicit articulation, in post-Conciliar teaching.

4 — Post-Conciliar Development

The immense influence of the Council, especially of *Gaudium et Spes*, is best seen in the development of the Church's social teaching in the subsequent decades (1965-1985), a development accurately reflected in the statements of the CCCB.

The Development of Peoples

March of 1967 saw the appearance of Paul VI's encyclical *The Development of Peoples, (Populorum Progressio,* PP)[15] recognized by many government officials, economists and theologians, as surpassing in originality and force any papal teaching of the century. He wrote with a passion reminiscent of Leo XIII and Pius XI, but his was a much more developed analysis of the world situation and of economic structures. He called for

— a direct transfer of wealth from rich to poor nations, anticipating later calls of the United Nations Organization (nn. 44-55);

— changes in the structures of world trade to give more equitable return to developing lands for their primary products (nn. 56-61);

— effective participation of poor nations in the international community, free from economic and political pressures of powerful nations and of international capital (nn. 61-65);

— institutions and associations to prepare, coordinate and direct international collaboration until the establishment of an effective world authority in international trade and commerce (nn. 76-80);

— a world fund, provided from savings through reduction of armaments, to relieve the most destitute (nn. 51-55).

Paul VI has been dismissed as utopian, since development has not delivered on its promises of the sixties. In that he was no more fallible than many developmental economists, but had the vision to insist on international collaboration and solidarity in concern for justice and the poor. It was — and is — in this area that the cause of failure lies.

The Medellin Conference

The following year, 1968, saw the Medellin (Colombia) Conference of the Latin American bishops, which was to prove so influential in the universal church. Liberation theology, an indigenous political theology, was already dominant in the social thought of most progressive elements in that Church. Paul VI was present to open the Conference and praised the bishops for their action against structures of injustice.

The sixteen major documents of the Conference[16] had influence far beyond the almost 300 million Latin American Catholics — and not least in Canada. Since 1960 there had been a national program of pastoral action and help in Latin America by the Canadian church with the result that thousands of Canadian bishops, priests, religious and laity visited Latin America and became engaged in pastoral and social work in the ensuing years.

Medellin marked something of a watershed in the Church's social teaching. Deductive rather than empirical in ethos, this teaching had always envisaged economic society as essentially organic, a natural collaboration of labour and capital to mutual benefit and for the common good. Along with a Christian aversion to violence, this induced an extreme reluctance, almost incapacity to recognize that in many places labour and capital stood in a fierce adversarial relationship, in which capital exercised a cruel oppression through control of government and military. The Latin American bishops finally recognized that the class struggle was a reality, not to be fomented for the dictatorship of the proletariat, but a struggle for *justice*; not to be waged in hate or by violence save in extreme cases (only too frequent), but a *legitimate* struggle, in which the church had often been co-opted to the side of power and wealth. The Conference felt challenged to profess its preferential option for the poor. To their glory they did so.

Two key ideas issued from the Conference:

— *liberation* instead of development, liberation from oppressors, domestic and foreign;

— *participation*, in power, government, opportunity for individuals, groups, peoples, to choose their own way to a modest sufficiency, free from domestic exploitation or the dominance of international capital.

Clear evidences of Medellin and of the liberation theology which burgeoned there can be discerned in the statements of the Canadian Bishops (cf. Doc. 20, 21, 24; especially in 26-30; 34, 38, 40, 42, 46, 48, 51).

A Call to Action

The year 1971 was prolific in Catholic social teaching. First came Paul VI's Apostolic Letter to Maurice Cardinal Roy of Canada, President of the Pontifical Commission Justice and Peace, *A Call to Action* (*Octogesima Adveniens*, OA).[17]

Medellin had not used the phrase "preferential option for the poor" though the reality was there, but Paul VI recognized that "the Gospel instructs us in the preferential respect due to the poor" (n. 23).

> In the social sphere the Church has always wished to assume a double function: *first* to enlighten minds in order to discover truth and find the right path to follow... *secondly* to take part in action and to spread... the energies of the Gospel... It is not enough to recall principles, point to crying injustices, utter prophetic denunciations. These lack weight unless accompanied by... effective action. (n. 48)

In a momentous innovation Paul VI distinguished different meanings of Marxism:

— for some it is the active promotion of violent class struggle for the dictatorship of the proletariat;

— for others, the collective exercise of political and economic power by a single party;

— for others, a socialist ideology based on historical materialism denying all transcendence.

As any of these it is of course incompatible with Christianity. Marxism however, also provides a method of examining social and political reality, linking theoretical knowledge and the practice of socio-political transformation. As such, though to be used with caution, it can be useful (n. 33).

> Socialism... assumes different faces in different continents and cultures, though it drew or draws its inspiration from ideologies incompatible with faith. Careful judgement is called for... To guide concrete choices, distinctions must be made between the various levels of expression of socialism, a generous aspiration, a quest for a more just society,... an ideology which claims to give a complete and self-sufficient picture of man... This insight will enable Christians to see the degree of commitment possible along these lines, while safeguarding the values, especially of liberty, responsibility and openness to the spiritual, which guarantee integral human development. (n. 31)

This opens a way for prudent collaboration with socialist parties or movements whose socio-economic programs do not differ substantially from a Christian program for social justice.[18] Some national conferences of bishops and Christian Democratic parties have not been unaware of this opening to the left.

There is an interesting paragraph in this letter which must have come as a surprise to those who had stereotyped Paul VI as a very cautious conservative. He remarks that the dominant ideologies, bureaucratic socialism, technocratic capitalism and authoritarian democracy (in national security states) were all experiencing incapacity to find their way to a socio-economic order of justice and sufficiency for all. He notes a rebirth of utopias — not of the fantastic variety such as More's *Utopia* or Campanella's *City of the Sun* — but the quest for alternative organizations of an economy, neither capitalist nor socialist according to present models, but rather, in his words:

> (the effort) of forward looking imagination to perceive in the present the disregarded possibility hidden within it, and to direct itself towards a fresh future, sustaining social dynamism by the confidence it gives to the inventive powers of the human mind and heart. (37)

The Canadian bishops would follow this lead in their frequent appeals since the early 70's, for openness to alternatives other than our contemporary liberal capitalism or a soulless classical socialism.

Justice in the World

That same year of 1971 the Third International Synod of Bishops issued its statement, *Justice in the World*.[19] Paul VI had invited the bishops, one hundred and seventy representing all the episcopal conferences, for advice on how to serve universal social justice. They asked and received permission to make their own statement, which was to prove very influential throughout the Church.

Its First Part was a radical criticism of development as not achieving justice, but maintaining a deteriorating difference between rich and poor nations and between rich and poor within nations. The Second Part gave a brief biblical theology of the Gospel Message and of the Mission of the Church, very creditable in view of the pressures of time. The Third treated the Church's praxis and witness to justice, its education to the same, with some practical recommendations. The Canadian delegation of bishops was prominent in the deliberations (cf. Doc. 27, 28, 29), following the directives of the General Assembly (Doc. 26), so that the statement was widely publicized in Canada.

Two passages are particularly to be remarked:

> Unless the Christian message of love and justice shows its effectiveness through action on behalf of justice, it will only with difficulty gain credibility with the men and women of our times. (P. II, n. 35)

But this is emphatically not to be thought a public relations ploy to make the Gospel or Church more "relevant". The perspective of the Synod was much different. It had fully accepted the position that as religious and therefore also moral leaders, standing in the Gospel tradition, and particularly in a world in which day after day, half of humanity went to sleep hungry, indefatigable promotion of justice was part of their witness and evangelizing office.

> Action on behalf of justice and participation in the transformation of the world fully appear to us as a *constitutive dimension* of the preaching of the Gospel, or — in other words — of the church's mission for the redemption of the human race and its liberation from every oppressive situation. (*Introduction* n. 6)

"Constitutive dimension" occasioned no difficulty in the Synod, but became the subject of theological debate later.

This position would seem to be a confirmation of Rahner's interpretation of Vatican II (cf. above) and of its corollary that in the contemporary world, because of its shocking instances of social injustice and a greatly heightened sensitivity to the same, evangelization, the preaching of the Gospel, must include, and as an *intrinsic* element, proclamation of and action for justice. Increasingly throughout the 70's the Catholic bishops, together with other religious leaders in Canada would reaffirm that their advocacy of social justice was part of their evangelizing office, of their preaching of the Gospel of justice and love.

Evangelization in the Modern World

The operational theology of the Canadian bishops received strong support in Paul VI's apostolic exhortation *Evangelization in the Modern World*, (*Evangelii Nuntiandi*, EN, 1975).[20]

In Catholic tradition of recent centuries, evangelization was essentially a proclamation of the Gospel, of the faith and of the Church's interpretation of the same. The witness of the evangelist or evangelizing community, their sanctity, charity, zeal, was thought something extrinsic to evangelization, though obviously important — something of a pre-evangelization or condition of its efficacy. Hence the dissatisfaction of some theologians with the 1971 Synod's designation of action on behalf of justice as "a constitutive dimension of the proclamation of the Gospel".[21] Pope Paul VI had been reported to have reservations about liberation as proclaimed at Medellin, but he had had time to clarify his own theological thinking and to refine his vocabulary. He rejected the criticism that witness and action for justice are extrinsic to evangelization.

His letter early moves into a biblical-theological account of the *liberating* mission of Jesus Christ, proclaiming liberation from everything which oppresses people, not only spiritually but politically, socially, economically, as part of the Good News, and hence of evangelization (nn. 6, 9, 28, 29). Paul VI recalls with sympathy the passionate language of many Third World bishops in the Synod of 1974 (on evangelization), describing the struggles of their peoples

> ... to overcome everything which condemns them to remain on the margin of life: famine, chronic disease, illiteracy, poverty, injustices in international relations, especially in commercial exchanges, situations of economic and cultural colonialism sometimes as cruel as the old political colonialism. (n. 30)

He continued:

> The church has the duty to proclaim the liberation of millions of human beings, many of them her own children — the duty of assisting at the birth of this liberation, of giving witness to it, of ensuring that it is complete. This is not foreign to evangelization. (*ibid.*, cf. nn. 31, 32)

The Puebla Conference

The third conference of the whole Latin American episcopate was held in Puebla, Mexico, in 1979. The socio-economic and political situations had deteriorated, with development failing to benefit the vast majority of the population and more repressive national security governments in place in most countries. In that Church there had been some reaction against the Medellin positions and the secretariat of its episcopal conference had become notably more conservative. Its preparatory Consultation Document occasioned an unprecedented continent-wide debate and was found wanting. In response to many demands, a new commission of bishops was appointed under the chairmanship of the moderate and greatly respected Cardinal Lorscheider, President of the Conference, which prepared a much improved Working Document.

The resulting Puebla Document (PD)[22] was a firm endorsement of Medellin, incisive in its social criticism and with even stronger "preferential option for the poor" (in those terms). In its section on Evangelization, the bishops stated:

> The Church's proper role is one of teaching, denouncing, and serving in the interests of communion and participation. Faced with the situation of (social) sin, the Church has the duty to engage in denunciation, objective, courageous and evangelical... Enunciating the basic rights of the human person today and in the future is an indispensable part of the Church's evangelizing mission. (PD 1268-70)

The reason is that the proclamation of a dynamic process of integral liberation "belongs to the very core of an evangelization seeking the authentic realization of the human person" (PD 480).

John Paul II

It has been questioned if John Paul II shared the view of evangelization enunciated in *Justice in the World*, affirmed by Paul VI and at Puebla. Pope for only three months, John Paul II was at Puebla and made his position clear in his opening address to the Conference. He warned — as had Paul VI (EN, n. 32) — against any reductionism equating evangelization to a social programme. Nonetheless

> If the Church is involved in defending or promoting human dignity, it does so in accordance with its mission... She has learned that an indispensable part of her evangelizing mission is made up of works on behalf of justice and human promotion.[23]

And this is no opportunism but the prompting of "an authentically evangelical commitment to those most in need."[24]

The following year, 1980, he made a lengthy visit to Brazil, "by far the most significant of the various pastoral visits made by John Paul II."[25] Having praised Puebla's option for the poor to a large body of bishops from the continental Conference, he told the Brazilian bishops:

> You know that the preferential option for the poor... is not an invitation to exclusivism,... but a call to special solidarity with the humble and weak, the suffering and weeping, humiliated and left on the fringes of life and society, in order to help them realize ever more fully their own dignity as human persons and sons of God.[26]

Time and again he insisted on the specific right of workers to form unions and defend their rights; of landless farm labourers to land and just agricultural legislation, all towards indispensable transformation of the structures of economic life, and always in the interests of the common good, of persons. He was "evidently intent on allaying any doubts about his support of those who fight for human and political rights".[27] He encouraged the bishops and clergy in this sense, praising their "image of poverty and simplicity, of closeness to your people, of integration in their life and problems — the image of bishops deeply evangelical".[28]

John Paul II's letter *On Human Work* (*Laborem Exercens*, LE, 1981) is not passionate but rather didactic, a profound analysis of human work in the contemporary industrial world. The roots are in earlier letters, *The Redeemer of Humankind* (*Redemptor Hominis*, RH, 1979) and *Rich in Mercy* (*Dives in Misericordia*, DM, 1980)[29] which expound his Christian anthropology. From the former:

> The Church considers an essential, unbreakably united element of her mission this solicitude for men and women, for their humanity, for the future of the human family on earth and therefore also for the course set for the whole of development and progress. (RH, n. 15)

"Essential, unbreakably united element" is almost stronger than "constitutive dimension".

In *On Human Work* he advocates new movements of solidarity of, with and for workers, wherever called for by degradation of the dignity of work, exploitation of workers, growing poverty and hunger. "The Church is firmly committed to this cause, for she considers it her mission, her service, a proof of her fidelity to Christ, so that she can truly be 'the Church of the poor'." (LE, n. 8) In the face of concrete language of this kind, debate about whether the proclamation of liberation and the promotion of justice is constitutive dimension, integral part or essential element of evangelization becomes tedious. It is proposed by the Church as a duty Christ left to the Church and to every Christian who would be a living member of that Church.

I have stressed the development and evolution of this ecclesial conviction that such advocacy of justice is a Gospel call peculiarly important in our day and part of the Canadian bishops' teaching office, since they have been questioned, "Tell us by what authority you do these things." (Lk 20:2)

For many religion has become so privatized, so exclusively a matter between the individual and God, that the church should concern itself with public worship, limiting its moral catechesis at most to an individualistic ethics, as though the areas of public policy, of the common good, of the economy, politics and justice were beyond the judgement of the Gospel or the concern of church leaders to whom many still look for counsel drawn from the inexhaustible source of scripture.

But together with other Canadian church leaders the Catholic bishops have stated their "authority to do these things":

> We stand in the biblical tradition of the prophets where to know God is to seek justice for the poor and the oppressed. (Jr 22:16)... The church cannot remain silent on the political and social issues of the day if it is to claim obedience to Christ and His message of "good news to the poor" (Lk 4:18).

II — THE SOCIAL TEACHING OF THE CANADIAN BISHOPS

1. Antecedent to the Conference

From the appearance of Leo XIII's encyclical *On the Condition of the Worker* (1981), the Church in Canada endeavoured to spread pontifical social teaching in various ways. The *École sociale populaire* was founded in Montréal in 1911, to publicize papal teaching and to educate an elite of workers and others. The *Semaines Sociales du Canada*, annual conferences on social teaching (modeled on the same in France), were inaugurated in 1920 by Father Joseph Papin Archambault, S.J., and continued to a final 38th session in 1962. Catholic trade unions appeared in Quebec in the early decades of the century leading to the formation of the Canadian Catholic Federation of Labour, active for a program of social reform along the lines of Catholic social teaching, until 1960 when it severed connection with the Church.

The early history of social action in Canada by the English-speaking Roman Catholic Church remains to be researched and written. There was widespread but rather uncoordinated activity in the late twenties, principally in the maritime provinces but progressing and spreading to Vancouver.

Pioneering in English-speaking Canada was the Antigonish Movement, sponsored in 1928 by the Extension Department of St. Francis Xavier University, under its director Father Moses M. Coady, backed by Father J.J. Tompkins as theoretician and A.B. Macdonald as organizer. Inspired by Catholic social teaching this movement promoted improvement in chronically depressed eastern Nova Scotia through adult education and self-help, especially in cooperative endeavours, credit unions, home-building, marketing co-ops for fish and farm produce. The so-called Antigonish Movement became internationally known as a model of self-help education, studied and applied in many Third World countries.

The Extension Department of St. Dunstan's College, Charlotte-town, followed the lead of St. Francis Xavier University in organizing some 1500 study groups from 1935 to 1949, enrolling more than 10,000 members and leading to the formation of more than fifty credit unions, twenty consumer cooperatives and as many farm produce cooperatives.

Throughout the period between the wars, pastoral, but also social concern for Catholic immigrants remained a major preoccupation of the bishops and was the focus of an incipient national network sponsored by the hierarchy, providing a precious introduction of clergy and church workers to the social problems of the day.

The minutes of the first meeting of the Catholic Conference after the approval of the Holy See (1948) record the wish, that the directors of the Social Action Department report on what was being done and formulate a practical programme to be submitted to the commission on Social Action. "These two functions apply to social action generally and to immigration particularly as a first and pressing work." Coadjutor Archbishop Gerald Murray, C.Ss.R. of Winnipeg urged the importance of the work being done for immigrant farmers by Father Warnke, O.M.I., and the Assembly voted him a stipend equal to that of the directors of the Social Action Department.

Notwithstanding this emphasis, the newly formed Department

of Social Action, in its first report to the Conference (1949), expressed
its aim of

> ... leading Catholics to a knowledge of social problems, the
> principles neglected and in need of restatement, the aims and
> techniques of movements engaged in that work and the in-
> spiration of group action in solving the social problem.

> ... To contribute to the development of social institutions and
> relations that are truly Christian in character, was undoubtedly
> the hope of the Canadian Hierarchy as it set up the Depart-
> ment.''

Both Conference and Department have always maintained a deep
interest in immigration, the problems of migrants, immigrants and
refugees (cf. Doc. 2, 8, 36, 41, 42) while extending their interest and
activity to the whole area of human rights and social justice.

On appointment as a director of the Department in 1948, Father
F.A. Marrocco (later bishop, and President of the Social Affairs Commission) began to lecture on Social Action in St. Patrick's College
of the Oblate Fathers in Ottawa. This led to the foundation in 1951,
of the Institute of Social Action in St. Patrick's College, under the
direction of Father L.K. Poupore, O.M.I. Its purpose was the dis-
semination of Catholic social teaching and its application to contemporary social problems, training in leadership for reform of the social
order and the initiation of practical action in that sense. The Institute was strongly supported by the Ottawa Council of the Knights
of Columbus and functioned into the sixties, active in the promotion of housing cooperatives, offering courses in organization and
administration of housing cooperatives — by 1965 750 houses had
been built — credit and labour unions.

These and similar initiatives in other cities, diocesan social action
and immigration offices, labour schools and social institutes in
Catholic colleges or universities, parochial study and action groups,
had considerable influence in raising the social awareness of laity
and clergy. A numerous scattering of qualified personnel was available to the CCCB when it undertook a more active propagation of
the Church's social teaching after World War II and especially after
the Second Vatican Council.

2. Activity of the Conference

In 1966 the francophone bishops of the Social Affairs Commission recruited a group of lay leaders and priests to collaborate with them on social questions under the title of *Conseil national de l'action sociale* (CNAS). They met every few months from the end of 1966 to June 1972, the important years following the Second Vatican Council and during the rapid transformation of the ecclesiastical and political scene in Quebec.[30] Collaboration of the Commission with the anglophone laity was promoted in a less structured way by successive directors of the Social Affairs Department, who developed ties with many individuals and groups, both lay and clerical, in diocesan social action offices, Catholic educational institutions, as well as with government agencies and citizens' groups.

This wider contact developed rapidly, and took on a strong ecumenical character in the sixties and seventies. In 1964-65 Fathers John T. Shea and William F. Ryan S.J., Directors of the Social Action Department, began meeting with their opposite numbers from other confessional offices, forming the National Committee on Church and Industrial Society. In 1968 the Canadian Council of Churches and the CCCB appointed a Strategy Committee with the mandate to propose "a practical strategy of unified action for all Christian Churches in their present program of social action, in particular concerning poverty, and their future programs which might evolve in an ecumenical spirit."[31] The report, submitted in May, 1969, was approved by both bodies. (Doc. 20)

This ecumenical initiative led to increasing communication and collaboration with the Canadian Council of Churches and its members, with many confessional and non-confessional organizations and groups, pursuing similar goals.[32] The fruit of this interaction may be seen in six ecumenical briefs and statements included in this collection (Doc. 20, 23, 34, 42, 54, 57).

3. Ethos and Content

The scope of the bishops' social teaching is as wide as the field of human rights: social, economic, political and cultural rights of individuals and of the family, of particular groups, regions, countries and groups of countries (the Third World).

In the period from the foundation of the Conference in 1943 to the close of the Second Vatican Council in 1965 (covering the publication of Documents 1-13 of the collection), the bishops note accurately enough a variety of social problems, but offer little in the way of analysis (cf. Doc. 1, 3, 6, 12). Suggestions are of the order of common sense: sobriety and restraint, practice of good citizenship, reverence for spiritual values, recourse to the social teaching of the Church, collaboration of management and labour, of public authorities and intermediate organizations for the amicable solution of problems (cf. Doc. 1, 3, 4, 5, 7, 11). Save for passing reference to the international scene, concern is limited to the Canadian horizon. The tone is pastoral, exhortatory, moralizing. These documents (without deprecating or depreciating such teaching) represent religious rather than social discourse.

The close of the Second Vatican Council and promulgation of its decrees occasioned a notable increase in the social justice statements of the bishops. This theme, however, is the subject of less than half of their teaching, which covers the whole range of pastoral concerns, liturgy, worship and prayer; marriage, the family and divorce; abortion, capital punishment, pornography and prostitution and much else. In this collection illustrating the social teaching of the Canadian bishops, in the manner of most writing on the subject,[33] the area is limited to their teaching on the rights and duties of individuals, groups and corporate bodies, relative to a just organization of the socio-political order. Some subjects which in a wider understanding could readily fall under the title of social teaching, e.g., education, capital punishment, penal and correctional legislation and practice, abortion, divorce, marital morality, etc. are omitted.

Forty-six of the fifty-nine documents assembled here are from this period and there is a striking maturation in content and approach. The bishops had been interacting over a period of three years with the more than twenty-five hundred bishops of the Council and the hundreds of theologians and experts in various fields who attended as consultants. This was a unique educational experience. On returning home they were not slow to assume something of a new role in their endeavour to lead the Canadian Church on the path traced by the Council.

One remarks immediately a heightened awareness of the universality of the church and of the Canadian church's responsibility for its well-being everywhere, a well-being not only religious but secular, in the sense developed above (I).

1. Some dozen documents are concerned wholly or in part with

the *general* destination and distribution of material goods, socio-economic and cultural development, problems of world poverty, disease, illiteracy. (Doc. 13, 17, 26-29, 34-36, 42, 45, 51)

2. Fourteen address respect for human rights throughout the world. (Doc. 19, 25-29, 30, 32, 40, 42, 47, 48, 50, 58)

3. The anomaly of widespread and continuing poverty in a rich Canada, especially in certain regions and among certain minorities, is the subject of twelve statements, which characterize the disparity of incomes in Canada as a moral evil. (Doc. 14, 16, 18, 20, 23, 31, 33, 35, 36, 38, 42, 43)

4. Eight statements note with feeling the marginalization of so many, practically without voice in the direction of their lives, politically or economically, their lack of participation in their societies, abroad and in Canada. (Doc. 20, 21, 22, 24, 26-29)

5. Irresponsible stewardship of the earth's resources is castigated in many statements, notably in Doc. 40 and 50.

More important than these perceptions of malfunction and inequity in the social order, national and international, is the growing insight that it is the dominant ideology and the economic mechanisms of the Canadian and world orders which create and maintain the injustice under which a majority of mankind labours. (cf. among others, Doc. 23; 24, nn. 4-9; 31; 34; 35, nn. 3, 9, 18f; 38; 40; 42; 44; 46; 49, nn. 7-14; 55; 56) More and more in one form or another, the bishops' critique of the socio-economic order in Canada prompts them to question its legitimacy. Is this the kind of country Canadians wish it to be? Their statements are often action-oriented, calling for organization and concerted effort for reform, urging formation of, or engagement in citizens' groups for change. (cf. Doc. 20, 21, 26-30, 31, 34, 36, 42, 44-46) There was as well the disquieting realization that in its world trading activity as also in international politico-economic fora, Canada shared in the responsibility for the deteriorating First World/Third World or North/South imbalance. (cf. Doc. 34, I-II; 42, nn. 13-18; 47; 53, nn. 2.6, 3.5; 54, nn. 20-28; 57, nn. 24-31; 37-40).

The problem of world peace had been mentioned frequently in relation to world hunger and the violation of human rights, since the colossal expenditure on arms exhausts the budgets of developing nations and prevents the First World from giving greater and more effective aid. It is only in 1981, however, that the bishops consecrate a statement to that subject (Doc. 52). Then, alone or with other church leaders, they follow this up with three lengthy briefs, demonstrating well-informed grasp of problematic situations and a very respectable analysis. (Doc. 53, 54, 57)

Two statements on the responsibilities of investors, particularly in Third World enterprises, show a similar appreciation of social facts and structures, of the movement of capital to scenes of easy exploitation of workers, and of permissive environmental legislation. (Doc. 47, 48)

This concern for justice beyond Canada's borders does not blind them to the realities within the national horizon. The seventies had seen a considerable improvement in social services, the "safety net" available to the poor and disadvantaged in Canada, but the deepening recession of the early eighties and the means adopted by governments to fight inflation as "enemy number one", threatened to erase many of the gains. In two statements of 1980 and 1982, *Unemployment: The Human Costs* and *Ethical Reflections on the Economic Crisis*, the bishops returned to this topic of unemployment, its tragic consequences for so large a portion of our population, not least the young, the injustice and apparent inefficacy of the monetarist remedies legislated to fight inflation and speed recovery. (Doc. 49 and 55)

No statement of the Conference before or since generated the interest, the harsh criticism or strong approval, derision or defense, occasioned by *Ethical Reflections* (Doc. 55), and in so many circles of the national life: business, banking, the universities, political parties, management, labour, citizens' groups, the churches and all the national news media. It was evident that the bishops had spoken to the nation and in a sense which provoked many, but elicited the strong support of a numerous and varied constituency. They were *not* voices crying in the wilderness. Echoes and repercussions in the form of public debates, hearings, panel discussions, popular meetings, continued for months. It is difficult to recall any challenge to government, to the wisdom of the establishment and the national conscience which so effectively proclaimed the normative value of ethics, of right and justice, in public affairs and economic policy. The bishops had realized their desire "for public debate about economic visions and industrial strategies, involving choices about values and priorities for the future direction of this country" (Doc. 55, n. 26).

In the following year they seized the favorable occasion of continuing interest to make their submission to the Macdonald Commission (Doc. 56). This evidences an acquired experience and confidence and its three parts constitute the most comprehensive statement of the social teaching of the Conference:

— *Perspective* (of the bishops) — "not technical experts in economic matters... but moral teachers";

— *Problem* — "some of the major problems to be faced concerning the future of Canada's socio-economic order";

— *Challenge* — the fundamental one involving "a combination of moral vision and political will".

Such in summary are the complex and massive national and international problems which preoccupy the bishops after the Vatican II immersion course in their ecclesial role as leaders of a national church in a world church, a world become a global village, of rising expectations, of newly appreciated human rights and dignity, but of increasing hunger, oppression and violence. What are the ethical principles in whose light the bishops invite their co-religionists and all of good will to reflect on our social order?

4. Basic Ethical Principles

The ethical and ultimately Gospel principles basic to the bishops' teaching might be stated thus:

1. *The Primacy of Persons*

Persons are not for the service and development of the economy, a nation's or the world's: the socio-economic order is to serve persons. That order must be subordinated and directed to the common good, ultimately by legitimate authority, local, national and eventually international, with reverence for the principle of subsidiarity through intermediate bodies and with respect for the dignity of every individual. Human finality is not limited to the round of production-consumption. Economic laws are not absolutes but empirical statements of what happens if persons act thus or so. Useful in the choice of means, they cannot be allowed to dictate moral goals, the goals of persons or of their societies. Canadian Church leaders, the CCCB among them, subscribed to this absolutely fundamental truth quoting Prime Minister Pierre Trudeau's query to the Canadian people (1971):

> Why... do western governments continue to worship at the temple of the Gross National Product?... Shouldn't we be replacing our reliance on GNP with a more revealing figure — a new statistic which might be called "Net Human Benefit"? (Doc. 34, II)

2. *The Primacy of Work*

Because of their human dignity, workers must remain the responsible subjects or masters of their activity, which can never be equated to a tool of production or to so much mechanical or marketable energy. Work is human as the worker is human, and so finds a place in the moral order. The rights of workers have priority over the maximization of profits, over growth of capital or the introduction of new technology to that end. It is through work that workers provide for personal, family and other community needs, enter into social relationships and contribute to the common good; perfect themselves by such activity, and, in theological perspective, become partners with God in bringing creation to perfection. For this reason individuals, groups and citizenry must retain some real and reasonable control over the socio-economic order, exercising a disciplined freedom at various levels. It is to favour such freedom and responsibility that the bishops have encouraged worker-participation in management, shared ownership, profit-sharing, cooperatives of all kinds, and small to medium enterprises as against great conglomerates.

3. *The Primacy of the Common Destination of the World's Goods*

They reiterate with vigour the teaching of the Church, deriving from scripture and the Judaic tradition, that all goods and riches of the earth are, by primary destination, the patrimony of the whole human family. Private ownership, which is strongly defended, is but a means to the better stewardship of such goods, their development and distribution. Ownership and use are subordinate to this prior finality. This principle strikes radically at the foundation of economic liberalism in national economies and at the current practice of international trade, in which north exploits south, the rich and powerful, the poor and the weak.

It is on this divine destination of the wealth of the earth that the bishops base their call to responsible stewardship. No generation has the right contemptuously to poison the environment and exhaust its resources, violating the rights of future generations.

In the last two decades, particularly in the seventies as the "war on poverty" in Canada gained momentum, one remarks a change in tone in the bishops' statements. A veteran commentator of Canadian Catholic social teaching [34] notes the contrast between earlier messages (prior to the Second Vatican Council), whose tone was "pacifique et paternel", with those which followed, "beaucoup plus vigoureux, au point de se faire dans les dernières années... franchement contestataires de l'ordre établi". The bishops accept that popular citizens' groups, in opposition to "intolerable conditions which depersonalize and alienate, might become a counter-power" and see that this can be a form of the hunger and thirst after justice of which the Gospel speaks. (Doc. 21, nn. 12 f.)

Probing questions and blunt challenges are posed to Catholic constituents, to the country at large and to government.

> The insensitive conscience of the rich is perhaps the greatest evil of our times... This requires a spiritual revolution... a conversion freeing us from our sordid egoism. (Doc. 13, n. 11)

The word "struggle" is increasingly frequent.

> If we do not play our part in these struggles to correct conditions that contribute to poverty in Canada, we neglect our basic Christian duty to love God and our neighbour effectively. (Doc. 16, n. 11)
>
> Christian life is a lie if it has no part in the anguish of those who suffer from unemployment, discrimination, poverty,... no part in the aspirations of those who cherish hope for the realization of a just society. (Doc. 18, n. 1, and cf. nn. 4, 6)
>
> We have called this persisting state (of poverty and inequality) a "social sin"... underlining the finding of the Special Senate Committee on Poverty that "our society and economy not only tolerate poverty but also create, sustain and even aggravate it." (Doc. 33, n. 7)

With other church leaders, the bishops queried the Prime Minister and Cabinet:

> We must ask whether, as government leaders, you hear the voices of the poor as often and as effectively as you hear the voices of the rich. (Doc. 42, n. 28)

Some have thought the tone and passion of their advocacy occasionally strident. There is no doubt that they write with force and conviction, and perhaps bothered by some sense of frustration. As has been remarked,[35] to combine the roles of biblical prophet, ethical teacher and constructive socio-economic critic is difficult, and particularly so if attempted in the same discourse. The prophet is almost necessarily denunciatory, stressing evils which mark the times and social order, the sins of individuals or of groups, calling to conversion. Passion is necessary. The ethical teacher or social critic must be analytic, rational, appealing to intellect rather than heart. It is easy to fall between two stools.

That popes and bishops speak in the names of their churches, universal, national or local, increases the delicacy of their position. Every prophet who hopes to be heard must live the conversion preached, in this instance to frugality, solidarity with the poor, self-sacrificing devotion to their interests, risking the disfavour of the establishment — all this under penalty of futility. The position of the ecclesiastical prophet is even more delicate. Unless the church or church people are seen to be living the prophetic message, or at least clearly striving to live it, and in action which has something of a corporate character, credibility suffers. It is not easy however to lead a massive institution to such conversion.

An apparently related criticism of the efficacy of Catholic (as of other confessional) social teaching is the suspicious query, "But do the bishops speak for the people in the pews?" A Catholic sociologist who has studied the churches' social teaching in Canada voices a regretful negative.

> The social justice concerns of the churches are not wholeheartedly supported by the vast majority of the church membership. And so it is relatively easy for politicians and business leaders to reject the demands of the churches for social justice, since they know that the church leaders and interchurch agencies do not fully represent the general membership of their churches.
> ....
> To date they (social justice statements) have had relatively little success in making Canada a "just society".[36]

The basis of such a judgement is not exposed. However, biennial elections in the United Church of Canada have continued to return very socially progressive Moderators and other officers to the national administration. Some conservative reactions in other churches have made little or no headway against strong advocacy for social justice.

"The Church has feet of lead" is a Roman commonplace, cited almost complacently, and large established religious bodies are generally traditional and slow to change. How would one judge success in such ecclesial promotion of justice, an area of Christian duty which had not been generally stressed in Canadian churches before 1970 and wherein many pastors and preachers felt and feel uncomfortable and hardly competent? If over a period of years fifty percent of regular church-goers were influenced in the sense of greater compassion and sensitivity to justice, would that not be a satisfactory success? Is it achieved? Who can say? Does exhortation to sobriety, truthfulness, sincerity, marital morality, or to all the lovely litany of virtues proposed by Paul to the Galatians (5:22) fare much better?

The proliferation of confessional and non-confessional organizations for justice in Canada and abroad is a striking feature of Canadian life in the last two decades. The collaboration between confessional and purely secular groups is close and there is considerable overlap of membership. Has the justice advocacy of the churches been without effect in this? There is some evidence that both government and business have not been unaffected by the positions the churches have adopted.

Certainly statements will not make Canada a just society. There must be organized effort and pressure by many groups working patiently and perseveringly to educate and influence both governments and the electorate. Vigorous advocacy of justice by the churches legitimates such organization and promotion, supports and encourages dedicated workers, protects them from attack, keeps progressive programmes in place and helps to solicit and provide the funds which are the necessary sinews of such a struggle. But the Catholic bishops and the other church leaders have a motive which goes beyond any of these and would suffice, if success were even more obviously questionable. It is their faith conviction that such promotion of social justice is part of their office of evangelization, of mediating the word of God, or proclaiming the Good News. "Woe to me if I do not preach the Gospel." (1 Cor 9:16).

> As bishops, we do not claim to be technical experts in economic matters. Our primary role is to be moral teachers in society. In this capacity, we attempt to view economic and

social realities primarily from the perspective of the Gospel message of Jesus Christ and his concern for the poor, the marginalized, and the oppressed. From this perspective, we believe there are fundamental ethical questions to be raised about values and priorities that govern any socio-economic order. Thus we have a responsibility to stimulate ethical reflections on the values, priorities and structures of this country's socio-economic order. (Doc. 56, n. 7)

For further description and analysis of the recent social teaching of the Canadian bishops, I would refer the reader to Gregory Baum's succinct and judicious *The Shift in Catholic Social Thought*[37], and its bibliography.

III — THE CANADIAN CONFERENCE OF CATHOLIC BISHOPS[38]

The Second Vatican Council in its decree, *The Bishops' Pastoral Office* (1965) established Episcopal Conferences as an ordinary structure of pastoral administration and action in the Roman Catholic Church. The Episcopal Conference is defined as ''a kind of council in which the bishops of a given nation or territory jointly exercise their pastoral office... through forms and programs of the apostolate adapted to the circumstances of the age.''[39]

The Canadian hierarchy had already moved to the foundation of such an association in 1943, and the Canadian Catholic Conference was recognized and approved by the Holy See in 1948. In 1977 the name was changed to the present Canadian Conference of Catholic Bishops. As pastoral need indicated, other (not subordinate) conferences developed, assuming responsibility for regional study and action: the Atlantic Episcopal Assembly (AEA), the Assemblée des Évêques du Québec (AEQ), the Ontario Conference of Catholic Bishops (OCCB) and the Western Catholic Conference (WCC). The CCCB focussed rather on national and international matters. Such a national Conference does not normally exercise any juridical authority over the local bishops and archbishops, who retain full competence in their respective churches.

All diocesan bishops of any rite of the Roman Catholic Church (and their equivalent in law), all coadjutor and auxiliary bishops, and any titular bishops who exercise in Canada an office assigned by the Apostolic See or by the Episcopal Conference, are members of the Conference. Until 1986, when its statutes were amended to conform with the new Code of Canon Law (canon 450), members included all the above who exercise or *had exercised* such office, including those retired. The number is close to one hundred and increasing as new dioceses are created.

Structures of the Conference[40]

The General Assembly is the body of highest authority, ruling on any question in the competence of the Conference. It elects the President, Vice-President and members of the *Permanent Council* (prior to 1986 called *The Administrative Board*, and in its earliest years, *The National Board*).

The Permanent Council comprises the President and Vice-President, two bishop members of the Pastoral Team, four representatives of the episcopal regions, one representative of the anglophone and one of the francophone sectors of the Church and four *ex officio* members, the archbishops of Quebec, Montreal and Toronto and the Metropolitan of the Ukrainian rite Catholics in Canada. Meeting quarterly the Council supervises the direction of the Conference and the implementation of the Assembly's decisions.

The Executive Committee meets six times yearly and is composed of the President, Vice-President and two General Treasurers elected by the Permanent Council from among its members. They are responsible for the promotion and coordination of activities and for financial matters.

The Presidency alternates between the two sectors of the Conference, an anglophone President being assisted by a francophone Vice-President and vice versa. The term is for two years. The President is spokesman for the Conference, leads its delegations at meetings with other bodies, represents it to the Holy See and through its General Secretaries supervises its work.

The Pastoral Team is composed of six bishops, the two General Secretaries and a multi-disciplinary staff of six from the Secretariat personnel. It is responsible for study, research and overall pastoral planning, and particularly for the preparation of the Plenary Assembly and other meetings of the bishops and for various study and action projects of the Conference.

Two *General Secretaries*, one from each linguistic sector, are the chief executive officers of the Conference, holding authority directly from the General Assembly to which they are responsible and depending immediately on the President in the exercise of their functions. The services of the Secretariat include Public Information, Publications and Production, Administration, Library and Archives.

Six *National Episcopal Commissions* serve both linguistic sectors in the areas of Canon Law, Ecumenism, Ministries, Missions, Theology, and Social Affairs. Three Episcopal Commissions for the areas of Social Communications, Christian Education and Liturgy are twin commissions, with distinct sections in liaison, serving the two linguistic sectors.

The National Episcopal Commission for Social Affairs

This is the largest of the national commissions and is composed of eight bishops, representative of the two sectors and of different regions. It is supported by a bilingual office under two lay co-directors. In issuing its statements, the Commission has used different titles at different times: Social Action Department, Social Action Commission, Episcopal Officers of Social Action, Episcopal Commission for (on, of) Social Affairs, Social Affairs Commission. Originally there had been two distinct anglophone and francophone Social Affairs Commissions. These became one in 1973 and have continued so.

Beginning in 1956, social statements of the CCCB were usually issued in September as Labour Day Messages or Statements. The series ended in 1976, the Conference finding it more convenient to issue such documents as occasion or need arose. From 1965 to 1973, the francophone commission, in odd number years, the anglophone in even number years, was responsible for the initial drafting and final editing of the Labour Day Messages, though there were liaison and collaboration.[41] Evidences of translation can be found in some of the English texts. For their last three years (1974-1976) the Labour Day Messages were approved by and issued in the name of the Administrative Board (as had occurred on occasion earlier).

The Commission for Social Affairs and its support office have the responsibility to follow socio-economic-political events at home and abroad and to keep themselves informed thereon. When it is judged that some statement is indicated, an established Code of Procedures determines the process. It is required that the President of the Conference agree in principle to the initiation of the project. Research and drafting are confided to a team of experts which includes one or more of the bishops of the Commission, members of the Social Affairs Office, and other experts as needed. The whole Commission is kept informed of progress and approves the final text.

If the statement is to be issued in the name of the General (Plenary) Assembly or of the CCCB, the text is submitted to all members before publication; if in the name of the Permanent Council (Administrative Board) or of the Executive Committee, then to their members. A simple majority is decisive.

If the text is to be issued as from the Social Affairs Commission, effort is made to have the text in the hands of all the bishops before it is given to the press, but the Code of Procedures does not require that it be seen by the members of the Conference before publication, though the President must see and approve it. During the preparation of the statement he may also consult other members, for example at meetings of the Permanent Council (4 annually), the Executive Committee (6 annually) or other Commissions meeting in Ottawa, as well as through intra-Conference communications.[42]

The Commission currently claims three major areas of study and reflection.[43]

1. *Faith and Justice Perspectives*

— biblical themes and teaching related to faith and justice, and ecclesiology and evangelization in this light;
— issues of human rights and justice in the Church and in religious institutions;
— continuing reflection on the ethical perspectives and social analysis in dossiers listed in (2) and (3) below. Of major interest is the growing domination of capital and technology over labour and the common good, in Canada and abroad.

2. *Justice Issues in Canada*

— economic: endemic high unemployment and remedial strategies; the interests of workers, especially in industries of rapid technological evolution; alternative economic models and strategies;
— social policy: retrenchment in social services, welfare, public health policies and programs; spreading and deepening poverty; national security issues;

— resource development: energy and land use; farmland take-overs, agri-business; social effects of mega-energy projects; issues of environment, acid rain, noxious wastes;

— Native Peoples: land and other claims; aboriginal rights in the Constitution; native self-government.

3. *Justice in the Third World*

— violation of human rights and scrutiny of Canadian government and business policies supporting such injustice;

— critique of Canadian immigration and refugee policies regarding right of asylum and immigration;

— peace and disarmament issues, including repercussions on Third World development of policies on nuclear armament and arms trade with the Third World;

— issues of economic development, advocating general or specific initiatives in underdeveloped countries.

Edward F. Sheridan, S.J.

NOTES

1. Five statements (Documents 28, 36, 40, 44, 46 of this collection) are to be found in a pamphlet now out of print, *Witness to Justice* (Canadian Catholic Organization for Development and Peace, Toronto, no date). Five (Doc. 40, 44, 46, 49, 55) in Gregory Baum and Duncan Cameron, *Ethics and Economics* (Toronto, James Lorimer, 1984).

2. Richard Arès, SJ, *Messages des évêques canadiens à l'occasion de la fête du Travail, (1956-1974)*, Montréal, Les Éditions Bellarmin, 1974. Five of the CCCB texts (Doc. 32, 44, 46, 49, 55) are in Gérard Rochais édit., *La Justice sociale comme bonne nouvelle*, Montréal, Les Éditions Bellarmin, 1984.

3. *L'Église canadienne* since 1968, Éditions Fides, Montréal; *Documentation sociale*, a bulletin of the CCCB, Ottawa.

4. Cf. Christopher Lind, "Ethics, Economics and Canada's Catholic Bishops" *Canadian Journal of Political and Social Theory*, vol. 7, n. 3, 1983, p. 150; A.M.C. Waterman, "The Catholic Bishops and Canadian Public Policy", *Canadian Public Policy*, University of Guelph, Ont., IX, 1983, n. 3, 374, and the comment of Bruce W. Wilkinson in the same, X, 1984, n. 1, 88; *Ecumenism*, Montreal, the whole n. 71, Sept. 1983, 12 comments; Walter Block, "On Economics and the Canadian Bishops", *Focus*, n. 3, Fraser Institute, Vancouver, 1983; *Canada's Unemployed: the Crisis of Our Times*,

Report of the Hearing Panel on *"Ethical Reflections on the Economic Crisis"* (with summary of the more than 100 written submissions, almost half from associations, groups, etc.), Catholic Archdiocese of Toronto, M5B 1Z8. Cf. also Baum and Cameron, *op. cit.*, note 1 above, pp. 94-97.

    5. On this development, cf. Gregory Baum, *Catholics and Canadian Socialism: Political Thought in the Thirties and Forties* (Toronto, James Lorimer, 1980); the same in *Ethics and Economics* (Toronto, James Lorimer, 1984), "Shift in Social Teaching", pp. 19-93; Richard Arès, SJ, "Le Souci de la justice chez l'épiscopat canadien", *Académie des sciences morales et politiques*, Montréal, *Travaux et communications*, vol. 1, Sherbrooke, Éditions Paulines, 1973, pp. 30-53; Arthé Guimond, "La pensée sociale des évêques canadiens de 1956 à nos jours", *L'Église canadienne*, vol. 15, n. 1, 3 sept. 1981, p. 11 ss.; Jacques Racine, "Les discours de l'Église en matière économique", *Communauté chrétienne*, vol. 21, n. 121, jan.-fév. 1982, pp. 35-42. Remi de Roo, Bishop, *Cries of Victims Voice of God* (Ottawa, Novalis, 1986); Michael Ryan, *Christian Social Teaching and Canadian Society*, IV edit. (St. Peter's Seminary, London, Ont., 1986; a good brief exposition of Catholic social teaching with bibliography on the Canadian scene.

    6. On the social teaching of the Church in recent times cf. David Hollenbach, SJ, *Claims in Conflict: Retrieving and Renewing the Catholic Human Rights Tradition* (Paulist Press, New York-Toronto, 1979); the same in *The Faith that Does Justice: Examining the Christian Sources for Social Change*, edit. John C. Haughey, SJ (Paulist Press, 1977); Donal Dorr, *Option for the Poor: a Hundred Years of Vatican Social Teaching* (Maryknoll, New York, Orbis Books, 1983); Rodger Charles, SJ, and Drostan MacLaren, OP, *The Social Teaching of Vatican II* (Oxford, Plater Publications, 1982); Joseph Gremillion, *The Gospel of Peace and Justice: Catholic Social Teaching Since Pope John* (Maryknoll, New York, Orbis Books, 1976); John Desrochers, CSC, *The Social Teaching of the Church* (64 Miller's Road, Bangalore, India, 560 046);

    7. Leo XIII, *On the Condition of the Worker (Rerum Novarum)*, 1891, in *The Papal Encyclicals*, edit. Claudia Carlen, IHM (Wilmington, N.C., McGrath Publishing, 1981), II, 241.

    8. Karl Barth, *The Christian Community and the Civil Community*, in *Against the Stream* (London, SCM Press, 1954), p. 36.

    9. There are many editions of the documents of the Second Vatican Council; that generally used here is of Walter Abbott, SJ, *The Documents of Vatican II* (New York, Guild Press, 1966). Since sections of the documents are identically numbered in the original and in all editions, any edition may be used.

    10. Karl Rahner, SJ, "Towards a Fundamental Theological Interpretation of Vatican II" in *Theological Studies*, Washington, 1979, XL, n. 4, p. 717.

    11. Karl Rahner, *ibid.*

    12. Karl Rahner, *op. cit.*, p. 719.

    13. Document 56, n. 8.

    14. The point had been made, rather ahead of his times, by Pius XII in his Pentecost Message of 1941, "The Social Question in the New Order", cf. *Catholic Mind*, New York, 1941, XXXIX, June, p. 10.

    15. In Carlen, *op. cit.* note 7 above, vol V, 183.

    16. Cf. *The Church in the Present-Day Transformation of Latin America in the Light of the Council*, vol. 2, *Conclusions*, (Washington, Latin American Bureau of the U.S. Catholic Conference, 2nd edit., 1973).

    17. Cf. *The Pope Speaks*, Washington, 1971, XVI, 137.

    18. In his encyclical, *On Reconstructing the Social Order*, 1931, Pius XI had noted favourably some changes in socialism since the time of Leo XIII, but then, as though

alarmed by his temerity, had hardened his stance; in Carlen, *op. cit.* in note 7 above, III, pp. 432-34, nn. 111-222. John XXIII too had remarked that in certain cases collaboration with socialists "for the attainment of practical results" might be admissible; cf. *Peace on Earth*, 1963, in Carlen, *op. cit.*, V, p. 125, nn. 159-60.

19. Cf. *The Pope Speaks*, Washington, 1971, XVI, 377.

20. Cf. *The Pope Speaks*, Washington, 1976, XXI, 4-51. Also in Joseph Gremillion, *op. cit.* note 6 above, p. 593.

21. Cf. Charles M. Murphy, "Action for Justice as Constitutive of the Preaching of the Gospel: What did the 1971 Synod Mean?", *Theological Studies*, Washington, 1984, XLIV, 298.

22. Cf. John Eagleson and Philip Scharper, *Puebla and Beyond: Documentation and Commentary*, (Maryknoll, N.Y., Orbis Books, 1979), pp. 123-285.

23. John Paul II, *Opening Address*, cf. Eagleson and Sharper, *op. cit.*, note 22 above, III, 2, p. 66.

24. *op. cit.*, III, 3, p. 66.

25. Donal Dorr, *op. cit.*, note 6 above, p. 223.

26. *Osservatore Romano*, English edit., Vatican City, Aug. 11, 1980, p. 10.

27. K.A. Briggs, *The New York Times*, July 7, 1980.

28. *loc. cit.*, note 26 above.

29. Cf. Carlen, *op. cit.*, note 7 above, V, 245 and 275.

30. Cf. Bernard M. Daly, "Labour Day Statements of the Bishops of Canada 1965-1982", an excellent and informative paper read to the Canadian Catholic Historical Association (355 Church St., Toronto, Ont., M5B 1Z8), and unfortunately unpublished. It provides much information on the working of the Conference, the preparation of many of its statements and on the development of its social teaching.

31. Instructions of the CCCB and of the Canadian Council of Churches to their Strategy Committee, in Foreword to *Towards a Coalition for Development*, Doc. 20. The Foreward is not given below. Cf. also Bernard Daly, *op. cit.*, note 30 above, p. 22.

32. Cf. Bernard Daly, *op. cit.*, note 30 above, pp. 7 f. During his visit to Canada, 1984, Pope John Paul II praised warmly this ecumenical collaboration in the promotion of justice and human rights; cf. his address at the Ecumenical Meeting, St. Paul's Anglican Church, Toronto, Sept. 14, nn. 5 f., in *The Canadian Catholic Review*, Saskatoon, vol. 2, n. 9, Oct. 1984, p. 46.

33. Cf. authors cited in note 6 above; also Gérard Rochais, *op. cit.*, note 2 above, p. 21.

34. Richard Arès, SJ, *op. cit.*, note 5 above, p. 51.

35. Cf. Jacques Racine, *op. cit.*, note 5 above, pp. 39 f.

36. John R. Williams, *Canadian Churches and Social Justice* (Toronto, Anglican Book Centre and James Lorimer, 1984), pp. 9 and 11.

37. In Gregory Baum and Duncan Stewart, *Ethics and Economics* (Toronto, James Lorimer, 1984), pp. 17-93.

38. Information on the Canadian Conference of Catholic Bishops is drawn from *The Directory 1986* and *The Report 1984-85*, CCCB, Ottawa, K1N 7B1; and from Bernard M. Daly, *op. cit.*, note 30 above.

39. The Second Vatican Council, *The Bishops' Pastoral Office in the Church* (1965), n. 38, 1).

40. CCCB Report 1984-85, p. 6 ff.

41. Cf. Bernard Daly, *op. cit.*, note 30 above, pp. 6 and 46.

42. Cf. also, Gérard Rochais, *op. cit.*, note 2 above, p. 16.

43. CCCB Report, 1984-85, pp. 12 f.

Document 1

FUNDAMENTAL PRINCIPLES AND URGENT PROBLEMS

Author — The National Board of the Canadian Hierarchy,[1]
January 18, 1945

Dearly Beloved:

1. Under the providential guidance of our Holy Father and completely at one with our venerated brethren of the Catholic Hierarchy of the United States of America, of Australia, and of England and Scotland, we offer, in this critical time, our word of direction. Our first concern is the repeated insistence to be placed on some fundamental principles and then we claim your attention to our mind on the more urgent problems of the day.

I — FUNDAMENTAL PRINCIPLES

2. Many have explained the causes, the futility and the injustice of wars of aggression. They have set down the conditions of a just peace. They have suggested the structure of a harmonious international order.

3. In spite of all this constructive effort, the average human mind still remains somewhat clouded as to the real and vital issue. Thus to cleric and to lay person, to members of families, to religious and to civil societies, to all who are intelligent and free, sane and responsible, we say in all earnestness, this is a world problem, your world problem.

4. Your eternal salvation, your temporal peace depend without qualification on how you accept and discharge your conscientious personal responsibilities to your God, to yourself and to your neighbour, in this conflict for world domination. Realistically and objectively it is abundantly clear that there always has been and is, only one real struggle in human lives. It is the warfare between the forces of good and evil. With intensity and in extent hitherto unknown to man, disorder opposes unity, falsehood attempts to replace truth, and injustice and hatred seek to deprive man of his only source of happiness, a life of justice and love. Helpless with the intoxication of power, but with diabolical cunning and cleverness, these agencies of evil seek to deceive and to control individuals and nations. They are strong and well organized in material and physical resources, even to the power of sanction. They are weak in the realm of the moral and the spiritual. Hence the one formula for peace to men of good will is prayer and study and sacrifice.

5. God still governs the world in the wisdom of His Divine Providence. On those who share His authority and whom He has gifted for their offices there now rests a more serious duty of leadership and inspiration. Bishops, pastors, priests, parents, religious and lay teachers, and, in their stations those whose care it is to protect and promote the common good, all must serve heroically in the defence of Christian life and of the peace it brings.

6. Human nature was instituted by God. A human person is constituted essentially of an immortal soul and a body. Both need their proportionate reasonable care. This is had in the exercise and discharge of rights and obligations which flow from their nature. This is personal freedom. Simple, clear and unmistakable truth on this prerequisite to human happiness must be afforded to every responsible person.

7. The family is the fundamental unit of human society. It was instituted by God. He made the laws which direct and govern it. Disregard for these laws leads to inevitable decay in social life.

8. The state exists for the common good. It is a natural instrument to promote and safeguard the rights of the individual and of the family in view of the good of all. Its authority comes from God. Its law is a moral law, governing moral beings. It must give justice to all.

9. To all nations belongs the right to life and independence. This means political freedom, economic development and protection of neutrality. Reparation for the violation of those rights is to be made by the laws of justice and reciprocal equity.

10. To racial minorities belongs the right to their culture and to their language. Their access to economic resources may not be restricted nor their natural fertility limited or abolished.

11. These are the principles which must be known and practiced in every phase of human life. Falsehood and error, selfishness and expediency do exist in too large measure. More regrettable and fatal to any plan for a new order of peaceful life is the organized effort of these powerful agencies for evil which capitalize on this condition of human weakness. They hide their real purpose and identity. They appear in the guise of friends. They are the real enemies of justice, love and peace.

12. There are still many good souls, good families, good men and women in positions of trust, or how could these onslaughts of evil have been withstood? Fidelity and honour in discharge of duties whether of prayer, work, suffering or even death have been the human salvation of Christian democracy. Nations disintegrate only through moral decay.

13. So, dearly beloved, we enjoin you, "Watch and pray". Watch through your faith in God, and through the exercise of prudent judgment. Your sacrifices give you the right to weigh the burdens to be placed upon you. Your love of truth and your practice of justice and charity in word and most of all in deed, will finally prevail. Pray that men and nations may quickly return to the knowledge, love, and service of God. He is the author of life and love, and the Prince of Peace.

II — PROBLEMS OF THE DAY

14. *International Order* — We beseech most earnestly the all-powerful and merciful God to grant that peace soon to the world, and to direct the leaders of nations in the way of organizing an orderly peace founded on justice, morality and religion. We are happy to give our complete support to the declaration on the inter-

national order made by our venerated brethren of the Hierarchy of the United States on Noverber 19, 1944. [2]

15. *Poland* — We express again the hope that the Allied Nations will not abandon heroic Poland to her fate. For it was the defence of Poland which first motivated our entry into the war and which was the greatest incentive of our valiant forces. The late Cardinal Hinsley, Archbishop of Westminster, said with reason that the treatment accorded to Poland would be a touch-stone of the loyalty of the Allied Nations in their efforts to re-establish liberty and justice in the world. Poland, in effect, in resisting so courageously the Nazi oppression, has earned the right to the admiration and protection of all civilized nations. The same measure of sympathetic understanding is offered to all nations who have suffered the tyranny of aggression.

16. *Peril of Communism* — We warn once more against materialistic and atheistic communism which now personifies in the world all the unleashed forces against the Church and against the moral values of which she has the care, namely, human dignity and Christian liberty. The courageous part which the Russian people have played in turning away from the world the frightful Nazi domination must not blind us regarding the world revolution which the leaders of international communism always seek. Governments and simple citizens alike have the very grave obligation of checking amongst us communistic infiltrations under whatever external appearance they present themselves. Otherwise they are preparing for our dear country, for which so many of our sons offer each day their life and their future, the worst disorders and calamities. It seems to us at least comforting, that even outside Catholic circles a part of public opinion is on guard against this kind of danger of international dictatorship to whose hidden attacks our country is not alone in being subject.

17. *Order and Justice in Canada* — We desire above all to see interior peace reign in our beloved country, a peace based on concord and reciprocal esteem between the diverse elements which constitute Confederation, both English and French, a peace coming also from the watchful care of and generosity towards, all the racial and religious minorities which are spread through our vast country. For that which makes a true democracy as opposed to state absolutism and totalitarian rule, is not only or even precisely, the dominant

will of the greatest number, it is the sincere pursuit of the common good while respecting the dignity and the liberty of the human person, it is the constant exercise of distributive justice towards the individuals and groups which compose the political and national community.

18. *School Legislation* — In this regard we are bound to assert most strongly that the school legislation of most of the provinces seems to us to call for radical improvements, with respect especially to the Catholic and French element, if it is wished that they truly reflect the spirit of cordial agreement which presided at the Canadian constitution. In fact, as long as the same flagrant inequalities exist between the treatment which the Province of Quebec has given religious and racial minorities on the one hand, and on the other hand that which the other provinces have imposed upon them, it appears to us useless to speak of equality of advantages and of sacrifices, useless also to hope to see reigning in our midst that mutual confidence which is indispensable to the peace and prosperity of the nation.

19. *Social Legislation* — We exhort strongly all public authorities to establish, as soon as possible, or to improve accordingly, where work is already started, the laws and institutions capable of assuring social peace. We recommend specially the protection of the organized professions, and the necessary care for improved standards of rural life and for the welfare of the working class. Most urgent of all is the immediate attention, gratefully offered, to the proper rehabilitation of the men and women of our armed forces.

20. *Marriage and the Family* — If it is gratifying to see that public attention is beginning to turn towards the economic security of the family, we can only deplore the repeated attempts to loosen the sacred bonds of marriage. We condemn without hesitation all the attempts, conceived at times by public bodies from whom one should expect more foresight, to introduce divorce into the provinces which still repudiate it, or to make it more frequent and easier in the others. We invite in particular Catholic associations to make heard their protests against these efforts to de-Christianize marriage and family life, and to demand that the legislative and judicial authorities treat this double institution according to Christian teaching and to the best traditions of our country. We express the hope of seeing as soon as possible, the family, dismembered and broken by

the sad necessities of war, recover its integrity and balance as planned by God, and of seeing as soon as possible the wives and mothers re-enter the home of which they are the guardians. We appeal finally with all our strength for a sound national family program, that is, for a policy of protection and assistance to the family, the living cell of the whole social body.

21. *Harmony and Charity* — We exhort all our fellow citizens of every religious denomination to avoid and to silence as far as possible all provocations of hatred, discontent and mutual misunderstanding. That they foster and promote, in speech and most of all by example, the union of all forces, above all Christian forces, for the triumph of gospel ideals in the work of social reconstruction which is beginning. That all engage in helping to establish that harmony so necessary to the Canadian nation, if it wishes to remain equal to the marvellous destiny which Providence seems to have assigned to it in the concert of the nations of the New World.

22. *Christian Unity: the Mystical Body of Christ* — We recommend instantly the practice, blest and encouraged by the Holy See, of the Octave of Prayers for Christian Unity (January 18-25), in order to gather into the unity of faith all those who, under whatever title it may be, recognize the authority of divine revelation. And we urge all the faithful to meditate and to live the doctrine of our incorporation in Christ, the doctrine which His Holiness, Pope Pius XII, gloriously reigning, has so magnificently set forth in his recent encyclical, *The Mystical Body of Christ, (Mystici Corporis)*, 1943. For it is in the return to this mysterious participation in the divine life that we Christians are to find the secret of our personal sanctification and of every exterior action for re-Christianizing the world.

23. *Appeal to those in Public Life* — In these hours, so serious for the future of our Christian civilization, we hasten to address ourselves in anguished appeal to all in public life. We know the burden, onerous at times, of their office: on them falls the direction of the national and international community. But we know too that He from Whom come all authority and all power does not refuse His grace to one who does all in his power. And it is from the depths of our souls that we send up our prayers to heaven on behalf of our rulers. May they always adhere to that ideal for legislators which His Holiness, Pope Pius XII proposed in his latest Christmas message:

... an elite, spiritually eminent and of strong character; men chosen for their solid Christian convictions, straight and steady judgment, with a sense of the practical and equitable, true to themselves in all circumstances; men who in periods of transition, generally stormy and disturbed by passion, by divergent opinions and opposing programs, feel themselves doubly under the obligation to send circulating through the veins of the people and of the state, burning with a thousand fevers, the spiritual antidote of clear views, kindly interest, a justice equally sympathetic to all and a bias toward national unity and concord in a sincere spirit of brotherhood.[3]

NOTES

1. At the time, the National Board of the Canadian Catholic Conference comprised the residential archbishops and the bishop-chairmen of the episcopal commissions. The name and structure were superseded by the Administrative Board (renamed Permanent Council in 1986), composed of fourteen bishops elected by the General Assembly. The Permanent Council is second in authority only to the General Assembly.

2. *The Catholic Mind*, New York, 1945, XLIII, 1.

3. *Acta Apostolicae Sedis*, Vatican, 1945, XXXVII, 16, Italian text. English version, *The Catholic Mind*, New York, 1945, XLIII, 70.

Document 2

ON IMMIGRATION
AND ON PERSECUTION OF MISSIONARIES
IN COMMUNIST COUNTRIES

Author — The Canadian Hierarchy, October 9, 1952

The archbishops and bishops of Canada gathered in Ottawa for their annual meeting have discussed important questions of the day and feel it their duty to speak to their people on these subjects.

I

Immigration is a social question with many aspects. The Church does not wish to pass judgment on the details of policy regarding immigration, but does point out to all that immigration is a moral question, subject to moral laws which should direct and inspire those whose duty it is to determine a policy of immigration.

1. Broken homes constitute a deplorable and disastrous problem, particularly when the head of the family is separated from wife and children; public and voluntary agencies should make an immediate and determined effort to reunite these families whose members have permission to enter the country.

2. Since God created the entire earth for man's use and benefit, the countries which have unoccupied land should open such territory to people of overpopulated countries.

3. The policy that governs the flow of immigration should be truly

democratic and any regulations that would restrict, in an arbitrary manner, the emigration of people from an overpopulated country or of refugees from persecuted lands would be contrary to the fundamental principles of justice and true peace.

II

The Canadian archbishops and bishops are saddened at the thought that persecution directed against the Church and her missionaries in the countries under communist domination is ever on the increase. Catholic bishops are sentenced to death as hardened criminals; men and women engaged in missionary work are being imprisoned, tortured and mistreated; the faithful, victims of deception, are being unjustly forced to join a national church, the leaders of which are themselves apostates. Those who profess the Christian faith are pressed to join a political party which denies everything supernatural.

The archbishops and bishops request their Catholic people, in these time when every problem has an international import, to unite in prayer and penance with their persecuted brethren. Our faith cannot be limited by national boundaries. It must be a source of strength and comfort to our persecuted brethren and a bond of union with them in their sufferings.

Document 3

LABOUR DAY MESSAGE — 1956
ON LABOUR UNIONS — AUTOMATION
HOUSING — ADVERTISING
CONSUMPTION — CREDIT

Author — The Canadian Catholic Conference

Introduction — Saint Joseph the Worker

1.   Pope Pius XII recently approved the casting of a medal to commemorate the current year of his Pontificate. One side of the medal depicts Catholic workers presenting gifts to the Pope on May 1st, 1955, in St. Peter's Square at Rome. The inscription on the medal reads: ''The Zealous Collaboration of Workers and Employers''. The casting of the medal was occasioned by the proclamation of St. Joseph as Patron of Workers, and by the establishment of May first as the Feast of St. Joseph the Worker. On this continent, by special permission of the Holy See, the Mass of St. Joseph the Worker may be offered also on Labour Day, although May first is the day on which the Feast is celebrated.

2.   By his approval of the medal, the Supreme Pontiff drew world attention to a highlight of this year, namely, the progress made in labour-management relations, and thus reminded the world that collaboration is basic to justice and charity.

3.   Nowadays, when powerful economic and financial combinations are pushing the little man into obscurity, the Holy Father champions man's natural rights. He insists that the common man be remem-

bered. How appropriate then was the Holy Father's choice of St. Joseph as Patron of Workers, for St. Joseph has been called the greatest common man of history. Like him, today's workman usually leads a hidden life. His very obscurity often hides from the world his God-given dignity and worth and his contribution to the common good.

4. St. Joseph is no stranger to Canadians nor is his intercession something new. He had already been known as Patron of Canada for three centuries when Pope Pius XI placed under his protection a world threatened by materialism and by communism, its evil offspring.

Labour Unions

5. With the coming of another Labour Day we recall the words of the Holy Father who, speaking of respect for the higher interests of the workers, said: "Progress is slow, much too slow, on this essential point, in most countries and on whole continents".[1]

6. There is today a marked tendency for similar professional groups to join forces. Every time that this trend brings new strength to labour it should bring, in consequence, an increased sense of responsibility toward the common good.

7. Man has a natural right to form unions; without them he cannot, in the economic order of our times, obtain justice. The Canadian bishops have consistently encouraged workers to join unions and to participate actively in them. But, in the words of the Holy Father:

> Do not allow yourselves to become overenthusiastic or deluded by the growing number of names on your roster... Ask rather, what each of these names is worth... You will be able to congratulate yourselves fully and without reserve on the progress of your association only when the life of your single specialized groups and each of their members is linked harmoniously from below to the organization which operates from above.[2]

8. Two thousand years ago Christ examined the conditions of His time and found them wanting. He preached a radical doctrine, that

is, a doctrine directed to the roots of the evils. The Vicars of Christ have likewise denounced the conditions of our times. But, like Christ, they have done more than this. They have given us a positive program for the reconstruction of the social order. Labour too must be positive. Its task is clearly to use its new strength and authority for the betterment of the existing social and economic order, namely, to promote a program of social change that will bring reality more nearly into conformity with the ideal.

9.   There is need for labour to show initiative in such vital fields as labour-management relations, economic cooperation, housing, and in the general field of finance, with special emphasis on credit, insurance and taxation. In short, organized labour must move into that area where morality, economics and social behaviour are inextricably meshed. If this is done, many of the still unorganized workers of Canada will be attracted into the household of organized labour. In this year's message, we will limit our words to a few of the above problems.

Automation

10.   Labour must, as does the Church, have a serious concern for what this "second phase of the industrial revolution" means for man as a human being. As the Holy Father has repeatedly stated, all technical advances must be used with a sense of moral and social responsibility. The Church recognizes that automation can be a very great blessing for mankind. His Eminence Cardinal Dell'Acqua, writing on behalf of the Holy Father to the 43rd *Semaine Sociale de France (Marseilles)*, July 1956, said:

> The Church... asks the faithful to see in the astounding progress of science the realization of the plan of God, who has entrusted to man the discovery and exploitation of the wealth of the universe: "Fill the earth and subdue it" (Gn 1:28)... Is it necessary, however, to abandon oneself with blind confidence to those perspectives of technical progress and economic expansion? "Productivity is not an end in itself," the Holy Father said recently.[3]

11.   Automation will raise a host of new problems, problems that must be solved if technological progress is not to degenerate into

another instrument of corruption: a raising of general living standards, the use of increased leisure, the transfer of workers from one area of employment to another, with its dangers to family life. In the study of these problems lies an opportunity for labour to make a huge contribution to the welfare of human society.

Housing

12. It was not so very long ago that the Holy Father, Pope Pius XII, had occasion to lament the widespread scarcity of reasonably priced housing:

> What a burden it is on the Christian conscience when those planning to marry, the newly married, and the parents of growing families cannot find shelter, or can find only housing that is inadequate and often too dear.[4]

13. This is a problem that strikes at the very heart of society. In this country many families of moderate income, by the practice of thrift and frugality, and by forming cooperatives, have succeeded in building themselves decent family houses. But only the fringe of the problem has been touched. Much remains to be done that cannot be done by individuals, but must be accomplished through the collaboration of social-minded groups with municipalities and with governments at all levels. Housing programs have been strongly endorsed by public bodies and by resolutions of the major Canadian labour organizations. These are hopeful signs. Again we give the words of the Holy Father:

> In regard to housing, as in other matters, public authorities should favour and not oppose private enterprise. And in the case of low-cost housing especially, they should favour cooperatives.[5]

Advertising — Consumption — Credit

14. An increasingly serious modern disease is the desire to consume beyond the limits of reasonable need. Modern advertising, stimulated by ever increasing production, strives ceaselessly and by every means to create a climate of opinion in which men and women

are never satisfied but must, to be "normal", buy more and more. To make this possible, credit is freely extended by merchants and others so that most things may be had on installment plans. In the struggle to meet these payments (to which substantial interest charges have been added), those whose earnings are sufficient for all reasonable needs find themselves living from hand to mouth and falling into the hands of money lenders. The Holy Father has spoken bluntly:

> Morally healthy people are those who in all their material needs put necessary things before the merely useful or pleasurable. They do not let themselves be dragged into unrestrained consumption, a cancer of present-day social economy.[6]

We urge on all the development of a sense of responsible thrift. Credit unions are an excellent means to this end and are at the same time an introduction to, and an encouragement of, that social and economic cooperation between citizens that is truly Christian.

15.   Labour and government alike should recognize their social responsibility to devise, advocate and promote means of encouraging thrift, curbing the abuse of credit by loan companies and limiting the wasteful incitement of irresponsible publicity.

16.   These are some of the problems. Their solution demands the application of moral principles by all segments of society and the willingness of all to adopt programs of action in conformity with these principles.

17.   In conclusion, may we again exhort all and especially organized labour, to accept fully the new responsibilities placed in their hands by Providence. We pray particularly that St. Joseph, the Patron of Workers, will inspire organized labour to provide the world with a shining example of how democratic, Christian control and use of material riches can bring about universal well-being and that "peace of Christ in the Kingdom of Christ" which is the hope of humanity.

NOTES

1. Pius XII, *To International Conference on Human Relations in Industry, The Pope Speaks,* Washington, 1956, I, 52.

2. *To Italian Workers, The Catholic Mind,* New York, 1948, XLVI, 610.

3. *The Catholic Mind,* New York, 1956, LIV, 661.

4. *To the Roman Institute for Low-Cost Housing, The Catholic Mind,* New York, 1954, LII, 309.

5. *Ibid.,* 310.

6. *Ibid.*

Document 4

CHRISTIAN CITIZENSHIP IN PRACTICE

Author — The Canadian Catholic Hierarchy, November 15, 1956

1. During their annual meeting in 1953, the Canadian hierarchy reminded Catholics of certain fundamental moral truths upon which sound family life is founded, truths the general practice of which adds greatly to the common good of society. And, morality being indivisible, it follows that those who take their family responsibilities seriously are more likely to be good citizens than those who neglect them.

2. Furthermore, it is vain to imagine that self-centeredness in its many forms can easily be overcome; nor is it sufficient to overcome it only in the home, where its destructive effects are especially harmful. For though it may be banished from the home, self-centeredness may well continue to flourish in our social and community life, in direct opposition to the ideals of citizenship.

Importance of Citizenship in a Democracy

3. This year we wish to outline the principal obligations involved in the practice of the virtue of citizenship. The importance of this virtue cannot be denied, especially in a democracy, of which system of government it has been said that none demands higher standards of its citizens. It is true in the case of individual virtues, since there can be no sound, healthy society unless the men and women who compose it are honest, temperate and generous in their private lives. It is no less true of citizenship as a whole, for without this social virtue a citizen would be mediocre even if his private life were beyond reproach.

4. Unfortunately, it happens that many honest people, who believe themselves to be good Christians, appear to be far less conscious of their civic responsibilities than they are of their family and professional obligations. Knowingly or otherwise they think and act as if the force of the moral law did not extend to their whole life, public as well as private. Even without realizing it, they display a lack of citizenship the results of which are only too visible and may, in the long run, seriously endanger not only individual moral values but the well-being of society itself.

Citizenship and Justice

5. What then is this virtue so often misunderstood by those who have the greatest opportunity to put it into practice? It may be quite simply defined. It is the firm resolve to subordinate one's personal interests, or any other special interests, to the common good of society. Thus understood, citizenship is directly derived from justice in its highest form, i.e., general or social justice, since its function is to direct the practice of all the other virtues towards the common good, or to render to that "other person" (society) that which is rightfully due.

6. In fact, we owe a true debt to society. If we remember our origins and recognize our limitations, we shall be obliged to admit our dependence upon society. Our very life, and those material advantages which make life worth living, come to us by means of the family which is itself an integral part of society. And having received so much from society, it is only just that we should give back to society what she requires from us if she is to fulfill her obligation to all her members. Citizenship impels the individual to discharge this debt honourably, whether by keeping the civil law, paying taxes or serving the community by accepting public office.

Citizenship and Charity

7. Being concerned with the good of one's neighbour, citizenship is engendered by that charity of which St. Paul wrote that it "is not self-seeking" (1 Cor 13:5), which means, according to St. Augustine, "that it prefers the common good to its own. That is why," he adds, "you will measure your progress by the greater care you

will give to the common good in preference to your personal advantage." It will readily be understood then, that Christians, for whom the great commandment is that of charity, must be outstanding by the quality of their citizenship, whether they exercise it as governors or as governed.

Citizenship Necessary for All

8.   The Christians of the first centuries belonged almost entirely to the class of those who were ruled, as distinct from the ruling class of their day. Mindful of Christ's teaching to "render to Caesar the things that are Caesar's and to God the things that are God's" (Mt 22:17), the Apostles preached submission to established authority. They stressed the fact that all authority comes from God and merits obedience, provided that it commands nothing contrary to divine law.

9.   In time however, Christians were called upon to take part in the government of their respective countries and to exercise temporal power. The Church then explained to her children the true nature of this power, which was to be used in conformity with God's plan. We are told by St. Paul that civil authority is a means used by God to lead men to good. Just laws enacted by authority are made binding by divine law itself: "Thou must needs then be submissive, not only for fear of punishment, but in conscience." (Rm 13:5)

10.   In order legitimately to exercise power over his fellows, a man must act with a view to attaining a good higher than himself, of which he is but the trustee. It was explicitly stated by Pope Leo XIII that "civil authority must never be used, on any pretext whatsoever, to the advantage of one person or of a small group, because it was instituted for the common good."[1]

Civil Authority and the Common Good

11.   The duty of responsible leaders of government is not only to ensure the individual good of every citizen, but also to establish those external and social conditions which will permit all to achieve, by their own efforts, the degree of human perfection to which they may legitimately aspire. Thus, in the matter of material prosperity

for instance, the state should not be expected continually to increase the allowances or grants paid directly to individuals, but rather should seek vigilantly to develop and sustain general economic conditions which permit every citizen to provide adequately for his needs and for those of his family.

12.   Governments must not use their political strength to usurp the functions of private enterprise, nor should they attempt to do the work of those organizations which act as intermediaries between the citizen and the state. The role of government is rather to support their efforts, to coordinate them, to arbitrate, when necessary, between groups whose interests conflict, and to dispense justice impartially to all.

13.   Yet in some cases preference may legitimately be given to citizens in poorer circumstances, as a means of modifying social injustice which cannot be entirely eradicated.

Blind Partisanship Contrary to Citizenship

14.   In any system of government involving different political parties, citizens must beware of that deformation of citizenship which is blind partisanship. Party leaders may justifiably try to convince voters of the benefits they believe will flow from the election of their party to power, but in so doing they must still set an example by their respect for truth, justice and fraternal charity. And, should they be elected to govern, this same undeviating concern for the common good will prevent them from favouring special interests to the detriment of the commonweal.

15.   It need hardly be added that religion must not be used to bolster any specific political ideology. Pope Leo XIII wrote: "But to sully the Church by party strife, or to desire to make her an ally in overcoming opponents in such strife, would be the work of men who rashly abuse religion."[2]

Christian Unity above Party Allegiance

16.   The Church leaves her members free to belong to the parties of their choice, as long as the doctrines or methods of the parties

are not opposed to their religious faith, as in the case of the communist party. On the other hand, she calls upon Catholics of all political persuasions to forget their political differences and to unite whenever the issue at stake is a law necessary to safeguard public morals, divine law or some basic freedom such as the freedom of education.

Present Need for Education in Civics

17. What we have said concerning the demands made by citizenship should suffice to emphasize the need for continuing comprehensive and widespread education in civics. This need is nowhere more pressing than in our own developing country. The almost revolutionary changes brought about by Canada's industrial expansion have, in the brief space of fifty years, transformed us from a predominantly rural nation into one of large urban populations. The consequences of these rapid changes (which are far from ended yet) are evident. Even in the country, life is no longer what it was, as the influence of city life increasingly makes itself felt.

18. In the gathering strength of their numerical growth, working men have used the trade union movement as a lever to compel recognition of their rights and to better their condition. Economic expansion has multiplied the contacts between our two main ethnic groups while, at the same time, immigration has brought us people of many other races, all hopeful of finding opportunities to make a good livelihood for themselves in their new homeland. Those responsible for education have more and more directed and adapted it to the conditions and pressing needs of a changing economy, while striving to avoid the sacrifice of traditional cultural values.

19. By developing her immense resources, Canada has attained an enviable position among the nations. This does not mean however, that she has yet achieved a social equilibrium of which we may be proud. Too many families are still deprived of adequate housing and lack the minimum material resources needed for the rearing and education of their children. There has moreover, been a noticeable weakening of moral standards among those who have benefited most from our general economic prosperity. This is doubly disquieting, for not only does it jeopardize the eternal destiny of the many individual souls concerned, but it also diminishes the spiritual and moral fabric of the nation.

20. It will be seen that our economic progress itself gives no guarantee of national well-being. If all our citizens are not imbued with that true sense of civic responsibility which makes them place the common good above their own interests, social peace and the balanced development of our nation cannot be achieved.

Education in Citizenship

21. Because self-centredness is the principal obstacle to the practice of citizenship, we cannot begin too early to combat it. Above all, it is in the home that children should first be led to experience the deep satisfaction of serving others. This training should be continued throughout the years of school, by using the opportunities provided in teaching geography, history and religion to reinforce this natural truth. Our National Citizenship Day which will be held on May 17th, 1957 is also a splendid occasion for us to recall the privileges and obligations inherent in our Canadian citizenship.

22. Far from being indifferent to citizenship, our faith ennobles it by saturating it with the spirit of Christianity. It is the duty of those who preach to emphasize this truth by showing that the law of Christ must rule every human activity. It is the function of Catholic Social Action to foster the growth of citizenship by developing a spirit of community between men.

23. However, the finest incentive to the proper accomplishment of civic duties should be the example set by those who govern. Their cardinal obligation is to acquire the competance and cultivate the virtues demanded by their state of life. No one has expressed this truth better than the Holy Father when, in 1950, he said to members of the Italian Parliament:

> You realize — as everybody should realize — how much strength we need to receive from God, so that when exercising authority, we shall remain firm in the fight against self-centredness and pride, in order always to place the general good before the particular advantage of the individual, group or party, in order to act always from motives inspired by justice, charity and faith.[3]

Document 4

24. In view of these words of authority, need we speak further of the necessity for prayers for divine help; help for all who wish to remain faithful to the teachings of Christ, both in the practice of citizenship and in the discharge of their own individual duties?

NOTES

1. *The Christian Constitution of States (Immortale Dei)*, 1885, *The Papal Encyclicals*, edit. Claudia Carlen, IHM (Wilmington, N.C., McGrath Publishing, 1981), II, 108.
2. *The Chief Duties of Christian Citizens (Sapientiae Christianae)*, 1890, cf. Carlen above, II, 218.
3. Search has failed to discover the text of this address.

Document 5

LABOUR DAY MESSAGE — 1957[1]
AN APPEAL TO SPIRITUAL VALUES

Author — The Canadian Catholic Conference

1. The archbishops and bishops of Canada take this occasion of the Labour Day celebration of work and workers, to communicate a message dictated by the consciousness of their responsibility as Church leaders. We gratefully recall the immense contribution made by the daily labour of every worker to the nation's progress, to the Christian well-being of the family and to the development of the individual.

2. The cause of the world's anguish is that it does not "seek first the kingdom of God and His righteousness" (Mt 6:33). People go astray because they wander in the dark rather than follow the luminous path of truth. They are divided because their egoisms dissolve the bonds of love. "They trust in their wealth and boast of the abundance of their riches" (Ps 49:6). Limiting their hopes to worldly goods, they deprive themselves of life's authentic riches. The endless struggle in which such spirits are engaged, exploits and destroys, and those who engage in it are "unable from the good things that are seen to know Him Who is, and to discover the Creator in His creation" (Ws 1:13). Too often materialism, infatuated by its godless technology, science and culture, raises a tower more monstrous even than that of Babel, but whose fragility involves the world in a frightful insecurity. Material goods sought for themselves are fallacious riches which only impoverish, a deceitful liberation begetting slavery.

3. His Holiness Pope Pius XII, in his encyclical *On The Pilgrimage of Lourdes*, denounced yet again this degrading evil:

> The world of today which offers so many grounds for pride and hope, experiences as well a fearsome temptation to materialism, one often denounced by our predecessors and ourselves. This materialism is not only the condemned philosophy which presides over the political and economic life of a good part of humanity; it rages also in the love of money whose ravages spread in proportion to the growth of modern business and which dictates so many of the decisions burdening the lives of people; it is evidenced in a cult of the body, an excessive attachment to comfort and flight from any austerity of life; it can incite even to contempt for human life and its destruction before ever it has seen the light of day. It is at the root of an unbridled pursuit of pleasure, flaunted without shame and attempting to seduce, by written word and visual arts, souls still pure. It is discernible in a lack of care for one's fellows, in an egoism quite ready to crush, an injustice careless of the rights of others: to be brief, in a way of life which orders everything, with a view only to material prosperity and earthly satisfactions. Said the rich man, "I will say to my soul, 'Soul, you have ample goods laid up for many years; take your ease, eat, drink, be merry!'" But God said to him, "Fool! This night your soul is required of you!" (Lk 12:19 f.)[2]

4. To dam this ever rising tide of disintegration, human as well as Christian, all must face the truth, divine truth, in perfect honesty. It is this truth which must preside at the construction of our world, just as it is God who is the author of all creation. The divine message remains ever the same, the hierarchy of values unchanged. It is truth which frees us. Those sovereign goods which the glorious Redeemer has confided to His Church are indispensable for human, as for Christian development.

5. That is why the Church, mindful of her mission, tries to be present everywhere, bringing that without which it is impossible to build any sort of life. What she provides contributes to a society in which citizens and families can enjoy true liberty, economic and social security, and the possibility of a truly humane culture; in a word, builds a world at the heart of which Christ is the uncontested King of individuals, of families, of institutions, indeed of all human relations.

6. Let us strive to give an unequivocal example of all the civic and Christian virtues. Let us so live as to gain the immeasurable riches to which light eternal guides us. Our faith, teaching us the respect due to the dignity of the human person, raises us above any servile response to the sanction of force, guaranteeing the rights of the individual and of the family. The Church is not distrustful of technology. She recognizes its necessity and value, but she wishes that it remain ever the servant of riches which transcend technology. Let all those in authority, in the political domain or in other social sectors, place their constant effort in the service of the unfolding of God's plan. May all our institutions of education, our labour organizations, our movements of Catholic Action continue their beneficent efforts to increase that body of apostles whose indefatigable devotion enlightens, encourages and compels affection.

7. To build and consolidate, to make labour effective, to assure social security, progress and harmony, while preparing ourselves for a perfect happiness, let us recall the words of the Psalmist:

> The law of the Lord, is perfect, reviving the soul; the testimony of the Lord is sure, making wise the simple; the precepts of the Lord are right, rejoicing the heart; the commandment of the Lord is pure, enlightening the eyes; the fear of the Lord is clean, enduring forever; the ordinances of the Lord are true and righteous altogether. More to be desired are they than gold. (Ps 18:7-10)

8. In this jubilee year of the centenary of the Apparitions of Lourdes, may the Immaculate Virgin enlighten consciences and open every heart to the message of the love of her divine Son. And let us have confidence also in Saint Joseph the Worker, living model of that justice which should reign everywhere.

NOTES

1. It proved impossible to discover the original official English text of this Message. A new version from the French in the archives of the CCCB is offered here.
2. Pius XII, *On the Pilgrimage of Lourdes: a Warning against Materialism*, 1957, *The Papal Encyclicals*, edit. Claudia Carlen, IHM (Wilmington, N.C., McGrath Publishing, 1981), IV, 343, nn. 45-48.

Document 6

LABOUR DAY MESSAGE — 1958[1]
UNEMPLOYMENT:
PART OF ECONOMIC WARFARE

Author — Social Action Department, Canadian Catholic Conference

1.   What has been called "the crisis of our times" has been precip-
itated by the leaders of the U.S.S.R. in a clear declaration of economic warfare, the stated objective of which is the final destruction
of all forms of society not based on atheistic materialism. This economic warfare, which has already begun, will be waged with calculated ferocity and may well be more menacing to us than the hydro-
gen bomb and the intercontinental ballistic missile. The strategy of
this warfare is to bring about civil chaos; the tactics include provok-
ing class hatred, unemployment and all forms of disorder where
they do not already exist. The struggle is between total control by
a godless state on the one hand and various combinations of free
enterprise and democracy on the other.

2.   Nuclear warfare threatens, quite simply, the end of human life
on this planet, after a relatively short period of almost unimagin-
able horror and destruction. Economic warfare may lead to our being
nibbled to death, as it were. The alternative is for free citizens to
work ceaselessly to devise and employ means of sharing our physical, mental and spiritual resources in collaboration for the common
good. At no time in our history has there been greater need for intelligent, dedicated Christian leadership at all levels and in every institution of society.

3.   Unemployment mars the thankfulness and rejoicing that should

be characteristic of Labour Day. Its causes are varied and complex and no attempt is made, in this short message, to detail them. This running sore on our economy is, in part, due to the failure to employ fully our human talents for collaboration with our fellow men for the benefit of all humankind.

4. It is pertinent at this point to recall the fact that money is meaningless except as a symbol of real wealth, that is, goods and services. Higher wages do not benefit wage-earners when their receipt is accompanied by a matching rise in the cost of goods and services. Similarly, a greater production of goods is of no value to industry if people lack the money to buy the goods. Social justice demands that the benefits of man's efforts be widely shared for the common good.

5. Even in the simplest forms of society, concerted, cooperative effort for the common good is necessary. It is immeasurably more necessary now, even vital, when our society is composed of large and highly complex groups. But harmonious cooperation of all economic groups within a country cannot be achieved by state control. It must arise from the educated social consciousness of the groups themselves, if it is to conform to the social nature of man. This ideal of an organic society, fitted to meet the common interests of diverse groups, was clearly stated by Pope Pius XI[2] and is known on this continent as the Industry Council Plan.

6. This is the age of "bigness", big business, huge labour unions, increasingly centralized government, consolidated control of the media of communication and so on. It is unreasonable to hope that this trend to bigness will reverse itself; it is unrealistic for one group to attempt by misrepresentation or oversimplication to attribute responsibility for all social and economic problems to another group. This is particularly true in the area of labour-management relations, where the highest degree of understanding and mutual trust is essential if our society is to survive.

7. In the midst of the many and appalling dangers which threaten us, we need not lose courage. Our latent strength is our belief in the dignity and destiny of man, that he is not an economic cypher, nor a mere tool to be used and scrapped. As a Christian, he is a child of God who, motivated by the fundamental law of charity,

must work constructively and with all his resources of mind and heart, with his fellow men for the good of all.

8. In this way he will exemplify true democratic citizenship; he will prove his practical love of neighbour; and he will help to promote on this earth that ideal for which he prays when he says in the Lord's Prayer: "Thy will be done on earth as it is in heaven."

NOTES

1. This is the only instance in which the English Labour Day Message is quite different in theme and content from the French. I have been unable to discover any reason for this unusual procedure. The French Message can be found in *Messages des évêques canadiens à l'occasion de la fête du Travail (1956-1974)*, edit. R. Arès, SJ (Montréal, Les Éditions Bellarmin, 1974), p. 23. The title of the Message given there is *Attitude chrétienne face aux problèmes sociaux*.

2. Pius IX, *On Reconstructing the Social Order (Quadragesimo Anno)*, 1931, *The Papal Encyclicals*, edit. Claudia Carlen, IHM (Wilmington, N.C., McGrath Publishing, 1981), III, 427-31, nn. 76-97.

Document 7

LABOUR DAY MESSAGE — 1959
FOR A GREATER COLLABORATION
BETWEEN MANAGEMENT AND LABOUR

Author — The Canadian Catholic Conference

1. Grave dangers threaten the world today, dangers which have their roots in profoundly different ideologies. Catastrophe will only be averted by a close collaboration, based on justice and charity, between all who control our social and economic life. If Christian social doctrine is ignored by the world, our fate will be either slavery or destruction. Only by action inspired by Christian unity can we find our way out of today's agonizing dilemma.

2. During the last world war, management, labour and governments in Canada had to work together in the national interest. Does not the gravity of our present situation demand the same spirit of sacrifice, the same solidarity? Among the requirements for the economic and social order in any country is harmony of the forces of production. This can be achieved, humanly speaking, only through the existence and the stability of associations uniting workers on the one hand and management on the other. These groups must be strong, active, democratic and free from all undue outside influence. Thanks to such organizations, inspired and guided in their activities by Christian social principles, one and the other are enabled to hold free discussions and to establish independently and equitably the status of labour.

3. The considerable power which these management and labour groups enjoy imposes grave responsibilities upon them. They must

avoid the use of their strength as a purely defensive or offensive weapon. If they do not, there is war between one side and the other. On the contrary, they have the duty, in view of their great influence, of better serving the interests both of their partisans and of the whole nation collectively. Trade unions and management must channel their efforts so as to render true service to the common good.

4. Class distinctions do in fact exist, but according to the social doctrine of the Church there are no insuperable barriers between classes. Class consciousness, which derives from conscious solidarity in the pursuit of common interests, is in itself a natural and even a praiseworthy thing, so long as it does not imply any contempt for the rights and needs of other groups. But to confuse class consciousness with class warfare, which is its abuse and distortion, would be as unjust as to equate enlightened patriotism with aggressive nationalism. Management organizations and those of the workers thus have the duty of avoiding all class antagonism, all systematic disparagement. Any doctrine which states that such warfare is inevitable is directly opposed to Christian doctrine and aspirations.

5. In our country we have no experience of open and systematic warfare between management and labour. We should appreciate this good fortune. Nevertheless, the situation in Canada still falls short of the Christian social ideal. If there is no bitter struggle between the leaders of management and labour, neither is there any practical, effective, constructive collaboration, except during times of armed conflict. It is not sufficient for Christians to reject class warfare in theory. They must will and create class collaboration, in fact and in spirit. Management and workers must try to meet on concrete common grounds of thought which are capable of becoming grounds of action. There can be no common action without a minimum of common ideas. It would thus be normal for those who profess the Christian social doctrine, whatever their condition of life, to try to reach certain identical practical conclusions. This does not exclude a divergence of interest and certain conflicts which can be resolved only through compromise.

6. We earnestly wish that the leaders of management and labour in Canada would come together to exchange ideas. There is no lack of subjects for discussion: the problem of unemployment, the exploitation of natural resources, social legislation, for instance, all provide opportunity for management-labour discussion. Such initiative

could but create good faith, increase mutual trust and bring about a solution to certain of our problems.

7.   It is up to the leaders of workers and of management themselves to seek out occasions for meeting. They must contrive to bring about collaboration, occasional or permanent. Whether this is done through specialized management-labour commissions or through economic councils and permanent work councils, great benefit can come from such initiative. The state too has the responsibility of encouraging such collaboration between managers and workers, by inviting representatives of both sides to sit, as often as possible, on administrative or consultative commissions.

8.   The situation in Canada is privileged from this point of view, since it permits us to avoid two excesses which have caused great damage in other countries, that is: war between management and labour and exaggerated intervention of the state which substitutes itself for the leaders of workers and management. In either case management and labour have remained facing each other simply as opposing and hostile forces. Open discussion and sincere colla-boration are the means of avoiding such abuses and of reaching the harmony and collaboration required both by the natural law and by Christ's teaching. Nature has in fact everywhere sown unity and harmony. In the human body, despite the diversity of its members, we find unity and balance in the relations of the parts. So too has nature willed that in society, workers and employers should live the obligation of working for the common good. As our Holy Father Pope John XXIII has written, echoing the words of Leo XIII (*Inter Graves*, 1891):

> This prospect will be realized when the social doctrine of the Church is put into effect, and if all "endeavour to preserve in themselves and to arouse in others, from the highest to the lowest, that mistress and queen of all virtues, charity. For sal-vation, so eagerly awaited, will be the fruit of a great outpour-ing of charity, since Christian charity, containing in itself the whole Gospel and willing to sacrifice itself for others, is the most powerful antidote to the pride and egoism of the world."[1]

NOTE

1. *On Truth, Unity and Peace (Ad Petri Cathedram)*, 1959, *The Papal Encyclicals*, edit. Claudia Carlen, IHM (Wilmington, N.C., McGrath Publishing, 1981), V, 10, n. 49.

Document 8

LABOUR DAY MESSAGE — 1960
LABOUR AND IMMIGRATION

Author — The Canadian Catholic Conference

1. Still mindful of all the good things that have been said and done on behalf of refugees during World Refugee Year, we would like to use our Labour Day Message to indicate the desirability of continuing our activity in this area and of developing still further right attitudes towards refugees and immigrants in general. Our words are directed to labour because we realize that fundamentally labour has the right attitude towards refugees and immigrants and moreover, is able to exert a good influence on other segments of our Canadian society in this vital matter.

A QUESTION

2. It is well known that labour has officially supported the *Universal Declaration of Human Rights*, which states that "No one shall be arbitrarily deprived of his nationality nor denied the right to change his nationality", and leaders of organized labour have spoken out clearly for an immigration policy free of prejudice. Despite this, one still occasionally hears individual workers ask, "Why should we provide jobs for foreigners when our own men are out of work?"

THE ANSWER

3. The answer is quite simple. We should not provide jobs indiscriminately for workers of other nations when our own are out of

work; but we should provide a place in Canada, with an opportunity to work, for some whose circumstances are, and have been for years, far worse than those of even the unemployed Canadian.

4. It is simply a matter of recognizing a condition in which "Thy necessity is greater than mine", and offering the help that is so sorely needed, even if it means depriving ourselves of opportunities for work we also need, but not quite so sorely, or of accepting a standard of living lower than the one we now enjoy in Canada. We are not convinced however, that helping needy immigrants would necessarily result in such hardships. The divine promise of a hundredfold blessing applies to nations as well as to individuals.

PROTECTION OF IMMIGRANTS

5. We would like to commend those who have assisted immigrants in any way and especially those who have taken steps to protect the new Canadian worker from injustices on the part of unscrupulous employers. Fortunately such injustices have not been widespread, thanks to a prevailing sense of decency and the protective influence of organized labour, of government, and of the press; but vigilance is always commendable because injustice is always to be condemned. An injustice to workers anywhere is an injustice to workers everywhere; and that too, is another reason why all groups and classes should be interested in the well-being of those who need to migrate to Canada, and solicitous for their welfare when they have arrived. "If a stranger dwell in your land, and abide among you, do not upbraid him; but let him be among you as one of the same country; and you shall love him as yourselves." (Lv 19:33-34)

AN UNDERLYING PRINCIPLE

6. There is a principle regarding the right to migrate that we feel ought to be stated. Correct attitudes can more easily be formed and practical programs better elaborated, if we know the general direction we ought to take. First of all, few people want to leave their homeland; and it is the duty of the state to give every reasonable help in creating economic conditions that will allow citizens to remain at home. In this regard our governments are to be commended for the assistance they have given and are giving to some

less developed nations, thus making it possible for more people to remain in their own country and improve their own economic and social conditions.

7.   When however, an area is unable to support its population, for lack of economic resources, then that state has a duty to help people to emigrate and to find a new home. No nation may justly refuse its people the right to emigrate. When people want to move, they must be left free to do so, even though emigration may be regulated and legitimate means may be used to encourage citizens to stay at home.

RESPECT FOR RIGHTS OF WOULD-BE IMMIGRANTS

8.   What is perhaps of more immediate and actual importance to us in Canada, is our duty to respect the rights of would-be immigrants. The late, beloved Pope Pius XII stated the principle in these words:

> The Creator of the universe made all good things primarily for the good of all. If then in some locality, the land offers the possibility of supporting a large number of people, the sovereignty of the state, although it must be respected, cannot be exaggerated to the point that access to this land is, for inadequate and unjustified reasons, denied to needy and decent people from other nations, provided of course that the common good, considered very carefully, does not forbid this.[1]

THE COMMON GOOD

9.   It is the business of the state to regulate the flow of immigration with a view to the common good; but it is the duty of all to recognize that there is a common good, more universal than that of a particular nation or group within a nation. There is the common good of humanity itself. And certainly it is in the interest of this common good, that human beings who have been suffering inhuman hardships, be given an opportunity to live in a manner befitting their human dignity, as children of God, regardless of race, colour or creed, even though it should mean if necessary, a lower material standard of living for all in the nation of their adoption. Not charity

only, but justice demands the recognition and the implementation of this principle.

CHAMPIONS OF HUMAN RIGHTS

10.   It is a well recognized fact that from the ranks of labour have emerged some of the great champions of human rights. Organized labour will always deserve the respect and gratitude of all right-minded men while it continues to give leadership in the struggle for justice and charity for all. We would encourage Canadian labour to maintain and promote vigorously its policy of universal brotherhood under the Fatherhood of God and to work for a steady influx of needy immigrants to our Canadian homeland.

11.   We invite our governments to extend further their own efforts in the same direction. We urge our provincial governments in particular to maintain a strict watch over all those who might be tempted to exploit labour in general and immigrants in particular for selfish ends. It is the duty of government ever to protect the weak from the strong.

UNEMPLOYMENT AND IMMIGRATION

12.   We share the concern of all in the matter of unemployment. It is a constant cause of suffering and hardship to our unemployed citizens and their families. It is proposed as an objection to the admission of immigrant families. That is a reproach to our ability to organize society efficiently, as required by the demands of justice and charity.

13.   We warmly commend the Senate study on unemployment now under way and the efforts of the Departments of Labour to improve the situation. We would however, join with others in recommending that a standing committee be set up to study and seek appropriate solutions for this pressing problem; and that it be made up of representatives from government, labour, management and from other bodies having a direct interest therein. This urgent problem,

aggravated by the introduction of new methods of production without due regard for the welfare of the human persons involved, deserves the full, immediate and continued attention of the best minds available to wrestle with it.

NOTE

1. Letter to Archbishop John T. McNicholas, *Acta Apostolicae Sedis,* Vatican, 1949, XLI, 69 f.; *National Catholic Register,* Los Angeles, Feb. 6, 1949.

Document 9

LABOUR DAY MESSAGE — 1961
THE SOCIAL TEACHING OF THE CHURCH

Author — The Canadian Catholic Conference

On this Labour Day, Christian social principles command our attention as the only ones capable of restoring order in society. The study of these principles is the responsibility of all. In this regard, Labour Day this year has a special importance. The seventieth anniversary of the social encyclical *On the Condition of the Working Classes (Rerum Novarum)*, 1891, and the appearance of a similiar great encyclical, *Mother and Teacher*, press upon all the invitation to study the social teachings of the Church and to become more and more aware of their responsibilities in this field.

The anniversary of *Rerum Novarum* was the occasion, in Rome particularly, of great demonstrations. The workers felt the urge to give thanks again to the Church for this document on the condition of labour which had signaled the hour of liberation for the proletariat. It had helped establish a better balance in the distribution of this world's goods. Leo XIII had stood up with courage against the prejudices of his time, against the philosophy of economic liberalism. He had recalled to governments and employers their grave obligations to the poor and to the workers and proclaimed in a clear voice their right to organize. He did not speak in vain.

The results inspired by this great social charter are numerous and varied, especially in the western world: workers have obtained better working conditions, professional organizations have multiplied, social legislation has been developed to bring better protection to the weak. On the other hand all the directives of Pope Leo XIII have not been applied. There is still present the spectre of unemployment. Families are still condemned to live in slums and many workers continue to receive a wage that does not meet the demands of justice and equity.

This is the reason why the successors of Leo XIII, especially Pius XI and Pius XII, have so often recalled his teachings. So too Pope John XXIII in his letter, *Mother and Teacher*: "That encyclical *(Rerum Novarum)* is rightly hailed, even to the present day, as the *Magna Charta* for the reconstruction of the socio-economic order".[1]

To speak of the problem which he considers a major one in our society, Pope John XXIII borrows a phrase from *Rerum Novarum*. He points to the misery and wretchedness of the people in many underdeveloped countries. In virtue of the oneness that all share, no person may remain indifferent to people who are struggling with poverty and misery and are not enjoying the basic rights of human beings. The duty of coming to their aid with the greatest possible unselfishness is imperative. It is so imperative that there will be no fruitful or lasting peace as long as the economic and social condition of these people differs so greatly from the condition of people in the more developed nations. The Christian conscience must not rest in the face of a plague of hunger that affects two-thirds of mankind.

True disciples of Christ cannot remain insensible and inactive in the face of the misery of others. They must recognize their obligations in justice and charity to their neighbors even though these live on the other side of the earth. It is our duty to prove in a concrete manner that the love of God leads directly to the love of neighbour. The Church in the name of human dignity, has shown herself champion of the oppressed in the industrial world. Today she reaffirms the right of the underprivileged nations to live with dignity among their more wealthy neighbors.

Like Leo XIII, Pope John XXIII would make us conscious of the need to work with everyone, individuals, groups, and public authorities, to resolve an ever-growing number of economic and social problems peculiar to our time:

1. Again there is expression of pity for the lot of workers, even of those in industrialized countries, at least of certain regions and sectors. Their wages should be determined according to justice and equity. That means wages which will permit the worker to maintain a truly human standard of living and to face with dignity his family responsibilities. For them too, social progress ought to go hand in hand with economic development.

In harmony with the common good it is necessary to promote worker enterprises, to develop agriculture along family lines and to foster cooperatives as a means of integrating these two. In both medium and large enterprises, the workers' desire to take an active part in the life of the enterprises where they are employed is a legitimate aspiration. It corresponds to natural needs inscribed in the human heart, and is in harmony with an unfolding historical development in economic, social and political life.

2.   The situation of farmers also receives the attention of the Holy Father. The productivity of their work as well as their level of living is too often below that of many who live in cities. It is necessary then to work for those economic policies which will allow farmers to improve their productivity and to assure them greater security and a fuller participation in the general prosperity. More favoured workers cannot remain indifferent to the lot of their farmer-brothers or of others who do not enjoy equally favourable economic and social conditions.

3.   Among all workers including farmers, a further extension of their right to unite would permit their better integration into our society and genuine participation at all levels of economic and social life. They could thus be associated in elaborating and executing those economic and social policies that are necessary to their welfare. In our country, even if labour unions are quite widely developed, we ought to realize that our society has not fully accepted the idea of unionization and that too many workers, rural and urban, still do not belong to organizations of their own. This situation impedes the direct action of unions and effectively prevents them from playing the role which belongs to them, that of helping to solve the many complex problems of our economic society.

4.   Another problem finds its true solution in the encyclical *Mother and Teacher*, namely the relationship between a growing world population and the available means of subsistence. The basic solution to this problem must not be sought in expedients which are contrary to the natural order established by God and attack the very source of human life. It will be found in new scientific efforts on the part of man to increase his mastery over nature. The progress already realized by science and the development of new techniques open up unlimited horizons.

5.   The need to establish just economic and social policies demands an ever-increasing intervention on the part of public authority. This poses a serious question. How can we maintain our liberty and a true sense of social responsibility and at the same time find a valid solution to our various problems? The Church rejects both a suffocating statism and an individualism which leads to anarchy. Neither state absolutism nor unrestrained competition can be considered the basis of a social order that will be in keeping with the demands of human nature. Such an order cannot be developed without the free involvement of those affected. The establishment of policies that correspond to the needs of our time, always respecting man as the subject of social life, requires the state to encourage its citizens to accept their responsibilities and to provide the institutions that are favorable to joint action.

6.   Social institutions are founded in a crusading spirit for the service of men and the realization of their aspirations. Too often, as they become better established, they are liable to forget their origins and their ends. Preoccupied with assuring their own stability above all else, they come to value persons as means to an end, rather than as the active subjects of social life. Associations of employers and employees, like all other groups, must not give their members the impression that they are mere objects existing for the sake of the organization. The organization exists for them.

On the occasion of this Labour Day Message, it is our wish that all become aware of the luminous teaching of Pope John XXIII in his encyclical *Mother and Teacher*. The directives found there, so full of wisdom and prudence, are the only ones capable of re-establishing order in society and of assuring to all peoples an era of prosperity, joy and peace.

NOTE

1. *Mother and Teacher*, 1961, *The Papal Encyclicals*, edit. Claudia Carlen, IHM, (Wilmington, N.C., McGrath Publishing, 1981) V, 62, n. 26.

Document 10

LABOUR DAY MESSAGE — 1962
SOCIALIZATION

Author — The Canadian Catholic Hierarchy

1. A problem of conscience pervades the minds of our people. It renders the present insecure and the future uncertain in a time calling for courageous and positive action. This problem is the conflict of values, the issue of individual freedom versus social progress.

2. As guide and instructor of consciences, the Church spoke through John XXIII last year to point to a resolution of this dilemma. In his social encyclical, *Mother and Teacher* (1961), he squarely posed the issue of socialization and individual freedom. The past year has witnessed the intensification of this problem in Canada so that we feel it timely to speak further on the question of socialization.

3. Remarkable changes have taken place in the past two decades through new developments in power, productivity, transportation and communication. Industrial civilization has really just begun, for a new civilization tends to come into being when a hitherto rare or occasional event becomes more general or common. One rocket in orbit does not make a space-age but can be its forerunner. With the acceptance of research as the key to scientific discovery, we may expect change as a regular feature of our life. These changes moreover will extend to many parts of our life and to the life of newly developing countries as yet unaffected.

4. There are many signs that the particular is becoming general in the social structure of our present civilization. Social development is flowing into our lives through new channels. Politics and industry

are not the only pipelines of social progress. In the words of Pope John XXIII:

> In recent times this tendency (socialization) has given rise to the formation everywhere of both national and international movements, associations and institutions with economic, cultural, social, sporting, recreational, professional and political ends.[1]

5. This tendency to organize into groups for various common purposes, including progress, is most simply described as socialization. It is the expression of the social nature of man, evidence that "it is not good for man to be alone." (Gn 2:18)

> It is also the result and the expression of a natural, wellnigh irresistible urge in man to combine with his fellows for the attainment of aims and objectives which are beyond the means or the capabilities of single individuals.[2]

6. Totalitarian and materialistic socialism is an extreme, a heretical form of socialization. In itself, socialization no more necessarily leads to this kind of socialism than the natural desire for freedom necessarily leads to the other extreme, individualism. Indeed, socialization, with all the organizational activity which it implies, is the natural solution to the dangers of both extremes in our society. Pope Leo XIII denounced the loss of organic social life by nineteenth century man. He was thinking of men set before machines, their houses lying within the shadow of the factory, and only nationalism and political socialism to fill the vacuum left by the lack of group activity in their lives. Socialization is the re-vitalization of this lost organic life.

7. The great scientific advances of recent years have freed man from those narrow "laws" that nineteenth-century liberalism thought necessary for the development of society, as well as from the all-embracing arms of socialism and communism. For the first time in the history of industrial society we find ourselves realizing that industrial development need no longer form and control in its wake the person, the family, and free groups. Technological development has become so much an instrument of man and can so clearly be put at his service, that the person, the family, and the free group can now begin to control the order of this development as never before.

8. As this becomes truly possible, private property, the worker, and the right to free association by cooperation, should no longer be on the defensive in our society. In short, while technology displaces many traditional types of labour, socialization can make ordinary man more productive, and can challenge the creative and artistic man in exciting new ways. We have hardly begun to tap the organizational potential of the citizen in the democratic order, of the employer and the employee in industrial society, of the family in the local community, of the professions in social planning. Until we do so, technological society will not be a human civilization insofar as it will not bear the imprint of these very human expressions. For socialization gives human features to the planning required by industrial society. Man smiles as he stands before his own creations.

9. Our society cannot possibly advance on all fronts, and therefore become a truly human society, if there is a basic misunderstanding about the nature and functions of social organization. The organization is meant to serve man, not man the organization. To misunderstand this is to throw us back upon the individualism-versus-socialism conflict of the nineteenth century. How much this conflict is still with us is evident on the international scene in stifled trade and immigration, and in an inability to find a place for such a cultural economic experiment in socialization as the European Common Market. It is equally evident on the national scene in the case of Medicare, in the persistence of bitter industrial disputes and the extent of permanent unemployment.

10. There are of course many encouraging signs: the sense of responsibility for the impact of industry on society manifested by the recent study conferences chaired by the Duke of Edinburgh; the tour of Productivity Council representatives to Western Europe; the increasing concern among labour, management and government officials for a suitable programme of education for the industrial worker; the more frequent reflection upon the family by social planners and social workers; and the more diversified experiments in general education.

11. Energy, action and goodwill however are only wasted when our society is without a social philosophy adequate to the age. For this reason we strongly recommend that the social teaching of the Church be studied now with greater intensity than ever before. Within the Church the fruits of socialization, made manifest in the

liturgical movement, the lay apostolate and the ecumenical movement, have been accompanied by a theological revival. So too our
society must learn a formula of active, free and intelligent participation, as its members organize themselves in those social groupings
that will be expressive of a social philosophy fit for man in this new
age.

NOTES

1. *Mother and Teacher, The Papal Encyclicals*, edit. Claudia Carlen, IHM, (Wilmington, N.C., McGrath Publishing, 1982), V, 66, n. 60.
2. John XXIII, *ibid.*

Document 11

LABOUR DAY MESSAGE — 1963
INDISPENSABLE COLLABORATION
BETWEEN PUBLIC AUTHORITIES
AND INTERMEDIATE ORGANIZATIONS

Author — The Canadian Catholic Conference

INTRODUCTION

The importance of close and harmonious collaboration between public authorities on the one hand, and the various associations, organizations, and institutions established independently of government initiative, and generally called "intermediate bodies", on the other, has always been stressed in Catholic social teaching. Two reasons prompt us to devote our annual Labour Day Message to this basic theme. We wish to set it out in terms as concrete as possible, and to review it in the light of the recent and memorable social encyclicals of the late Pope John XXIII, *Mother and Teacher*, 1961, and *Peace on Earth*, 1963.

Our Rapidly Changing Society

In a country in such total evolution as ours, when so many plans, programs and reforms are being drawn up at the same time in all sectors and at all levels, municipal, provincial and federal, it becomes imperative to unite all the energies, talents and goodwill available for this extensive task.

It is important moreover, that all who are involved, both governed and governing, share, discuss and approve studies, decisions and actions that can have far-reaching consequences. Any action that is only one-sided, though taken by government with the best of intentions, runs the risk in the long run of discouraging the free flow of public opinion and suggestion, and of snuffing out the citizen's sense of responsibility and initiative, so indispensable to the general well-being of society.

Safeguarding the Democratic Way of Life

In a political system, the spirit of democracy is manifested not only in the right of citizens to vote freely and from time to time, but also in the effort of the elected representatives to exercise their mandate in close and continuous collaboration with their electors.

> To express his own views of the duties and sacrifices imposed on him and not to be compelled to obey without being heard — these are two rights of the citizen... From the solidarity, harmony, and other good results thus produced between the citizens and the government, one may decide which democracy is really healthy and well-balanced, and what is its life energy and power of expansion.[1]

In the modern state, intermediate bodies have become for all practical purposes the principal and most reliable means of expression at the disposal of the public; therefore they should be heard and respected as such.

The voice of the isolated voter makes little impression in our day. Only intermediate bodies assuming all their responsibilities can save our country from the horrors of arbitrary action or that political tyranny which other so-called democratic countries have sadly experienced. It is only by working together, and not by opposing each other, that our civil authorities and intermediate bodies can maintain a truly democratic system of government.

Let us consider in concrete terms some of the responsibilities incumbent on both the intermediate bodies and the public authorities, which by their nature demand close and indispensable collaboration.

I — SOME RESPONSIBILITIES OF INTERMEDIATE BODIES

The intermediate bodies should:

a) recognize that their responsibilities are increasing.

Paradoxical as it may appear, these responsibilities must increase in proportion to the "more frequent and extensive intervention by public authorities in the economic and social fields,"[2] so characteristic of our age and making itself felt everywhere. The effective and representative work of groups therefore, must be more evident than ever. Any evasion or systematic obstruction of their role by government intervention would be regrettable and harmful to the balanced evolution of our country.

b) broaden their horizons with a view to closer cooperation in seeking and promoting the common good.

Individual citizens and intermediate groups are obliged to make their specific contributions to the common good. One of the chief consequences of this is that they must bring their own interests into harmony with the needs of the community, and must dispose of their goods and services as civil authorities have prescribed, in accord with the norms of justice, in due process, and within the limits of their competence. This they must do by means of formally perfect actions, the content of which must serve the common good, or at least be capable of being directed toward that good.[3]

c) pursue and promote a most careful collaboration with civic authorities.

Such cooperation should always be close, clear and constructive, conducted in that real spirit of solidarity stressed in John XXIII's *Mother and Teacher*. In fact, the life of society can be prosperous and orderly only if private citizens, intermediate bodies and public authorities work in harmony and unite their efforts.

d) take whatever steps or make whatever statements they consider necessary, provided they be truly useful, the fruit of serious study and discussion, representative of the views of their members, free from partisan politics and obviously for the common good.

e) set up where possible committees or councils for study and research.

These may be private or the joint effort of several associations, working with university centres and government bodies. This would lead to a clearer analysis of facts, a better evaluation of situations, more timely and effective action, and when necessary, constructive suggestions for legislative and administrative measures.

f) place in responsible positions qualified and experienced persons capable of facing, analysing and solving the actual problems.

As our civilization is characterized above all by the remarkable achievements of science and technology, ''one cannot enter these organizations and work effectively from within unless one is scientifically competent, technically capable and skilled in the practice of one's own profession.''[4]

g) bring the officers and members of each group into closer association to assure that the former are truly representative.

Studies have shown that very often in large groups, as they grow and become more complex, considerable gaps appear between the opinions expressed by the officers and the real opinions of the members.

It is important therefore, in our opinion, that such a situation be corrected without delay wherever it is found to exist. Such disunity leads to confusion and, in the long run, lessens the practical influence of the intermediate bodies with the public in general and the civil authorities in particular. Hence the importance of maintaining a continuous exchange of information between officers and members, by means of a proper program of education. Otherwise, how can one know that the public statements of the leaders truly correspond to the real needs and aspirations of the members?

h) try by all means to bring together all the professional and non-professional groups that are already so numerous in our society and still continue to multiply.

Too often there is division, or repetition that endangers their efficiency, weakens their practical influence with public authorities and even, at times, interferes with their pursuit of the common good. We cannot give enough encouragement to all these groups to look for practical ways of coordinating their efforts, of undertaking joint action at times, and even of regrouping their forces.

i) make an effort to have the intermediate bodies representing different sectors of our society show due respect for one another.

It would seem desirable to set up permanent liaison committees, or something similar, in order to establish regular contact among them and to facilitate a mutually helpful exchange of views and experiences. This would avoid useless provocations and contradictory statements that are always harmful to the common good. As Pope John XXIII suggests:

There are some souls, particularly those endowed with generosity, who, on finding situations where the requirements of justice are not satisfied in full, feel enkindled with the desire to change the state of things, as if they wished to have recourse to something like revolution. It must be borne in mind that to proceed gradually is the law of life in all its expressions. Therefore in human institutions too, it is not possible to renovate for the better, except by working from within and gradually.[5]

May this Labour Day Message, devoted to that "indispensable collaboration which ought to prevail between public authorities and intermediate groups," do nothing to discourage the most worthy efforts being made, or to disparage the real progress already achieved. May it be on the contrary, a clear expression of the sincere desire of the Canadian Catholic Hierarchy to contribute to our country's progress.

It is our earnest wish at this time to recall in precise terms these mutual responsibilities, convinced as we are that they are essential to the harmonious development of our country and to its general prosperity.

II — SOME RESPONSIBILITIES OF PUBLIC AUTHORITIES

The public authorities should:

a) fully recognize the existence of associations or intermediate bodies and the need for them.

For the achievement of ends which individual human beings cannot attain except by association, it is necessary and indispensable to set up a great variety of intermediate groups and bodies in order to guarantee the dignity of the human person and safeguard a sufficient sphere of freedom and responsibility.[6]

It even devolves upon the public authorities to contribute to the creation of a state of affairs that would "facilitate the establishment of intermediate groups which will make social life richer and more effective."[7]

b) see to it "that the citizens no less than the intermediate bodies, in exercising their rights and fulfilling their duties, enjoy genuine juridical protection in their relations with one another and with the public officials."[8]

c) seek and foster a real collaboration with the intermediate groups.

Instead of seeing these groups as a threat or a luxury, the public authority rather should draw upon them as a source of light and experience, ally them to itself, seeing them as an indispensable support and aid to that work which is proper to the state, namely the realization of the common good in the temporal order.

d) enter into partnership with these groups in the preliminary study, discussion and formulation of laws and regulations.

As Pius XII declared:

> To express his own views on the duties and sacrifices imposed upon him; and, not to be compelled to obey without first being heard — these are two rights of the citizen which find their expression in democracy, as its name implies.[9]

e) create where needed other consultative bodies, superior councils or permanent commissions, similar to those already existing in our country.

These have the immense advantage of bringing together representatives of different groups and of establishing relations among them and with the public officials. It is important above all that these bodies be truly operative. They must therefore be given all the financial and technical assistance they need to work effectively.

f) encourage all higher officials and technical consultants, specialists and jurists in the service of the various government bodies, to meet often with the leaders and members of these groups.

This will help them to keep in touch with actual problems and with practical difficulties that may accompany new legislation.

g) have recourse, continually and officially, to the intermediate groups for their collaboration in both the application and control of laws and regulations.

As Pope John XXIII observed, "In the political life of the commonwealth, it is of great importance that all ranks of citizens feel themselves daily more obligated to safeguard the common good."[10]

Such collaboration is necessary to avoid conflicts caused by the unsuitability of certain measures, or by inevitable differences of interpretation. It is necessary also in order to involve a larger number of competent persons and associations that may be especially interested in the development of a given sector and capable of working closely with public authorities for the realization of the common good. In fact, it belongs to the state to encourage in its citizens a sense of the common good. This requires a many sided education it is true, but it normally develops best in concrete action.

h) make known to the citizens and to the intermediate bodies as clearly as possible the true dimensions of the problems to be solved and the precise import and expediency of the measures to be taken.

It is important that all who will be affected by new laws know their meaning and spirit, as well as their implications and specific requirements. They can then discuss them calmly and with profit, and freely give their accord.

> The dignity of the human person also requires that every man enjoy the right to act freely and responsibly. For this reason, in social relations especially, man should exercise his rights, fulfil his obligations and, in the countless forms of collaboration with others, act chiefly on his own responsibility and initiative. This is to be done in such a way that each one acts on his own decision, of purpose and from a consciousness of his obligation, without being moved by force or pressure brought to bear on him externally. For any human society that is established on the sole basis of force must be regarded as simply inhuman, inasmuch as the freedom of its members is repressed, when in fact they should be provided with appropriate incentives and means for developing and perfecting themselves.[11]

Here then are made explicit some of the reciprocal duties which we believe devolve upon intermediate bodies and public authorities. On our respect for them depends in large measure the constant progress and equilibrium of our Canadian society. "Not revolution but harmonious evolution" declared Pius XII, "will bring about salvation and justice."[12]

CONCLUSION — TWO CONTRIBUTING FACTORS

In a period of rapid change and manifold reform such as ours, two general supplementary conditions can contribute to free exchange among all parties and to a better realization of the common good: maintaining a certain calmness in discussion and a progressive evolution.

Calmness in Discussion

At this point in Canadian history there are multiple occasions for differences of opinion on initiatives to be taken and steps to be followed. It could hardly be otherwise in a society that wisely acknowledges the right of each one to choose freely and to express himself openly. Nevertheless it is important that we avoid unnecessary tensions and conflicts. It is good to distinguish between fruitful discussion and partisan debate. As Pius XII declared:

> When people call for "more and better democracy," such a demand can have no other meaning than that the citizen be ever better enabled to hold his own personal opinion, to express it and to make it appreciated in a fashion conducive to the common good.[13]

We would therefore encourage all citizens, all directors of intermediate bodies and all political leaders to maintain a fitting calm in their discussions and in their daily relations. Moreover, personal contacts and discreet negotiations are preferable to public statements that too often provoke and upset people. Together we can work for that order envisioned by Pope John XXIII, "An order that is genuinely human, whose foundation is truth, whose measure and objective is justice, whose driving force is love, and whose method of attainment is freedom."[14]

Progressive Evolution

In closing, let us recall that the sincere desire to make rapid progress, to accomplish worthwhile goals, even to make up for lost time, should not lead to the error of skipping necessary steps. Too much haste in economic and social progress can stir up resistance that could be avoided. Too easily it brings on debate and conflict that throw individuals and groups into discord. Then, sooner or later, having learned by failure on the hard road of experience, it is found necessary to retrace one's steps and go forward again, this time avoiding the short cuts.

NOTES

1. Pius XII, *Christmas Message, 1944, Acta Apostolicae Sedis,* Vatican, 1945, XXXVII, 13; *The Catholic Mind,* New York, 1945, XLIII, 67.

2. John XXIII, *Mother and Teacher, The Papal Encyclicals,* edit. Claudia Carlen, IHM, (Wilmington, N.C., McGrath Publishing, 1981), V, 64, n. 49.

3. John XXIII, *Peace on Earth,* cf. Carlen above, V, 113, n. 53.

4. John XXIII, *ibid.,* p. 123, n. 148.

5. *Ibid.,* p. 125, nn. 161-62.

6. John XXIII, *ibid.,* p. 109, n. 24.

7. John XXIII, *ibid.,* p. 114, n. 64.

8. Pius XII, *Christmas Message, 1942, Acta Apostolicae Sedis,* Vatican, 1943, XXXV, 21 f., n. 4; *The Catholic Mind,* New York, 1943, XLI, 57, n. 4.

9. *Christmas Message, 1944, Acta Apostolicae Sedis,* Vatican, 1945, XLIII, 13; *The Catholic Mind,* New York, 1945, XLIII, 67.

10. *Mother and Teacher,* cf. Carlen above, V, 70, n. 96.

11. John XXIII, *Peace on Earth,* cf. Carlen above, V, 110, n. 34.

12. *Pentecost Message, June 13, 1943, Acta Apostolicae Sedis,* Vatican, 1943, XXXV, 175; *The Catholic Mind,* New York, 1943, XLI, July, p. 4.

13. *Christmas Message, 1944, Acta Apostolicae Sedis,* Vatican, 1945, XXXVII, 13; *The Catholic Mind,* New York, 1941, XLIII, 68.

14. *Peace on Earth,* cf. Carlen above, V, 124, n. 149.

Document 12

LABOUR DAY MESSAGE — 1964
AUTOMATION

Author — The Canadian Catholic Hierarchy

INTRODUCTION

1. Labour Day, 1964, finds us seriously involved in a technological world; the threat of the machine replacing man is with us. It is therefore necessary to re-affirm man's dignity, to stress in clear terms man's pre-eminence in production over machines and technology. Of special significance at this time are the words of Scripture: "Fill the earth and subdue it" (Gn 1:28), which remind us that God intended that man, as His own true image, should imitate His creative love and learn to dominate and control nature to make it serve the needs of all his brothers. God did not intend that man should himself become the victim of his own creative powers.

2. Thus the subject of our Labour Day Statement this year, automation, is a serious concern for every segment of Canadian society, especially for those persons who are beginning to suffer the negative effects of this new technique in production.

3. Automation, a method of improving human productivity through machines, finds application not only in industry but also in the business world where computers are beginning to replace clerical workers. Such widespread introduction of automatic processes has grave implications. Increasing numbers of persons are beginning to suffer unemployment and displacement by the application of these new processes. The threat to the dignity of these men and

women is a cause of serious concern to organized labour, industry and government who view with warranted alarm the immediate and long-range effects of this new power in business, industry, and society itself.

4. Our purpose in dealing with the subject of automation is to remind those agencies responsible for its implementation of the need to consider the human and spiritual implications of this new technology. Man is the centre and source of society and his needs and dignity must be protected. Pope John XXIII admonished us in his encyclical letter, *Mother and Teacher* (1961), that science and technology should serve man and his development and not become his master. He stated that the gigantic forces placed at the disposal of technology require man to recognize the overwhelming importance of spiritual values and consequently to see that these scientific and technical advances serve man and his development and do not dehumanize him or lead him to destruction.[1]

EFFECTS OF AUTOMATION

5. Among the good effects of automation we observe that it not only increases productivity but also decreases production costs. It improves working conditions and can eliminate routine and hazardous jobs. It makes possible the creation of new industries and products. It provides for shorter hours and increases leisure time. This leisure time, profitably spent, will enrich man physically and spiritually, enable him to grow intellectually and creatively and to make his family relationships more meaningful.

6. In the long run automation can provide the key to the attainment of some of labour's chief goals, a shorter work week, higher wages and better working conditions, with due respect for the processes of collective bargaining between employer and employees.

7. Automation and technological progress then, are considered essential to the general welfare, the economic strength and defense of the nation. Furthermore, through the intelligent application of these methods, for the first time in his history, man can be released from drudgery and poverty.

8. Just as there are a great number of people who focus attention

on the brighter side of automation, there are also those who believe that the impact of automation in the reduction of jobs, is and will be much greater than is commonly believed; that automation is a major factor in eliminating jobs; that it displaces people directly and indirectly; that it requires very little maintenance; that it is likely to reduce rather than to increase the demand for skills and aptitudes, because it is a fact that many workers are not retrainable. Often the workers displaced are the least adaptable, the older, the lower paid, and the unskilled. They cannot afford to move to another location or they are psychologically incapable of beginning a new life in a strange area.

9. It is also argued that employees fear automation not so much because it will deprive them of a living but because it will give them too much leisure. This psychological fear of leisure is really based on anxiety concerning what a sudden shortage or absence of work would do in a work-oriented society. To be deprived of work in such a society is equivalent to becoming a social outcast, suddenly unneeded and unheeded.

RECOMMENDATIONS

10. The Church, in keeping with her constant concern for man's total welfare, has much to say about the use of these newer methods in science and industry. In an address of May 14, 1953, Pope Pius XII spoke of the Church's interest in man's triumph over nature through science when he stated that the development of automation

> ... should be considered with prudent and healthy optimism. If the machine which only yesterday was still a gradually improving and stronger tool in the service of man, can henceforth replace the hand which grasps and guides, the eye which observes and controls and even, for certain purposes, the consciousness which watches and the memory which preserves an always available past, if the machine is substituted not only for the worker, but also for the bookkeeper and to a certain extent for the technician, thus opening to industry unsuspected possibilities — for all this we should only give thanks to God who has enabled man to accomplish such work.[2]

11. In his encyclical letter, *Mother and Teacher*, the late Pope John

XXIII spoke of the scale of values to be observed in subordinating technical progress to man's dignity and spiritual destiny:

> Certainly the Church has always taught and continues to teach that scientific and technical progress and resultant material well-being are truly good and, as such, must be regarded as an all important sign of progress in human civilization. Nevertheless in the Church's view, these things should be valued according to their true worth, i.e., as means of achieving more effectively a higher end, that of facilitating and promoting human perfection in both natural and supernatural orders.[3]

12.   In a Statement of the Holy See to the Halifax Social Life Conference in 1961, mention is made of the manner in which automation is to be applied to our social needs, so that no single group of workers or individuals will suffer from its effects:

> Attention must be paid to the fact that, following upon ever wider application of processes of automation, the means of production, particularly in certain sectors of industry and personal service, are subject to rapid and far-reaching changes. This in turn can have immediate negative repercussions upon working people, especially in what affects the stability of their employment. It is therefore an exigency of social justice that this application be made in such a way that the immediate negative results of automation should not be borne exclusively by the workers or by certain groups of workers. Rather should such negative results weigh equally, or even more heavily, upon the investors of capital and when opportune, even upon all the members of the political community, since all, in the final analysis, benefit by such changes of automation. This can the more surely be obtained when the workers, through their unions and organizations, are present and have a voice in the implementation of processes of automation.[4]

POSSIBLE SOLUTIONS

13.   Automation can fit well into God's plan of enabling mankind to use the riches of nature to tap the secrets of His creative love. The prophecies of gloom need not come true. The answers of course, are not stubborn optimism on the side of management, extreme pessimism on the side of labour or a long state of indecision on the

part of unions, business and government. We are faced with the basic problem of employing a vast number of men and women in a manner that will enable them to maintain their human dignity and provide a sense of personal worth necessary to self-respect and a feeling of being needed and wanted in the community.

14. Our attitude should be to welcome the new technology, to work out its installation and operation by consultation and cooperation. This applies particularly in the matter of the retraining and the transfer of workers. Above all, those few or many workers who are unfortunate enough to be employed on jobs which are eliminated by automation should not themselves have to pay the cost of this progress. The new wealth created by automation will be very great; in the nation as a whole there will be more than enough to prevent any group whatsoever from being victimized.

15. Business, labour and government have active roles to play in solving the problems presented by automation, but to ensure a satisfactory solution there must be cooperation among these agencies. The climate of confidence and mutual understanding which must prevail and which is so necessary for this work of cooperation, was described by Pope Pius XII in his address to the First Congress of the International Association of Economists on September 9, 1956:

> It is also one of the happy traits of the present epoch that it accentuates the feeling of interdependence among the members of the social body, and leads them to recognize that the human person reaches his true dimensions only on condition that he recognize his social and personal responsibilities and that human problems — or simply economic ones — will find their solution only through the medium of understanding and sincere mutual love.[5]

CONCLUSION

16. Automation has crept into industry without the majority of people being really aware of it. The cumulative effects of all the changes that are being made in industry today in a seemingly piecemeal manner, will suddenly be felt with an impact for which, unless there is some serious thinking and resolve concerning the human consequences, we will not be prepared. Technical development must be

combined with ethical concern; in other words, technological advance and social progress must go hand in hand. Technological progress is not an unmixed blessing. It should be welcomed to the extent that it leads to a progressive rise in the living standards of workers and takes place within a national policy of full employment. The gains of automation must be shared with the workers through expanded purchasing power and shorter hours of work. Automation will result in some unemployment; therefore measures must be taken to improve the condition of the displaced worker. Poverty and its twin, drudgery, can be avoided if only society will use the new technology for the benefit of everyone instead of solely for corporate profit.

17. The church welcomes advances in automation if it be for the benefit of man. Pius XII said that even though automation produced many goods it was not really beneficial until it proved that it could produce better men. This is the key to the Church's stand on automation. The Church would also hope that all men participate in the benefits of automation. It must benefit the common good of all and not of only a select few. The common good however, is not achieved when many become casualties through displacement and subsequent unemployment as a result of circumstances beyond their control. Automation has unlocked another dimension of God's limitless bounty and goodness in providing for the human and material needs of His children. Now it is for them to learn to share this new-found wealth generously among all members of the human family.

NOTES

1. Cf. *The Papal Encyclicals*, edit. Claudia Carlen, IHM (Wilmington, N.C., McGrath Publishing, 1981), V, 64, n. 47; 86, nn. 246 f.; 256.

2. In spite of the date given, effort to locate this text has been unsuccessful.

3. In Carlen above, p. 86, n. 246.

4. *Letter of Amleto Cardinal Cicognani*, Cardinal Secretary of State, at the request of Pope John XXIII, to Archbishop Gerald Berry of Halifax, Aug. 28, 1961, in the archdiocesan archives. Cf. *The Mail-Star*, Halifax, N.S., Oct. 14, 1961; *The New York Times*, Oct. 14, 1961, p. 22.

5. *Acta Apostolicae Sedis*, Vatican, 1956, XLVIII, 673; *The Pope Speaks*, Washington, 1956, III, 244.

Document 13

LABOUR DAY MESSAGE — 1965[1]
SOLIDARITY IN THE DISTRIBUTION
OF THE WORLD'S GOODS

Author — The Canadian Catholic Hierarchy

1. Canadians traditionally celebrate Labour Day on the first Monday of September when we reflect on the dignity of human work, stressing its importance in people's lives. We consider the economic and political aspects of work, as well as its spiritual and moral implications. For Labour Day this year, we would like to suggest some reflections on a matter of particular importance these days: international solidarity in the distribution of the product of man's labour.

2. Man's labour was intended by God to place the resources of the entire universe at the service of all men. Until now, unfortunately, it has succeeded in satisfying the needs of only a fraction of mankind. The creator wanted man's labour to foster unity among men, but because its product has been so unjustly divided, men are split into two groups — the "haves" and the "have nots". Why does such a situation exist and continue to sow the seeds of division and discord?

3. The two encyclicals of the late Pope John XXIII, *Mother and Teacher* (1961) and *Peace on Earth* (1963), the preoccupations of the Second Vatican Council (1962-1965), the appeal of Pope Paul VI from Bombay (1964), the designation of 1965 by the General Assembly of the United Nations as International Cooperation Year, — all these require us to give serious thought to the grave problem of hunger in the

world, and encourage us to discover how we can provide more effective help to the hungry.

THE SITUATION

4.   To underline the importance of the problem raised by the unsatisfactory distribution of the world's riches, many examples could be cited. These all draw special attention to the needs of a particularly disfavoured group of mankind. For example in 1965, the deaths of millions of persons can be traced directly or indirectly to malnutrition and hunger. More than one-half of our fellow human beings are forced to live on an inadequate diet, and this situation seems to be growing steadily worse. The least developed countries now are estimated to have only one-fortieth of the per capita income of the developed countries and may well have only a hundredth in the years ahead, thus widening still further the abyss that divides the privileged and the underprivileged. In the twentieth century, one child in three is born with no chance of living a normal life. Life expectancy is directly related to the degree of economic development in a country.

5.   Is it really possible that we have a billion and a half starving people on our consciences and yet do not react more sharply? If the problem itself is frightening, is it not equally terrifying to see the indifference of so many people, and of so many Christians who calmly soothe their consciences while whole nations flounder in misery?

PRINCIPLES

6.   Some important principles should inspire the efforts of all people of good will in this matter. The first is that all human beings are essentially united in one great family. Whoever we are, regardless of race, language or sex, and regardless of where we were born, we are all brothers and sisters, called to the same destiny in this world and in the next. Born of one and the same Father, having the same nature, redeemed by the same Saviour, all are endowed with the same rights among which is the right to life and to decent living conditions. In this one great family the sufferings of a few members must be the sufferings of all, and must be alleviated by

those who have the means to do so. The economic resources of the world should be administered and distributed to serve the welfare of the whole human family and not the interests of only a few; collective egoism like individual egoism must be rooted out.

> God created men as brothers, not enemies. He gave them the earth to be cultivated by their toil and labour. Each and every man is to enjoy the fruits of the earth and to receive from it his sustenance and the necessities of life.[2]

7. The goods of the world therefore, are destined for the use of all men. Those who own property, individuals as well as nations, must realize that ownership of property involves a duty towards all. No one has the right to abandon a brother or sister in need; and if, in a given country, a decent minimum share of available resources can be determined for each citizen, a similar standard must exist at the level of the whole human race. Indeed distributive justice among nations is founded on this respect for the inalienable rights of the human person, and on the fact that the goods of the world are destined for the use of all. This however can be achieved only through concerted efforts on the part of all nations.

8. There is a serious obligation in justice to share our goods with those who are hungry. For too long foreign aid to the less developed countries has been considered an act of kindness or generosity, not a requirement of justice. Failure to recognize the extent of this obligation is perhaps due to the fact that only recently have men become conscious of the existence of a universal common good. Today more than ever, it is clear that a country which would refuse to aid the less developed countries, or would do so in a niggardly fashion and not according to its true capabilities, would sin gravely against international social justice. This obligation becomes all the more urgent in proportion as some nations spend great resources while other nations are caught in the grip of ever pressing needs. We think too often in terms of giving gifts to the less developed countries when we really should be thinking in terms of mutual trade.

9. Most of the countries which today seek our material help are highly civilized, and in the course of centuries have enriched the cultural and spiritual patrimony of mankind. We have all profited and continue to gain from their civilizations and cultures. These non-

economic values are certainly worth the share of our material riches that we consent to part with; indeed, they are worth more.

10. Faced with this situation of the unjust distribution of riches in the world and the evils it engenders, especially mass hunger, men have no choice but to see that they are one and to work towards effective international cooperation.

AN APPEAL TO CONSCIENCE

11. First of all, we appeal to the consciences of all Christians and of all persons of good will. Christ's teaching is clear: "Let him who has two coats share with him who has none; and let him who has food do likewise." (Lk 3:11) Pope John XXIII had this to say in his letter *Mother and Teacher:*

> We are all equally responsible for the undernourished peoples. Therefore it is necessary to awaken men's consciences to the sense of their responsibility which weighs upon everyone, especially upon those who are more richly blessed with this world's goods.[3]

The insensitive conscience of the rich is perhaps the greatest evil of our times. It is imperative that no one ignore mankind's present state and its contradictions; each must acknowledge responsibility for changing it. This will require a spiritual revolution that will lead us to consider our neighbour as our equal, possessing the same rights as ourselves; a conversion that will free us of our sordid egoism and allow us to become sincerely altruistic; a conversion, in a word, that will fill us with brotherly love which, in our times will express itself in sharing and trading with others.

12. Let all be on their guard however, against making peace with conscience too easily by handing out a thin coin here and there. That is not enough. Instead they must direct their efforts to creating a civilization in which men will feel close to one another. They must concern themselves with the underlying and often structural causes that are at the root of international imbalance. Finally they must provide for personal involvement in combined efforts, whereby everyone, on every level, may recognize and assume personal responsibility. Every Christian must consider participation in this struggle against misery and injustice, not as a marginal activity but

as a normal dimension of a fully lived Christian life. Did not Christ couple an eternal reward to such a concept of Christian living?

AN APPEAL TO NATIONS

13.   Whole nations as well must feel themselves responsible for one another in this gigantic struggle against hunger. The moving appeal of Pope Paul VI at Bombay still sounds in our ears:

> We entrust to you, gentlemen of the press, our special message to the world. Would that the nations could cease the armaments race, and devote their resources and energies instead to fraternal assistance to the developing countries! Would that every nation, thinking "thoughts of peace and not of affliction" (Jr 29:11) and war, would contribute even a part of its expenditure for arms to a great world fund for the relief of the many problems of nutrition, clothing, shelter and medical care which afflict so many peoples.[4]

We touch here an extremely important point. When we realize that expenditures for military defense in the leading industrial countries will soon equal — yes, even exceed — the sum total of the gross national revenues of all the less developed countries, we cannot help seeing in this situation a violent disorder capable of producing the worst of catastrophes. Our fellowmen ask only to be allowed to live, and despite the fact that the world grows daily richer, they are increasingly exposed to destruction.

14.   Our prayers and our hopes cry out to God that the nations may progress in the way of mutual aid and cooperation in order to solve what has been described as "one of the most difficult problems facing the modern world — namely, that of the relations between the economically advanced countries and those in the earlier stages of development."[5] This cooperation must take place in the name of justice, in a climate of brotherhood and not of paternalism, with openness to a policy of mutual trade, respecting the characteristics of each country and without trespassing on its legitimate autonomy, in a disinterested manner, concerned only for what is best for mankind, the whole human family, each integral person.

SOME PRACTICAL SUGGESTIONS

15. We would like to suggest here some practical measures that could well occupy our attention and lead to combined efforts on the part of all Canadians:

(1) Public and private agencies should provide all possible information about the needs of the underdeveloped countries, the initiatives that might be undertaken to help them, and the projects already under way.

(2) Everyone should strive to enlighten and involve public opinion in this matter. We commend the great work already being done in this area by the communications media, press, radio and television.

(3) Families and schools should strive to educate our youth to a sense of brotherhood and international solidarity. So many occasions are offered to parents and teachers in everyday happenings and circumstances to form young people who genuinely feel that they are members of the great human community.

(4) A warm, fraternal welcome should be given to citizens of the third world who emigrate to our country to earn their share of the bread that was lacking in their own.

(5) We must encourage and facilitate the mission of Canadian specialists, technicians, teachers, etc. to lend an able hand to other nations.

(6) Governments in our country must realize more and more the supreme importance of our participation in all undertakings to bring help to peoples in need. We are a rich country, blessed by Providence. Can we sincerely say that we are doing our fair share? The suggestion already made, that an international fund be established to fight against hunger in the world, should have a favourable hearing by our political leaders.

(7) Participation in the activities of existing international organizations should be especially encouraged. In this regard, we take occasion to urge all Catholics to assure the full success of the International Cooperation Year in our country.

CONCLUSIONS

16. If we are to have peace, we must prepare the conditions of peace. One of these conditions is surely the realization of a just international order from which hunger, caused by unbalanced distribution of the world's riches, will be banished. The complexity of the problem that we face should not prevent us from making a beginning. Ignorance, laziness and selfishness in this matter take on a special gravity today and failure to work toward a solution is reprehensible. "I was hungry and you fed me; I was naked and you clothed me." (Mt 25:35) We recall these words of Christ. If the peoples of the world would but heed the Gospel and by concerted and intelligent effort accept the responsibility of advancing the economically weak nations, the effect would be electrifying and the world would never again be the same.

17. While the Christian message bears directly on the kingdom of God, nevertheless it is essentially related to the welfare of mankind, for at its centre is the commandment of love. Let every individual and every people laying claim to the Christian spirit put it in practice and the whole world will stand in admiration. Mankind faces the greatest opportunity in history to present a spectacle of charity of world dimensions. Will it close its heart to the anguished cries which rise on all sides? We beg the Lord that Canadians hear those cries on this Labour Day and not let them die without an echo.

NOTES

1. Prior to 1965, though the Episcopal Commission for Social Affairs disposed of twin staffs, anglophone and francophone, the Labour Day Messages had been very collaborative efforts. From 1965 to 1973 inclusive, in the odd number years, the francophone staff was responsible for the initial draft and final edition of the Messages, with mutual consultation and collaboration, the anglophone staff being similarly responsible in even number years. The Messages of 1974-76 (when the series of LDM's ended) did not follow this pattern, since a restructuring of the General Secretariat of the Conference resulted in the merging of the two staffs in a single bilingual Social Affairs Office.

2. John XXIII, *On Truth, Unity and Peace (Ad Petri Cathedram)*, 1959, *The Papal Encyclicals*, edit. Claudia Carlen, IHM (Wilmington, N.C., McGrath Publishing, 1981), V, 7, n. 23.

3. In Carlen, above, V, 77, n. 158.

4. *The Pope Speaks*, Washington, 1965, X, 158 f.

5. John XXIII, *Mother and Teacher*, in Carlen above, p. 77, n. 157.

Document 14

LABOUR DAY MESSAGE — 1966
POVERTY IN CANADA

Author — The Canadian Bishops

1. In the spirit of the Second Vatican Council, concluded some months ago in Rome (Dec. 8, 1965), the Catholic Church in Canada identifies herself with "the joys and the hopes, the griefs and the anxieties of the men of this age, especially of those who are poor or in any way afflicted."[1] In our annual Labour Day Message this year we turn out attention to the plight of our fellow Canadians who are caught in the vicious circle of poverty that enchains so many of our citizens. Although progress has been made in the past years in recognizing the rights of working people, little has been done to help the plight of "the other Canada", the poor in our country, who lack employment altogether and/or are deprived of a just share of the national wealth.

2. Last year our annual Message considered the urgent problem of a more just distribution of the world's goods in the international community and touched on the problem of poverty on the world scene. While we realize that poverty in a rich country like ours is not to be compared with the massive poverty of Asia, Africa and Latin America, which remains our overmastering concern, nevertheless this year we wish to deal with the problem of poverty here at home. We do so not primarily to preach to others nor to offer ready-made solutions, but humbly to bring the light of the Gospel and the Church's experience to bear on this stubborn human problem which is already being tackled by science as well as by so many men of good will. This will survey briefly the actual situation, pro-

pose a Christian judgment and suggest some guidelines towards
the elimination of poverty in our country.

THE SITUATION

3.   Who are the poor in Canada? According to recent research by
the Planning Secretariat of the Prime Minister, the poor are: low-
income, unemployed family heads — the 23% of the Canadian families with income of less than $3,000; thousands of fatherless fami-
lies and Indian and Eskimo families, and, in some parts of Canada, families of fishermen, farmers, and loggers; the uneducated
— 1,024,785 Canadians are "functionally illiterate", that is, not sufficiently educated to play a full role in society; the aged — the median
annual income for men falls from $2,000 to $900 as men pass from
their late sixties to their late eighties; large families — the father of
the larger family, in spite of his greater responsibilities, tends to
have the least education and so less earning power; the disabled
— 1,300,000 Canadians are permanently handicapped to some
degree.

4.   In addition, there are those who suffer from poor health and
from poor housing. The poor give less health care to their children
and thus reduce their potential working and earning power. Housing is most inadequate among the aged, in broken families and
among the Indians.

PRINCIPLES

5.   To make a Christian judgment of this phenomenon of poverty
in Canada, we should recall that "God intended the earth with
everything in it for the use of all human beings and peoples".[2] Therefore social justice requires that all men work together to eliminate
those social conditions that foster poverty and deprivation. If we
do not play our part in these struggles to correct conditions that contribute to poverty, we neglect our basic Christian duty to love God
and our neighbour effectively. "He who has the goods of this world
and sees his brother in need and closes his heart to him, how does
the love of God abide in him?" (1 Jn 3:17)

6.   The Fathers of the Church proclaim the penalty for an inactive

charity: "Feed the man dying of hunger, because if you have not fed him, you have killed him."[3] And Pope Paul VI in a pressing appeal last February said:

> No one can today say: "I did not know." And, in a certain sense, no one can any longer say: "I was not able, I was not obliged." Charity extends its hand to all! How can anyone dare say: "I did not want to."?[4]

In fact, the most specific promise of salvation ever pronounced is for those who feed the hungry.

7.   The eminent Protestant theologian, Karl Barth, has reminded us that not only is relief of poverty and hunger a duty of individual Christians, but the institutions of society, including Church and State, must consider it a primary duty:

> The Church is witness to the fact that the Son of man came to seek and to save the lost. And this implies that casting all false impartiality aside, the Church must concentrate first on the lower and lowest levels of society. The poor, the socially and economically weak and threatened, will always be the object of its primary and particular concern, and it will always insist on the State's special responsibility for these weaker members of society.[5]

8.   In working to provide for their immediate physical needs of food and shelter and to improve their employment situation through technical training and education, we must above all respect the poor as persons, as children of God, and not merely as objects to be bettered by social engineering. Today economics and Christian theology happily speak with one voice: an affluent society which does not foster development of both personal talents and physical resources is wastefully un-Christian. Rather than being hypnotized by economics, we must extend our creative capacities to the limit, as befits children of God, made in His image and given His mandate to manage His creation for the benefit of all our fellowmen.

9.   What is being done in Canada in its war on poverty? What can be done? Recently many Canadian institutions have courageously accepted the challenge of poverty in our country. Governments, Canadian business and organized labour, as well as other agencies have begun to work seriously to eliminate poverty and its causes.

We are particularly impressed with the benefits promised by "The War on Poverty" undertaken by governments at all levels, the Agriculture Rehabilitation and Development Act, the Canada Pension Plan, the Canada Assistance Plan, Medical Care legislation, Family Allowance provisions, etc.

10.   Yet, there remains so much to be done. Has the war on poverty seriously been launched? In terms of involvement, joint activity and personal commitment, what does such a war mean to each of us?

11.   One fact is certain. The problem of poverty can be solved. With the vast resources of raw materials, technical know-how and motivation in this country, it is possible to overcome the need from which so many are suffering. Christ's word, "You have the poor with you always" (Mt 26:11), while serving as a constant witness to our selfishness, should also act as a stimulus to strive by every means to reduce the gap between wealth and poverty and spread our material abundance more equitably. The Gospel urges us to strive constantly to make poverty everywhere the exception rather than the rule.

APPEAL TO CHRISTIANS

12.   In conclusion, we urge all Christians to join together, mobilizing the full talent, energy and resources of the entire Christian community, to enter into the campaign against poverty in Canada. In this day of widespread cooperation among the Churches, is not poverty one area where we can work together in designing joint programs of action both in our pastoral missions and in our dialogue at the community level, for a common Christian witness? In this battle against poverty, the disciple of Christ must be the first, the most zealous, the most effective, the most fraternal, the most radical. Not only should each person accept his share of responsibility for the existence of poverty among us, but he should use his time, energy, talent and resources to turn the tide so that every Canadian can share in the benefits and hopefully aspire to provide for his children the great opportunities that an affluent society can offer.

13.   Without diminishing in any way our sympathy and generosity for the poor of other nations, we must begin here at home to assist those whom opportunity has passed by and who are trapped by

forces beyond their control. If we engage in this attack on poverty as individuals and groups, not only will we contribute immediately to the establishment of a more equitable balance of opportunity for all but we will thereby render ourselves more worthy to receive the reward promised to those who recognize the person of Christ in the poor.

NOTES

1. Second Vatican Council, *The Church in the Modern World,* 1965, n. 1; cf. *The Documents of Vatican II,* edit. Walter M. Abbott, SJ (New York, Guild Press, 1966). Quotations of the documents in this collection are generally from the Abbott edition, one among many. Since reference is always to the section number in the document, future reference will be simply to document title and section number.

2. *Ibid.* n. 69.

3. *Ibid.* n. 69 and cf. note 225. The axiom is found in *Decretum Gratiani, C. 21, dist. LXXXVI, (Corpus Iuris, ed. Friedberg, I, 302),* where it is attributed to St. Ambrose, in a lost work *"On Feeding the Poor".* It is also found in St. Anselm, cf. Friedberg, *loc cit.*

4. Allocution to a general audience, Feb. 9, 1966, *The Pope Speaks,* Washington, 1965-66, XI, p. 66.

5. *Against the Stream* (London, SCM press, 1954), p. 36; in essay *The Christian Community and the Civil Community* (1946).

Document 15

ON THE OCCASION OF THE HUNDREDTH YEAR OF CONFEDERATION

Author — The Assembly, the Canadian Catholic Conference,
    April 7, 1967

1. After a century of Confederation, the people of Canada are counting the gains and losses which have marked the last hundred years of their history, and are asking themselves how they may ensure a future which will match their hopes. The Church, deeply involved as she has been in Canadian life from its earliest beginnings, cannot be indifferent to the urgent questions of the present day. This is why we have thought ourselves obliged to add our reflections to those of so many others, in the hope of making a contribution of our own in the task of determining all that the present situation is asking of Canadians.

2. The problems which concern our people are numerous. There are the threat of inflation, the persistence of areas of poverty, instability in the economy and in political life. For a good many however, the most serious and delicate problem is that of finding a remedy for the tensions engendered by the coexistence in Canada of the two great linguistic and cultural groups, which, by a rather curious state of things, stand as two majorities, each a challenge to the other.[1]

3. This conflict is far from a new thing for the Church. She sees it within her very bosom, so to speak, since her flock is composed of a large section of the two great groups whose encounter creates the Canadian problem. In certain of its aspects, the question may be merely political and technical, but it is also profoundly human

in character, supposing as it does great ideals, and affecting human beings body and soul. For this reason, and because the solution of the difficulties which Canadians are facing, will depend in great measure on the moral attitudes which each adopts, we judge it our duty as pastors to define the spirit which must guide Canadians, if they are to be loyal to the Gospel. It is our prayer that this action of ours may meet the expectations of the many Christians who have been waiting for the authority of the Church to give attention to the gravest of their problems and to throw some light upon it.

4. The thoughts which we shall here set down are manifestly not intended to lend approval in the name of the Gospel to any given political regime, much less to absolve persons or associations from their duty of continuing effort in the task of determining how to discharge political responsibilities in a positive and Christian fashion. On the contrary, it is our view that all competent persons and organizations should embark upon active research. Indeed one of the aims of this letter is precisely to awaken in everyone a desire for enlightened political enterprise.

5. A clear grasp of the problems which Canadians are now facing is no easy matter. Serious minds are well aware of the complexities. Indeed they are experiencing the need of informing themselves as thoroughly and exactly as possible, and of weighing all the consequences of proposed action, so that both persons and ideals may be respected. Enlightened politics also demands that men rise above the level of passion, and take account of the truth that political regimes and legal structures are means, not ends, and therefore susceptible, as history shows, of constant reform.

6. The prevailing uneasiness in our society leads to widely differing positions. Even a superficial analysis of public opinion reveals deep divergence of views regarding the right means to lasting and satisfying solutions for the problems with which we are faced. The more we ponder the question which makes the object of this letter, and the attitudes which it provokes, the more our minds are driven to this primary conviction: no matter what sort of constitution may guide the peoples who inhabit our land, the facts of geography and history, and the forces of actual economic and social conditions, will oblige them to maintain relations with one another, and these relations must be inspired by the ideal of peace. All men of good will will nowadays hold the conviction that no matter what the difficul-

ties, mankind must agree never to employ any but peaceful means to overcome them, and must see the solving of these difficulties as the actual building of true peace. Are we deceived in our confidence that this primary conviction of ours will receive the assent of all Canadians? We think not. Our Canadian people have so often demonstrated their firm resolve to be guardians of peace throughout the world, that we are sure they will be loyal to their principles in their own land.

I — PEACE AND JUSTICE

7. True peace is more than silent guns. It is a climate of joy and contentment of soul. We must see it as the fruit of order and, above all, of justice which is the prime requisite of human order. Injustice is a hateful thing which fosters hate. In its own fashion, it is a form of violence and an endless source of revolt. To hope to found peace on injustice is an illusion. Canadians ill disposed towards peace might do well to ask themselves if they are not also ill disposed towards justice.

Justice and Equality

8. In our day, the word justice usually stands for "equal opportunity for all", and everyone is aware that this is the goal of a healthy social life. There is no question of a demand for absolute and fixed equality of income and position: such an ideal is utopian and very few men think that its attainment would be a good thing. But we do maintain, that beneath differences of race, culture, religion, profession, age and sex, all share equally the same human nature and enjoy the same basic rights. And we do wish to see an honest, realistic and effective search for a form of government which will make it possible to prevent those inequalities between persons, which are extreme and can find no basis in justice.[2]

9. This keen and growing awareness of the common dignity of all persons has found expression in our time in the great declarations of the rights of man. The importance of these declarations no one can deny. On her part, the Church is also aware that respect for the rights of the person is a condition of peace: John XXIII's encyclical *Peace of Earth* (1963) begins with a list of these rights.[3] The

conciliar Constitution, *The Church in the Modern World*, also sets them down, after having devoted its first chapter to recalling the dignity of the person.[4]

The Hope for Equality

10. It is a feature of the twentieth century that the drive for justice is no longer carried on by persons only, but also by peoples, regions, and ethnic communities. And the fact that it is now possible, by means of statistical surveys, to determine with something like mathematical precision the standard of living of various regional, racial, linguistic and cultural communities, so that all sorts of comparisons can be made, deepens the resolve of such communities to seek a form of government which will allow them to expand in a fashion comparable to that of the societies by which they are surrounded. And of course it is only right to take account of the aims of whole groups, if it is sincerely desired to meet the hopes of individuals.

Banishing Private and Public Selfishness

11. All who sincerely want peace must entertain no illusions concerning the following principle: peace depends on united, realistic and dogged effort to establish the reign of justice, of a justice which is forever drawing nearer to the ideal, and which guarantees to groups as well as to individuals their fair share of the benefits of progress. Everyone must also realize that this pursuit of justice cannot be effective without rejection of the notion that selfishness, collective or individual, is a law of life and progress, and is therefore defensible. The view which accepts as normal a state of things in which each person, each region, and each social body, is content to seek only its own welfare, without concern for others, is false. To hope in a social order erected on such a conception as the surest way of attaining the best type of society is to indulge in a dangerous illusion. Such ideas must be rejected. They are hostile to the spirit of Christianity and are contradicted by fact. Worse still, they encourage indolence in the pursuit of social justice and form a subtle threat to peace. It has been asserted that democracy cannot exist except in a certain spiritual climate. The same is true of peace. If we wish to make sure of peace we must revise our basic attitude toward wealth and property. The motto which must guide individ-

uals, national groups and governments is not "every man for himself"; it is rather "each and all for the common good". There are even grounds for asserting that the well-off, whether these be persons, peoples, or regions, must be ready to accept some revision of their privileged condition, even if this entails real sacrifice.

12.   We called attention to these principles some years ago, when reminding Canadians of their duty towards countries less fortunate than our own, and especially of the duty to open our frontiers with generosity to immigrants, making no distinction of race, language, or religion.[5] Since that day, we have been pleased to observe genuine progress, both in opinion and in legislation. But what we want to stress now is that Canadians ought to apply within their own borders this same principle of the unity of all mankind. For, within their own country there still persist extreme inequalities between classes of society and between certain regions.

The Chief Malady of Canadian Society

13.   These is no concealing the fact that the chief malady of Canadian society consists in the deep discontent felt by a growing number of French Canadians at the difficulties which their community must face in its attempts at growth, and in the uneasiness which the claims of the French-speaking group arouse in other parts of the country. It is our desire to help Canadians, as they deal with this mutual unrest, to overcome a weakness which may well be shared by both parties: that of failing to understand the rights and the ideals of the other group, and of selfishly walling themselves up in something like a caste.

14.   The French-Canadian community is a linguistic and cultural group with roots three centuries old in the soil of Canada, the soil which has served as the "cradle of their life, labour, sorrow and dreams". Here is a people deeply attached to their own identity, proud to be the inheritors in North America of one of the great cultures of history. They are also vividly aware that they make up a community enjoying a unity, individuality and spirit of their own, all of which yield them an unshakable right to their own existence and development. Although this French-Canadian community may represent a numerical minority as against the whole of the country,

it forms not only a majority, but a compact and significant body within the vast extent of Quebec.

15.   The characteristic traits just mentioned explain how it is that the French-Canadian community so easily sees itself as a nation, and there is no need to remark how often the use of this term leads to serious misunderstandings between the two chief communities of Canada. It is no part of our present duty to settle a question of vocabulary, which is rather delicate in any case, and becomes more so when moving from one language to another. This at least must be granted however, that no peace can come to Canada without honest recognition of the social fact which is the French-Canadian people and effective recognition of the rights of this people.

16.   It is beyond dispute that the French-speaking group of Quebec has a right to existence, to normal development in all spheres of life, to civil and political institutions suited to their genius and peculiar needs, and to that autonomy without which their existence and prosperity would enjoy no good guarantee. But at the same time, one must not forget that the legitimate aspirations of Quebec may be justly fulfilled only when there is full respect for the greater common good, and for the inviolable rights of others.

The Problem of Minorities

17.   Besides the problem of the French-Canadian community, there is that of the minorities. No matter what political system they may devise, Canadians will never be able to rid themselves of minority groups, whether within the frontiers of Quebec or elsewhere in the country, whether the minorities be English-speaking, French-speaking, or of some other identity. We deem it timely to recall the firm declaration of John XXIII:

> It is our duty to state most explicitly, that every policy which tends to block the life and growth of minority groups is a grave crime against justice, and graver still when its aim is to wipe out such minorities. On the other hand, nothing is more in harmony with justice than any line of action by public authority which aims at a better life for ethnic minorities, especially as concerns their language, culture, customs, resources and economic enterprises.[6]

18.   Not all minorities in Canada are in the same situation. Fair treatment must be given to each, and we must learn to accept the sacrifices which such treatment may demand in the cost of certain services, of which education is a primary example.

19.   It is now recognized that the Indians and Eskimos have often had to endure, and sometimes still endure, the effect of prejudice, ignorance, indifference, and even injustice. Since these are the descendants of the first inhabitants of America, they enjoy a unique right to the respect and understanding of all, and to the benefits of the kind of positive policy in favour of minorities of which John XXIII was speaking.

20.   In the case of certain groups which are especially numerous and influential, the principles of justice emphasized by the Pope also hold good in a fashion beyond question and impose special requirements. By our conduct we must learn to acknowledge how valuable is the contribution made by such peoples to Canadian life. With respect to French and English language minorities, we must remember that both belong to communities which in other parts of the country enjoy majority status and the characteristics of genuine peoples; and this situation is the result not only of political dispositions, but of sociological realities. When one reflects on the problem of minorities in Canada, it becomes clear that a political system which, in analogous situations fails to assure the same treatment to French or English language minorities, is with reason intolerable.

Sympathy and Practical Steps

21.   It is admittedly difficult to find a political set-up which will allow the French community of Quebec, more and more aware of its own identity, to enjoy the conditions necessary for its own development, while respecting the well-being and the rights of other Canadians. Hence there is no need to remark that these reflections of ours are not intended of themselves to clarify the whole of the Canadian problem, much less to solve it. No words of ours can eliminate conflicts which, by reason of unavoidable circumstances, cause the rights and welfare of certain groups to stand in natural opposition to those of certain others. But we deem it necessary to invite all parties to make themselves honestly aware of the sociological characteristics of the Canadian scene, to restore in all hearts a deep regard for the rights

of others, and a feeling for the common good in the widest sense. Finally, we call upon our fellow countrymen to settle the differences which divide them in the spirit of the wish of John XXIII: "as men should, with the aid of mutual understanding, of a detached assessment of the facts, and by fair compromise." [7]

II — PEACE AND BROTHERHOOD

22. Justice is not enough to bring about and to guarantee the kind of peace of which we are speaking: such peace is also the effect of an esteem which goes far beyond all that justice can do. Brotherhood is the second foundation of peace. [8]

23. There is a natural instinct which urges us to look upon all men as brothers, but only rarely is the basis of this human fraternity distinctly perceived. Here is perhaps the reason why the concept of brotherhood has produced more good rhetoric than good conduct. Indeed, a vague spirit of fraternity based on nothing more than the fact of a common existence and fate, and a sharing of the same planetary adventure, will be a pretty fragile thing. As for a brotherhood which finds its roots in nothing better than our prehistoric origins, remote and obscure as these are, will have no power over the human heart, above all when our origins are interpreted as the effect of mere chance.

A Christian Demand

24. As support for belief in the brotherhood of man, Christian faith offers convincing reasons of an entirely different order. For the man of faith, human fellowship does not rest on some remote and fortuitous origin, but on the supreme, actual and personal fatherhood of a God who has resolved that all of us shall be His children by virtue of a design great in mercy. In this God, according to the phrase of Saint Paul, "we live and move and have our being." (Ac 17:28) The fact that men share similar earthly toils, hopes, and sufferings, is of course an invitation to brotherhood, but how much closer becomes the tie which unites us, when we know that all of us, when the hazards of this life have been left behind, are called to the joy of meeting the Father!

25. Throughout the world, Christians are bound to search out more and more the meaning of the bonds which make us all one, and to press for spiritually vital methods of living in harmony with others. It can happen, at certain times and places, that this great responsibility is laid upon them more urgently than ever. This is true in Canada today. Our country is passing through painful and crucial times, while the overwhelming majority of its citizens are Christians.

Fellowship Concrete and Universal

26. A genuine spirit of brotherhood imposes two duties which seem to stand in paradoxical opposition: the duty of giving such spirit concrete forms in the here and now, but also of maintaining its all-embracing universality.

27. No one may call himself the brother of his neighbour, if he is content to express this relationship in mere formal abstractions, verbal declarations or empty wishes. No man can lay claim to the spirit of brotherhood, if his love spends itself only on humanity in the abstract, or in noble dreams of comradeship with men far off, while his attitude towards those at hand is mean and hostile. True fraternity must bring about mutual dependence in immediate and concrete shape. It must take realistic forms, making itself tangible in vital concern for the good of a definite group, region or family. But on the other hand, even at its most practical, under pain of being in conflict with the Gospel, brotherhood cannot close itself to any other or others. No group has the right to hold itself the centre of everything, deaf to the appeals of others, taking no account of their needs. We know well that the tragedy of human history is precisely that man has constantly given in to the temptation of restricting the notion of brotherhood to those of his own particular kind.

28. These reflections, though general in character, should be of some use to Canadians. It has been rightly noted how concerned they are for international harmony, and how generously they work for it. In various conflicts outside their own country, their efforts at conciliation have proved the accuracy of these observations. But the people of Canada must learn how to make their concern for fellowship take effect in their own everyday life, since in their very homeland they witness the clash of national, regional and social in-

terests. They must not offer the ironical spectacle of men, capable of generosity towards the whole world, yet incapable of treating fairly the man at their elbow. The Canadian people's instinct for concord and mutual understanding on the world scale must lead them to demand, within their own community, the abolition of clannish groups which tend to become nothing better than examples of collective selfishness.

Fostering Union and Accepting Diversity

29.   If men are to be brothers, two further needs must be met: care for the similarities which draw them together, and acceptance of differences.

30.   As we have remarked already, it is clear that the demands of human brotherhood cannot be understood properly without attending to the common traits of nature, origin and destiny which bind us to all our fellows. As a consequence, we must be constantly sensitive to everything which unites us to others, thus obliging ourselves, under all differences of race, nationality, culture, language, customs, and property, to identify the brother so profoundly like ourselves. If we are Christians, this resolve will lead us to recognize among all men a deep and mysterious unity, and will render us capable of fellowship with all, even when defending the rights of the community to which we happen to belong.

31.   Nowadays people are inclined to wonder how it could happen that the wars of the past so often set Christian peoples against one another. These fratricidal conflicts, and the injustices which led to them, strike the Christian of 1967 as thoroughly irrational and even shocking. In somewhat the same way, here in our own land, it seems incomprehensible that the religion of Christ has so often divided us, instead of bringing us together. Christian thinking of today, inspired by the ecumenical movement, inclines us to pass harsh judgment on these attitudes of the past and to regret them keenly. Such judgments and regrets are wholesome signs: they show that we are rediscovering essential Christian principles. It is to be hoped that we shall not employ them as a mere camouflage for secret inclinations to repeat the old crimes.

32.   There remains another side of brotherhood which we cannot

ignore without mutilating the ideal. Although built upon a community of origin and destiny, brotherhood nevertheless supposes true differences. Both unity and diversity are necessary elements of fellowship. We can treat as a brother only a person other than ourselves. And brotherly conduct therefore demands that we gladly allow others to be unlike ourselves. It goes without saying that such an attitude supposes both generosity and delicacy of feeling.

33. In their present circumstances, Canadians should ask themselves if they are indeed concerned to let others be what they are, not only in individual encounters, but also in dealings between those groups differing in language and culture which comprise the Canadian people. The years that lie ahead will be darkened by futile and ruinous quarrels, if the various groups which make up our country, and especially the two principal ones, will not allow one another the right to be different. There must be honest acknowledgement that each has a destiny of its own, and deserves from the others respect for its rights and for the conditions needed for their exercise.

Brotherhood and Non-Violence

34. The people of our time, like those of all former times, often waver between sincere acknowledgement of the irrational character of violence, and the temptation to make violence respectable when employed in the service of a loyal community, a country, or some just cause. Without attempting to elaborate here a principle which would hold good for all possible solutions, we firmly believe that one of the most important calls made on the contemporary conscience is to understand that the old ways must be set aside in favour of non-violence, the only way compatible with true brotherhood.

35. During his visit to the United Nations, Paul VI made a moving appeal to the world: "No more war! Never again!"[9] All Canadians heard this noble cry. If only the echo of this call remains stronger in their souls than all temptations to violence, including the temptation to have us believe that violence produces effective results which can be legitimately sought! Granted the means actually enjoyed by Canadians to make justice prevail, their plain duty is to reject all thought of violence, even of violence that is deliberately limited in scope or only tactical in aim.

Watching our Words

36. It is by our deeds that we prove the genuineness of fraternal sympathy; but it is also a matter of common knowledge that by mere words we can improve good relations or destroy them. True fraternity has an idiom of its own. It is a serious duty to learn how to speak it, and to make sure that its rules are respected as carefully in dealings between groups as is normal in dealings between individuals.

37. If two groups between whom there is tension, will not talk to each other, they will soon be misrepresenting each other to the point of caricature. Judgments about the rival community become crude, unjust and arbitrary. Shortcomings on the other side are magnified, while genuine virtues are perversely ignored. Such attitudes dangerously envenom human relationships. As John XIII reminds us: "History reveals that people are never so deeply stirred as by anything, great of small, which touches their honour; and it is right that they should be sensitive about such things."[10]

38. We believe that all Canadians should keep strict watch over their opinions concerning others, above all when such opinions bear on whole regions or groups and are expressed in public. Everybody should see the urgent duty of doing away with prejudices, half-truths, crude or unfair judgments, and attitudes of contempt. Courage and energy in defense of rights are not to be confused with a certain mental and moral violence as hostile to brotherhood as that which takes physical form.

39. There are times, of course, when persons or groups are deserving of censure. In such instances, care should be taken at least to avoid exaggerated language. And instead of being content to impute failings or shortcomings to others, might it not be well to ask ourselves if some of the responsibility does not rest with us, and if we could not perhaps take a hand in eliminating the evil? In any case, it is certain that a fair judgment of others is much more probable if we recall that "the frontier between good and evil runs through the heart of every human being".

40. Often enough it is ignorance which explains hostile and unfair opinions. Such ignorance should not be difficult to combat by promoting meetings, cultural exchanges, and exact and reliable infor-

mation. Mutual explanations, made with frankness and respect, should also be invited, and everything possible done to open the way for such encounters.

41. It is here that political leaders, educators, journalists, and all who can influence public opinion, must accept their special responsibility. They must promote mutual understanding, balanced judgment and concern for the common good of the society of which national groups form a part, as well as for the common good of mankind.

42. These are our thoughts in this year which marks the centenary of Confederation. We do not mean to conceal the dangers which threaten us, nor to allow anyone to ignore the tasks and obligations which must be met if we are to deserve peace. With all of our people, we beg God's blessing and His aid in keeping us faithful to our heavy obligations as human beings and as Christians.

NOTES

1. Cf. *Preliminary Report of the Royal Commission of Inquiry into Bilingualism and Biculturalism* (Ottawa, The Queen's Printer, 1965) p. 135.
2. Second Vatican Council, *The Church in the Modern World*, 1965, n. 29.
3. Cf. *The Papal Encyclicals*, edit. Claudia Carlen, IHM (Wilmington, N.C., McGrath Publishing, 1981), V, 108, nn. 11-27.
4. Second Vatican Council, *ibid.*, nn. 29-31; 60; 65-72; 73-75.
5. *Labour Day Message*, 1960, Document 8 above.
6. *Peace on Earth*, 1963, in Carlen above, V, 117, nn. 95 f.
7. *Ibid.*, in Carlen above, n. 93, p. 117.
8. Second Vatican Council, *The Church in the Modern World*, n. 78.
9. *Address to the Assembly of the United Nations*, Oct. 4, 1965, *The Pope Speaks*, Washington, 1966, XI, pp. 51-53, n. 5.
10. *Peace on Earth*, in Carlen above, V, 117, n. 89.

Document 16

LABOUR DAY MESSAGE — 1967
THE ECONOMIC CONDITION
OF THE CANADIAN FAMILY

Author — The Canadian Catholic Bishops

1.   The fact that the International Conference on the Family is being held in our country at this time prompts us to devote our annual Labour Day Statement to some reflections on the important subject of the economic situation of the family.

2.   In the briefs which we presented recently to certain governmental committees [1], we insisted that every feasible measure be taken to strengthen this basic institution of our society, the family. We must face the fact that the economic conditions under which a large number of Canadian families live today, present almost insurmountable obstacles to that harmony and stability required in family life for the full human development of the members.

THE CHURCH'S CONCERN FOR THE FAMILY

3.   The Church, devoted as she is to the service of man and his destiny, is concerned about the economic problems that face the family. Founded by Christ to carry out His redemptive plan and thus lead men to salvation, the Church is concerned with everything in life and society that can facilitate or impede this plan. She grieves to see families deprived of the resources essential to create a milieu favourable to spiritual progress and to a wholesome social order.

4.   Within the network of human relationships that is the family,

the father, mother, and children live in a state of continuous dialogue. But a lack of financial resources can cause a climate of tension which destroys these harmonious relations. The family should
be a privileged atmosphere helping the individual to grow into what
each is to be, and to fill an appropriate social role at each different
stage of life, childhood, adolescence, maturity and old age. Yet how
can it support its members at these different stages if it does not
have the means?

5.   Since it is through the family that we become part of society,
a family handicapped economically is unable to participate fully in
social life and risks providing society with marginal and second-rate
citizens. Finally, a family harassed by financial worries cannot provide the stability it normally should even in a rapidly changing
society. The human and social values endangered by economic insecurity are a matter of deep concern to the Church.

INCOME AND ITS USES

6.   The principal standard of measurement of the economic situation of a family is its income, and so we now turn our attention
briefly to certain statistical data in this area.

7.   The last general census indicated that more than 50% of the
heads of families included in Canada's work force earned less than
$4,000 annually. When we look at their total income, we find that
23.73% of Canadian families not engaged in farming, live in misery
(i.e., earning less than $2,000); that 10.45% earned between $2,000
and $2,997 and were classed as "poor" families; that another 15.24%
did not reach the $4,000 level and were classed as "living in
privation."[2] Misery, poverty, privation, that is the lot of more than
a third of a population that lives in a very affluent country, to say
nothing about the lot of many families who live on farms.

8.   Attention is drawn to a related problem, that of the use of
income. And here we mean the whole process of our consumer civilization that calls for examination. There is a fundamental contradiction in a system which considers the family primarily as an agent
of consumption, but each individual citizen primarily as an agent
of production. Thus the family is the victim of a milieu wherein an

exaggerated drive for profit and other economic values tends to rule supreme.

9. While recognizing the value of advertising, we must say that flashy, alluring advertising directed even at children all too often creates desires, expectations and new wants which are purely artificial and lead to an extravagant manner of life. This tends to create a mentality of chronic dissatisfaction, of egoism, and of closing one's heart to others. Under this social pressure, the responsibilities of parents and the education of children are only too often neglected for illusory advantages. Greater self-control, a stronger grip on one's whole life, and a more critical spirit towards seductive advertising would permit families to make better use of the income at their disposal.

10. We wish to encourage those organizations and movements which are presently doing excellent work in aiding families to continue their efforts. We follow with interest the steps now being taken to protect consumers and to provide individual Canadians with better advice on how to spend their money.

JUDGMENT AND ASSIGNMENT OF RESPONSIBILITIES

11. We judge it intolerable that in a society described as "affluent", so many families derive little advantage from economic progress. We cannot accept a situation wherein families which have assumed the responsibility of providing our society with citizens, find themselves by this very fact in a state of economic inferiority. We decry a mentality that fosters a false scale of values.

> The fundamental purpose of this productivity must not be the mere multiplication of products. It must not be profit or domination. Rather, it must be the service of man, and indeed of the whole man, viewed in terms of his material needs and of the demands of his intellectual, moral, spiritual and religious life.[3]

And therefore productivity must serve the family, since the latter is so important for the growth and maturation of the individual and for the equilibrium of society.

12. In our view, shared by many Canadians in all walks of life, the

family plays a key role in the harmonious development of man and in the stability of society. Each citizen then must do his part in providing the necessary economic resources for these goals. As the political expression of a people who for the most part live in families, the state must support social policies that are genuinely family-centered. The family is an essential element in the social structure since it provides the members of society. Social policies centered exclusively on individuals as the basic units of society would be radically misdirected. Political leaders must foresee the consequences for the family of all legislation and government policies. It is their duty to take special measures to help families meet the challenge of life imposed on them by major changes in industrial and urban living.

13.   Family life has changed in many ways. Children now remain at home, in the care and at the expense of their parents, longer than formerly. In some cases, married women have no choice but to work in order to maintain the family's standard of living. The cost of living is continually on the rise and many heads of families have been unable to acquire adequate training which could lead to more remunerative jobs.

14.   Who is responsible for these problems? Is it not in many ways the fault of our whole society? If families are to provide members for society, should not society assure families the conditions necessary for a quality of family life free from tensions and characterized by economic security and stability? Hence the necessity of legislation which helps meet the needs of the family at the different stages of its evolution. We are thinking here of the problems of newly formed households that have to go heavily into debt; of those families whose budget is taxed by the arrival of each new child; of those parents whose children remain at home longer because their education is lengthened; of broken homes, of aged couples, etc.

15.   We appreciate the positive measures already taken, and we would encourage public authority to establish family policies which correspond to the needs of our times. Those responsible for economic and industrial change and development should take into account the tensions which such change and development may cause for our families. The latter however, must remain the primary agents of their own social betterment. An isolated voice has little chance of being heard; individual initiative carries too little weight. In our

era of socialization, collective action is becoming the indispensable method of facing and solving problems. We strongly encourage families to unite in their own active organizations, having a collective responsibility for the Canadian family. They should avoid scattering their energies and, while respecting a healthy pluralism, should provide themselves with representative institutions which will influence legislation. They should participate, as do other groups on occasion, in the power structures of our society.

16.   Although we have insisted on the role of the state and on the need of collective action, we still recognize the primary responsibility of the individual in the development of his or her own family. An adult must be responsible. Even if strongly conditioned by the culture, each remains free and must generously assume the task of supporting the family. All must resist the pressure of advertising leading to an unwise use of income, and of the temptation to sacrifice family values.

SPECIAL RECOMMENDATIONS

17.   By way of conclusion we propose certain recommendations which, it seems to us, would improve the lot of those families now under economic handicap in our country.

We recommend:

(1) that support be given to the development of family associations and movements;

(2) that governments establish agencies concerned specifically with the family, and that representative family organizations be invited to participate in these institutions;

(3) the creation of a diversified system of family benefits adapted to the needs of families;

(4) that present family allowances be increased;

(5) that serious consideration be given to the improvement of those elements that deeply influence the standard of family life, especially in the areas of education, leisure, housing, health, protection before the law, etc.

For our part, we propose to ask that a certain number of priests specialize in the study of family problems. As a result, within the limits of their competence, they could work more effectively with others engaged in family programs.

CONCLUSION

18. We repeat the appeal voiced by all the bishops of the world at Vatican II, that Christians — and we are thinking here of all the churches in our country — work actively together, in union with all their fellow Canadians, to promote the genuine values of marriage and the family by the witness of their own lives as well as by concerted action with all men of good will. ''Thus when difficulties arise, Christians will provide, on behalf of family life, those necessities and helps which are suitably modern.''[4]

19. We know only too well that working people are often the victims of the situations we have just described. On the occasion of this Labour Day, we express our heartfelt wish that public opinion may become increasingly sensitive to the welfare of the family. We hope that individuals, leaders of unions and employer groups, family associations, and the state, itself, will join forces effectively to face up to the economic problems presently overwhelming so many families.

20. The Church has always shown a keen interest in the family and since the Second Vatican Council is more conscious of its duty to be present in the modern world. It cannot therefore but be vitally interested in any matter that pertains to the family. Such is the reason for these reflections. May they help all Canadians to assume their full responsibility in the maintainance of healthy and happy family life and in building a better world.

NOTES

1. *Statement of the Canadian Catholic Conference on Contraceptives,* presented to the House of Commons Standing Committee on Health and Welfare, Sept. 9, 1966, cf. Proceedings, no. 18, Oct. 11, 1966, pp. 576-81; *Statement of the Canadian Catholic Conference on Divorce,* presented to the Special Joint Committee of the Senate and House of Commons on Divorce, April 6, 1967, cf. Proceedings, no. 24, April 20, 1967, pp. 1510-1513. Both in the Archives of the Canadian Conference of Catholic Bishops, Ottawa.

2. *La Troisième Solitude,* étude sur la pauvreté dans la région de Montréal, le Conseil du Travail de Montréal, 1965, p. 25.

3. Second Vatican Council, *The Church in the Modern World,* n. 64.

4. *Ibid.* n. 52.

Document 17

ON DEVELOPMENT AND PEACE

Author — The Canadian Catholic Bishops, March 14, 1968

INTRODUCTION

1.   One year ago in his Encyclical, *The Development of Peoples*, Pope Paul VI addressed to all mankind a stirring appeal on behalf of the underdeveloped world. He stated: "The Church deems it her duty to help all men explore this serious problem in all its dimensions and to impress upon them in this hour of crisis the need for concerted action." [1]

2.   Development of the needy nations is "the road to peace" [2] offered to all men. It challenges humanity as the greatest opportunity of history. His Holiness issued this call to peaceful combat to the affluent nations without whose help the underdeveloped world cannot escape its misery. How can we remain blind to the tragedy of the suffering of two-thirds of the peoples of the world? During the next ten years hunger could claim more victims than have all the wars of history. Only the concerted action of all mankind can conquer this menace to the security, even to the survival, of humanity.

3.   As Christians we cannot remain strangers to this tragedy that involves the Mystery of Jesus Christ in Whom all are brothers and sisters. We are Christians only to the degree that we show compassion for the hungry and suffering peoples of the world. With this in mind we address this letter to you in the hope of awakening your Christian conscience.

THE PRESENT EFFORTS

4. Either alone or in association with others or through the various services of the United Nations, many wealthy nations have already gone to the help of disinherited peoples. Prompted by generous love for their fellowmen, many private groups have also been formed to serve the unfortunate people of the world.

5. Unfortunately these efforts are clearly insufficient and are often poorly planned. Filled with anguish at the population explosion, experts are sometimes more preoccupied with a negative policy of limiting births than with a positive program of developing food resources. Moreover, the aid provided by rich countries is often prompted by self-interest. Priority is granted to economic aid benefiting the countries giving the aid. More is spent for military aid than for works of peace.

6. Though praiseworthy in some respects, our Canadian effort has never been sufficient. We have regarded this problem with far too much indifference; some among us are opposed to any external aid. Canadians simply must not tolerate the scandal of such massive misery which provides a violent contrast to the high standard of living we enjoy. To remain indifferent or to be content with symbolic aid would be to sin gravely through egoism. It would reveal disquieting signs of moral and spiritual underdevelopment. "Avarice, in individuals and in nations, is the most obvious form of moral underdevelopment." [3]

MISSIONARIES AND DEVELOPMENT

7. It would be unfair to intimate that Canadians have done nothing until now to aid in the development of less fortunate countries. In addition to the contribution of various levels of government and private associations, mention must be made of the work done by the missionaries.

8. Although the primary task of the missionaries is to proclaim the Word of God, they have shown themselves sensitive to the material and human needs of the peoples whom they serve. This has led them to engage in a multitude of tasks that contribute to the

development of these countries. The record of this missionary activity is impressive: schools, hospitals, agricultural training centres, promotion of rural development, cooperatives, handicraft centres, small industries, centres of community development, press and radio services, adult education, etc.

9. This record is not without shadows cast by unintentional mistakes, for the priority of needs has sometimes been misjudged. Nevertheless missionary activity has manifested the qualities so necessary in enterprises of development, selflessness, cooperation with responsible people in the countries being helped, sincerity and high motivation. In proposing new ways for Canadian Catholics to come to the aid of suffering peoples we are well aware of what has been achieved through their aid to missionary activities, and we express our gratitude to them for their devotion and generosity.

ORGANIZATION FOR DEVELOPMENT AND PEACE

10. At a meeting of our National Conference held in October 1966, the Canadian Bishops laid the basis of the project that we now wish to commend to your support. At that time, in collaboration with leading Catholic laymen, we launched an organization dedicated to international cooperation in the socio-economic development of needy nations. This organization, it is hoped, will engage all Canadian Catholics in every diocese and every parish in contributing to a common fund whose primary purpose is the development of needy nations. Far from wishing to work in seclusion we keenly desire to learn from and work in close harmony with other churches, private associations, and with governmental and international services.

11. The board of this new foundation is to be known as the Canadian Catholic Organization for Development and Peace. The very name signifies the truth so frequently proclaimed by Pope Paul VI that without the development of the poorer nations there can be no peace.

12. In union with all Christians and in accord with the desire of Jesus Christ, we hope this new enterprise will help open all minds to the vision of the good life that all men might enjoy, and will release new energies for the creation of a renewed humanity. In

urging support of this work, we recall the inspiring action of our brother bishop, Cardinal Paul-Émile Léger, who decided to leave his high post as Archbishop of Montreal to work among the lepers of Africa.

13. It is hoped that the Canadian Catholic Organization for Development and Peace (CCODP) will work in close cooperation with the Pontifical Commission Justice and Peace in Rome. We also hope that universities will set up institutes of research on the problems of developing nations, and that there will be other centres of research and an increase in the number of competent specialists in the field. Some institutions have done marvellous work already.

14. In the present circumstances, it is not enough merely to invite Canadians to be generous and to show good will. This is a challenge of a new and different kind. Planning is necessary, and the objectives of the operation must be clear and definite.

INFORMATION AND EDUCATION

15. It is essential that mankind evolve a new economy for the nations of the world. This is by no means an impossible task. Through science and technology we can reform the universe by bringing about a more equitable sharing of wealth and raising the standard of living everywhere. We must seek no less than a global organization of this planet's economy.

16. Since this is eminently a political operation, we encourage government at every level to take a resolute hand in the cause of world development, to plan it and to involve the whole population in this noble and genuine pursuit of peace. The public must be informed of the nature of the problem and of the progress made. Canadians must strive to enlist all other nations in a campaign to make the world more human.

17. Prosperity has a tendency to close the human heart. It kills sensitivity and breeds egoism. Wealth can be as dangerous as a perverse drug, creating illusions and leading to personal destruction. The public, stimulated by all media of information, must be awakened to reality. Cultural and educational institutions must instill in their students the will to grapple in an intelligent, generous manner with the most urgent human problems.

18. We dedicate ourselves to the task of urging all Canadians to approve governmental generosity in foreign aid programs. This calls for acceptance by all citizens of the sacrifices involved in contributing a higher percentage of Canada's gross national product to nations suffering from poverty and want. All of us must go beyond concern for home and neighborhood and give the support of our love to those in need wherever they are found, since we share a common nature and destiny.

> It involves building a human community where people can live truly human lives, free from discrimination on account of race, religion or nationality, free from servitude to others or to natural forces which they cannot yet control satisfactorily. It involves building a human community where liberty is not an idle word, where the needy Lazarus can sit down with the rich man at the same banquet table.[4]

For those who now enjoy abundant security and wealth, this calls for greater generosity and willing sacrifice. Are we prepared to support at our own expense projects and undertakings designed to help the needy? Are we prepared to pay higher taxes so that public authorities may expand their efforts in the way of development? Qualified members of the younger generation must ask themselves if they are ready to join the steadily increasing stream of talent that is already flowing to distant lands in order to help people struggling to emerge from human degradation.

TRAINING AND ASSISTANCE

19. The problem of development has usually been treated almost exclusively as an economic and technical matter. Too little attention has been paid to the training of leaders at home and volunteers for abroad who will dedicate their lives to this basic and urgent task. We must therefore apply ourselves to searching out and training leaders who will instill in Canadians and in our social organizations the determination to serve the underdeveloped world. By collaboration in a collective philosophy of life reaching even to the international level, ''... they will activate the preparation of a new international law which today is recognized as indispensable.''[5]

20. The CCODP will subsidize specific projects for socio-economic development in selected regions of the world. In achieving this goal

our work must not overlap or compete with other agencies already in the field. Coordination, planning and efficient effort will evolve. We must endeavour to support projects undertaken by other Canadians along similar lines, to create new ones and to inspire many who would not otherwise do so to contribute generously to this cause.

21. The national fund that is to be set up is to be used for the purposes suggested in this letter. No account will be taken of the religious belief or ideologies of the people to whom aid is given. The only consideration will be the intrinsic value of the projects, their conformity with criteria of priority, and the evaluation of their human and social effectiveness. These are the considerations that led the Canadian bishops to launch the CCODP, now an independent lay organization drawing its membership from responsible citizens in every part of Canada and showing an image of the post-Conciliar Church in which the laity work in close collaboration with bishops and priests.

LENT OF SHARING

22. We address this urgent appeal to you during the season of Lent. At this time of year our thoughts turn to the suffering of our Saviour who shed His blood for love of all persons and peoples. We are convinced that we who dare to call ourselves His disciples must share His universal love and compassion, embracing generously the sacrifices that love entails. "If any man will come after me let him deny himself and take up his cross daily and follow me." (Mt 16:24)

23. May this season of Lent move us to support in prayer and action the cause of the underdeveloped world. May God the Father of our Lord and Saviour Jesus Christ through the inspiration of the Holy Spirit awaken us all to a deep consciousness of human brotherhood. Deeply aware of the terrible suffering of the people of our time, may we rest uneasy until all of us who enjoy abundant security, conscious of our Christian calling, come to the rescue of the underdeveloped world.

NOTES

1. Paul VI, *The Development of Peoples, The Papal Encyclicals,* edit. Claudia Carlen, IHM (Wilmington, N.C., McGrath Publishing, 1981), V, 183, n. 1.

2. Paul VI, *ibid.,* n. 83, in Carlen, p. 198.

3. Paul VI, ibid., n. 19, in Carlen, p. 186.

4. Paul VI, *ibid.,* n. 47, in Carlen, p. 191 f.

5. L.J. LeBret, *L'Église dans le monde de ce temps* (Mame, Paris, 1967), p. 276.

Document 18

LABOUR DAY MESSAGE — 1968
THE CHURCH'S SOLIDARITY
WITH WORKERS AND WITH VICTIMS
OF SOCIAL INJUSTICE

Author — The Episcopal Commission for Social Action[1]

1. This Labour Day, the Church, the People of God, marks its solidarity with that large sector of our population which is made up of workers. Labour Day is also an occasion for all of us to remind ourselves that a Christian life is a lie if it has no part in the anguish of those who suffer from unemployment, discrimination, from poverty in any of its forms, if it has no part in the aspirations of those who cherish hope for the realization of a just society.

2. The scandal of poverty and injustice at the world level is flagrant: 20% of the world's people living around the North Atlantic have at their disposal 80% of the world's total riches. But even Canada with all its wealth still presents in many respects a sad picture for those who thirst after justice and human dignity for all. One out of every three Canadians lives socially, economically and culturally on the margin of our Canadian community.

3. In particular, the present housing situation and the gross inequities arising out of regional underdevelopment in Canada fly in the face of justice and are an ugly sore disfiguring the body of one of the richest countries in the world. The Canadian community cannot absolve itself of responsibility for this situation.

4. We live in exciting and frustrating times. For the first time in

history, economists tell us that all men can enjoy prosperity and well-being, that newly discovered knowledge and technology can turn our long-cherished dreams and hopes into living reality at home and abroad. We could if only we would: what is lacking is neither knowledge nor ability, but love, conviction and will. Indeed, as has been remarked so often, "The real problem is not the poor, but we, the affluent." The perpetual drama is lack of collective awareness of the poor and what it means to be poor. We still are not willing to favour unreservedly their full participation in the decisions that concern them, as their human dignity requires.

5. The Christian message is starkly clear. God is surely speaking to us through the signs of the times, through the events of everyday life. He is urging us insistently: "Feed your hungry brother! Clothe your naked brother! House your unsheltered brother!" Concretely this means for us today: "Pay better wages! Provide a higher level of education, easier access to medical care, and possibilities of leisure for all!" It means even more: "Undertake radical changes in the structures of your society, fully realizing that this involves upsetting the *status quo* and disturbing many people in established positions!"

6. In the past, Canadian workers, especially through their organized movements, have striven courageously to lift the downtrodden, the victims of injustice in our country. Let them not falter now, not turn in on their own comfort. There are too many needs and hopes that still go unsatisfied. Many people, as was evident at the recent interdenominational conference on "Christian Conscience and Poverty" (Montreal, May, 1968), are urging the Church to be more faithful to her mission of being the "social conscience" of our society. No Christian can shut his ears to these heartbreaking appeals.

7. Humanity is today confronted with a gigantic task, that of promoting a fully human development for every human being. To go forward in this task, it is not sufficient to mouth principles of justice and charity, however worthwhile and necessary these may be. No! Concrete action is called for on the part of every citizen. The workers and the poor themselves are the first responsible for improving their own lot, but industrialists, social organisms of every kind and governments at every level must join forces with them in strategic and sustained cooperative action. And in this action they

can count on the firm commitment of the People of God within all the Churches.

8. In our world that no longer knows frontiers or distances, a world increasingly and necessarily physically one, too many men still live as "neighbours but strangers". For this world, the Church has the highest of aspirations; she dearly longs to breathe into it a soul of unity and love. This mission is at the heart of the gospel message which founds man's ultimate hope for a better world.

NOTE

1. At the time and for some years later, the Episcopal Commission for Social Affairs was composed of ten bishops, five Anglophone and five Francophone, elected by the whole Canadian episcopate.

Document 19

HUMAN RIGHTS: THE ROAD TO PEACE

Author — The Episcopal Commissions for Social Action and of Health and Welfare, December 18, 1968

1. The Church shares with the United Nations the conviction that the effective protection of human rights is an essential condition of national and international peace and progress. Pius XII set respect for fundamental rights as the prerequisite of peace. Paul VI saw the progress of mankind in the protection of individual freedoms. John XXIII began his encyclical *Peace on Earth* with a commentary on the rights and duties of the human person, stressing that respect for the one and fulfillment of the other are essential to order among men and to the peace of society.

2. Like other great social and political declarations of our time the United Nations Universal Declaration of Human Rights (1948) is a challenge to the human conscience to transform the forces of our society, particularly those forces which unduly exploit individuals and nations and which lead to deprivation and discrimination. These great documents not only spell out the hopes of millions denied their rights. They translate these hopes into irresistible demands.

3. Dag Hammarskjold, placed the spiritual forces of the world at the very heart of the movement to achieve human rights. He wrote:

> Attempts are made to link the development of human rights exclusively to the liberal ideas which broke through to predominance in the Age of Enlightenment. To do so however, seems to me to overlook the historical background of those ideas. It means also cutting our ties to a source of strength that we need

in order to carry the work of human rights to fruition and to give those rights, when established, their fitting spiritual content.[1]

4. Voicing the concern of these spiritual forces, Paul VI, in a message to the United Nations Conference on Human Rights (Teheran, 1968), remarked that there is still "an enormous road to be travelled" before human rights are secured, and before such injuries to man's dignity as social injustice, extreme poverty, and ideological oppression can be halted.[2]

5. The journey in Canada has begun. More and more areas of concern are being pointed out. In the matter of true constitutional protection there is no Canadian Bill of Rights. The present one is only a legislative enactment. In the case of native cultures within the country (Indian-Metis, Eskimo), there exists a need for proper measures to conserve their identities and their capacities for self-development. In education, the right of parents to have their children educated in a system consonant with their religion and culture must be honoured. The language rights of the founding cultures must be respected in law, commerce, education and the provision of equal opportunity. In labour and in services for the public there must be no discrimination because of race, creed or colour. In the case of women's rights, equal pay for equal work and equal opportunity for advancement must be guaranteed. In the vast network of social services, whether they be remedial or preventive, policy ought to build upon the preservation of freedom and initiative and not upon a degrading form of dependence. In international aid and in the development of emerging countries Canada has those duties to fulfill which fall naturally upon one of the wealthier and more technically advanced countries of the world.

6. The implementation of measures to ensure the rights of the disadvantaged is always dependent upon the motivation of those who enjoy advantages. The framing of the Universal Declaration of Human Rights twenty years ago has done much to keep that motivation conscious. In highest praise of it Pope John XXIII wrote:

An act of great importance performed by the United Nations Organization was the Universal Declaration of Human Rights. For in it the dignity of the person is acknowledged. There is proclaimed as fundamental the right of free movement in the search of truth and in the attainment of moral good and justice; and also the right to a dignified life with all the other subsidiary rights that this implies. It is our earnest wish that the day may come when every human being may find therein an effective safeguard for the rights which derive directly from his dignity as a person, and which are therefore universal, inviolable and inalienable.[3]

NOTES

1. Search has failed to locate this quotation.

2. Message transmitted by the Director of the Papal Delegation, Reverend Theodore Hesburgh, CSC, Rector of the University of Notre Dame, Indiana. cf. *Acta Apostolicae Sedis*, Vatican, 1968, LX, 283.

3. *Peace on Earth*, cf. *The Papal Encyclicals*, edit. Claudia Carlen, IHM (Wilmington, N.C., McGrath Publishing, 1981), V, 123, nn. 144 f.

Document 20

POVERTY AND CONSCIENCE: TOWARDS A COALITION FOR DEVELOPMENT[1]

Author — Report of a Joint Strategy Committee of the Canadian Council of Churches and of the Canadian Catholic Conference: To All Concerned Canadians, May 30, 1969

I — BACKGROUND

We will not let ourselves be pushed around any longer... The inequalities and injustices of which we are the victims exist because we are kept out of the centres of decision-making, where the society of the rich decides our future.

> Montreal Conference on Christian Conscience and Poverty, May, 1968, United Citizens' Statement

1. Everywhere in today's world of destructive/creative chaos, people are in a hurry to be fully alive. Youth and the poor especially want to have more, know more, and do more so as to *live more*. They are seeking freedom from daily want, a share in social power and a better quality of life *now*. The deprived are saying to the privileged, "Damn your charity, give us justice!" Those in need are impatient because there is no longer any valid excuse for injustice and discrimination. Abundant resources and technical know-how can provide necessities and opportunities for all, given enough *moral will* and *political courage*. Hence the great expectations. Hence the revolutionary mood because these expectations are frustrated.

2. Most of humanity is still caught in the trap of poverty. The gap

is widening between the rich and poor nations, between the affluent and the deprived within each nation. In Canada, the "Just Society" is still a dream. The reality is a disgrace, which sees 4,000,000 to 5,000,000 Canadians enslaved by economic and social want. Public priorities still put the power of money before the needs of people.

3.   Yet this crisis holds a promise. Organized protest is building up a momentum toward development, the process that frees people from want to seek a full life. This rising movement offers new opportunities for justice, if only people will seize them.

4.   This crisis-opportunity confronts the one-sixth of mankind who call themselves Christians. Potentially, they represent history's most powerful lobby for human development. Will they respond with a "pussycat purr or a tiger's roar"? Some Christians are beginning to take a critical look at themselves:

5.   * *Beirut, April 1968* — The first international conference sponsored jointly by the World Council of Churches and the Vatican explored "World Development: Challenge to the Churches". The conference of social scientists and world leaders challenged

> ... Christian citizens everywhere to pledge their support to development as a settled commitment, to campaign or lobby for development by all means at their disposal, and to give governments, parties, leaders and agencies no peace until the whole human race can live with reasonable ease and hope in its single planetary home.

6.   * *Montreal, May 1968* — The first national conference co-sponsored by 12 churches, the federal government and several provincial governments, examined "Christian Conscience and Poverty". Five hundred delegates decided that

> ... the widening of differences between rich and poor has become so marked that Christians personally and the Christian Church as an institution are called upon to make deep and rapid changes in their way of thinking and living.

(Churches of Christ [Disciples], Greek Orthodox, Lutheran Council in Canada, Mennonite Central Committee [Canada], Roman Catholic, Anglican, Baptist Federation, Pentecostal Assemblies, Presbyterian, Religious Society of Friends [Quakers], Salvation Army, United Church.)

7. * *Summer and Fall, 1968* — At assemblies and conferences, several of Canada's major churches pledged support to the war against poverty.

8. * *Toronto, November, 1968* — Leaders of the 12 co-sponsoring churches met to consider the possibilities of a coordinated response. They decided that an interchurch committee should draw up a "practical strategy of unified action" by May 15, 1969.

9. * *Fall and Winter, 1968-69* — Meanwhile, there were new stirrings across Canada. From the Atlantic to the Pacific, local and regional groups of concerned Christians initiated programs for development.

10. * *Strategy Committee, December, 1968 to May, 1969* — In December the Canadian Council of Churches and the Canadian Catholic Conference (CCC and CCC) each appointed four representatives to the strategy committee recommended by the Toronto meeting. In early 1969 the members and their assistants studied, consulted, debated and prepared this report.

II — AS OF NOW...

Our standard is human dignity, human opportunity, human freedom; in short, the fully human. We do not claim to know all that is in man or all that is involved in the fully human... But we press for human development (and as part of this, economic and social development), because we believe that man's future is open and that the future of many men should and could be more open than it is at present. We believe that all men have the right to develop themselves with their fellow men in community.

> Beirut Conference, World Development: Challenge to the Churches, April, 1968, Report, pp. 17-18

1 — The Present Contribution

11. We acknowledge the contribution which the Christians of Canada now make to the cause of human development.

12. Recent examples include initiatives to airlift emergency supplies into Biafra, and the support of self-help projects through such agencies as the Anglican Primate's Fund, the Canadian Catholic Organization for Development and Peace, and the overseas development fund of the United Church.

13. Congregational support of world and home missions is an important Christian response to human needs. Education, health, welfare, and family services are supported on a large scale. Add institutional and personal works of mercy in cities and outlying areas. Add the generous donation of time and talent made by individual Christians through voluntary and public agencies; this, even though often not recognized, is of major social significance.

14. While it is impossible to place any precise monetary value on these contributions, something in excess of $25 million annually would appear to be a modest estimate, exclusive of education costs and donated time.

15. The present contribution is cause for some satisfaction. Yet it is clearly not enough. For one thing, it is fragmented. Each church is preoccupied with its own projects, and even within a given denomination, there is often little or no coordination between one level and another. Again, the emphasis is on helping to *alleviate* the effects of poverty, rather than on helping to *eliminate* causes of human misery. The building of a just society requires more than patchwork, however skillful. Finally, widespread criticism of the "comfortable church" shows that suffering humanity expects much more of Christians. Above all, many still look to Christianity *for reasons to hope, for motives to serve one another.*

2 — Some Working Assumptions

16. * *Poverty* is the sum total of human needs and hungers. In this broad sense all of us are poor. The majority of mankind is denied even the basic necessities of existence. Under present priorities, arms before aid and money power before people's needs spell poverty for most. The majority is enslaved by a conspiracy of circumstances, cut off from adequate opportunities to better their lot. This human misery is indivisible in the nation called Earth. Our neighbour is every man whose need we know and whom we can assist, whether he lives "at home" or "abroad".

17. * *Development* is the process of continuous human growth, the integrated sum of human achievements and satisfactions, economic, social, political, cultural, and spiritual. Human development policies involve new approaches and new social priorities. The process of development moves beyond "band-aid" remedies to root out causes of human want; it moves beyond the "rich man's burden" mentality to a fraternal attitude of mutual support. This process opens new doors to participation in decision-making. Development policies set people free to seek a full life, each in his own way and at his own pace.

18. * In *Christian perspective* development is seen as a continuation of creation, in which man has an increasing responsibility to "subdue the earth" to human service. For Christians, Jesus Christ exemplifies the fully human man who lived and died for others, in free obedience to the Father of all. The social imperatives of his New Commandment are seen now as primary. "The glory of God is man fully alive." (Irenaeus, second century, *Against Heresies*, Bk. 5.)

19. * Given this perspective, a growing number of Canadian Christians are making a *renewed commitment to social action now*: action centered on people, at all levels, in various forms; action together and in partnership.

20. * *Action centered on people:* The basic premise of the report is that people come first. Wide participation is the key. When many more people share actively in decision-making, new social priorities will emerge for building a better society. In today's technical world, both the "poor poor" and the "affluent poor" hunger for a full life. The Christian community can help discern human values and pioneer in programs of "animation" to awaken "people power". The main resource which the church has to contribute, now as in the past, is human capital, committed, competent men, women, and youth in families, schools, work life, and public affairs. They are seeking new outlets for social action.

21. * *Action at all levels:* Each church, congregation, religious organization or agency, and each Christian shares in this common responsibility. Each can "plug in" at the appropriate point, local, diocesan, provincial, regional, national or international. Social progress requires united action at national and world levels, and personal involvement at the grassroots.

22. * *Action in various forms:* There is ample room for different initiatives and experiments by Christians inside, alongside, and outside church channels. There is a place for both person-to-person actions and for united action to revise public priorities and reform social systems.

23. * *Action together as Christians:* A greater social contribution requires Christian cooperation, while respecting the autonomy of each church. United action does not call for a centralized super-structure, but it does require an interchurch "clearing house" (at one level or more) to coordinate the common effort.

24. * *Action in partnership with other Canadians:* Even if Christians work together, it would be ghetto-minded and totally unreal for the churches to try to "go it alone". It would be wasteful folly to attempt what governments or other agencies are better equipped to do. To win the long war against want, a partnership of public, voluntary, and religious agencies is necessary. Such a "coalition of concern" exists, at least potentially, in every community. One of the first tasks is to help mobilize this coalition for united planning and action.

3 — Framework for United Action

25. The Strategy Committee was not set up to analyse the general problem of poverty, or to research particular aspects. The committee itself made a further decision: "What is required is *a strategy rather than detailed tactics.* The strategy should indicate the development of a process and leave it to members of the churches to implement."

26. *We identified four main guidelines to united action,* which are described in paragraphs 29-50. Within their broad framework, Canadian Christians can make a greater contribution to development: working within each church; better still, cooperating with other Christians; best of all, serving alongside fellow citizens in the total community.

27. To ensure that this strategy becomes a reality during the 1970's, *essential first steps in 1969* are recommended in paragraphs 51-60.

28. We believe we have proposed what is possible and therefore realistic.

III — INTO THE 1970'S:
GUIDELINES TO A UNITED STRATEGY

The work of development will not be finished in a day or a year. This is a work for this century and beyond.

Beirut Conference, Statement, p. 13

1 — Review Resources and Revise Priorities... Ministry of Penance

Christians personally and Christian churches as institutions must make deep and rapid changes in their ways of thinking and living.

Montreal Conference, Summary of Resolutions

29.   A "practical strategy of unified action" requires at the outset, in every area of Christian life, a detailed stock-taking of resources and a questioning of individual and collective conscience. Periodic review and evaluation are necessary, since Christian commitment is a continuing process. Long-range planning is also required.
    What's involved:

* *Review Resources*

30.   Make an inventory of existing manpower (human capital), revenues, investments, buildings, other assets, etc. Examine operating and capital budgets.

Determine how these resources are used now in terms of time and money spent, and in relation to human needs in the community. What's the present profile of priorities?

* *Examine conscience: "Where our priorities are, our heart is."*

31.   What does the pattern of priorities say about our way of living now as Christians? In the face of human need, what should be the role of Christian conscience?

Are any changes in priorities indicated? If so, what changes? Is there any consensus?

Are we really serious about making such changes? If so, which ones for a start?

Are we also prepared to reform our own attitudes and ways of living so as to conform to these new priorities? If so, what does this renewal involve?

When and how do we begin to put new priorities into effect? What step-by-step plan of action should we adopt?

2 — Commit More Resources to Development... Ministry of Sharing

Let each one examine his conscience. Is he prepared to support, out of his own pocket, works and undertakings organized in favor of the most destitute? Is he ready to pay higher taxes so that the public authorities can intensify their efforts in favor of development?

Paul VI, *Development of Peoples*, n. 47

32.   Putting new priorities into effect is the ''crunch test'' of the Christian community's credibility. More than token commitments and once-a-year offerings are involved. While resources are limited, the opportunities for generous sharing are limitless, especially in terms of the churches' main capital: people.

33.   This is not to suggest that the churches should try to ''go it alone'', or try to duplicate what governments and other agencies are better equipped to do (and in which many Christians now serve). Rather, it is a question of Christian groups *serving as leaven*, pushing toward a just and compassionate society.
      What's involved — some possibilities:

   * *Commit human resources to development*

34.   *Shift the emphasis from ecclesiastical housekeeping to serving in the community*, at local, regional, national, and international levels. Redeploy Christian manpower: free men, women and youth to give priority time to the cause of human development in whatever ways are most effective.

One proposal, for example, calls for Christian task forces to work alongside depressed groups ''to learn from the minorities' point of view the conditions of their life, and the attitudes and conduct of the dominant group which underlie these conditions''. Other prospects: assist in leadership-training and in self-help programs; sponsor candidates in urban-training courses, co-operative projects.

Also required by this commitment are just salaries and working conditions for employees of churches and religious agencies.

* *Commit buildings and other properties*

35. Shift from the attitude of "When in doubt, build" to "Where there is need, open the door".
Response options include:

Declare a moratorium on new building, subject to annual review.

— Whenever possible, favor interdenominational building.

— Build modest churches, not triumphant monuments.

— Consider interdenominational leasing of space in new complexes.

— Delay interior completion and furnishing of new buildings. After all, creation is not finished. Channel the savings to development projects.

— Review capital financing in terms of its burden on the poor, in the congregation and the community.

— Consider longer-term financing for new buildings.

— Adapt existing facilities to community uses, such as daycare centres, recreation centres for youth and the aged.

— Make more property sites available for lower-income housing, or other community services.

— Gradually phase out of property ownership.

* *Commit financial resources*

36. Open the books! Examine revenues, reserves, investments, and prospects for new funds. Decide on generous commitments.
Options include:

— Switch some existing investments into low-yielding development projects.

— Provide "seed money" for demonstration projects. In housing, for example, raise "seed" funds for lower-income or cooperative programs which will accent living conditions, not profits; housing with "Children Welcome" signs.

— Re-examine the issue of property taxation, asking what public policy will best serve people's needs. In this light face the question of taxation of church properties. In lieu of property taxes, congregations could adopt some form of voluntary assessment and contribute the funds to development programs.

— Earmark an increasing percentage of annual revenues for development. As a beginning, Christian congregations across Canada in 1970 could earmark at least 3%-5% of annual church income for development programs outside the traditional missionary field. This would raise as much as $10 million for investment in people and self-help projects. (It would also put "our money where our mouth is" when advocating that Canada allot 1% of the gross national product to international aid.)

— Interchurch cooperation to raise funds for world development is another possibility. As a start, during Lent 1970 Canadian Christians could conduct a joint campaign for world development and could jointly support some deserving programs.

37.   In these and other ways during the 1970's the Christian community in Canada can risk becoming a "poor Church" or at least one that is more in keeping with the life style of the Servant Lord.

3 — Animate People... Ministry of Hope

Peace is the development of people.
Calgary Interfaith Motto

38.   Most economic and social problems at their roots are "people problems". At every level of society there exist social indifference and inertia on the part of the vast majority; poor communication, even between next-door neighbours; and worst of all, a deepening alienation between various "we" and "they" groups. This alienation is almost total between the affluent and the deprived. They live in different worlds.

39.   Hence the need for a process of contact, dialogue, communion,

participation. This calls for new expressions of the Christian ministry of reconciliation and hope.

40. Christians can serve as a *catalyst*, striving to bring alienated groups together to discover one another and identify their common problems. As a "value centre" and an "enabler", the church can serve as an *animator* to awaken people's hopes and stir their will to organize and take action.
What's involved:

* *Within the Christian community*

41. Give priority to social education for all age groups. Emphasize the imperatives of the Gospel. Show the relationship between worship and social action. Aspects include social formation in small groups of students, workers, or married couples, catechetical programs on social responsibility, and training in group leadership. Among promising new approaches are neighborhood "living room dialogues" on public issues.

— Support and reenforce individual Christians who serve in public programs for human development.

— Invite Canadian theologians and social scientists to prepare a "theology of development", showing the relationship between the Christian mission and human progress.

* *In the total community*

42. Help organize public forums outside partisan politics, for free debate of key issues in which human values and public priorities are at stake. The churches' education and communication services could head the initiative, preferably in cooperation with the mass media.

— Help sponsor programs of social animation to release and focus "people power". Examples include the "Town Talk" plan of organizing a community-wide dialogue, the small-groups process called "Project People", the animation technique devised by *le Conseil des Œuvres de Montréal* to stimulate participation in deprived urban districts, the pioneering Antigonish Movement of economic self-help through cooperatives and credit unions, the methods developed by the federal New Start program and the

Saul Alinsky approach of confrontation used by industrial and minority groups.

43.   By these and other means, the Christian community can contribute to the development of people, the new name for peace.

4 — Initiate Political Action... Ministry of Justice

The Church must actively support the powerless in our society as they seek their share in decision-making and in determining their own destiny.

Montreal Conference, Summary of Resolutions

44.   When it comes to building a just society in Canada and "the global village", moral will is a vital missing element. The powerful of the world lack sufficient political will to make development a top priority. The powerless lack sufficient information and organization to make an impact on the wielders of power.

45.   As an "oasis of freedom", the Christian people can make a notable contribution here, accepting the risks involved.

46.   The Church is called to be a gadfly, a *radical questioner* of the *status quo* including its own social status; a *voice of conscience* which raises the gut issues, rebukes every injustice, challenges public opinion, and rallies the moral will, in the manner of the ancient prophets, of Jesus Christ and of such modern martyrs as Martin Luther King, the Kennedys, and Camilo Torres.

47.   At the same time, the church's ministry of justice commits it to become an *authentic spokesman and lobby for the dispossessed.* This will be possible only as the deprived are invited into the mainstream of church life to share equally in decision-making.
What's involved:

   * *All levels*

48.   Without paternalism, assist the urban and rural poor, minority groups, members of depressed regions, the aged and the handicapped to organize and focus their power. As allies, Christians can

support these groups when they take their problems before the general public and elected representatives.

— Present interchurch briefs on critical issues of development to federal, provincial, and municipal governments. Join with voluntary agencies whenever possible.

— Issue statements and comments on key public issues while they are "hot", *before* policies are made. An informed diversified Christian contribution to public debates will assist elected representatives to select priorities, provided these statements avoid safe generalities and identify specific human values at stake. Issues calling for more Christian comment include Canada's slow progress towards a world aid goal of at least 1% of the gross national product, the 6 to 1 arms/aid imbalance, tax reform, family needs, including the need for new forms of house financing; discrimination problems in education, jobs, and housing; the questions of guaranteed annual income and medicare, and the social impact on Canadian life of world technology and international corporations ("private governments").

* National Level*

49.   The Canadian Council of Churches and the Canadian Catholic Conference could present an annual brief to the federal government on critical issues of development, expressing support for some existing programs, and advocating new public priorities. For example, the two national groups could make a joint submission to the Senate Committee on Poverty.

— Whenever possible, national church groups should join with other voluntary agencies, such as the Canadian Welfare Council, in making united representations to the federal government.

— Research studies are needed on the human consequences of public policies and priorities in such fields as science, defence, education, family life and housing. Theologians and social scientists could undertake such "human dimension" studies into their effects on rights, values and relationships.

— Church leaders are asked to set up a Coalition of Canadians for Development (CCD) to coordinate and service the unified strategy proposed here. (Details are given in the next section.)

IV — 1969 PRIORITIES: ESSENTIAL STEPS

Delegate at Montreal conference, 1968: *"I came here expecting to see a tiger set free. Instead, it's a fat, toothless and gutless pussycat."*

Dr. Charles Hendry, co-president: *"The process is the reality. In this case, the process has only begun."*

Madame Pauline Vanier, co-president: *"I'm impatient, gentlemen!"*

Stage by Stage

50. *"How* do we do these things? How can we carry out a unified strategy?" Specific answers will be discovered on the job. As a general principle, a workable process is essential at every level and stage. This requires:

— *Leaders who can give priority time* to putting the show on the road and keeping it on the move.

— *Limited and well-defined goals.* People set realistic objectives they can reach, step by step.

— *Evaluation as part of the process.* Assess results at every stage.

Priority Steps Now

51. Limited specific goals for 1969, which are possible:

All Levels

52. 1. Intensive, extensive *promotion and circulation* of the Report, including media coverage, and distribution to the churches and all interested groups. The communications and public relations departments of the churches are requested to undertake this service as a major responsibility.

53. 2. *Positive, decisive responses to the Strategy Report* by the two CCC's, churches (denominations), congregations, and by Christians in other groupings. To begin with, national church leaders are asked

to name a small *steering committee* to achieve the first stages of the process outlined below.

54. 3. As tangible proof of genuine concern, Christian groups across Canada are invited during 1969 and early 1970 to take *initial steps towards a generous commitment of resources to development.*

Some minimum possibilities:

* *Begin a review of resources and priorities, and a serious questioning of conscience* at interchurch or denominational institutes during the fall-winter months of 1969-70. Any realistic review will examine church resources in the light of human needs in the community and beyond, such as education, employment, health, housing and leisure needs.

* Local parishes/congregations or dioceses/presbyteries *could earmark at least 3%-5% of their total 1970 income for development projects* outside the traditional missionary field. This fund, which might reach $10 million across Canada, could be given to "investments in people", such as the support of laity and clergy in animation and self-help projects; or to related programs designed to release human potential among minorities or deprived youth.

* Alternatively, congregations and parishes could adopt some form of *voluntary assessment in lieu of property taxation; or delay the interior completion and furnishing of new church buildings.* The funds or savings realized in 1970 could start a "seed money" reserve for lower-income housing; or else might be used to sponsor youths in updating courses, adults in retraining programs, community personnel in development leadership.

* During Lent 1970 Canadian Christians could conduct an *interchurch campaign for world development funds,* and could jointly support some overseas projects.

55. 4. Organizations, agencies, departments, training and education centres, and other groupings within the churches are invited to *make the Strategy Report a main reference point in their planning and programming* for the rest of 1969 and thereafter.

56. 5. Christians in public groups are encouraged to *start or sup-*

port new initiatives in human development. Here too the Report can be a main point of reference.

National

57.   6. The two CCC's are urged to *submit a joint brief to the Senate Committee on Poverty.*

58.   7. Church leaders are asked to begin setting up a *Coalition of Canadians for Development (CCD)* to promote, coordinate and service the unified strategy.

* Such an agency was recommended at the Montreal Conference, anticipated in the Toronto consensus, and proposed in various forms by the members of the Strategy Committee, who are in general agreement that until some such agency exists, a unified strategy cannot become a reality. At the same time the committee agreed this facility should serve, *not* oversee, the many initiatives undertaken.

* The proposed CCD would consist of a *board of directors* or advisors, and a small *action bureau*, or "operations desk".

* The CCD would be *funded, equipped and mandated to carry out these functions:*

— Publicize and promote the report.

— As a clearing house, receive and transmit relevant information. Maintain liaison with each church at different levels, with voluntary and public agencies, government, and interested groups.

— Coordinate projects as required.

— Provide consultative services and program resources on request, and on a cost-fee basis.

— Prepare progress reports and evaluations for the two CCC's and the churches.

— As a national catalyst, otherwise stimulate and support the unified strategy.

* The proposed CCD would come into being in stages. *The following steps are proposed to achieve the "start up" of CCD in 1969* through the agreement of the churches:

— Appoint an interim *Board of Directors,* beginning with several personnel from national social action departments or their equivalent. Instruct the interim board to meet as soon as possible after appointment to select an executive and make arrangements for a permanent board. *(By Jan. 1, 1970, it should include representatives from the sectors of population most actively concerned with poverty problems,* such as deprived minorities, youth, welfare planning bodies, citizens' groups, government agencies, business, labour, and farm groups.)

— Establish the CCD *Action Bureau in Ottawa,* including bilingual secretarial service and office space.

Initial operations could be handled by an executive staff person from the Canadian Catholic Conference and by the Ottawa officer of the Canadian Council of Churches, when appointed. Their regular responsibilities should be curtailed sharply during this interim service.

Permanent leadership for the bureau would arise from decisions by the board of directors and the sponsoring churches.

Churches could be approached to detach other staff for short-term, long-term, or permanent assignments with the CCD, as required. Such personnel would be supported financially by their constituent churches, but they would come under the direction of the CCD board.

(Note: Such a "detaching" process would help CCD meet the problem of deploying staff in the various regions of Canada, including the development of French-Canadian groupings.)

Churches could also be asked to revise their staffing plans so that other personnel needs of the CCD could be met.

Regional/Community

* *If and when required, set up regional/community offices for CCD.*

59. These seven steps or their equivalent in 1969-70 would *establish*

a beachhead, providing the minimum personnel and programming needed for the unified stategy to emerge and then gather momentum in the 1970's.

60.   In this expectation, let us risk our comfort.

V — RENEWAL THROUGH SERVICE

61.   What do you mean by crushing my people? By grinding the faces of the poor? This is what the Lord of hosts says. (Isaiah 3:15)

Let me have no more of your noisy hymns... Instead, let justice roll on like a mighty river. (Amos 5:23-24)

Go first and make peace with your brother; then offer your gift at the altar. (Matthew 5:24)

The Son of Man did not come to be served; he came to serve. (Mark 10:45)

Love one another as I have loved you. (John 13:14)

... (Commitment to development) includes readiness to render our time, skills and wealth, and perhaps to lay down life itself, for the achievement of a more just and compassionate society. He who makes all things new is drawing us on. (Fourth Assembly, WCC, Uppsala)

It is towards that new history, a peaceful, truly human history as promised by God to men of good will, that we must resolutely march. (Paul VI, UN Address, 1965)

Only he who shares his bread may come to the Lord's table. (A. van den Huevel)

The Church is her true self only when she exists for humanity. As a fresh start she should give away all her endowments to the poor. (Dietrich Bonhoeffer)

Thesis

62. Christian cooperation in the creative task of development is a living witness to the Good News.

63. By such cooperation the Christian community is renewed, becoming more faithful followers of the Servant Lord.

64. In the global neighbourhood, which man must build to survive, only a serving church will be credible and relevant.

Questions

65. These discussion-starters could be used by groups when making a review of priorities and an examination of conscience.

1. Do the norms above (61) describe Christians of today?

2. If not, where and why do we fall short?

3. What does the rest of humanity expect of Christians in the struggle against poverty?

4. How can the Christian community contribute most effectively to the cause of human development?

5. What could be done by our parish/congregation/organization?

6. How can individual Christians best contribute through voluntary groups, occupational organizations, political parties, public agencies?

NOTE

1. In December, 1968, the Canadian Catholic Conference and the Canadian Council of Churches struck a committee of eight with instructions to propose "a practical strategy of unified action for all Christian churches in their present programs of social action, in particular concerning poverty, and their future programs which may evolve in an ecumenical spirit" (Foreward of the Report, p. 2).

The members of the committee were: George E. Davy, Toronto, Chairman of the Program Committee of the General Synod, Anglican Church of Canada; Rev. Charles

Forsyth, Toronto (Co-Chairman), Secretary of the Board of Evangelism and Social Service, United Church of Canada; Rev. Arthur Gowland, Toronto, Secretary of the Board of Evangelism and Social Action, Presbyterian Church in Canada; Romeo Maione, Montreal, Director of the Canadian Catholic Organization for Development and Peace; Rev. Clifton Monk, Winnipeg, Executive Secretary of Social Services, Lutheran Council in Canada; Abbé Robert Riendeau, Montréal, Directeur, Département du Bien-Être et de la Santé, Conférence Catholique Canadienne; Louis Roy, Montréal (Co-Chairman), Société financière pour le Commerce et l'Industrie; Rev. William F. Ryan, S.J., Ottawa; Co-Director, Social Action Department, Canadian Catholic Conference.

The Committee presented its report publicly May 30, 1969. It was formally approved by both the Canadian Catholic Conference and the Canadian Council of Churches in June, 1969. (Cf. Bernard M. Daly, *Labour Day Statements of the Bishops of Canada 1965-1982*, a paper read to the Canadian Catholic Historical Association, Ottawa June 9, 1982. Unfortunately this very interesting and informative paper remains unpublished. Mr. Daly is presently Assistant General Secretary of the Canadian Conference of Catholic Bishops, a veteran of its permanent staff and of its social affairs activity.)

Document 21

LABOUR DAY MESSAGE — 1969
NEW POWER

Author — The Episcopal Commission for Social Action

1. What has been called "new power", the phenomenon of ever-widening participation in public dialogue and policy-making, has arisen in both civil life and religious society. We believe it opportune and fitting to choose this noteworthy "sign of the times"; as our theme for Labour Day, 1969.

2. The emergence of this new power indicates real progress towards a truly democratic society; it points to a distribution of power among groups which up to now have been without it. If, as we hope, this wider diffusion of power is translated into more participation in decision-making, and if it encourages a greater sense of responsibility, then it will contribute significantly to the development of people and to building a more humane society.

3. As we use the term, new power refers to the ever-increasing will of the powerless, the deprived and the forgotten to have a public voice, to express their dissatisfactions, to make known their longings and aspirations, to dialogue with the present holders of social power. This new force, springing from the basic needs of citizens, is frustrated by the anonymity of impersonal power structures, sclerotic and unresponsive to their vital aspirations. The citizens of today simply do not accept to be excluded from the centres of policy decisions which affect their daily lives.

4. New power refers also to the upward human thrust made by certain fortunate sectors of our population. Thanks to better inte-

grated policies of development, these citizens have been able to acquire more knowledge, more property, more power, and to carve out for themselves a secure place in the areas of education, politics and the economy.

5.   New power also reflects the keener sense of justice to be remarked in many, prompting them to repudiate all camouflaged forms of power, such as lobbying, favoritism, patronage and paternalism.

6.   Finally, new power means that the exercise of authority is now conceived rather in a spirit of service, than as the possession of high office or prestige allowing greater control or even domination of others.

Whence this New Power?

7.   The blossoming of this many-faceted new power can be attributed mainly to the fact that citizens today are better informed and democratic participation increasingly practised. The phenomenon also has its origins in the deficiencies or abuses which certain wielders of established power could not or would not avoid.

8.   It is not our purpose to condemn the powers that be *en bloc*, nor is it our intention to suggest that they lacked completely the best characteristics we see in the aspirations of new power. We note with satisfaction that a number of those holding power have updated their style of exercising it, have themselves adopted more democratic methods, and have encouraged to the fullest extent an exchange of views between the grassroots and those in positions of authority.

9.   Nor do we assume that the phenomenon of new power is itself perfect in every sense. It has its own share of faults. In particular, we question that blind fanaticism which thoughtlessly calls for acts of violence, revenge or wanton destruction. Certain attitudes and conduct seem more in accord with the jungle law of retaliation than with the conciliatory spirit of the Gospel. In such attitudes and actions the ordinary citizen looks in vain for that respect for his dignity which is his birthright. At the same time of course, it is true that established power can be, and sometimes is, guilty of legalized injustice and violence. This in turn invites violent reaction.

Values Contained in the New Power

10.   On balance, taking a positive approach, we see the phenomenon of new power as a favourable trend in both civil society and church life. It deserves encouragement and support, while effort is made to reduce excesses and remedy defects. The human, social and Christian values which this trend can promote are important agents for the complete development of "all men and of the whole man".

11.   This evolution seems to us to be an authentic sign of human vitality, in individuals and groups. We see in it at least potentially, the manifestation of a determined popular will to participate, to shape society's destiny, to be totally engaged in a responsible way and with an honest desire for liberty and self-determination.

12.   It is even acceptable that this new power can lead to contestation and conflict, and that it may at times become a counter power in opposition to unacceptable and intolerable situations which depersonalize and alienate people. We see this as a contemporary form of that "hunger and thirst after justice" of which the Gospel speaks.

13.   When this new power denounces such social abuses as pseudo-consultation and manipulation by subtly biased misinformation; when it organizes pressure groups and demands for all the basic right to be heard; when it calls for representative structures through which the economically deprived can express themselves; when it demands a share in making decisions of common concern; when it asks for dialogue to dispel misunderstandings and to clear the air; when it points out that the exigencies of life take priority over laws and systems; when it cries from the rooftops that people must come before money, how can it be doubted that such action bears the mark of a better humanism and is both inspired by, and can inspire, a spirit in keeping with the Gospel?

Involvement of the Churches

14.   The Christian knows that there can be no total commitment to or false worship of any power new or old. The Christian sees that all human power is relative, its exercise ambiguous; that God is not

necessarily in every revolution or any established system. The Christian looks beyond the angry, ugly clashes of power, wherein people are hurt, in search of that vision in which power and justice coincide. His criterion is always the same: does this particular exercise of power help to build a just and humane society in Canada and the global community?

15.   We hope that Christians become ever more appreciative of this reality which expresses some of the highest aspirations of mankind today. There has been considerable recognition of its promise. Let it suffice to mention three significant church statements.

Paul VI to the Assembly of the United Nations Organization:

> We must get used to thinking of man in a new way; and in a new way also of man's life in common; in a new manner too, of conceiving the paths of history and the destiny of the world.[1]

In the same vein is a statement of the Episcopate of France:

> A point of no return has been reached. From now on the exercise of authority will require dialogue and access by all to more responsibility. The authority necessary to the life of all society cannot but be strengthened thereby.[2]

There is also the commitment undertaken by the Christian Churches of Canada, in their proposed strategy of forming a Coalition for Development:

> The Church must actively support the powerless in our society as they seek their share in decision-making and in determining their own destiny... The Church is called to be a gadfly, a radical questioner of the *status quo* including its own social status; a voice of conscience which raises the gut issues, rebukes every injustice, challenges public opinion, and rallies the public will.[3]

16.   In this 50th anniversary year of the International Labour Organization, we recall the words of Paul VI, in his address to that body in Geneva, June 10, 1969:

> By your legislation you have assured the protection and the survival of the weak against the power of the strong... You

must in future control the rights of the strong and favour the development of the weak... You must also ensure the participation of all nations in the development of the world and be concerned as of today with the oppressed, just as yesterday your first thought was for the less favoured social categories... Never again will work be superior to the worker, never again will work be against the worker, but always work will be in the service of man, of all men and of all of man.[4]

NOTES

1. *Address to the U.N. General Assembly*, N.Y., Oct. 4, 1965; cf. *Acta Apostolicae Sedis*, Vatican, 1965, LVII, 884; *The Pope Speaks*, Washington, 1966, XI, 56.

2. *Declaration of the Cardinals and Bishops of the Permanent Council of the French Episcopate*, June 20, 1968, n. 5; cf. *Documentation Catholique*, Paris, 1968, LXV, 1186, n. 5.

3. *Poverty and Conscience: Towards a Coalition for Development*; Document 20, above, nn. 43 and 46.

4. *Acta Apostolicae Sedis*, Vatican, 1969, LXI, pp. 500 f., n. 22; p. 495, n. 11; *The Pope Speaks*, Washington, 1969, XIV, pp. 148, n. 22; 142, n. 11.

Document 22

INDIANS IN CANADA

Author — The Canadian Catholic Conference to the Government of Canada, November 28, 1969

WHEREAS the Canadian Government on June 26, 1969, has presented a Statement on Indian Policy, which lends itself to various interpretations and creates a state of disillusionment and unrest among the Indian people: and

WHEREAS the Government proposes to invite various Indian organizations "to discuss the role they might play in the implementation of the new policy, and the financial resources they may require" (cf. Statement, page 13, para. 2): and

WHEREAS the Indian people do not now possess adequate means to establish this dialogue as equal partners: and

WHEREAS the Catholic Bishops of Canada take a positive interest in the general welfare of the Indian people:

THEREFORE the Catholic Bishops of Canada

— express their concern for, and give sincere support to, proper consultation with the Indian people, over a sufficiently extended period, to allow them to evaluate the policy and its implications;

— pledge themselves to cooperate with the Indian people in their efforts to obtain fair treatment and insist that the Government of Canada, before enacting new legislation, negotiate with the Indian people an equitable settlement of treaty and other land claims and of other rights;

— request that the Government provide the official Indian organizations with "the financial resources they may require" to enable them to do research and to acquire the means necessary for a meaningful dialogue.

Document 23

TO THE SPECIAL SENATE COMMITTEE ON POVERTY

Author — The Canadian Catholic Conference and the Canadian Council of Churches, June 11, 1970[1]

INTRODUCTION

Everywhere in today's world of destructive/creative chaos, people are in a hurry to be fully alive. Youth and the poor especially want to have more, know more, and do more so as to live more. They are seeking freedom from daily want, a share in social power, and a better quality of life now. The deprived are saying to the privileged, "Damn your charity, give us justice!" Those in need are impatient because there is no longer any valid excuse for injustice and discrimination. Abundant resources and technical know-how can provide necessities and opportunities for all, given enough moral will and political courage. Hence the great expectations. Hence the revolutionary mood because these expectations are frustrated.

> *Poverty and Conscience: towards a Coalition for Development*,
> Interchurch Strategy Report (ISR), 1969, 1
> (Cf. Document 20 above).

1. We are here in response to the sign of the times described above. We acknowledge that the churches of Canada, various groups of Christians, share in the collective responsibility for human want in the midst of plenty, both in this country and the nation named Earth.

2. Because we stand in the Judaeo-Christian tradition we must

assume the duty to be watchful critics of society in every time and place. For we believe that only God is perfect; only on Him can men ultimately rely, and only to Him can men commit their unconditioned loyalty. To accept human laws and institutions as beyond criticism is to idolize them. On this point the Bible enjoins us to be radical questioners of all earthly authority. "You must judge whether in God's eyes it is right to listen to you and not to God." (Ac 4, 19)

3. We share also in the responsibility to seek solutions to social injustice. In this we are in the tradition of the great prophets of Israel, who insisted that men's first duty before God is "to break unjust fetters... to share your bread with the hungry and shelter the homeless poor." (Is 58:6-7) Christians should pay particular heed to this prophetic injunction, and suffering humanity expects that we will, since we claim to follow a Servant Lord who lived and died for others.

4. In the past Christian groups have been social pioneers. It was religious agencies, for example, which started many of the first schools, hospitals, and welfare programs before such services were widely accepted as public responsibility.

5. Can churches in Canada again serve as social pioneers in the technical society of today? In recent years Christian leaders have been searching for new social strategies. One product of that search is a practical program for united action in the 1970s. It is contained in the Interchurch Strategy Report (ISR) entitled *Towards a Coalition for Development*, which is included in the documentation. Since its publication in May, 1969, some 50,000 copies of this report have circulated across Canada. In response to the report, Christian groups in growing numbers are taking stock of their resources and making new social commitments.

6. This submission represents another step in our continuing search for effective social strategies. We offer some further insights, and report progress to this date in an "experiment in pluralism", namely the Canadian Coalition for Development. This new working partnership of religious groups and a wide range of other intermediate organizations in the voluntary sector was initiated by the Conference and Council.

Respectfully submitted,[2]

Canadian Catholic Conference   Canadian Council of Churches
   Executive Committee   Executive Committee

I — A PERSPECTIVE AND TWO WORKING NORMS

Most of humanity is still caught in the trap of poverty. The gap is widening between the rich and the poor nations, between the affluent and the deprived within each nation. In Canada, the "Just Society" is still a dream. The reality is a disgrace, which sees 4,000,000 to 5,000,000 Canadians enslaved by economic and social want. Public priorities still put the power of money before the needs of people.

> Interchurch Strategy Report (ISR), 2, Document 20 above.

7. Already you have received many definitions of poverty; we do not propose to offer another. Instead we endeavour to situate the problem of poverty within a vision of man and society, taking into account some of the human values and aspirations which many Canadians hold.

8. Most definitions of poverty betray an economic preoccupation. Certainly bread comes first, but human need encompasses much more than bread. Most definitions of poverty also offer an antiseptic and detached description of a human tragedy which cries out for passion and compassion. Nor do most definitions recognize that poverty in some sense afflicts all men. As the Interchurch Strategy Report of May, 1969, said:

> Poverty is the sum total of human needs and hungers. In this broad sense all of us are poor. The majority of mankind is denied even the basic necessities of existence. Under present priorities, arms before aid and money power before people's needs spell poverty for most. The majority are enslaved by a conspiracy of circumstances, cut off from adequate opportunities to better their lot. This human misery is indivisible in the nation called Earth. Our neighbour is every man whose need we know and whom we can assist, whether he lives "at home" or "abroad". ISR, 16

9. The same report attempted to broaden and humanize the popular concept of development, stating:

> Development is the process of continuous human growth, the integrated sum of human achievements and satisfactions,

economic, social, political, cultural and spiritual. Human development policies involve new approaches and new social priorities. This process opens new doors to participation in decision-making. Development policies set people free to seek a full life, each in his own way and at his own pace. ISR, 17

10. We agree with this description as far as it goes. However, it does not quite break away from the prevalent notion which sees development as an almost mechanical and inevitable process involving an efficient blend of education and technology. The definition does not point out that existing social systems have built-in biases which tend to perpetuate inequities. Nor does it acknowledge that justice demands nothing less than the creation by the people of new social structures in harmony with human fulfillment.

11. For these reasons, we prefer to speak of humanity's escape from poverty in all its forms as a gradual process of liberation. Liberation, first of all, involves the rejection of popular myths which now comfort the powerful and deny justice to the weak; the myth that public education is neutral, when in reality it is geared to the "success formula" and designed to preserve the *status quo*; the myth of "scientific objectivity", which tends to treat existing social practices as immutable laws; the myth which holds that the deprived are intrinsically inferior ("lazy", "unstable", etc.), when in reality they are kept powerless and voiceless by a conspiracy of circumstances favouring those already established.

12. Liberation is a constant biblical theme. The Scriptures speak of men's longing to be liberated from the slavery to which human sin has subjected them: misery and violence, oppression and ignorance, in a word, that injustice which has its origin in selfishness. The "hunger and thirst after justice" of which the gospel speaks anticipated the profound yearnings of contemporary humanity for an end to war and exploitation; for a halt to all those policies of madness which enslave mankind, pollute the environment, and even threaten life on Earth.

13. In interpreting this hunger of the human spirit for liberation, modern Christian leaders have called repeatedly for fundamental reforms to "reduce inequalities, fight discriminations, free man from various types of servitude and enable him to be the instrument of his own material betterment, moral progress, and spiritual growth".[3]

Youth and the oppressed especially long for opportunities to realize their dignity as children of God; for opportunities to become "new men" who are masters of their own life and makers of their own history.

14.   Obviously then, any educational or economic program which would have people simply "fit in" with the present technological maze and political muddle is not true liberation. Authentic policies of liberation will enable people to seek a full life, each in his own way and at his own pace in the company of his neighbours. The challenge of liberation is to enable persons now entrapped by circumstances to spring loose, to discover their potential, to seek opportunities for change and growth, and to assume the primary responsibility for their own future and share in building a just society.

15.   This requires organization, new power groupings, which give the deprived a public voice and an active role in decision-making. This in turn requires new attitudes on the part of the present wielders of public power, and in time, new social structures and methods which facilitate rather than handicap the quest for freedom and fulfillment. This involves contention, conflict, and suffering, the price necessary for human progress paid by such men as Jeremiah, Francis of Assisi and Martin Luther King. It is a price well worth paying. The prize is fullness of life.

16.   It may seem naive to foresee a day when virtually every person can become an active participant in the policy-making which affects his life. We call your attention to the emergence of articulate leaders among Canada's first native peoples and the remarkable growth of citizens' groups during the past year. These signs of the time indicate "new power" is fast becoming a reality.

17.   In Latin America meanwhile, where social inequities are much greater than here, a process of liberation such as we have described is beginning among the common people, with Christians among the pioneering leaders. And throughout the world there are new stirrings among students, workers, professionals and intellectuals. In any case, we are not afraid to be hopeful in proposing a new vision of man and an open future for humanity. Surely a new perspective is called for when existing systems keep 80% of humanity enslaved by want, including as many as one fourth of all Canadians.

18. We believe two working norms follow from this perspective of human liberation and social development.

1) *Full development depends on both public and private sectors*

19. We acknowledge and emphasize that public authorities have the major responsibility for advancing and coordinating the common good of the people. Today only governments have the powers and resources to initiate and sustain balanced development. Nevertheless, we challenge any assumption that policies of development should be decided exclusively within the narrow confines of partisan politics. And we challenge any assumption that public agencies of government alone can overcome poverty and achieve social progress. Programs which are planned and executed by governments alone have yet to show that flexibility which meets the diversity of local needs.

20. More important, it is imperative that each citizen, poor as well as rich, join in the search for a better quality of life. Poverty does not consist solely in economic hardship; it entails the erosion of human personality, the cramping of a person's sense of what a full life can mean. To combat poverty then, it will not suffice for the public sector to hand out money. Each person must learn to discover and articulate his own needs and seek to fulfill them.

21. The awakening of the sense of what is possible for man and of the responsible steps required to attain it, is primarily the task of voluntary organizations, not of governments. Voluntary intermediate groups, including religious bodies, should cooperate with, complement and supplement the efforts of governments; and when need be, should also challenge existing priorities and policies in the public sector. Thus voluntary organizations of citizens will exert an essential "countervailing presence".

22. The effectiveness of the voluntary sector however, is impeded by fragmentation, duplication of effort, and excessive internal housekeeping, such as maintenance of structures and fund-raising. Among other reforms, there needs to be a united effort which pools limited resources and personnel.

2) *New working partnerships are required*

23.   We are more than ever convinced that the Interchurch Strategy Report of May, 1969 was correct in calling for new working partnerships in the intermediate sector to help win the long war against want. As it said, "Such a 'coalition of concern' exists, at least potentially, in every community". (ISR, 24) The report recommended that the Canadian Council of Churches and the Canadian Catholic Conference should try to initiate such a coalition at the national level (ISR, 58). In June of last year the executive officers of the Conference and of the Council accepted this recommendation. Since then senior staff of the two bodies have been engaged in this new undertaking.

24.   The results to date are described below. We invite your comments and encouragement in this social pioneering; it is at once evidence of our hopes and our commitment to share in the progressive development of Canadian society and the global community.

II — THE COALITION EXPERIMENT

Wide participation is the key. When many more people share actively in decision-making, new social priorities will emerge for building a better society. ISR, 20

25.   Last summer the idea of a working partnership of churches and other intermediate organizations in the voluntary sector was explored with national leaders of business, cooperatives, labour, welfare and related fields. Their responses were favourable, providing that this cooperation did not involve yet another superagency and assuming that an open-ended, *ad hoc* approach was taken.

26.   A bilingual meeting of potential partners took place in Ottawa during October to explore the possibilities further. The leaders present readily agreed that their groups and others should work together to promote social development. They also reached consensus on three priority goals requiring united action:

— tax reform that gives a fair deal to low-income Canadians;

— effective cooperation with new citizens' groups at local levels;

— and a greater Canadian role in world development.

At a December meeting a fourth priority was selected:

— united support of native peoples.

27. Further exploratory sessions were held in Montreal and Ottawa early this year. At the same time a bilingual task group was devising a flexible mode of operation for the proposed partnership and was selecting possible action strategies on the four priority issues. The bilingual Founding Forum for the Coalition was held in Ottawa on March 13. Representatives of more than 30 national organizations, plus several citizens' groups, approved a "Provisional Statement of Intentions" for the Coalition, endorsed action strategies for 1970 based on the four priority goals, chose a representative executive, and authorized the setting up of small action bureaus.

28. Besides the Conference and the Council (including most of the eleven denominations making up the Council), partners in the Coalition include the Canadian Chamber of Commerce, Canadian Council for International Cooperation, Canadian Labour Congress, Canadian Welfare Council, Catholic Organization for Development and Peace, Confédération des Syndicats Nationaux, Cooperative Union of Canada, Fédération des Caisses Populaires Desjardins, and the National Indian Brotherhood. Prospective partners include the Canadian Association for Adult Education, Canadian Association of Social Workers, Canadian Jewish Congress, Canadian Metis Society, Indian-Eskimo Association of Canada, Mennonite Central Committee, and the National Farmers Union.

29. The Provisional Statement adopted at the Founding Forum describes the nature and spirit of this "experiment in Canadian pluralism". The Coalition functions as a working partnership of organizations "which meet on the common ground of shared human values" to carry out specific actions together. The partners make policy and take action through consensus, usually with the most competent partner in a given project taking the initiative and providing key resources. Partner organizations are free to "join in or opt out of any specific program, but not to interfere with the independence of the Coalition". Details of this open-ended style of joint operation are being worked out on the job.

30. As a kind of third force in the middle position between citi-

zens and government, the Coalition will "strive to become a new lever for the elimination of poverty" and for the promotion of a better quality of life. Especially through public forums, and with the co-operation of the mass media, the Coalition plans to "offer new opportunities for more Canadians to participate directly in public dialogue and decision-making". This emphasis on participation is evident in the priority action strategies the Founding Forum selected for 1970. As the minutes of the Founding Forum record, these include:

* *Tax Reform* — In the near future hold a national forum and "peoples' hearings" across Canada to recruit public support for various tax reforms of benefit to low-income Canadians. If a consensus is reached the Coalition will make a joint presentation to the federal government and Parliament.

* *Citizens' Groups* — At the local level, partner organizations are to urge their members to "plug in" with citizens' groups and help start community and regional coalitions. Nationally, the Coalition is ready to serve as one clearing house for information and resource material wanted by citizens' groups.

* *Native Peoples* — Join with the National Indian Brotherhood and like organizations in their efforts to have a direct voice in federal-provincial policy-making on Indian-Eskimo-Metis affairs. Have the Coalition Executive make direct appeals to federal and provincial governments.

* *World Development* — Take definite steps to mobilize public opinion in favor of a greater Canadian role in world development. Possibilities suggested: prepare a critical analysis of the Pearson Report, *Partners in Development*[4]; organize a national forum on world aid and trade policies.

31. It remains for the partners to make the Coalition work. The united actions attempted and the public impact achieved will reveal whether this new partnership is an authentic social force. The Coalition will succeed in the measure that it brings more Canadians into the policy-making process, from which new priorities for building a just and compassionate society emerge. This in turn requires the formation of voluntary coalitions at local, provincial and regional levels. An Alberta Coalition for Development is already functioning. We understand local coalitions are in the process of formation or in prospect in several major cities.

III — FIRST PRIORITY:
POLICIES TO GUARANTEE BASIC RIGHTS

32. To return to the preeminent role of public authorities in the continuing process of social development: Canada has abundant resources, a viable economy, and technological know-how. Yet this nation still has a long way to go before it can call itself a Just Society in which people's well-being is given first priority. Existing priorities must be out of joint when as many as one quarter of the citizens live near or below the "poverty line".

33. There is supporting evidence that public priorities are awry. For one thing, $1.8 billion are allocated annually for national defence while only about one-sixth of the amount is earmarked for the more positive works of development in the Third World. Domestically, based on estimated expenditures for 1969-70, the federal treasury is allocating 60 cents per capita for public housing subsidies, $13.59 for post-secondary education, and $29.12 for family and youth allowances, making a total of $43.31 per capita, compared to nearly twice as much, $86.22 per capita, for the national defence budget.

34. When basic human needs are given first place in federal spending, then policies to guarantee fundamental economic and social rights will take priority, together with improved legislation to safeguard the civil rights of the powerless and existing legislation guaranteeing political freedom and bicultural rights.

35. We are aware that some federal spokesmen point to the difficulty of reaching a national consensus on economic and social rights. This difficulty is a challenge to leaders to lead Canadians towards such a consensus. How else can this nation begin to realize in practice what Canadian representatives accepted in principle when they assented to Article 25 of the 1948 United Nations General Assembly's Universal Declaration of Human Rights?

> Everyone has the right to a standard of living adequate for the health and well-being of himself and of his family, including food, clothing, housing and medical care and necessary social services, and the right to security in the event of unemployment, sickness, disability, widowhood, old age, or other lack of livelihood in circumstances beyond his control.

36. To guarantee such basic rights, what do we favour in the way of economic and social policies? Rather than reiterate what has already been argued well, we record our substantial agreement with the comprehensive approach and most of the proposals found in the brief presented to you April 14, 1970, by the Board of Evangelism and Social Service, United Church of Canada. We respectfully recall to your attention certain specific recommendations:

1) To meet an urgent immediate need, Parliament should amend the Old Age Security Act so as to allow regular increases in benefits which at very least will keep pace with actual cost of living increases. The Guaranteed Income Supplement also should be adjusted upwards. Why should senior citizens, who have contributed so much towards the building of Canada, be expected to bear a disproportionate burden in the struggle against inflation? Why should their pension benefits lag behind, especially when elected representatives in the other Chamber recently assured themselves of generous pension provisions? This amounts to a shocking disparity of treatment. It would be intolerable if the present session were to adjourn without taking remedial action to ensure at least this measure of justice to senior citizens, who are among the most deserving and yet most vulnerable groups in Canada. Indeed, fairness demands parliamentary action to ensure that the pensions of senior Canadians keep pace with increases in national productivity.

2) In this session Parliament should amend the unemployment insurance program in order to provide a wider range of coverage and increased benefits, so that recipients will not be pushed towards or over the "poverty line". Continuing inflation and relatively high levels of unemployment, particularly in some regions, demand action now.

3) Concerning income-maintenance policies for the near future, we are in general accord with the position advocated, including the proposal "that *en route* to a guaranteed income program for Canada, the federal government should consider a major improvement in family and youth allowance benefits", which would be treated as taxable income so as "to maximize the benefits to the poor and the 'near poor'... while also maximizing recovery... from those who do not need them".

4) We concur with the same brief and also with our Coalition partner, the Canadian Welfare Council, in its submission June 4 to

the Standing Committee on Banking, Trade & Commerce, that social policy and tax policy should be "harmonized". Positive social policy and fair taxation go together as two sides of one coin. How and in what amounts tax revenues are raised and how they are spent should be considered together.

37. Concerning taxation, we welcome the federal government's initiative in proposing reforms in its White Paper of November, 1969.[5] How these proposals will affect lower-income Canadians, who now bear a disproportionate tax burden, should be a main focus of public and legislative attention. We also believe other tax reforms are required in federal, provincial and municipal levies. Nevertheless, bearing in mind the two sides of the coin, no matter how fair taxation may be, it cannot be a substitute for social programs designed to guarantee basic human needs. In this regard, one of the main purposes of all tax reform should be to increase revenues for more public investment in the development of Canadians, Canada and the global community.

38. A key question to be asked therefore, is whether the revenues foreseen under the federal tax plan would provide an adequate share of funds for the development programs needed two or five years from now. In any attempt to answer this question however, the proposed tax reforms should be examined alongside the promised White Paper on federal social policies. Unfortunately, this second White Paper[6] (the so-called Willard report) has yet to be made public at this writing. In the interim, we want to stress this: even if Parliament enacts more equitable tax measures, their effects could be largely negated if the collected revenues are used to finance public conveniences for the affluent (superhighways, airports) ahead of essential services for the deprived (income-maintenance programs, lower-cost housing, education opportunities).

39. This consideration brings us once again to the heart of the matter, the making of social policy and the setting of social priorities which "affirm persons". Something other than a mere perpetuation of existing economic and social policies, with their escalating costs, is needed. "More of the same" will not suffice when poverty and pollution problems proliferate. We are more and more persuaded that new approaches, new priorities, new styles of design and delivery are essential in such fields as income maintenance, hous-

ing, education, urbanization, civil liberties and civil order, and ecology.

* We count on your Special Committee to bring forward creative and concrete recommendations that will initiate a new social policy for Canada.

* To provide continuing analyses and renewed inspiration in policy-making, we believe there should be a Social Council of Canada of like status and purpose as the Economic Council.

* We are also confident that new social policies which effectively put people first will emerge more quickly as deprived citizens come to share actively in the process of policy-building. This will add the needed dimension of living experience to the expertise of the professional planners and legislators.

40. Here we repeat our conviction that the voluntary sector has an important role to play alongside public authorities. That is why the Canadian Coalition for Development is endeavoring to provide new opportunities for participation by more citizens, many of whom are still unorganized and therefore socially powerless. Specifically, the Coalition is committed to ''provide free forums to clarify issues, identify human needs, generate debate, and mobilize public will, in this way releasing creative energies for constructive social change''.

IV — THE QUESTION OF WILL

41. The resources and know-how are at hand to build a better Canada. However, efforts to narrow the economic gap between deprived and affluent citizens at home and abroad are seriously impeded by a persisting ''attitudinal lag'' on the part of many. The Interchurch Strategy Report of May, 1969 described this stubborn phenomenon:

> At every level of society there exist social indifference and iner-tia on the part of the vast majority; poor communication, even between next-door neighbors; and worst of all, a deepening alienation between various ''we'' and ''they'' groups. This alienation is almost total between the affluent and the deprived. They live in different worlds. ISR, 38

42. In short, there remains the need to rally sufficient moral determination and political courage to put human development first. On both the Canadian and world scenes (as the Pearson Report, *Partners in Development*, emphasizes) this question of will is of critical importance. In particular, short-sighted self-interest on the part of the affluent denies to the deprived what is theirs by right. As Mrs. Coretta Scott King has said, ''The lack of will power to help humanity is a sick and sinister form of violence.''

43. This lack of social vision and courage poses a particular challenge to religious groups. If Christians are to make a distinctive contribution to the struggle for human betterment, surely it must begin here, at the level of personal conscience and social concern, while also finding expression at the level of institutional practice. The Interchurch Strategy Report of last May acknowledged this:

> The Church is called to be a gadfly, a radical questioner of the *status quo*, including its own social status; a voice of conscience which raises the gut issues, rebukes every injustice, challenges public opinion, and rallies the moral will, in the manner of the ancient prophets, Jesus Christ, and such modern martyrs as Martin Luther King, the Kennedys, and Camilo Torres. ISR, 46

44. We realize that so far many Canadian Christians have not responded to this call. Within our own communities, a collective renewal of conscience is urgently required. And in the wider community which reaches around the earth, we are challenged, together with other religious groups, to become once again ''troublers in Israel''. Religious leaders recognize in this challenge a call to moral courage and public responsibility. We must show courage, saying what many within our own churches will find both dangerous and foolish because it is uncomfortable. And if we are authentic leaders, we will strive to bring many more Canadians into the struggle for a just and compassionate society.

45. In pursuit of such objectives the Council and the Conference are committed during the 1970's to promote four social strategies which are described in detail in the 1969 Interchurch Report. The four guidelines:

* Review resources and revise priorities, a ministry of penance;

* Commit more resources to development, a ministry of sharing;

* Animate people, a ministry of hope;

* Initiate political action, a ministry of justice.

46. One year after they were first proposed, we reaffirm our determination to press for the implementation of these guidelines and to initiate or support other creative social strategies, such as the Coalition experiment already described. We do so in the belief that "the glory of God is man fully alive"?[7]

NOTES

1. This brief was presented by a joint delegation, six from the Council and four from the Conference. The Senate Committee accorded the entire morning session to the joint CCC/CCC delegation.

2. Signatories were: The Executive Committee of the Canadian Catholic Conference, i.e. six bishops, the President, Vice-President, Treasurer, and three Counsellors.

The Executive Committee of the Canadian Council of Churches, i.e. the President, Second Vice-President, Treasurer and General Secretary, with representatives from each Member Church (11): The Anglican Church, The Armenian Orthodox Church of America, The Baptist Federation of Canada, The Churches of Christ (Disciples), The Greek Orthodox Church, The Presbyterian Church in Canada, The Reformed Church in America (Ontario Classis), The Salvation Army, The Society of Friends, The United Church of Canada, The Lutheran Church in America (Canada Section), and eleven other Members.

3. Paul VI, *The Development of Peoples*, 1967, *The Papal Encyclicals*, edit. Claudia Carlen, IHM (Wilmington, N.C., McGrath Publishing, 1981), V, 189, n. 34.

4. Lester B. Pearson, Chairman U.N. Commission on International Development, *Partners in Development* (New York, Praeger, 1969).

5. E. J. Benson, Minister of Finance, *Proposals for Tax Reform* (tabled Nov. 7, 1969; Queens Printer, Ottawa, 1969).

6. *Income Security for Canadians*, Dr. Jos. W. Willard, Deputy Minister of Health and Welfare, tabled by the Minister, John C. Munro, Nov. 30, 1970, Queen's Printer, Ottawa, 1970.

7. Irenaeus, second century, *Against Heresies*, Bk. IV, C. 20., n. 7.

Document 24

LABOUR DAY MESSAGE — 1970
LIBERATION
IN A CHRISTIAN PERSPECTIVE

Author — The Episcopal Officers for Social Action

Introduction

1.   A period of turmoil is often a prelude to social advance. Today's chaotic experiences may persuade humanity tomorrow to intensify the building of peace, that continuing work of justice which Canadians recall each Labour Day. Already, at the beginning of a new decade which has been foreseen as a "time of troubles", we discern the proddings of the Spirit in an accelerating process of human liberation.[1]

I — SIGNS OF THE TIMES

2.   On every continent and in most nations anguished voices are crying out for liberation from the slavery of war, economic want, political tyranny, sterile legalism, social discrimination, stifling paternalism, cultural disparity and spiritual alienation. These are some of the many forms of oppression brought about by the limitations of men and institutions. Impatient voices are calling for a change of heart and more humane policies now. We consider these yearnings to be a current expression of the "hunger and thirst after justice" of which the Gospel speaks. If these impatient hopes are denied, there may be a bitter harvest of global violence. On the other

hand, the new ferment represents a special opportunity for human betterment if only people of today seize the moment to build anew.

3.   A phrase from St. John's Gospel comes to mind: "... and the truth will make you free". (Jn 8:32) This teaching has retained all its timeliness. Truth is far from finding its fulfillment in the modern world. Who would pretend that any one of us has been completely freed from ignorance and misjudgments? While most have moved beyond functional illiteracy, contemporary man is often the victim of other kinds of ignorance which are subtly cultivated or wilfully maintained. The media of social communications frequently despoil truth by offering consumers biased information and false propaganda. Personal narrow-mindedness is also prevalent, that wilful mentality which refuses to open itself to the whole truth, and which refuses to understand and accept other persons as they are, without condition. As men and women become aware of these imprisoning kinds of ignorance, they long for the truth which liberates. They begin to see that individuals, groups and peoples must somehow transcend narrow attitudes and biased points of view in order to build the better society John XXIII envisaged: a truly human community based on the four foundations "of truth, of justice, of love and of freedom".[2]

II — QUESTIONS OF HUMAN VALUES

4.   After more than a century of unprecedented technological advance and a quarter century of rapid economic growth, millions are still denied the basic necessities of life, even in rich nations. Many of the well-to-do are finding material affluence an empty satisfaction. Many young people, rich as well as poor, are restless and discontented with the *status quo*. Discerning people in all walks of life are coming to see that the most important, and also the most difficult human enterprise, is that of learning to live together in harmony. This is the art of politics in its best and most profound sense. Here, scientific skill and technological know-how alone will not suffice. Hence the public focus is shifting to deeper questions of political will and social policy: will Canadians agree to share more at home and with other neighbors in the nation called Earth? Has modern man enough imagination and motivation to use scientific knowledge and technical power in a more human way? Can leaders and citi-

zens of all classes together devise systems and structures, policies and programs which will serve justice and enhance the quality of life? These are some of the "value questions", both personal and communal, which are coming to the fore.

5. Such very human questions are posed in the slogans and songs of disenchanted youth and protesting students throughout the world. True, they sometimes seem immoderate and intolerant, and often do not articulate their aspirations with any precision. Even so their criticisms are instructive. The more thoughtful reject the faceless, computerized future some technocrats are planning. They also reject the comfortable security which has lulled many of their parents into a stupor of complacency. It is not surprising therefore, that responsible leaders of the new generation are intent on a "value revolution".

6. Canadians who have been denied basic human needs and social influence are also fed up. In 1968 the Economic Council of Canada referred to the deprived citizen as "an unwilling outsider, a virtual non-participant in society".[3] Since then a growing number of Canada's poor have become politically conscious and have begun to group together in order to demand participation in all public policy-making which affects their lives. This is their human right, as we noted in our 1969 Labour Day Statement on *New Power*. According to a recent study, there are now more than 200 organized groups of lower-income citizens in communities across Canada.[4] Public authorities are beginning to listen and respond positively.

7. But what of the Sino-Soviet world, as in Czechoslovakia, where humane reforms were harshly suppressed? And what of the Third World? In many countries of Latin America, Africa and Asia, military-political establishments suppress any popular movement for reform. In Brazil, for example, systematic violence masquerades as a "defense against communism". No wonder the Catholic Bishops of Latin America, in their 1968 joint declaration of Medellin, Colombia, called for a continent-wide "awakening of conscience" (conscientization) and for the "liberation" of the populace. As they defined it, this process of liberation involves active participation in society's reconstruction together with a personal change of heart: "We will not have a new continent without new and reformed structures, but above all, there will be no new continent without new men, who know how to be truly free and responsible according to

the light of the Gospel"[5] We believe this twofold concept of liberation is universally applicable.

III — LIBERATION THROUGH PARTICIPATION

8.   In recent years the Catholic Bishops of Canada, through their national Conference, have often spoken in favor of development. While this term focuses on the more human aspects of societal growth, it is sometimes taken to mean that progress is always smooth and gradual. Here the concept of liberation is a corrective which challenges the comfortable myths of the privileged. It conveys those notes of urgency and impatience which characterize the expectations of the deprived. They are trapped and they want to be freed now.[6]

9.   In Canada as many as one quarter of the citizens, including most Indians, Metis and Eskimos, are still trapped within an imprisoning network of circumstances and constraints. These cut them off from fair opportunities for education, employment, decent living conditions and effective participation in public affairs. Seeing this, the Economic Council of Canada in 1968 spoke of the "sense of entrapment and hopelessness" found among Canada's poor:

> Even the best statistics can only hint at this. They cannot capture the sour atmosphere of poor health and bad housing, the accumulated defeat, alienation and despair, which so tragically are often inherited by the next and succeeding generations.[7]

Those who may still find "entrapment" too strong a word, have probably never experienced how demeaning such social constraints are to human dignity; how they sap a person's sense of worth and his hopes for tomorrow. How many of us have ever tasted the frustration and humiliation of the father or mother who cannot find work, who cannot meet family needs and who must line up at a public office to beg for help? Often they are not even extended those common courtesies which established citizens take for granted. Lacking any social leverage, the powerless in Canada and abroad have not had even a "fighting chance" to grow as persons and make their contribution to human progress.

10.   At long last the disinherited recognize that one key to libera-

tion is social participation. They see now that if ever they are to enjoy personal development and social opportunities there must be a much broader base of public power in which they too have a responsible voice. This is a welcome trend. True, in its first stage, the movement often appears largely negative, as the powerless contend with the powerful and seek to demolish obstacles in their path. The second stage, a building phase, should come as public authorities, established citizens, and the representatives of "new power" learn to collaborate in policy-making.

11. In the search for better social policies, for example, the responsible voice of new power can make a major contribution. In their joint brief to the Special Senate Committee on Poverty the Executive Committees of the Canadian Catholic Conference and of the Canadian Council of Churches put it this way:

> We are confident that new social policies which effectively put people first will emerge more quickly as deprived citizens come to share actively in the process of policy-building. This will add the needed dimension of living experience to the expertise of the professional planners and legislators.[8]

IV — LIBERATION THROUGH PERSONAL RENEWAL

12. Liberation also requires of everyone personal reform and renewed commitment, especially on the part of those who have much. The cause of liberation requires that conversion of heart which the Baptist announced and that humility of spirit which the Servant Lord proclaimed nearly twenty centuries ago.

13. Affluent Canadians are challenged as never before to escape the servitude of endlessly wanting more and more things; to put away that shortsighted self-interest which is satisfied with casual progress towards social justice in Canada, and with an even smaller measure of support for people in want beyond these shores. Those who enjoy this world's advantages and privileges will become liberated only when, out of love for God and neighbour, they freely consent to share goods and also power with those in Canada and the Third World who have less than their just share.

14. However, it is painfully evident that man is made in a way

which makes it very difficult for him to detach himself from his privileges. Thus a major responsibility falls on public authorities as custodians of the common good. They must implement, as soon as practically possible, social structures and policies which will ensure an equitable sharing of riches and distribution of power among citizens. The deprived expect nothing less. This claim to justice is supported by the Scriptures and emphasized anew by Vatican II and Paul VI: "God destined the earth and everything it contains for the use of every man and all peoples so that all created things would be shared fairly by all mankind".[9]

Conclusion

15. The movement for liberation from all forms of oppression is gathering momentum. Will the Churches respond in the generous and resolute spirit of the Gospel? Throughout the world, Christians are joining the front lines of the struggle for a genuinely human society. Across Canada for example, a creative minority is testing the four social guidelines for the 1970's proposed in the Interchurch Strategy Report of May last year.[10] These Christians are revising priorities, sharing more resources, animating fellow citizens and initiating new coalitions to seek social justice from local to world levels. May their ranks increase and the fruits of their labour multiply. "The glory of God is man fully alive."[11]

NOTES

1. Second Vatican Council, *The Church in the Modern World*, 1965, nn. 4, 11, 17, 75.
2. John XXIII, *Peace on Earth*, 1963, *The Papal Encyclicals*, edit. Claudia Carlen, IHM (Wilmington, N.C., McGrath Publishing, 1981) V, 128, n. 167.
3. Economic Council of Canada, Ottawa, *Fifth Annual Review*, 1968, p. 104.
4. Mario Carota, *The Citizen Group Movement Among the Lower Income Citizens of Urban Canada*, Canadian Association of Neighbourhood Services, (research funded by Dept. of National Health and Welfare, Ottawa), 1970.
5. *The Church in the Present Day Transformation of Latin America*, (edit. L.M. Colonnese, General Secretariat of CELAM, Bogota, 1970), vol. II, Conclusions, p. 41.
6. Cf. Document 23 above, nn. 11 ff.
7. Economic Council of Canada, *loc. cit.* above, note 3, p. 105.

8. Document 23 above, n. 41.

9. Second Vatican Council, *loc. cit.* above, note 1, n. 69; Paul VI, *The Development of Peoples*, 1967, *The Papal Encyclicals*, edit. Claudia Carlen, IHM (Wilmington, N.C., McGrath Publishing, 1981) V, 187, n. 22. Cf. Gn 1:28; Am 5:23 f.; Ac 4:34 f.; 2 Cor 8:8-15.

10. Cf. Document 20 above, nn. 29-49.

11. Irenaeus, second century, *Against Heresies*, Bk. IV, C. 20, n. 7.

Document 25

LABOUR DAY MESSAGE — 1971
A CHRISTIAN STANCE
IN THE FACE OF VIOLENCE[1]

Author — The Episcopal Officers for Social Action

1. Canadians are asking themselves more and more why there are so many manifestations of violence in the world and particularly in our country. We too are asking questions and we invite all citizens of good will to reflect with us on our shared responsibilities in the face of such violence, whatever its kind.

I — HOW PEOPLE SEE VIOLENCE

2. On our part we have already held initial consultations which led to the preparation of this statement. The consultations yielded numerous, diversified opinions, which taken together, see violence as a many-sided, multi-levelled phenomenon, not simply physical force.

3. Violence is seen in the unequal distribution of primary goods within society and sometimes within individual families. Sexual, cultural and ethnic discrimination are forms of violence. The lack of adequate food, clothing and shelter is a violation of human dignity which causes family breakups and sets brother against brother. Violence is the squaring of accounts through bloodshed. There is violence in the manipulation of minds and the coercion of wills. Violence is done to the small wage-earner who labours with such difficulty to improve his lot, in contrast to the ease with which those

who hold the reins of economic, political and professional power give themselves the best salaries and social prestige. The wasteful misuse or destruction of producer goods and consumer goods when there are starving people in the world is a form of violence. Violence is seen in the public assistance which is virtually consumed by bureaucracies before it reaches the people for whom it was intended. Violence is done when there is inexcusable delay on the part of those who are responsible for making policy decisions to rectify injustices. Violence is done when people's rights are trampled by fanaticism and crime. There is violence in the collective egoism of pressure groups. Violence is seen in the complacency of the affluent.

4.   Such social injustices give rise to much unrest. We are sensitive to the awakening of the poor and oppressed to these injustices. They are developing a sense of human solidarity and a deepening realization of the need for basic social reforms.

5.   No one has a ready-made solution to the many-sided problem of violence. Nor do we consider it our task to condone or condemn particular forms of violence. All of us must look instead for the deeper meanings, for the root causes in turn, require revolutionary thinking in the best and most profound sense. For Christians, this requires that we hear anew the radical message of Jesus Christ, which calls for the progressive humanization of relations among men and between societies.

II — SOME SOURCES OF VIOLENCE

6.   As already indicated, it is not easy to define the complex reality of violence. Tentatively, we shall describe violence as any force, physical or psychological, which is exerted on a man or group of men to obtain what neither argument nor law nor moral suasion would make it possible to obtain from them.[2] Violence involves the use of force or other pressures which attack the integrity of persons by preventing them from freely participating in responsible societal decisions.[3]

7.   Violence has always marred the history of mankind. New in our day however, is the widespread acceptance of almost automatic

recourse to the tactics of confrontation or the ultimatum. One way in which people get their bearings in modern society is by forming more and more organized groups. When this happens, there is a release of long-repressed frustrations, a clearer perception of inequalities, a more concrete identification of systems of exploitation, an awakening of expectations. Thus aroused, harnessed and focused, people's energies may be released in the cause of human liberation. But such a promising outcome is by no means guaranteed.

8. The strongly individualistic and acquisitive mentality which characterizes today's production-consumption society attaches greater importance to getting more things than to becoming more as persons. The mania for efficiency and the thirst for immediate results engender merciless competition. The consequent indifference to spiritual values, the decline of the "sense of wonder" and of the joy of celebration, mean that many persons are left with feelings of confusion and emptiness, and even in some instances, of alienation and despair. Deep-rooted prejudices and plain incompetence further aggravate the situation. Thus the accelerated process of organization can, and with increasing frequency does, become destructive rather than creative.

III — WHAT CAN BE DONE ABOUT VIOLENCE?

9. In conscience we cannot ignore the diverse manifestations of violence in our midst. As citizens, as Christians, whatever our individual roles in society, all of us, within the limits of our own knowledge and competence, must re-examine our personal and collective attitudes towards violence. We have a duty patiently to develop policies which can mitigate this evil and are conducive to the integral development of persons and peoples.

10.   — In a complex society in which we are more and more dependent upon one another, what key insights and order of values should inspire a renewed education on the social responsibilities of free citizens?

    — What effective forms of participation should be adopted in a technological age?

    — Can Canadians reach a viable consensus on common social goals, which is the basis of orderly, satisfying life in society?

— What criteria should govern the decisions made by heads of unions and corporations?

— What factors should tip the scales when the policies of federal and provincial governments are being decided?

— What priorities should mark our cooperation with developing countries?

— What concrete efforts by Christian communities will help liberate modern man?

11. "Injustice breeds violence."[4] The process is well known: deprivation, misery, humiliations, arbitrary restraints bring about a revolt of the oppressed and of others who are determined to fight for a just, humane world. This revolt in turn often elicits repressive action by the forces of law and order, which sometimes leads to physical and psychological excesses.

12. Nuances, subtle distinctions, "beating about the bush" — these should not be allowed to distract us from the central issue. Commitment to terrorist aggression and its ugly consequences are serious types of violence; but worse still are the institutionalized forms of violence and the economic, political and social injustices to which they give rise. Both forms of violence demand early and substantial response. And there is only one way to break the vicious circle of violence: expose the sources of unrest and eliminate injustices.[5]

IV — WHAT CAN WE LEARN FROM THE GOSPEL?

13. Every trend in Canadian society, both the most promising and the most dangerous, pushes us towards a continual evaluation of our ways of thinking about the world. In this it is essential that Christians be guided by the light of the Gospel, by the wisdom of the Spirit, in our efforts to hasten the liberation of mankind. Truly liberating action is essentially of the Gospel; passive submission to injustice is not.

14. But what of violent reactions to systematic injustices which in turn do further violence to human dignity? Violence of any kind implies irreconcilable hostilities among men. The Gospel however,

anticipates a total reconciliation of all persons among themselves and of all with God, through the liberating, salvific action of Jesus Christ. Violence too often means the imposition of some closed ideology even to the contempt of its adversaries. The New Testament however, announces that the person, not ideology, is the summit of all creation. Persons transcend civilizations, economic systems and political ideologies.

15.   Nevertheless, the Christian knows that man is always ambiguous. The Christian confronts the paradox of sin and hope, both within himself and in society. He experiences within himself the continuing struggle between violent reaction and reconciliation, between human selfishness and the grace of generous love. He comes to see that social injustices are the embodiment not only of past errors, of policy failures, of insufficient clarity of vision, but also of present, persisting sinfulness. Yet the mystery of Christ risen gives hope to the Christian. Despite human ambiguity, the Christian believes that a new history, brought about by converted hearts and transformed structures, can emerge and is already emerging amid confusion and pain.

16.   The genuine Christian cannot avoid committing himself to this gradual liberation of men and societies.[6] He cannot however, subscribe to violence as an end in itself or even as a means lightly to be adopted to achieve a worthy goal. How could he easily be party to any ideology or program which accepts that justice can be established by violence between persons or societies?

17.   In the struggle to obtain justice, amid the tensions and conflicts always inherent in the evolution of society, the Christian will prefer persuasion, the influence of public opinion and legislative process. He will try rather to awaken conscience and so to prevent fanaticism and hardness of heart.

18.   What if all non-violent means fail to bring justice? But who is qualified to make so crucial a judgment? We would suggest that only he who has no hate in his heart, who lives the Sermon on the Mount, can truly discern such a situation as actual.

19.   Even then, any recourse to violence will always be a highly ambiguous choice for the Christian. It can be undertaken only insofar as it is absolutely necessary as a last resort for the achievement

of a just, fraternal society. The Christian will choose violent means only with the greatest reluctance, for he is always mindful that the weapons of the Kingdom of God are not those of the people who violate it!

20. The demands of Christian faith can be harmonized with the best values in the democratic tradition; there can be concerted, peaceful efforts to liberate the whole person and all people.

21. Christians in each local community have the responsibility of translating into concrete actions the call to commitment contained in this message and in previous Labour Day Statements, *New Power* and *Human Liberation.*[7] Essentially, this commitment will take the form of collaboration in the awakening of consciences, social animation, in the organization of popular and professional movements, through participation in political life, all with a view to achieving an equitable distribution of goods and power, essential to human dignity.

22. Any intellectual commitment requires serious reflection. We especially urge diocesan councils, social and apostolic movements, parish councils, ecumenical and life groupings to adopt authentic forms of social commitment in their respective circles, to continue seeking non-violent and creative answers to injustices in the months ahead.

23. We ourselves assure all of the cooperation of our national office of social action. We also hope that within dioceses, specialized agencies will become engaged in this endeavour.

Conclusion

24. To sum up: Christians in collaboration with fellow citizens have the continuing obligation of improving the quantity and quality of their social and political commitments. In this common task it is urgent that Canadians identify and begin to root out the underlying causes of violence; mere condemnation of symptoms is never enough.

25. The goals of the new civilization which modern man is trying

to achieve commit all of us to traval a long, hard road. It is however, a road lit by faith in man and especially by the hope that has been revealed.

NOTES

1. This letter was prepared in the tense months following the violence and disorder in Montreal on the issue of Quebec independence. The British diplomat James R. Cross had been kidnaped Oct. 5, and Pierre Laporte, Quebec Minister of Labour on Oct. 10, by agents of the Front for Liberation of Quebec. The body of the latter was found in the trunk of an automobile, Oct. 18, while the former was released only Dec. 3. Prime Minister Pierre Trudeau invoked the War Measures Act, Oct. 16, to control street and other violence. Archbishop of Quebec Maurice Roy, Primate of Canada, issued a pastoral letter on violence in the name of the bishops of Quebec, Oct. 17. It was followed a few days later by a pastoral on the same subject by Archbishop Paul Grégoire of Montreal. The text of these letters may be found in *The Catholic Mind*, New York, 1971, LXIX, Jan. 1971, pp. 2 and 3. The French texts are in *L'Église Canadienne*, Montréal, III, n. 10, nov., 1970, pp. 327 ff.
2. Cf. Jean-Marie Domenach, *Semaine des Intellectuels Catholiques*, 1967: *La Violence* (Desclée de Brouwer, Paris), p. 30.
3. Cf. René Rémond, *ibid*, Introduction.
4. Letter of Archbishop Roy, cf. note 1 above.
5. Cf. Dom Helder Camara, Archbishop of Olinda and Recife, Brazil, *The Spiral of Violence* (London, Sheed and Ward, 1971) throughout but especially Part 3, pp. 56-83.
6. Cf. *The Liberation of Men and Nations*, a working paper of the Interamerican Bishops' Conference, May, 1971, cf. *The Catholic Mind*, New York, 1971, LXIX, Sept. pp. 13-29. This paper was released jointly by the Canadian Catholic Conference and the U.S. Catholic Conference, July, 1971, as a useful instrument for promoting dialogue, but not as an official position of either Conference. Principal authors of the first draft were Rev. Wm. F. Ryan, S.J., then director of the Center of Concern, Washington, presently English language General Secretary of the CCCB, and Rev. Jos. Komonchak, then professor at St. Joseph's Seminary, Yonkers, N.Y.
7. Documents 21 and 24 of this collection.

Document 26

JUSTICE IN THE WORLD

Author — The Assembly of the Canadian Catholic Conference,
September 20-24, 1971

1. In anticipation of the Third Assembly of the International Synod
of Bishops, opening in Rome Sept. 30, the Canadian Catholic
Conference of Bishops voted this week on twenty-five proposals
concerning "Justice in the World".

2. *Actions to Match Words* — The Bishops agreed that the Synod
should be oriented towards decisions leading to action in the cause
of justice. The Conference advised the Canadian episcopal delegation to the Synod to advocate action on social issues in the light of
the Gospel. At the same time the bishops adopted a motion committing the Canadian Catholic Conference (CCC) to "verify by
actions in Canada" the positions taken by the Canadian delegation
at the Synod.

3. *Financial Openness* — The Canadian delegation was asked to
advocate financial openness on the part of the Vatican, national
conferences of bishops, dioceses, parishes, religious orders and
related institutions. Further, it was agreed that representatives
of the organizations concerned should participate in a review of
pastoral priorities.

4. *Integral Development* — The Canadian bishops want the Church
at all levels to support popular educational movements that are
in accord with the Gospel for the development and liberation of
deprived peoples, especially in the Third World. The Synod should
also recognize that integral development includes the right of each
people to shape its own destiny.

5. *World Affairs* — The Canadian delegation will call on the Synod to enumerate and denounce abuses caused by excessive nationalism and the greed of certain multinational corporations. Flagrant examples of these abuses include the arms race and the exploitation of the weaker nations. The CCC also wants the Synod to affirm support of the United Nations as a first step toward effective international authority.

6. *Violence* — The Conference, affirming the principle of evangelical non-violence, is calling on the Synod to examine the root causes of many forms of violence. The Canadian delegation was asked to inform the Synod that some of the most serious forms of injustice are the exploitation of the poor, unscrupulous advertising, etc.

7. *Women* — The Canadian bishops said the Synod should advocate the removal of all discriminatory barriers against women in the Church. The Conference recognized that women are full and equal members of the Church with all the rights and responsibilities pertaining thereto.

8. *Faith and Social Action* — The CCC members agreed that effective Christian involvement in the cause of justice calls for the formation of a ''new man'' who brings religious faith into social action.

9. *Youth* — The Synod should urge the Church at every level to pursue a continuing dialogue with youth concerning their rights and responsibilities in the Christian community.

Document 27

ORIENTATION OF THE SYNOD TOWARDS ACTION

Author — Presentation of Archbishop Joseph-Aurèle Plourde, President of the Canadian Catholic Conference, to the International Synod of Bishops, Rome, October 19, 1971

Introduction

The point of departure for any serious effort in the human enterprise — educational, cultural, social and religious — is an avowed acceptance of the fact that all men and their work are now united in one destiny. We live or die together. We can continue to drift towards a common doom or we can work together in the struggle for peace.

1. I begin my presentation with this statement of the World Conference on Religion and Peace (Kyoto, October, 1970, Message). I will present first, general observations on the Relation (Synodal working paper), based on the deliberations and decisions of the bishops of Canada regarding *Justice in the World*. Then in the name of our Conference, I will expose how we conceive the fundamental role of the Church with regard to Justice in the World. A written report on the Canadian proposals on justice will be given to the Synod Secretariat. My confreres will take up later some of its more important points.

I — OBSERVATIONS ON THE RELATION

2.   We are pleased with the Relation because it is short and written in a sincere and authentic style. It delineates different roles in the Church and leaves scope for freedom and creativity. It recalls the moral dimensions of problems but without exaggerating their importance. The Relation however, also has its weakness. It does not contain a specifically Christian world vision and so is not sufficiently future-oriented. Ecumenical concern is almost totally lacking and this in an area where action in common by the churches is most highly desirable. Finally, certain basic problems seem to have been evaded, in particular, the limits of private property and the link between private property and economic and political power.

II — CHRISTIAN WORLD VISION

3.   The modern world does not need the Church's help to reflect on itself in theoretical terms. Both Marxists and capitalists, in spite of ideological differences, have devised precise analytical tools. If we want to be of service, we must orient our efforts towards what is specifically Christian, towards what only we Christians can do, by starting from the Word of God in Jesus Christ.

a) Indeed, only we know that man is "an extension of the family of the Trinity" (St. Augustine); that man, when God sees him as imaging God, is first of all Jesus Christ; that, in consequence, man is directed by the same dynamisms as the Trinity itself, namely the fullness of life in liberty, union and love.

b) Only we know that this image of God in us is to be realized in a divine *milieu*, which requires that our domination of nature and thus our technological and economic effort, must reach beyond the fight for survival and appropriation to a general sharing and full development of all men.

c) Only we know that this image of God, created integral but destroyed by selfishness and pride, is now restored by the death and resurrection of Jesus Christ. The result is that we are neither naively optimist nor pessimist with regard to man. He is totally but painfully oriented towards a future of liberation and full development, a future at once guaranteed and yet in continuity with his present actions wherein the Spirit is already at work. It is this hope that the Church must already live and witness to, so that her light may be believable to men even in their present experience of hardness of heart, of suffering and of death. We would have liked the general lines of this vision to be developed more clearly in the Relation.

III — THE CHURCH AND JUSTICE

4. If the Church is to be a light to the world, she must first of all live this justice to be believable. As St. Ambrose has said, "It is not by dialectics that God deigned to save his people". It is only the practice of justice that enables the Christian to discern this prophetic liberty with regard to the structures within which we have been formed and live. "He who lives the truth comes to the light." (Jn 3:21) It is here that we must begin to speak of strategies and programs. Men, today more than ever before, have to be freed from their mechanisms of selfish desires; for a greedy world will always be a divided world. As long as the rich nations do not find the strength of soul to gain mastery of their consumer societies, sharing will not be possible, exploitation and wastage of the resources of the poor will only be aggravated by technological progress; as long as national borders continue to mark the limits of opposed egoisms and are considered unchangeable absolutes, human solidarity will remain impossible. And as long as money remains the supreme force that directs public life — even if in private life people try to live by higher and more human values — nothing will change. Only the spirit of poverty, a real and voluntary austerity, will liberate man from the technological spirit, from the undisciplined use of new scientific discoveries which can destroy him. Unless we begin to practise such a spirit of poverty, we can always rationalize our actions, we will not bring the light of the Gospel to the world.

IV — BEGIN AT HOME

5. The Church must begin this practice of justice at home. It must demonstrate that it can reach beyond the consumer society, and live a life of sharing and detachment. It must demonstrate that its entire

resources, its manpower, its knowledge, its money, are at the service of the whole community, including the most underprivileged. We are pleased that the Relation insists on this so clearly. In carrying this out, the Church must refuse simply to use the model of big business. Its financial openness, its reassessment of investments, the inventory of its resources, must be done in harmony with the Gospel. Its efforts at education, conscientization and social animation must likewise take on specific forms. Its moral teaching must at all cost stop giving privileged treatment to private ethics, wherein sin is seen primarily as a private matter, rarely as association, conscious or not, with the forces of oppression, alienation and physical violence. Its own practice of justice must eliminate as soon as possible anything that tarnishes its image, whether it be discrimination (one of my colleagues has already alluded to discrimination against women), harassing procedure (I am thinking of the conditions imposed on priests who have been dispensed to return to the lay state), or of the social security of personnel who work for the Church. In each case, education for justice must begin at the domestic and local level and reach out to the international level. We ask ourselves moreover, whether, in order to play the role of responsible custodian of the Gospel, at both local and international levels, the Church ought not to denounce more forcefully those who call themselves Christians and yet directly violate both the Gospel and the rights of man by indulging in such practices as torture and puppet trials for political ends. Without going back to legal excommunication, must we not more often have recourse to fraternal correction which could go as far as excommunication by denunciation?

Conclusion

6.   These are not novel ways. They are the traditional ways of conversion and of hope. The difference is that today conversion is often only possible in a change of structures. What is today referred to as charity is in fact a matter of justice.

7.   From outer space the pioneering astronauts saw a planet without national boundaries, a good earth on which, perhaps alone in the universe, the miracle of life exists. Modern man must see the world in this way if he wants to survive. In some way or other and soon, he must reach beyond narrow nationalisms, whether they be the offensive nationalism of the great nations or the defensive nation-

alism of the small, and begin to create a world community. The Church will participate in this work only if it thinks globally, if it learns how to discover and to speak about what it knows of Jesus Christ, of the destiny of man and of the beginning of that reality here on earth in the practice of a justice which makes believable the fact that the world has a meaning.

Document 28

CHRISTIAN FORMATION FOR JUSTICE

Author — Presentation of His Eminence George Bernard Cardinal Flahiff, C.S.B., delegate of the Canadian Catholic Conference to the International Synod of Bishops, Rome, October 20, 1971

One of the striking phenomena of our times is how modern totalitarian powers imprison, torture and even kill men who speak out freely. Novelists and poets have been jailed, social leaders have been murdered, and in many countries priests who dared to challenge the *status quo* are today in prison. In biblical times not a few prophets were done to death.

This should suggest to the Church and to this Synod how important and difficult it is to educate people to justice. The Relation (Synodal working paper) emphasizes this task, and I, in the name of the Bishops of Canada, wish to re-emphasize it.

I — THE MODERN SITUATION

In former days, the Church could be content to educate the People of God to justice on the family or local level. But today we are so shaped by modern ideologies and especially by our increasingly structured milieu that to fail to speak is to have been co-opted by the system, to have become consciously or unconsciously a victim of its advertising and collective values, including its injustices. Our opinions are often nothing more than the product of adaptation psychology. One thing only is left for us to do, to play the marginal role of consoling victims of the system, to be a social band-aid which every system, socialist or capitalist, needs if it is to continue to function.

The time has come to ask ourselves whether or not much of the official support, especially financial, given to the Church by bourgeois society is not for this purpose. If we are unable to break out of the system, or unable at least to remain clear-sighted within it, so as to judge it and if necessary to reject it, we have become merely cogs in the machine. Fidelity to the Gospel of Jesus Christ demands that His people rise above slavery to any system, for neither an ideology nor a system can ever adequately represent the Kingdom of God. And yet Christians need not be chronic malcontents; we must learn to be forward-looking and creative.

In our new situation, in which the forces of alienation are multiplied by propaganda, what new questions should we be asking?

a) How can we help Christians to make a synthesis of their religious values (which they live on Sundays) and of their human, secular values (which they live on weekdays)?

b) How can we help Christian groups to discern good from evil in a system which has shaped them and within which they live?

c) How can we help both individuals and groups to move to action instead of simply bewailing the evils and the injustices that exist in the world?

II — A BASIC PRINCIPLE

When we ask ourselves, sometimes with no little anxiety, why the social teachings of the Church have had so little impact, I believe we may have to admit that we have too often believed that an academic knowledge of them was the most important, if not sufficient.

I suggest that henceforth, our basic principle must be: only knowledge gained through participation is valid in this area of justice; true knowledge can be gained only through concern and solidarity. We must have recourse to the biblical notion of knowledge, experience shared with others. We have too frequently separated evangelization from social action, and reserved social involvement to elites and eventually to the clergy. Unless we are in solidarity with the people who are poor, marginal, or isolated we cannot even speak effectively about their problems. Theoretical knowledge is indispensable, but it is partial and limited; when it abstracts from lived concrete experience, it merely projects the present into the future.

And here I would add another factor. Programs are stamped by the age of the persons who conceive and execute them. Church programs in which youth have not been involved will lack a sense of daring and courage as well as an acceptance of mistakes.

III — THE SPECIFIC ROLE OF THE CHURCH IN JUSTICE

Justice is not a theological but a human virtue. Why then should the Church be concerned with it in a specific way?

a) Christianity liberates. It liberates from sin; not only from personal sin, but also and perhaps chiefly from social sin, since social sin, like original sin, creates a situation wherein individual sin becomes easy and acceptable.

b) Christianity believes in man, even if it knows him to be a sinner, because it expects the gift of salvation and awaits a coming (an *adventus*, a *parousia*) over and above that future which we ourselves can make. And so we have a task to perform; we are not merely critics; we are fashioners of hope.

c) Christianity cannot be content with minimum proposals, defending the minimal rights of man. It must see human rights as dynamic and constantly evolving, not static, since it demands the maximum development for all, the right to the fullest possible development, whether it be for developing countries, or for women, or for the aged, or for the unemployed or unemployable. We have already proposed a commission on the ministries of women. It would be equally desirable to set up a permanent commission on human rights.

IV — TO MOVE TO ACTION

From the points already made it follows that the principal lines of action should be these:

a) To encourage, at all costs, the practice of justice, knowledge by participation. We shall begin effective formal instruction neither in the school nor from theory but from life, involvement and solidarity.

b) To encourage at all costs, social animation and through it, conscientization, first of all at the local level, that is with the real problems of the milieu in which Christians live. Only by experiencing and grappling with injustice in the local community will they come to an effective understanding of injustice among other poorer and more powerless peoples of the world.

c) To encourage the responsibility of all: and not paternalism only on the part of pastors and elites.

d) To encourage Christians to dig out factual information (the example of Ralph Nader in USA is remarkable in this regard).

e) To encourage also more scientific research, especially in national and international centres, associated or not with universities, but in centres which have a certain autonomy and a desire to work with all men of good will. Such research must above all, be action-oriented and in constant contact with the plight of the poor and the powerless.

f) To recommend a constant evaluation of present Church agencies (I am thinking now especially of the Commission Justice and Peace), so that they too in their research may not become excessively theoretical and too far removed from action.

Conclusion

The Church cannot be content to think of the world theoretically; it must transform it. Only if the Church commits itself wholeheartedly to the task of forming Christians through practice and solidarity will it become credible, especially to the young.

Jesus was hardly a professor, but He taught much about the perception of injustice and oppression; unlike them He chose not the comfortable life of quiet retirement but the demanding life of a witness to justice, the life which led to the redemptive cross.

Document 29

SUPER-STATES
AND MULTI-NATIONAL CORPORATIONS
IN A DEVELOPING WORLD COMMUNITY

Author — Presentation of Bishop Alexander Carter, delegate of the
Canadian Catholic Conference to the International Synod
of Bishops, Rome, October 20, 1971

One of the most attractive features of creation is its ability to
correct disproportionate development: monsters die. Yet this mechanism is not operative in human affairs: injustice begets violence
unless men exercise vigilance.

The Relation (Synodal working paper) correctly indicates that the
chief source of international injustice lies in the domination of the
poor and the weak by the rich and the strong. In their powerlessness, poor nations often see their life styles, their economies, their
political life, their whole world being shaped to the image and interests of the super-powers with their technology and their multi-
national corporations. And in too many cases this is done with little
regard for the interests of the small nations themselves.

Because the Relation does not insist on this point, and because
the Canadian Bishops, in their preparation for the Synod, considered it important, I speak to this relatively new problem of the disproportionate power, possessed and exercised by rich sovereign
nations and multi-national corporations, which hinders the building
of a world community.

I shall try to be practical and positive. Mere denunciations impress
no one but ourselves. A naive assumption that socialism is a pana-
cea and a cure-all will prove cruelly deceptive. The evil is deep in
all of us.

I — THE SITUATION

A few examples will show what bigness and power can do. Military expenditure in 1970, almost all in USA and Russia, amounted to over $200 billion, or 7% of the world's total production; it equals the total annual income of the billion people who live in Latin America, South Asia and the Middle East. It means that about $60.00 was spent on national security for each person in the world, and $60.00 is more than the total annual income of hundreds of millions of those people. In the same year the richer countries devoted less than $3.00 per capita of their population to development aid, while they mounted tariffs against the products of the poor countries that were twice as high as those against the products of the rich, although unemployment is five times greater in the former.

The size and power of multi-national corporations — as already signaled in Pius XI's Encyclical, *The Reconstruction of the Social Order* (1931) — are equally striking. The annual gross sales of overseas American corporations amount to almost $200 billion; this figure is surpassed by the gross national product of only Russia, Japan and the USA itself. If we rank together gross national product of nation states and gross annual sales of large corporations, 13 of the largest are not countries at all but private corporations. In the first 100, 50 are private corporations and only four African nations appear on the list: Nigeria comes 39th, after General Motors and Ford; Algeria, 61st, after General Electric; Morocco, 64th, after Westinghouse; and Ghana, 78th, after Union Carbide!

Evidently many of the largest powers in the world are not in the United Nations. Little wonder that the Prime Minister of my country, Mr. Trudeau, recently compared living next to the United States to sleeping with an elephant. Its slightest twitch can crush you like a mouse! Large multi-national corporations are accountable to no one for their stewardship except to shareholders, who, though in the majority Christian, are seldom acquainted with the operations of their companies abroad. An advertisement appearing in a daily Canadian newspaper not more than two weeks ago typifies the situation that exists between many rich and poor countries. It reads: "People are earning good profits in Nigeria. Why don't you? Abundant manpower is available at a rate as low as 7 US cents per man-hour... Pioneer industries enjoy long tax holidays" (*Globe and Mail*, Toronto, Oct. 1, 1971).

II — ANALYSIS OF THE SITUATION

Power, even great concentration of power, is not evil in itself. Nor have we any clear evidence that this power is exercised by unscrupulous men. Historically, national sovereignty has been the only force capable of mobilizing a society for economic and social development, by giving people an identity and pride of purpose. Multi-national corporations have been the only effective international agency for spreading modern technology and technological skill round the globe.

But both these great powers, sovereign nations and multi-national corporations, whether capitalist or socialist in ideology, are structurally inadequate and even inimical to the building of a just world community. Even good men are enslaved to inhuman systems, use their ''machine heads'' more than their ''human heads'', and with blind logic, put national security, high rates of economic growth, efficiency and maximum profits ahead of the basic needs and desires of the human race.

At a time when total nuclear wars are prepared not in years but in seconds, the super-powers are trapped in the national security straitjacket. They talk seriously of ''arms control'' not disarmament; and they permanently subordinate human and domestic priorities to those of economic growth adapted to national security. The fault is not personal but structural.

The history of foreign corporations operating in weak nations is replete with injustice: efficiency, profits and loyalty to their own country taking priority over the needs and aspirations of local people; taking too much and leaving too little; crushing local competition and gaining monopolistic power; making poor countries dependent on foreign sources for modern technology and even national defense; serving as instruments of their own country's foreign policy; and creating desires that cannot be satisfied by the poor country.

III — ROLE OF THE CHURCH

It is not the office of a bishop to offer technical solutions to these problems, but it is his task to bring insistently to the attention of those with power and competence their responsibility to work together to take charge of the inhuman situations which are now slipping out of control.

Clearly, unlimited national sovereignty in both large and small nations must be curbed before domination and dependence will disappear. National security must be internationalized and become the joint responsibility of a global community of juridically interdependent nations so that, with survival guaranteed, human needs and aspirations can finally have top priority in the councils of men of good will. At best nationalism provides limited sanctuary for vulnerable societies. Poor and weak nations will continue to need the buffer of national sovereignty as long as there is no effective impartial world force capable of protecting them against the intrusion of big powers in their political and economic life.

The dynamic creativity of the multi-national corporations must not be lost, but these giants must be made accountable for their actions. Their parent governments must not permit them to perpetrate in poor countries abuses which are outlawed at home. An international authority representing both capitalist and socialist nations should be created to draw up a code of international conduct, with a review board to which poor and weak countries can take their complaints. Perhaps too the Vatican diplomatic corps could exercise a useful function of persuasion in this matter!

New kinds of agreements should be encouraged whereby international corporations can become ''suppliers of know-how and services'' by contract, rather than foreign agents possessing permanent ownership of local resources.

Finally, it is an urgent task for Church leaders to form and inspire competent international men and women in all nations to carry out this human and very Christian task with a keen sense of world justice.

Document 30

SOCIAL JUSTICE IN THE CHURCH

Author — The Assembly of the Canadian Catholic Conference, April 21, 1972

The Second Vatican Council, Pope Paul VI and the 1971 International Synod of Bishops called for a more vigorous Christian witness to social justice. This week the Catholic Conference has addressed itself to certain questions of justice in Canada, both within the Church and in civil society. We focused first on our own household. We made a collective examination of conscience on life styles and the use of time and resources.

In our deliberations we identified some guiding norms, made some findings and agreed to several proposals. These we wish to share with fellow believers and the general public. Above all however, we invite Catholics throughout Canada to join us in a continuing examination of social conscience. In this way, the whole Church may become more faithful to the Servant Lord.

Some Guiding Criteria

While social norms are always relative, the directives of the Gospel remain constant and relevant. In an affluent society, Christians are called to give witness to the Gospel's radical ethic of solidarity, simplicity and sharing. Scandalous disparities between rich and poor, abroad and at home, reinforce the urgency of the Gospel summons.

Some Findings

With these norms in mind, we have begun to assess the present state of justice in the Canadian Church. We see signs of hope. Many Catholics continue to give generous support, often at much personal cost, to the Church and to the cause of justice. Others continue to give example of fraternal frugality. Still others are exploring new ways to consume less and share more. Without fanfare, numerous bishops and priests are modifying their standard of living.

Still, many Canadians live in a miserable poverty while others among us enjoy an affluence which gives scandal.

Some Proposals

1. All of us, bishops, priests, religious, laity, are challenged to practise greater moderation in the use of consumer goods and a more generous sharing in the spirit and service of the Gospel, even to the point of forgoing what many might think their due:

— bishops, who are called to a service of authority, must set the pace in such a revision of life, making sure that they share something of the experience of their Christian community;

— priests too are invited to evaluate their use of time given to pastoral work; the kind of vacations, recreations and travel they permit themselves; their use of such resources as housing, furnishings, cars, etc.;

— we look also to religious congregations to give unequivocal witness to the vitality of the Gospel;

— we invite families and single persons, young and old, to respond faithfully to the Gospel call to simplicity and sharing.

2. It is increasingly evident that changes in style of living depend on a change of attitudes. Such an awakening of conscience, "conscientization", demands a renewed emphasis on social education, adapted to the particular time and place. This social formation should emphasize meaningful liturgy, social catechesis, special school programs, animation in small groups and community involvement.

3. There is corresponding need for more social research. Examples

include applications of the social criteria proposed by Vatican II and the recent Synod, as well as research into the ways in which society's structures shape our thinking and acting.

4. The rights of Church personnel, whatever their station, should be reviewed periodically so as to ensure that they receive just salaries, fair working conditions and security on retirement.

5. Ways in which neighbouring dioceses might share specialized personnel and resources need to be explored.

6. In the interests of fraternal accountability, the Conference recommends financial openness throughout the Canadian Church.

7. Social usefulness should be a major consideration in making investments.

8. Catholic groups should seek more ways to respond without paternalism to the expectations of the marginalized poor. We bishops should collaborate with them so that their voices may be heard as they work out their own liberation.

9. We recommend local credit unions and cooperatives as effective examples of organized self-help.

10. We reaffirm support of the Canadian Coalition for Development, while emphasizing the need for similar coalitions of churches and other voluntary groups at community levels.

11. We recommend that the 1972 Labour Day Message reflect the insights of this Plenary Assembly and of Catholics active in social development. We suggest also that supplementary material on social justice be circulated for diocesan and parochial use.

Conclusion

Social justice in the Church, in Canada and in the world will remain a major and constant concern of this Conference.

Document 31

SHARING NATIONAL INCOME

Author — The Assembly of the Canadian Catholic Conference, April 21, 1972

The riches of Canada are unequally shared. This inequality, which keeps so many people poor, is a social sin. To analyse what causes or what could eliminate this scandal is to enter into vast economic and social complexities. It is also to re-examine, in the light of the Gospel, assumptions we all share to some extent about who man is and how society should be put together.

Without espousing any particular program, we invite Canadians to accept the social goal of an equitable redistribution of income. We also call for acceptance of the principle that each Canadian should be assured that level of income necessary for decent human living and full participation in society. To this end, we accept a responsibility to join with other community leaders in sponsoring and initiating local study and dialogue concerning both the technical complexities and the ethical implications of our underlying attitudes. This education for social justice would, we hope, persuade people to support governmental measures leading to equalization.

230

Document 32

ON PASTORAL IMPLICATIONS
OF POLITICAL CHOICES

Author — The Assembly of the Canadian Catholic Conference,
April 21, 1972

As our regular spring assembly draws to a close, we the Canadian bishops would like to share with you the decisions we have taken following the Synod of Bishops held in Rome in 1971 and its statement *Justice in the World*.[1]

The subject which we discussed concerned the realization of justice in the Church and in our country. As a result we focused our attention on justice in our economic system, in the life of the Church, etc.

We also considered a problem which directly concerns Quebec but which also has implications for the whole of the country. We are well aware that the bishops of Quebec are questioned by Christians, especially the young, in these terms: are we free as Christians and as Christian communities in our political choices? Is there any option we must exclude, any option we must choose? To such a question asked of us from a pastoral point of view we wish to give a pastoral answer.

We affirm that all options which respect the human person and the human community are a matter of free choice on the individual as well as the community level. This is in keeping with the most recent teaching of the Church.

As Pope Paul VI said in his recent letter to His Eminence Maurice Cardinal Roy:

It is up to the Christian communities to analyze with objectivity the situation which is proper to their own country, to shed on it the light of the gospel's unalterable words and to draw principles of reflection, norms of judgment and directives for action from the social teaching... It is up to these Christian communities, with the help of the Holy Spirit, in communion with the bishops who hold responsibility and in dialogue with other Christian brethren and all men of good will, to discern the options and commitments which are called for in order to bring about the social, political and economic changes seen in many cases to be urgently needed. In this search for the changes which should be promoted, Christians must first of all renew their confidence in the forcefulness and special character of the demands made by the gospel.[2]

As the Synod of October 1971, representing the Bishops of the world, expressed it:

In order that the right to development may be fulfilled by action:

a) peoples should not be hindered from attaining development in accordance with their own culture;

b) in mutual cooperation, all peoples should be able to become the principal architects of their own economic and social development;

c) every people, as an active and responsible member of human society should be able to cooperate for the attainment of the universal common good on an equal footing with other peoples.[3]

We must therefore make two things clear to our Christian people.

1. In the search for and the pursuit of varied or even contrary political options there are human and Christian values which must be respected and lived. This is true also for those who choose to remain outside such a debate or search. Beyond the virtues of love, peace, justice, solidarity and fraternity, all must respect and accept another even when he chooses options different from one's own. In the same way we must accept and respect choices that a people may make in various moments of its history.

2. "Political options are by nature contingent, and never interpret the gospel in an entirely adequate and perennial way."[4]

All of us therefore, bishops, priests, lay people, religious, the whole people of God must realize and remember that the Church intends to play its role in this context of change, search and discussion. And this role will always be in the service of mutual presence, justice, dialogue and communion. We assure you that the bishops of Canada will be at the service of the people of God, whatever political, economic, social and cultural option they choose.

NOTES

1. In *The Pope Speaks*, Washington, 1971, XVI, 377.

2. Apostolic Letter to Maurice Cardinal Roy, President of the Council of the Laity and of the Pontifical Commission Justice and Peace, *A Call to Action (Octogesima Adveniens): on the Eightieth Anniversary of Rerum Novarum*, 1971, in *The Pope Speaks*, Washington,1971, XVI, 137 ff., n. 4.

3. *Op. cit.*, note 1 above, Part III, n. 8 (n. 71 in texts numbered continuously), *The Pope Speaks*, 1971, XVI, p. 388.

4. Third International Synod of Bishops, Rome, 1971, *The Ministerial Priesthood, Part II, Secular and Political Activity*, Vatican Press, p. 19; *The Pope Speaks*, Washington, 1971, XVI, 369.

Document 33

LABOUR DAY MESSAGE — 1972
SIMPLICITY AND SHARING

Author — The Episcopal Officers for Social Action

Overview: Critique of Present Growth Patterns

1.   The once unquestioned goal of ever increasing production and consumption is now widely recognized as an ambiguous good. Thoughtful critics point out that unbalanced economic expansion induces industrial pollution and consumer waste, while its material and cultural benefits are distributed very unevenly among nations and within nations. This inequitable sharing is not only an injustice to the poor; it traps the affluent in an endless spiral of earning and spending.

2.   Some still cling to the "trickle-down" theory, arguing that the benefits of economic growth eventually are enjoyed by all. The evidence however discredits this assumption: despite increases in the gross national product, unemployment persists in most nations and inequalities continue to widen between rich and poor. Here in Canada, after 25 years of supposedly effective social legislation, the wealthiest 20% of the population have almost six times more personal income than the poorest 20%.[1] Even as the revenue of corporations increases, inadequate incomes, uncertain employment and poor housing persist in the hazardous world of the workingman and his family.

3.   Why such glaring inequalities? Is it because of some fickle fate which rewards the affluent and penalizes the impoverished? Is it the Father's will that the majority of his divided family should be

denied basic necessities of life while a minority prospers? Or is it because of human disorder, a disorder which is embodied in social systems and structures, in the international and national "rules of the game"? There cannot be any doubt about which explanation applies. "The problem is the abuse of power, the coercion of the weak by the powerful," internationally, nationally and locally.[2] The present custodians of this power, industrialized states, multinational corporations, and the power elite, are not about to volunteer to share their decision-making and massive wealth with the impoverished and powerless.

4.   Compelling events say otherwise, however. Limited natural resources, environmental pollution, mounting civil unrest and violence, a spreading malaise of spirit, and similar circumstances show that the moral imperative of justice is fast becoming the practical necessity of common survival. Rich nations, corporations, groups, families and individuals will, sooner rather than later, have to learn — or else be forced — to consume less and share more of this small planet's finite treasure.

The Christian Perspective and Response

5.   These compelling signs underline the perennial relevance of the Gospel's radical ethic of fraternal solidarity, personal simplicity and communal sharing. (Cf. Ac 2:44-45) In more popular language, "The name of the game is to care, to spare and to share". In fact, we could not think of ourselves as generous even if we were to follow this Gospel ethic. Simplicity and sharing are enjoined by justice. Besides, through sharing we might begin to learn that what "belongs" to us is really a benefit made possible by the cooperation of many others. Then we might also be freed from the squirrel cage of earning more to spend more; from pursuing the advertisers' mirage of the good life; from acting as if material goods, without justice and brotherhood, could satisfy our deepest needs.

Global Sharing

6.   The 1971 International Synod of Bishops stressed the necessity of restraint in man's stewardship of the earth, and concurrent with this, the need for a major redistribution of global wealth. At the

recent (1972) Third United Nations Conference on Trade and De-velopment in Santiago, speaker after speaker and report after report insisted that only a redistribution of power, through the effective participation of all nations, could lead to a just sharing of the earth's resources.

Sharing in Canada

7.   The bishops of Canada, meeting in plenary assembly this April, called on all citizens in the name of justice to build a good society through honest discussion and effective action. The invitation fol-lowed an examination of the unequal sharing of Canada's wealth which keeps so many poor. The bishops called this persisting state of inequality a "social sin". This moral language underlines the find-ing of the Special Senate Committee on Poverty that "our society and economy not only tolerate poverty but also create, sustain and even aggravate it".[3]

8.   The same point has been made in recent months in more dra-matic ways. Across the land there has been a heightening of indus-trial strife. In the bitterness, a new note is being struck, namely that better working contracts alone will not suffice. The economic and political system itself has come under attack not only because so many employees are denied incomes commensurate with corporate earnings and government revenues, but also because these men and women are denied an effective share in decision-making. Their lives and those of their dependents are shaped by remote managements and ministries; the workers themselves have no real say. This state of affairs is contrary to papal and conciliar social teaching, which has always insisted in the name of human dignity, that workers, no less than businessmen and professionals, should receive a suffi-cient income to provide decently for themselves and their families; and further, that society should be so constituted that all citizens can determine their own destinies.[4] It would, we should add, be tragic if a larger share were simply to lead to the slavery of frenzied consumerism.

9.   Many Canadians however continue to subscribe to the domi-nating set of social goals, standards and procedures which rewards first those already rewarded, not those most in need. This main-stream mindset has its own measures of human worth: individual-

ism is prized above cooperation, selfishness is ranked ahead of sharing, and acquisitiveness rather than simplicity is seen as the way to happiness.

10. These aims, pursued with shrewdness and efficiency, are lauded by business executives and encouraged by political leaders as the characteristics best suited to foster economic expansion. By following such standards, Canada's free-market economy has indeed achieved sustained growth. However, this has been accomplished at a mounting social cost. All people are not served; the system always is. Housing is a glaring example. The system does not allow enough families to have the kind of home the nation could afford for every Canadian in the 1970's. According to prevailing norms, land for housing is part of the free market; land costs soar beyond most citizens' means while a few make quick profits. Again, financing for housing is determined by the norms of a money market. Patchwork, *ad hoc* measures designed to rectify the housing problem do not succeed because they do not attack the heart of the matter, namely that financial considerations take priority over human necessities. All this happens in the name of freedom.

11. More than 40 years ago Pius XI emphasized that mere economic growth and profit-making, the hallmarks of individualistic capitalism, do not serve people well enough.[5] Canada, no less than the so called developing countries, has need of other models for development, models which accord first place to human fulfillment, cooperation and community. In the search for new social visions, Christians ought not to be the ones who drag their feet. If we do, we will have to recognize that we are implicated in "social sin".

12. As a beginning, Christians in Canada could work for major reforms in taxation and social policy needed to make economic growth subordinate to the higher social goal of an equitable distribution of income.

Sharing at Local Levels

13. In each local community there are immediate opportunities for creative initiatives in the cause of social justice. By way of suggestion the April assembly of bishops invited Catholic groups and community coalitions to "seek more ways to respond without paternal-

ism to the expectations of the marginalized poor".[6] As one instance of what can be done, parishes and interchurch groups could sponsor public forums at which all sectors of the community could freely debate key social issues. Such collaboration would help ensure that the voices of deprived minorities are heard "as they work out their own liberation".[7]

Sharing in the Church

14. Appeals for simplicity and sharing in civil society are hollow unless, at the same time, there is a determined endeavour to practise these within the household of the Church. For good reason then, the recent Synod advocated an examination of conscience by all Catholics. This spring, the Canadian bishops invited fellow believers to join in "a collective examination of conscience on life styles and the uses of time and resources".[8] In so doing, the Assembly acknowledged that bishops themselves "must set the pace in such a revision of life style, making sure that they share something of the experience of their Christian community".[9] Noting that "change in style of living depends on a change of attitude", the Conference also stressed the central importance of social education to awaken Christian consciences.[10]

Conclusion

15. Consensus gives reality and force to social arrangements. No one person can change the social consensus. But if we work together we can change it. And while it is true that social structures must be reformed, there is no easy shortcut; each citizen must also change. Attitudes must change, hearts must change. Each family, small group, parish, ecumenical and civic organization can do something significant to help bring to the forefront of public affairs men and women who serve by sharing and so build true community. With such leaders, the struggle to raise consciousness levels, modify life styles, revise social priorities, and redistribute wealth will be effective because they will be rooted in people's lives in community.

16. The beatitudes promise happiness to those who seek justice and are "poor in spirit" (Mt 5:3,6). The simplicity denoted by poverty of spirit does not involve harsh austerity. Rather, it means

accepting a living standard of frugal comfort which breaks free from enslavement to more and more manmade things. Nor does generous sharing mean "less for me and more for you". Instead, it means breaking free from the narrow prison of individualism to experience a life in community which nourishes for all more of those values which count most in this life: fraternal support, friendship, love, authentic growth. This in part is the good news which the New Testament celebrates and which Jesus Christ exemplifies.

17. Generation after generation the Spirit calls Christians to become the "new humanity" who live and serve as Jesus did. Today this saving, transforming call summons Canadians to help build a world of caring, sparing and sharing among all peoples of the human family.

NOTES

1. *Poverty in Canada: Report of the Special Senate Committee* (Ottawa, Information Canada, 1971), p. 15.
2. Dr. Eugene Carson Blake, Secretary-General, World Council of Churches and Maurice Cardinal Roy, President, Pontifical Commission Justice and Peace, *Message to United Nations Conference on Trade and Development III*, Santiago, Chile, 1972.
3. *Poverty in Canada*, note 1 above, p. xxvii. Cf. also *Sharing National Income*, Document 31 above.
4. Cf. Leo XIII, *On the Condition of the Working Classes (Rerum Novarum)*, 1891, in *The Papel Encyclicals*, edit. Claudia Carlen, IHM (Wilmington, N.C., McGrath Publishing, 1981), II, 241 ff., nn. 3, 13, 37, 43-46; Pius XI, *On Reconstructing the Social Order (Quadragesimo Anno)*, 1931, in Carlen above, III, 415, nn. 71, 83, 110; John XXIII, *Mother and Teacher (Mater et Magistra)*, 1961, in Carlen above, V, 65, nn. 55-57; Paul VI, *Call to Action: on the 80th Anniversary of Rerum Novarum (Octogesima Adveniens)*, 1971, *The Pope Speaks*, Washington, 1971, XVI, 144 ff., nn. 14-16; Second Vatican Council, *The Church in the Modern World*, 1965, nn. 26, 65-69.
5. Pius XI, *On Reconstructing the Social Order (Quadragesimo Anno)*, 1931, cf. Carlen above, III, 432, n. 109; Paul VI, *The Development of Peoples (Populorum Progressio)*, 1967, in Carlen above, V, 187, n. 26.
6. Document 30, above, n. 8.
7. *Ibid.*
8. *Ibid.*, Introduction.
9. *Ibid.*, n. 1.
10. *Ibid.*, n. 2.

Document 34

DEVELOPMENT DEMANDS JUSTICE [1]

Author — Canadian Church Leaders to the Citizens of Canada, March, 1973

INTRODUCTION

As church leaders in Canada, we have come together for the purpose of making an urgent appeal to the Canadian people about the problems of world development.

We do not come with any special technical competence or solutions regarding the complex problems involved. We come instead with ethical questions about the values and goals underlying our present models for development. Our common concern for humanity throughout the world demands that justice be realized in the development of people and nations. This common ecumenical concern was clearly articulated recently by the general secretary of the World Council of Churches:

> We cannot speak of the church's mission to proclaim the gospel of Jesus Christ without seeing that the gospel has political implications. We cannot speak about renewal of persons and groups without facing the issues of power and authority, or of service without coming to grips with the struggle for justice.

We challenge the widespread assumption that the problems of development are solely or even mainly technical matters. On the contrary, the problems of development are primarily ethical questions pertaining to choices of social goals and human values. In our prevailing models for development, value choices have been made about what constitutes the good life and what constitutes a good community. We invite our fellow Christians and other citizens to join us in a public discussion of the value choices underlying our models for development in Canada and the western world.

We also challenge the assumption that leaders in government and business institutions alone have the prerogative to interpret the values and decide the goals of our development programs. All Canadian citizens should have the opportunity to participate in determining what our development goals as a nation should be. We therefore urge our fellow Christians and other citizens to join us in participating more actively in shaping new Canadian goals for world development.

I — THE DEVELOPMENT GAP:
CRITICAL PROBLEM OF INJUSTICE

The poor of the world, including the poor in Canada, are justly outraged by the widening gap that persists between those who have and those who have not.

In Canada, the gap between the rich and the poor has not changed despite major expansions in our gross national product. If anything, the gap has widened. The top one fifth of the Canadian population take home twice their share of the national income while the bottom one fifth continue receiving only a third of their share.[2]

In the world, it is the same story. Major increases in the aggregate wealth of the world have not narrowed the gap between the rich and the poor countries of this planet. One quarter of the world's population, including affluent Canadians, continue to control and consume three quarters of this planet's finite resources and services.

This development gap between the rich and the poor can no longer be taken for granted as "the way things are". There is nothing inevitable about the realities of being rich and poor in the world today. Nor can the gap be explained away by references to divine law or the inscrutable decrees of nature. The gap is the product of our own making as men of history. We have the responsibility of choosing the kind of social order we want to develop as a human family.

The development gap is first and foremost an ethical problem. Our planet contains all the resources and services necessary to maintain a decent living for the present world population. Yet there are gross inequities in the distribution of these resources and services among the peoples of the world. The development gap is no less than a critical problem of injustice for mankind.

The causes of the development gap are many and complex. On the surface, it is clear that the gap itself is created and maintained by our prevailing models for development. In turn, these models for development are based on the economic system of the industrialized countries, and more specifically of the western industrialized countries, including Canada. Herein lies the major cause of the development gap between the rich and the poor. It is our economic system which is primarily responsible for the inequitable distribution of society's resources and services. The Special Senate Committee on Poverty in Canada reached the same conclusion when it declared in 1971:

> The economic system in which most Canadians prosper is the same economic system which creates poverty... What society gives with the one hand it often takes away with the other.[3]

Our established models for development therefore, are firmly grounded in the economic system of the industrialized countries. Here development is conceived mainly, if not exclusively, in economic terms. The primary goal is to maximize economic growth. The underlying assumption is that ever expanding production and consumption is the road to the good life. Moreover, it is commonly held that all people will eventually benefit from increases in the gross national product. According to this "trickle-down" theory of distribution, an increase in aggregate wealth will automatically result in benefits for everyone. In short, equity is believed to be a natural by-product of growth.

This model for development was imported as the paradigm for development in the Third World countries of Africa, Asia, and Latin America. Following the disintegration of the colonial empires, most of the newly independent countries found themselves with a crippled economy dependent on either a single agricultural product (e.g., coffee) or a single raw material (e.g., tin). Following the industrialized model for development, the new countries explored various means for expanding their economic growth. Efforts were made to gain a reasonable share of the world market for their individual products and to encourage foreign investment and aid in their countries in order to acquire the capital requisite for economic development. However the desired goals for economic development were never achieved. The Third World countries soon learned that the rules of the development game were mainly formulated by the governments and corporations of the industrialized countries, including Canada. The rules were formulated for the main purpose of maximizing the economic growth of the industrialized countries. As a consequence, the amassed profits from foreign investment automatically became concentrated in the hands of the investors in the industrialized countries who owned the capital and the technological resources. At the same time, the profit margin of the poor countries in the Third World has been far too small to compete for the capital and technology required for their own indigenous economic development.

Of course there have been exceptions to these rules in the development game. But the general application of the rule is all too pervasive and true. The industrialized countries have employed a variety of institutional mechanisms for creating, maintaining, and extending the gap between the rich and the poor. Among the major mechanisms have been the dominant patterns of (1) international trade, (2) corporate investment, and (3) foreign aid.

1 — International Trade

The first mechanisms are the dominant patterns of international trade. The industrialized countries, including Canada, dominate the trade patterns between nations through the exercise of their own economic and political power. Since the second world war, there has been a steady deterioration in the terms of trade between the industrialized countries and their suppliers of agricultural and raw materials in the Third World.

On the one hand, the industrialized countries have repeatedly refused to pay adequate prices for basic agricultural commodities (e.g., coffee, rice, cocoa, tea, sugar) and raw materials (e.g., tin, copper, petroleum). On the other hand, the industrialized countries have increasingly charged the poor countries escalating prices for their finished products. For example, in 1954, Colombia could exchange 10 bags of coffee for one jeep. By 1967, the same jeep cost 39 bags of coffee. In other words, production in Colombia would have to increase four times in order to purchase the same amount of finished products from the industrialized countries.

2 — *Corporate Investment*

A second institutional mechanism is the dominant pattern of corporate investment. Foreigh owned corporations from industrialized countries, including Canada, have invested a large amount of capital and technology in the countries of Africa, Asia and Latin America. Many of these corporations have received generous tax concessions as incentives for using their capital and technology to develop the kind of indigenous industry that would meet the development needs of the Third World country. However, most of these corporations have been mainly concerned with maximizing their own profits rather than the economic development of the Third World.

As a result of the patterns of corporate investment, many of the Third World countries have increasingly found themselves trapped in a state of economic dependence. They discovered that their control over their own raw materials and their own processes of industrialization was decreasing. Far more capital was leaving the country in the form of profits and tax concessions than was coming in through investments (an estimated three dollars for every dollar invested). Moreover, many of the entrepreneurial skills and resources in the country were serving the foreign companies rather than the development of indigenous industry. In effect, the needs of the foreign company were being met by the investment of capital and technology rather than the more basic needs of the country itself.

3 — *Foreign Aid*

A third institutional mechanism is the dominant pattern of foreign aid. The dominant patern has been "tied aid". The industrialized countries, including Canada, usually grant aid on a unilateral basis with the result that they can determine exactly what the aid will be used for and what the conditions of its use will be. The receiving country is usually required to use the aid grant for purchasing the products of the donor country. For example, approximately two thirds of Canadian government aid is required to be spent on Canadian products and services.

For many Third World countries, foreign aid amounts to a net loss. Often, more money leaves the nation to pay off aid loans than the amount of money coming into the country in the form of aid programs. All this has contributed to the progressive debt incurred by the Third World countries. In 1968, the total debt incurred by poor countries of the Third World amounted to $47.5 billion. By 1972, the debt had risen to $60 billion.

These then are some of the major mechanisms employed by the industrialized countries in the development game. Their one net effect has been to maximize the economic growth of the industrialized countries and, at the same time, continue the economic underdevelopment of the poor countries in the Third World. Taken together, these mechanisms function to create, maintain, and extend the development gap between the rich and the poor throughout the world.

The injustices of the development gap and its causes compel us to re-examine the goals and values that underlie our prevailing models for development. We Canadians have chosen economic growth as the primary goal of our model for development. But equity has certainly not been the by-product of growth, at home or in the world. Is it clear that economic growth is to be valued above everything else? Especially when the cost of maximizing economic growth is increasing inequality, or increasing dominance and dependence, between the peoples of the world?

II — ALTERNATIVE MODELS FOR DEVELOPMENT: CRITICAL CHOICE

Among the peoples of the Third World, there is a growing resistance to the prevailing industrialized models for development. There is a desire to reaffirm the values of their traditional societies and their capacities for self-determination.

Increasingly these countries are resisting the pressures for modern industrialization where the human cost is too high. Many people in the Third World are rejecting the goal of maximizing economic growth, especially where the cost is increasing domination and dependence. The late Lester B. Pearson anticipated this emerging resistance over 15 years ago when he said:

> Perhaps only in North America every man feels entitled to a motor car, but in Asia hundreds of millions now do expect to eat and be free. They will no longer accept colonialism, destitution and distress as preordained. That may be the most sig-

nificant of all the revolutionary changes in the social fabric of our times.

In recent years, a variety of Third World countries have begun a serious search for alternative models for development. Several Third World models have been proposed which, in essence, call for a modest yet adequate level of living for all citizens. In contrast to the western industrial models, the primary goal is not maximizing economic growth with supposed "trickle down" benefits to the poor. The goal is to attain a balanced growth with an equitable distribution of income across the board.

Tanzania's President, Julius Nyerere, spoke for many Third World peoples when he articulated the vision of Tanzania founded on a traditional society. By a traditional society, Nyerere referred to the notion of "an extended family in which all contribute to the prosperity of the whole". He envisioned a society in which every one is a worker, and where each member regards everybody as his brother. In 1970, he outlined the implications of this vision of society for development itself:

> The purpose of development is man. It is the creation of conditions, both material and spiritual, which enable man the individual and man the species to become his best... (We are committed) to the belief that there are more important things in life than the amassing of riches, and that if the pursuit of wealth clashes with things like human dignity and social equality, then the latter will be given priority... This may seem to be a very academic point, but in reality it is very fundamental.

While following these guidelines for development, Tanzania has rejected foreign aid with strings attached and foreign investment that inhibits self-determination. Third World countries like Tanzania are no longer willing to sacrifice their humanity in order to become modern industrialized nations. The growing resistance against the western models for development is reinforced by the belief that the Third World countries can achieve adequate living conditions for all their citizens without economic dependence on the industrialized countries. Along these lines, Makbul ul Haq, advisor to the World Bank, advocated in 1972:

> The developing countries have no choice but to turn inwards, in much the same way as communist China did 25 years ago, and to adopt a different style of life, seeking a consumption

pattern more consistent with their own poverty — pots and pans and bicycles and simple consumption habits — without being seduced by the life styles of the rich. This requires a re-definition of economic and social objectives which is of truly staggering proportions, a liquidation of the privileged groups and vested interests which may well be impossible in many societies, a redistribution of political and economic power which may only be achieved through revolution rather than through an evolutionary change.

These Third World alternatives pose a major challenge for all of us in Canada and the western world. They offer us a vision of a new world order; not a world based on ever expanding growth, pro-duction and consumption, but a world based on equity, on "caring, sharing and sparing".

In effect, the voices of the Third World are telling us that "De-velopment Demands Justice". And justice, in turn, demands a major redistribution of economic resources and decision-making power in the world today.

This is no longer simply a moral imperative. The finite resources of this planet are rapidly being exploited to the point of exhaustion by current levels of consumption and production. Violence and civil unrest continue to mount among the oppressed peoples of the world who are demanding their fair share of the earth's resources. What was once considered a moral imperative for justice is rapidly being recognized as a practical necessity for the survival of our common humanity on this planet. Economist Barbara Ward recently articu-lated these realities:

> To live simply, to love greatly, to give without stinting, to see a brother in all mankind — this is no longer a remote theory of social behavior. It is the inescapable recipe for planetary survival.

Today, we Canadians are faced with a critical choice between alternative courses for the future. We can decide to continue our present course of maximizing economic growth, earnings, and con-sumption: or we can decide to join the poor in the struggle for a just distribution of economic resources and political power in the world.

Throughout the history of Canada, we have heard a chorus of demands for justice in the development of this country. We have a diverse and rich tradition of protest against the injustices of increasing economic growth and expansion, by the native peoples, by the Quebecois, by the farmers in the west and the coal miners in the east. Much of this tradition is still alive and active at this very moment. In recent years, some people have moved from a critique of the industrialized model for development to a creative search for alternative models. This trend was given official recognition recently when the Prime Minister himself (the Honourable Pierre Trudeau) asked the Canadian people in May, 1971:

> Why... do Western governments continue to worship at the temple of the Gross National Product?... Shouldn't we be replacing our reliance on the GNP with a much more revealing figure, a new statistic which might be called "Net Human Benefit"?

The goal of "Net Human Benefit" however, requires specification in terms of our relations to the Third World. It must be considered in terms of what will be required to advance the purpose of narrowing the development gap between the rich and the poor. We must ask ourselves what kind of alternative policies for development are required to narrow the development gap in the world. For example:

1. Are we prepared to start paying fair prices for basic agricultural products such as coffee, cocoa, rice, and sugar? Are we prepared to give trade preferences to the commodities of Third World countries, thereby giving them a more equitable share of our market?

2. Are we prepared to place less emphasis on maximizing profits in our foreign investments and more emphasis on developing viable economic institutions that meet the particular needs of the developing countries and preserve their right of self-determination?

3. Are we prepared not only to increase the quantity of foreign aid but also to improve its quality by not tying it to the purchase of Canadian goods and by channelling more aid through the United Nations and grass roots agencies?

We must recognize however, that such alternative policies for development will require major changes in the economic structures of our society and the social order of our lives. We must ask ourselves whether or not we are prepared to accept the social and personal implications of these changes. For example,

1. What kind of structural changes are required in our economic system in order to bring about a more equitable distribution of economic resources?

2. What would happen to the economy if affluent Canadians adopted a more modest way of living? What would happen to the manufacturers, the workers, the advertisers, the media people? What kind of political trade-offs would be required?

3. How many relatively affluent Canadians are prepared to level off or even cut down on their living standards? How many would be prepared to accept the personal and family consequences of a national policy for limited growth, restrained consumption, and generous sharing?

Such questions compel us as Canadians to re-examine our personal values and our social goals as a nation. This kind of critical re-examination of goals and values is worthwhile at any time. But today, the development gap between the rich and the poor is advancing rapidly. A re-examination of our national goals and values for development is absolutely essential at this particular moment in the history of mankind.

NOTES

1. *Development Demands Justice* is the title of three distinct documents:

a. a brief two page statement prepared by the relief and development agencies of several Canadian Churches (Anglican, Lutheran, Presbyterian, Roman Catholic and United) and of the Canadian Council of Churches;

b. a longer document (14 pp.), based on the former, prepared for "presentation to the citizens of Canada", by six church leaders participating in Ten Days for World Development, March 9-19, 1973; Dr. N.B. McLeod, Moderator, United Church of Canada; Bishop W.E. Power, President, Canadian Catholic Conference; Dr. M.V. Putnam, Moderator, Presbyterian Church in Canada and Dr. D. MacDonald, Administrative Secretary; Archbishop E.W. Scott, Primate, Anglican Church in Canada. Ten Days for World Development has offices at 85 St. Clair Ave. East, Toronto, M4T 1M8.

c. a more technical document (19 pp.) prepared by the same leaders for "presentation to the Government of Canada and members of Parliament", to which were added two *addenda* (3 pp.); the first of Project GATT-Fly (an inter-church initiative) to the Ministers of External Affairs, of Finance and of Industry, Trade and Commerce; the second, of the Interchurch Consultative Committee on Development and Relief, being a Statement on the Development Education Programme of the Canadian International Development Agency (CIDA). This third document was presented to the Federal Government and Members of Parliament. It is the second of these three documents which is presented here.

2. There is an error in these statistics; the truth is more dismal. The top 20% of the Canadian population received in 1973 approximately 40% — twice their proportional share — of the national income. The bottom 20% received approximately 4% — *one-fifth* of their proportional share — of the national income. Overall taxation makes practically no difference in these relative shares. This proportional division of income in Canada has not varied significantly since statistics have been kept (1951), but is probably less favourable to the poorer sector in 1986 than in 1974 when this document was written. Cf. *The Hidden Welfare System* (1976), *Bearing the Burden Sharing the Benefits* (1978), *The Hidden Welfare System Revisited* (1979), (all Ottawa, National Council of Welfare), and the bibliography therein.

3. *Poverty in Canada* (Ottawa, Information Canada, 1971), p. xv.

Document 35

LABOUR DAY MESSAGE — 1973
INEQUALITY DIVIDES
JUSTICE RECONCILES

Author — The Episcopal Officers for Social Action

I — DISORDER: INEQUALITY UNDERMINES SOLIDARITY

1.   After consulting fellow believers across Canada,[1] the Bishops of the Canadian Catholic Conference responsible for social action wish to explore with all of you some implications of our 1972 Labour Day Statement on *Simplicity and Sharing.* If it is important to point out social injustices,[2] if it is necessary to face up to the moral and practical demands of equitable sharing[3], then it is urgent that we try to identify our main sources of strength, and at the same time analyze the social values predominant in Canadian society.

2.   The global family to which all of us belong is characterized by different histories, diverse cultures, individual talents. Yet in the uniquely personal quest for wholeness each individual is dependent on other members. In today's complex, technological age this interdependence has so increased that essential human relationships have become worldwide, in commerce, in politics, in cultural life, in religion and in interpersonal affairs. This now universal need to "care, spare and share" together is however, undermined by a major disorder found to some degree in every kind of society. In North America for example, the prevailing social norm is not cooperative interdependence but rather competitive survival of the fittest, the law of the jungle. The jungle rule of "more for me, less for you", built into many economic, political and social structures, denies equal

opportunities for human development. Thus various inequalities in daily life are perpetuated. Furthermore, awareness of the human family's necessary interdependence is undermined.

II — UNEQUAL OPPORTUNITIES FOR HUMAN DEVELOPMENT

3.   Unequal opportunities and their divisive consequences are evident on all sides. Why for example, must Canadians on fixed incomes bear the brunt of ever higher living costs, while corporate profits keep climbing? Why is adequate housing beyond the financial reach of so many families, while land speculators and developers reap more benefits? Why is it that one out of every four Canadians must struggle for the basic necessities of food, clothing and shelter, while some others claiming to provide these needs wax rich?[4] Why does the low-income earner have difficulty bettering his or her lot while it is relatively easy for the already affluent to raise their living standard still higher?[5] Why is it hard for many families to erase their debts while finance companies and banks prosper? Why, after years of social security measures, do such disparities persist? Why, despite policies designed to equalize opportunities, do some regions of Canada grow wealthier while others do not? And abroad, why do international trading arrangements almost always favour the industrialized nations, Canada included, at the expense of the poorer nations supplying raw materials?[6]

4.   Such inequalities are the work of men and the politico-economic systems they fashion. Even as global interdependence accelerates, such inequities, now known universally through modern communications, appear to multiply.

5.   One root cause of this disorder is a too narrow pursuit of the common goal "to do more, know more and have more in order to be more",[7] to be somebody! Unfortunately it seems that our society is mainly preoccupied with the material aspects of what it means to "be more". Many influential decision makers and trend setters would have us believe that the way to be "somebody" important is to acquire more, in order to consume more. In Marxist states, even religious freedom and family rights are often denied or restricted in the pursuit of similar material goals. Wherever it prevails, this excessive "consumerism" challenges the Christian conscience.

III — RESULT: SOCIAL INEQUALITIES

6. In our society buying power has become a widely accepted symbol of social status. As a consequence, there is now a psychological as well as a material gap between the rich and the poor, between those who reputedly "succeed" or "fail". It is a gulf which appears even more difficult to bridge than the social separation between peoples of different languages and cultures.

7. In these and similar ways, the uneven race to produce more wealth and consume more things fragments the human family at every level. Furthermore, prosperity itself seems to render some of the affluent insensitive to the sufferings of the deprived. "The response of the rich, the able, the secure," Barbara Ward has written, "seems to grow feebler as the risks and the despairs (of the poor) grow worse."[8]

8. This indifference is not the only consequence of the prevailing tendency to measure the worth of persons, their innate value, in terms of income level and buying power. Judgments based on such shallow criteria encourage various kinds of social discrimination. Subtle and not so subtle forms of discrimination segregate rich and poor physically and mentally, frequently in housing developments, sometimes in schools, law enforcement, and health care. Can any one among the affluent claim never to have succumbed to this pernicious tendency to look down upon the deprived or to treat them in a patronizing fashion?

9. Such inequities are the evil harvest of individual fears and selfishness, reinforced by public policies and structures which embody these human failings. Such inequalities mock the divine will, deny the fundamental dignity and equality of all members of the human family and betray aspirations for justice and peace. In the name of the Servant Lord whom we profess to follow, Christians cannot continue to tolerate, much less contribute to, these social disorders in our midst. Instead we must lend our efforts to the universal task of building, stage by stage, the house of peace on Earth, the home of our human family.

IV — THE GOSPEL GOAL OF COMMUNITY

10. Human solidarity, given flesh each day in different forms of fraternity, is the touchstone for both personal and communal development. Whether speaking of Adam or of our condition as redeemed sinners, the Good News affirms the oneness of all (Cf. Ac 17:26; Rm 5:15; Gal 3:28). If we take this Gospel seriously, then we should be among the first to try to envisage what could happen were the unity of the human family and global sharing accepted as the guiding norms of social conduct.

11. This unity in God precedes and transcends all social systems devised by mankind. Divine fatherhood is prior and gives ultimate meaning to human brotherhood. Nor can any human design annul what has been so ordained. In the words of the Second Vatican Council:

> With respect to the fundamental rights of the person, every type of discrimination, whether social or cultural, whether based on sex, race, color, social condition, language, or religion, is to be overcome and removed as contrary to God's will.[9]

12. God condemned Dives not because he was rich but because he was indifferent to the sufferings of the poor Lazarus (Cf. Lk 16:19-31). In response to this Gospel lesson, Christians should help lead the way in reaffirming human solidarity. This can be done best by fraternal initiatives to promote social justice among persons, peoples and nations. And here a providential occasion is at hand: reconciliation is the theme chosen by Pope Paul VI for the 1975 Holy Year. Local churches throughout the world, including the Church in Canada, can begin now to renew their commitment in faith to the work of reconciliation.

13. We invite all to a conversion of mind and heart, beginning with a critical examination of personal living habits and attitudes and the popular social norms used to measure our achievements as citizens, spouses and parents, young people and elderly, laity and religious, as Christians.

14. The Sermon on the Mount is the perennial Christian charter for human relationships. It is a charter whose radical ethic rebukes

competitive greed (Cf. Mt c. 5). As yet, comparatively few Christians appear prepared to become prophetic witnesses to the fraternal harmony promised in the beatitudes, even though such cooperative interdependence is now a practical necessity for global survival as well as a moral necessity for wholeness of life.[10]

V — SOLIDARITY IN THE CHURCH

15. The Church of Jesus Christ is called generation after generation to become a convincing sign of community in the world, giving witness to that unity for which our Lord prayed so fervently to the Father (Cf. Jn 17:21). Even so, internal divisions persist and for the most part we have no one to blame but ourselves. Consider the frank appraisal of Canada's Cardinal Primate:

> Mutual intolerance and excommunication too often rage within the People of God, as well as the... systematic refusal of communion with other Catholic brethren who do not have the same political views or who do not belong to the same social or cultural category. This... contradiction between Catholics' inner and outward behavior must be eliminated, under penalty of lying, counter-witness and ineffectiveness.[11]

16. Despite present efforts of renewal, our generation is clearly not exempt from the reproaches St. Paul made to the Christian at Corinth, who had allowed social dissension to divide the Eucharistic community (Cf. 1 Cor 11:18-22). Catholic bishops, priests, religious and laity, in cooperation with fellow Christians, have respective responsibilities, a shared commitment, to continue praying for, and working towards, that loving fellowship in the Lord which is the hallmark of Christian living and an integral component of salvation (Cf. Jn 13:34-35; 15:5). Practical expressions of this Christian ideal can best be devised through collaboration at the local level.

VI — SOLIDARITY IN CIVIL SOCIETY

17. The responsibility to build community extends to civil society. Many persons committed to social renewal are already exploring new roads to solidarity. Are these civil efforts sufficiently supported by Christians?

18.   Dovetailing our efforts with fellow citizens, Christians are committed by the Gospel and modern social teachings to help initiate, support and uphold public policies which aim at social equity and harmony. All citizens should share in devising such policies. The critical test of any society's justice and humanity is how it treats its weakest members: the unborn, the aged, the handicapped, minorities, and others who are especially vulnerable.

19.   A similar but much greater challenge exists at the international level. Under the present rules of the global power game, the "rich men's club" of industrialized nations, including Canada, has most of the bargaining advantages, advantages of power exercised in large part by giant multi-national corporations.[12] How, in such circumstances, can the Third World countries of Asia, Africa and Latin America secure just trading terms, preferential agreements which enable them to begin closing the development gap in their own distinctive ways? Present prospects are not encouraging, despite the urgings of the 1971 International Synod of Bishops and of Canadian interchurch leaders during this year's observance of *"10 Days for World Development"*. Similarly, in the 25th anniversary year of the United Nations' *Universal Declaration of Human Rights,* which member country can truthfully claim that all rights and duties proclaimed therein are faithfully honoured in practice? As instances, consider the rights of the family and each people's right to distinctive cultural development. Will such rights be respected in policy decisions when the delegations of governments meet at the 1974 United Nations Conference on Population? Will the Canadian government for one, speak out for such rights? These are some of the global questions, questions concerning the human family and each family ultimately, which Christians should put to their public representatives.

20.   In this country the *Working Paper on Social Security in Canada* proposes certain steps towards some measure of income equality.[13] How many of us have given these proposals much attention? Probably still fewer among us who are affluent, have seriously considered whether there is involved here a social responsibility to pay more taxes if necessary, and perhaps even a responsibility to consume less, to help make possible policies of equalization at home and just trade practices abroad. In every region, province and local community, similar questions of social justice confront us.

21.   Many thoughtful Canadians, including some young people, now question the human costs of the prevailing North American system, increasing greed and waste, widening inequalities, deepening divisions and a spreading malaise of spirit. At the same time, there is evidence that a new consciousness is emerging, perhaps even a conversion of conscience is beginning. Structural reforms are also required; after all, new wine requires fresh skins (Cf. Mt 9:17). The Gospel calls upon Christians to share in this continuing transformation of persons and of institutions.

VII — AN APPEAL

22.   In this 10th anniversary year of Pope John XXIII's last testament, *Peace on Earth,* we want to unite our efforts with you, fellow Christians and citizens, so that together we may reaffirm in practice those perennial values which "remove the barriers that divide and reinforce the bonds of mutual love".[14] All of us know or experience inequalities, injustices, which should be removed and divisions which should be healed. Together, invoking the Spirit who takes us beyond our human limitations, let us begin to build new bridges of reconciliation.

NOTES

1. Before this text was drafted, a number of Catholics across Canada were asked to cite social inequalities in their respective areas. Numerous examples were reported. A summary is available at nominal cost from the Canadian Conference of Catholic Bishops, Ottawa, K1N 7B1.
   2. Cf. Third International Synod of Bishops. *Justice in the World,* nn. 20, 35 f., 57; cf. *The Pope Speaks* (Washington, 1971), XVI, pp. 380 ff.
   3. Cf. *Simplicity and Sharing,* Document 33 above.
   4. Cf. *Poverty in Canada,* Report of the Special Senate Committee on Poverty (Ottawa, Information Canada, 1971), p. 11.
   5. Cf. *A Christian Stance in the Face of Violence,* Document 25 above.
   6. Cf. *Development Demands Justice,* Document 34, above.
   7. Paul VI, *The Development of Peoples,* 1967, in *The Papal Encyclicals,* edit. Claudia Carlen, IHM (Wilmington, N.C., McGrath Publishing, 1981), V, n. 6, p. 184.
   8. Barbara Ward, *The Angry Seventies* (Vatican City, Pontifical Commission Justice and Peace), pp. 61 f.

9. Second Vatican Council, *The Church in the Modern World*, 1965, n. 29.

10. Barbara Ward, *op. cit.*, p. 61.

11. Maurice Cardinal Roy, President of the Pontifical Commission Justice and Peace, *Reflections on the Tenth Anniversary of the Encyclical Peace on Earch*, 1973, *The Pope Speaks*, Washington, 1973, XVIII, 38.

12. W. Hettich, *Les problèmes de la répartition* (Ottawa, Economic Council of Canada, Nov., 1971) p. 2.

13. Department of National Health and Welfare (Ottawa, Information Canada, 1973).

14. In Carlen cited above, note 7, V, 127, n. 171.

Document 36

LABOUR DAY MESSAGE — 1974
SHARING DAILY BREAD

Author — Administrative Board, the Canadian Catholic Conference[1]

INTRODUCTION

1. Man does not live by bread alone, but without bread he cannot live. This human condition is graphically evident in a grave public issue now confronting Canadians in a special way. Not enough food available for most of humanity: that is the issue. Enough food at reasonable prices for all people: that is the goal.

2. As the elected representatives of the Catholic Bishops of Canada and in their name, we wish to share with you, fellow citizens, some reflections on the ethical implications of the worsening food problem. We propose for your consideration some questions regarding both personal life styles and public policies. We hope that these reflections and questions will contribute, along with those offered by other concerned Canadians, to examinations of conscience, to public debate, and to generous decisions by individuals, families, groups, and policy-makers.

3. In particular, we invite Christian colleagues to join in this enterprise. The food problem in Canada and in the world challenges especially those of us who pray, "Give us this day our daily bread", and who commune with the Servant Lord in consecrated bread. On our part, we envisage this statement as only one step in a growing response by Christians and fellow Canadians of other faiths to the demands of social justice.[2]

4. Practically every household in Canada is familiar with the food price squeeze. Increasing retail prices of food disrupt the budgets especially of Canadians with low incomes. A recent study by the National Council of Welfare found that price tags on foods usually consumed by poor families, such as hamburgers, potatoes and pasta, had risen much more rapidly than other retail food prices.[3]

5. Yet this Canadian aggravation does not begin to equal the suffering by people in Third World countries of Asia, Africa and Latin America. There the task of feeding multitudes has reached a critical stage, principally because global reserves have dropped from enough to feed humanity for 69 days in 1970, to enough for only 27 days this year. Consequently, the prices poor countries must pay for food imports have escalated in response to the lowest supplies since the Second World War.[4] At the same time domestic production of food in these developing nations has been drastically hampered by astronomical increases in the cost of fuel and fertilizer.[5]

6. As a result, growing numbers of men, women and children are trapped in a tightening vise of malnutrition and hunger. A recent assessment by the United Nations concludes that more than 400 million people (nearly 20 times the Canadian population) are not getting enough food to meet their minimum needs of nutrition.[6] Other studies estimate that between 25 and 75 million face the prospect of death by starvation. Statistics alone cannot begin to convey the magnitude of this suffering. As Canadians, few of us will ever know what it is like to be haunted by the spectre of starvation.

RESPONSIBLE STEWARDSHIP

7. We do know we cannot in conscience stand idly by while fellow humans die from hunger. That would be a cruel denial to our neighbors of the most fundamental of all needs, the need to eat in order to live. Furthermore, the world food crisis puts to the test the Judeo-Christian vision of one human family under God. Whatever else may be said about the social thrust of the Scriptures, the fraternal responsibility to feed brothers and sisters who are hungry is a central imperative. This imperative theme is a dominant thread in the biblical tapestry — from the story of Joseph's plans to store food in famine-stricken Egypt to the narratives of the sharing of loaves

and fishes by Jesus; from the bold vision of the ancient prophets to the description of the first Christians, who together celebrated the Eucharist, "the breaking of the bread", and who "shared their food gladly and generously."[7] These early Christians lived the spirit of the Gospel in everyday life by "caring, sparing and sharing".[8]

8. In the Scriptures, bread is a fundamental symbol of all God's gifts and mankind's task. Bread is the "test" of both worship and brotherhood. For Christians, Jesus Christ is the Living Bread who kneads together the relationship between God and man, between people and daily bread, between the human spirit and eternal life, between justice and love. Beyond material sharing, the Gospel insists on the deepest meaning of bread and its ingredients, the quality of the salt and the yeast in the dough in the everyday world. For Christians, Christ holds the key to both quality of bread and vitality of soul.[9]

9. Today the food problem at home and abroad impels us as Canadians to join Prime Minister Trudeau in examining whether we are "good stewards of what we have."[10] How responsibly do we use the great wealth in our custody, land, water, technology, food? Do those of us who are believers recognize that "God intended Earth and all that it contains for the use of every human being and people"?[11] Do we acknowledge that "All other rights whatsoever, including those of property and of free commerce, are to be subordinated to this principle"?[12] And do we accept the implication of this recognition: "Feed the man dying of hunger, because if you have not fed him you have killed him"?[13]

10. In a special session of the United Nations this past spring, the poor countries made a dramatic appeal to the rich nations to alleviate increasing shortages in food and other essential resources. On that occasion, Pope Paul VI urged the participating governments to take major strides towards responsible stewardship of the Earth's resources. The Holy Father called upon governments to fashion "new, more just and hence more effective international structures in such spheres as economics, trade, industrial development, finance and the transfer of technology". At the same time the Pope appealed to affluent citizens "to adopt a new life style that will exclude excessive consumption, excessive in that it often deprives others of necessities, has harmful effects on the environment, and weakens the moral fibre of the users".[14]

11. Modify living habits; reform economic structures: here are two key guidelines to global stewardship. This responsible stewardship first of all requires a closer look at the causes of the worsening food problem. Analysts point to a range of complex factors, such as climatic disasters, population growth, monetary instability and rising oil prices.[15] Add to these the arms race, a scandalous enterprise that sees hundreds of billions of dollars spent annually for death-dealing weapons, not for life-giving programs of development. These and other factors contribute to the present food crisis. Yet the underlying causes generally are found in the consuming and marketing practices of economic systems, practices which continually widen the gap between humanity's rich minority and poor majority.[16] As bishops, we do not claim technical competence in such matters, but we do feel obliged to examine some of the ethical implications. Hence we invite fellow citizens to reflect with us on these major factors of consumption and marketing, and to consider some consequent questions.

THE CONSUMPTION FACTOR

12. Observers agree that one of the main causes of the world food problem is the pattern of extravagant consumption found in the industrialized countries, including Canada. The average person in North America now consumes directly or indirectly five times as much cereal grain, a principal source of protein, as the average citizen of Latin America, Africa or Asia. Most of this North American intake is consumed in the forms of meat, eggs and milk.[17] Indeed, the affluent minority in the world feeds as much grain to animals as the deprived majority of humans eats directly! A North American steer consumes as much as 21 pounds of inexpensive grain to produce one pound of expensive beef.[18]

13. In effect, "the rich man's meat takes away the poor man's bread". Basic foods that could help overcome malnutrition and starvation are fed instead to livestock in order to satisfy our luxurious eating habits. It has been noted that the average Canadian now consumes annually ten pounds more beef, seven pounds more pork, and five pounds more poultry than he did five years ago.[19] This rate of increase places intolerable demands upon basic resources and represents one of the major causes of the global food crisis. Worse

still, human beings starve while North Americans indulge in special foods for household pets.

14. As consumers, as Christians, we are faced with a basic question: can we begin to reduce the demands we place on food resources by modifying our personal eating patterns? This kind of question, as also the need to transform economic structures, was critically examined in Quebec earlier this year by more than 1,000 groups participating in "Chantier '74".[20] By wasting less food and altering eating habits, Canadians could make some contribution towards an equitable sharing of the world's food supply. It has been estimated for instance, that if Canadians ate one less hamburger per week, one million tons of grain would become available to feed an additional five million people.[21]

15. As consumers then, as Christians, are we prepared:

(a) to question the goals of an economic system which urges us to consume extravagantly and to waste, rather than to share available food resources?

(b) to resist advertisements and other forms of social pressure which generate affluent eating habits?

(c) to practise the tradition of fast and abstinence by reducing our consumption of food, especially meat? For example, to consider and experiment with new, vegetable-based foods which can provide nutritious substitutes for beef, pork and poultry?

(d) to channel the savings we achieve by moderation, whether money or goods, to neighbours in need through effective voluntary agencies? The annual "Share Lent" program of the Canadian Catholic Organization for Development and Peace and like projects sponsored by other Canadian churches and groups are examples.

(e) to develop new educational programs in families, churches and schools oriented towards changes in consuming patterns and personal lifestyles? Such programs could for instance, examine the cultural significance of eating together, as families, as friends, as colleagues. Is it not time to change the emphasis from the physical pleasures to the fraternal values of eating together?[22]

THE MARKET FACTOR

16. International observers emphasize that alternative forms of personal consumption will be ineffective unless there are also fundamental changes in the marketing system which now governs the production and distribution of food throughout the world.[23] Canada's minister of agriculture, who predicts that global food production should triple in the next 25 years, says "The weak link in the chain today is the marketing system..."[24] The present market is designed primarily to make profits, not to feed people. The supply and distribution of food is determined mainly by effective demand, not human need. Effective demand is usually defined in terms of ability to pay. Food supplies are often controlled in such a way as to drive up prices. Some food industries have gone so far as to destroy their produce when they could not get the market price they wanted.

17. Recent studies indicate that some countries and corporations have been largely responsible for present food shortages and inflated prices.[25] In 1972 two grain corporations with large storage facilities were able to withhold 95% of the American soybean crop from the world market. In the following year, the market price for soybeans paid by consumers tripled, thereby providing huge profits for the two corporations.[26] During the same period, the price of wheat quadrupled on the global market. A record-breaking U.S. wheat sale to the Soviet Union in 1972 caused a sharp reduction in global food reserves, which in turn brought about a dramatic rise in wheat prices.[27] While these higher prices benefit Canada as a major wheat exporter, many poorer countries are compelled to do without adequate wheat supplies simply because they are unable to pay the going prices.

18. As citizens, as Christians, we are faced with this fundamental question: can we continue to rely on present market forces to set prices and determine the distribution of so essential a commodity as food?[28] This November the United Nations is convening a World Food Conference in Rome to consider this global issue. Canada has an opportunity and therefore a responsibility to play a decisive role at the conference. This country and the United States together "control a larger share of the world's exportable supplies of food grains than the Middle East does of oil".[29] This places Canada in a strate-

gic position to exercise leadership at the Rome conference. While Canada has steadily increased food aid shipments to less developed countries, much more could be done. New leadership is required to establish alternative programs for the production and distribution of food in the world community.

19. As citizens, as Christians, are we prepared to ask our policy makers:

(a) to make substantial contributions towards the creation of a world food bank (of wheat, rice, and coarse grains, plus fertilizer, fuels and other agricultural resources)? Current proposals call for regional storage depots that could be drawn upon by countries facing emergency food problems.

(b) to make more concessional sales of wheat to poor nations at below market prices while subsidizing Canadian producers? Canada has used a two-price system to benefit domestic producers and consumers. But Canada has yet to provide comparable advantages to the less developed states which purchase wheat.

(c) to increase the purchasing power of the poor countries by paying just prices for their exports? The prices Canada currently pays these nations for their commodity exports (e.g., tea, jute, coffee, cotton, bauxite) are generally not adequate to meet rising food prices and production costs.

(d) to provide more effective forms of agricultural assistance which will help developing countries to produce more food for their own peoples? Much of the assistance that is provided now does not meet the needs of the small farmer in these states.

(e) to increase the purchasing power of low-income Canadians, including small farmers and fishermen, by developing effective programs for the distribution of income in this country? Various proposals for a guaranteed income have been designed for this purpose.

(f) to break economic and cultural patterns which downgrade agriculture and drive farming families off the land? Present practices ignore fertile land which cannot be worked by large scale, capital-intensive machinery and methods. Is it not time to question the priority given to physically easy city jobs and to being a consumer? Is it not time to emphasize the personal and social values of creative physical work and primary production?

(g) to increase research studies on effective stewardship of the soil and the seas, and on balanced development of the rural and urban sectors of Canada?

CONCLUSION

20.   For our part, we say again that this statement of concern is only one step in a continuing process. As well, we want to join with other members of the Catholic community, fellow Christians, people of other faiths and fellow citizens in facing the challenges posed by the world food problem. Together as concerned Canadians, we should be able to develop more creative ways of sharing daily bread.

21.   Specifically, we recommend to pastors, families and small groups in the Church that the Holy Year of Reconciliation could be fittingly observed by a generous sharing of food and other goods. In the same spirit, the Year of Jubilee described in *Leviticus* called for communal sharing to eliminate social inequalities, as an acknowledgment that Almighty God is the author and giver of all goods.

22.   "For I was hungry..." Today's urgent cry for daily bread by most of humanity demands much more than statements of concern. Alternative living habits are necessary; fundamental social changes are imperative. For those of us who are Christian, our response will be a critical test of our faithfulness. What verdict will be rendered by suffering humanity and the Lord of history?

NOTES

1. Cf. note 1, Document 13, above. This and subsequent Labour Day Messages (the series ended in 1976) were approved by the Administrative Board of the Conference, second in authority only to the Plenary Assembly.

2. Cf. Third International Synod of Bishops, 1971, *Justice in the World*, Pt. II, *The Pope Speaks*, Washington, 1971, XVI, 381 ff.

3. Cf. *Prices and the Poor* (Ottawa, National Council of Welfare, April, 1974), pp. 6-7.

4. Cf. Lester R. Brown, *The Global Practices of Resource Scarcity* (Washington, D.C., 20036, U.S. Overseas Development Council).

5. Cf. Sirimavo Banderanaike, Secretary of State for Sri Lanka, to Special Session of the U.N. General Assembly, April 17, 1974.

6. Cf. *Preliminary Assessment of the World Food Situation: Present and Future*, Preparatory Committee of the U.N. World Food Conference, May, 1974.

7. Cf. Gn 41:25 ff.; Mk 6:35-44; 8:1-10; Is 58:6-8; Ac 2:42-47.

8. Cf. *Simplicity and Sharing*, Document 33 above.

9. Cf. J. Grand'Maison, *La seconde évangélisation* (Éditions Fides, Montréal, 1972) vol. II, 164-66.

10. Office of the Prime Minister, the Honourable Pierre Trudeau, Press Releases, Dec. 27, 1973; May 12, 1974.

11. Second Vatican Council, *The Church in the Modern World*, 1965, n. 69.

12. Paul VI, *The Development of Peoples*, 1967, n. 22, in *The Papal Encyclicals*, edit. Claudia Carlen, IHM (Wilmington, N.C., McGrath Publishing, 1971), V, 187, n. 22.

13. Quoted in Second Vatican Council, *ibid.* and cf. note 225 there; also Document 14 above, note 3.

14. Paul VI, *Message to Kurt Waldheim, Secretary-General of U.N. Organization, Osservatore Romano* (English edition), Vatican, April 4, 1974.

15. Cf. Edmondo Flores, "Why there is a Crisis" in *Ceres* (Unipub, Food and Agriculture Organization of the U.N., N.Y.), March-April, 1974, pp. 9-11. Two Canadian ecumenical coalitions, the Inter-Church Project on Population (ICPOP) and GATT-Fly, have also prepared position papers on related aspects of the food problem. These are available from GATT-Fly, 11 Madison Ave., Toronto, Ont., M5R 2S2.

16. Cf. Frances Lappe, "The World Food Problem", *Commonweal*, New York, vol. XCIX, n. 18, pp. 457 f.

17. Cf. Lester R. Brown and Erik P. Echolm, "The Empty Bread Basket", *Ceres*, March-April, 1974, p. 59; cf. note 14 above.

18. Frances Lappe, *ibid.*, p. 457; cf. note 15 above.

19. Statistics in *The Financial Post*, Toronto, July 21, 1973.

20. Chantier '74, *La Consommation*, 1974. Cf. Roger Lapointe, *Regard sur la société de consommation*, Éditions Fides, Montréal.

21. Adaptation for Canada of statistics cited by U.S. Senator Hubert Humphrey, *Center of Concern Newsletter*, Washington, 20017, June, 1974.

22. Cf. Julien Harvey, "L'homme de la consommation", *Relations*, Montréal, jan., 1974, pp. 16-18.

23. Cf. Barbara Ward, "A Kind of Sharing", *Development Forum*, United Nations, Geneva, July-August, 1974, reprinted in *Social Thought*, Canadian Catholic Conference, Ottawa, July-August, 1974.

24. Office of Hon. Eugene Whelan, Federal Minister of Agriculture, Ottawa; *Notes for an Address*, Aug. 8, 1974.

25. There have been U.S. Congressional studies of recent U.S. grain shipments to the U.S.S.R. A United Nations panel studying the operations of multinational corporations was requested to give special attention to the role of several grain corporations.

26. Cf. *Toronto Star*, Oct. 3, 1973, and the *Financial Times*, London, Jan. 9, 1974.

27. Cf. *The State of Food and Agriculture 1973*, Annual of Food and Agriculture Organization of U.N., Unipub, New York.

28. Cf. testimony of Lester R. Brown, of U.S. Overseas Development Council, Washington, to Rockefeller Commission on Critical Choices for Americans, cited by James Reston, *New York Times*, July 7, 1974.

29. *Ibid.*

Document 37

AN INVITATION TO WOMEN TO EXPLORE THEIR MISSION IN THE CHURCH

Author — The Assembly of the Canadian Catholic Conference, September 16-20, 1974

In preparation for the International Women's Year, 1975, the General Assembly of the Bishops of Canada offers to the women of Canada its respectful greetings.

In March of 1972, the Canadian Catholic Conference established a Committee on the Role of Women in the Church and Society. This Committee communicated with our Executive and Administrative Board on several occasions. The Assembly hereby expresses its thanks to the Committee and invites it to continue its work. In view of the recent development of episcopal regional structures, the latest report of the Committee has been transmitted to the regional level for more effective discussion and implementation. The local churches have been invited to follow this work actively and to send back their recommendations to us.

Due to the sociological context, members of both Church and society have failed in the past to recognize sufficiently the dignity and responsibility of women as members of the human family called to share equally in the mission of Christ. The acknowledgement of this situation and the desire to correct it according to the spirit of the Gospel,[1] represent a welcome sign of the times.[2]

The women of Canada are invited to participate with us in a nationwide effort to explore further their mission in the Church. Their talents, prayers and assistance are needed in leading the Church in Canada to a fuller appreciation of their role.

The whole Church requires the collaboration of all women. They in turn are assured of our intentions to work toward that kind of personal development and structural evolution which will enable the Church and society to reflect more fully the partnership of women and men in Christ's mission.

NOTES

1. Cf. Gal 3:28; Col 3:11.
2. Cf. Second Vatican Council, *Dogmatic Constitution on the Church*, 1964, n. 32; *The Church in the Modern World*, 1965, n. 29.

Document 38

TOWARDS SHARING NATIONAL INCOME

Author — The Executive Committee, the Canadian Catholic
Conference, May 22-23, 1975

In 1972, the Catholic Bishops of Canada called for a "Sharing
of National Income" in this country. We deplored the fact that "the
riches of Canada are unequally shared" and pointed out that "this
inequality which keeps so many people poor, is a social sin".[1]

On that occasion, we invited fellow Canadians "to accept the
social goal of an equitable distribution of income". As a matter of
principle, we maintained that "each Canadian should be assured
that level of income necessary for decent human living and full participation in society".[2]

From this standpoint, we welcome the recent initiatives of our
Federal and Provincial governments to draft legislation on guaranteed income. The proposed legislation outlines two programs. The
first is a scheme of direct payments to those people who are unable
to derive any income from normal work; the second is a program
of supplements for the working poor.

In general, we support these proposed legislative initiatives as
one step towards an equitable distribution of income in this country.
To be effective however, it is important that such legislation be oriented towards the goal of closing the income gap between the poorest
fifth and the wealthiest fifth of the Canadian population. At the same
time, it is imperative that the level of guaranteed income be adequate for a decent human living and full participation in Canadian
society.

In particular, we are encouraged by the attempt to introduce, for
the first time in this country, a program of income supplements for
the working poor. In recent years, the plight of the small farmer,

the small fisherman, the non-unionized labourer, the casual or the seasonal worker and others has been especially acute in the face of spiralling inflation.

We join with the other churches and community groups in asking our fellow members of the Catholic community in Canada:

a) to study these proposed governmental initiatives, federal and provincial, for a guaranteed income;

b) to express their concerns regarding these programs to our federal and provincial legislators;

c) to urge an early implementation, to offset the effects of inflation on the poor.

NOTES

1. Cf. *Sharing National Income*, Document 31, above.
2. *Ibid.*

Document 39

ON IMMIGRATION AND POPULATION POLICIES

Author — The Episcopal Commission for Social Affairs, July 11, 1975

Introduction

1. In the current debate about immigration and population policies, we are being asked in a general way what kind of future society we want. Difficult specific questions are being explored, about entry of immigrants, growth of cities and future total population size. Such questions touch some basic Christian concerns. We think it timely to discuss these and to invite reflection and action on them during the current debate.

Differing Viewpoints

2. An underlying question has to do with assuring a balance between available resources and the number of people. How one defines this situation is a matter of gravest importance. Quite different conclusions follow from the view that there are too many people than from the view that resources are inequitably distributed.

3. People migrate because they sense that they can do better somewhere else. Thousands from other countries come each year to Canada as a land of affluence and promise. Other thousands move from poorer outlying areas of this country to our metropolitan centres in search of a better share of our wealth. Migration, the movement of people either into this country or from place to place within

it, is one indication that there are inequalities and disparities of resources and opportunities.

4. While it is clear that God has distributed the riches of the earth according to a varied pattern, He intends the earth and all it contains for the use of every human being and people.[1] Therefore, we must always look most seriously at manmade differences between the few who hold and enjoy great wealth and power and the many who are deprived and destitute. "But if anyone has the world's goods and sees his brother in need, yet closes his heart against him, how does God's love abide in him?" (1 Jn 3:17) What then will be our response to people who wish to migrate to escape deprivation and to better their life chances?

Controlled Economy or Controlled People?

5. Recently Canadians have been pictured as opposed to controls on prices, wages and other elements of the economy. At the same time however, there is a preoccupation with the idea of controlling the number and movement of immigrants. What does this mean, if we seek to keep markets free and migrants controlled?

6. Fear of people seems to lie at the root of this willingness to limit or exclude newcomers. They are seen as competitors for jobs, goods and services, and so as threats to our present lifestyles and future aspirations. One reflex therefore, is to try to protect and maintain what we have by excluding others.

Building a New Society

7. The voices of the poor should give us pause. Within Canada and at the world level, there is a growing awareness that wealth is deliberately concentrated in some areas and in some hands to the neglect of others. Those who seek better opportunities by leaving the Atlantic provinces, or rural Quebec and Ontario, or the prairies, do so with full knowledge that the areas they leave could be better off and support more people. Likewise, on a world scale, there is a growing realization that manmade differences between overdeveloped and underdeveloped regions could be overcome. This is the basis of the *Declaration on the Establishment of a New Economic*

Order, adopted at the May 1974 Sixth Special Session of the United Nations General Assembly.

8.   Whether for Canada or for the world then the question is, who shall control and benefit from the world's resources? In the current debate, we should look to the building of a new economic order, domestically and internationally, when we consider what kind of future society we want. The amenities and attractions now concentrated in metropolitan areas could be shared with deprived outlying regions. Migration prompted by socio-economic disparities could be made unnecessary. A redistribution of wealth and not the control and exclusion of some people, could be made the goal towards which we plan and work.

Love, Not Fear

9.   Let us therefore strive to overcome fear of newcomers and strangers, whether from outside Canada or within it. As one step in rebuilding a just world, let us share with our sisters and brothers who are in greater need. So that God's love may abide in all of us, let us not fear to change our own lifestyles and our use and control of resources, so that created goods may be justly redistributed. Let us be active in telling members of parliament that we do not want restrictive and protectionist immigration and population policies. Let us pray that the kind of future society we build may be less scarred by greed and self-seeking and more marked by fraternity and sharing, by openness, hope and love.

NOTE

1. Leo XIII: "The earth, even though apportioned amongst private owners, ceases not thereby to minister to the needs of all." *The Condition of the Working Classes (Rerum Novarum)*, 1891, in *The Papel Encyclicals*, edit. Claudia Carlen (Wilmington, N.C., McGrath Publishing, 1981), II, 243, n. 8 (n. 7 in some editions).
    Pius XI: "... the vast differences between the few who hold excessive wealth and the many who live in destitution constitute a grave evil in modern society." *On Reconstructing the Social Order (Quadragesimo Anno)*, 1931, in Carlen above, III, 425, n. 38.
    Pius XII: "... the national economy... has no other end than to secure without

interruption the material conditions in which the individual life of the citizen may fully develop." *Pentecost Message, "On the Fiftieth Anniversary of Rerum Novarum"*, Catholic Mind, N.Y., 1941, XXXIX, June, p. 9.

John XXIII: "... the economic prosperity of a people should be measured not only in terms of its agregate wealth, but also and much more, in terms of real distribution of wealth according to the norms of justice." *Mother and Teacher*, in Carlen above, V, 67, n. 74.

The Second Vatican Council: "God intended the earth and all that it contains for the use of every human being and people." *The Church in the Modern World*, 1965, n. 69.

Paul VI: "All rights whatsoever, including those of property and of free commerce, are to be subjected to this principle." *The Development of Peoples*, in Carlen above, V, 187, n. 22.

Document 40

LABOUR DAY MESSAGE — 1975
NORTHERN DEVELOPMENT:
AT WHAT COST?

Author — Administrative Board, the Canadian Catholic Conference

I — INTRODUCTION

1. A cry for justice rings out today from the Native Peoples who inhabit the Canadian North. Dramatically, on a massive scale the Native Peoples of the North find themselves and their way of life threatened by the headlong search for new energy sources on this continent.

2. At the same time, other voices are raising serious ethical questions about the enormous demands for energy required to maintain high standards of wealth and comfort in industrial society. A variety of public interest groups are calling for greater care of the environment and responsible stewardship of the energy resources in this country.

3. We Catholic bishops of Canada want to echo these cries for justice and demands for stewardship in the Canadian North. They tell us much about ourselves as citizens and consumers, about the industrial society of North America, about the Native Peoples of the North. As Christians we cannot ignore the pressing ethical issues of northern development. For the living God, the God we worship, is the Lord of Creation and Justice.

4. We wish to share with you, fellow citizens, some reflections and

judgments on the ethical problems posed by the industrial development of the Canadian North.[1] We hope that these reflections and judgments will contribute to more public debate and stimulate alternative policies regarding the future development of the North. We also ask that these expressed concerns be tested in the public arena along with other points of view.

II — THE NORTHERN DILEMMA

5.   Since "time beyond memory", the vast land mass that covers the northern tips of our provinces and the sub-Arctic regions has been home for many of this country's Native Peoples, Indians, Inuit, Metis. Through time, these Native Peoples developed social, cultural, economic, and religious patterns of life which were in harmony with the rhythms of the land itself.[2]

6.   This land has been the source of livelihood for a significant portion of Northern Native Peoples, along with a number of early white settlers. It has been the basis of their traditional economy of hunting, fishing and trapping. For the Native Peoples the land is more than simply a source of food or cash. The land itself provides a permanent sense of security, well-being and identity. For generations this land has defined the basis of what the natives are as a people. In their own words, "Our land is our life".[3]

7.   After countless generations of occupation, use and care the Native Peoples of the North have come to claim their rights to these lands.[4] While some northern natives are giving up their life of hunting, fishing and trapping, these lands remain essential to their future economic development. For these northern lands are a natural storehouse of some of the most valuable resources on this continent, potential reserves of oil and natural gas, powerful river systems and rich mineral deposits.

8.   But now the "energy crisis" in the industrial world is posing a serious challenge to the people and resources of the northern lands. The search for new supplies of oil, gas and electricity on this continent is largely focused on the untapped energy resources of the Canadian North.

9. In recent years, provincial governments, crown corporations and private companies have been planning large scale projects to harness the power potential of the northern rivers. Dams, power plants, railroads and highways are now under construction in several provinces:

— the James Bay hydro project in northern Quebec;

— the Churchill-Nelson hydro development in northern Manitoba;

— the Churchill Falls hydro project in Labrador;

— the hydroelectric plants in northwest British Columbia.

10. Simultaneously, the Canadian North has been sighted as a major region for potential reserves of oil and gas. Assisted by the federal government, the giants of the oil industry, Exxon, Shell, Gulf, Mobil, Sunoco and others have led the way, through their Canadian subsidiaries, in making discoveries and initiating plans to build several major industrial projects: [5]

— the Mackenzie Valley pipeline in the Northwest Territories to bring natural gas from Alaska and the Canadian arctic to southern Canada and the United States;

— the Polar Gas pipeline designed to bring natural gas from the high arctic to the Maritimes and the United States;

— the Syncrude project to develop the Athabaska tar sands in northern Alberta.

11. In this way the Canadian North is fast becoming centre stage in a continental struggle to gain control of new energy sources. The critical issue is how these northern energy resources are to be developed, by whom and for whom. We are especially concerned that the future of the North not be determined by colonial patterns of development, wherein a powerful few end up controlling both the people and the resources.

12. Some present examples of industrial planning give us cause for grave concern. [6] For what we see emerging in the Canadian North are forms of exploitation which we often assume happen only in Third World countries: a serious abuse of both the Native Peoples and the energy resources of the North. [7] Herein lies the Northern

dilemma. What has been described as the "last frontier" in the building of this nation may become our own Third World.

III — DEMANDS FOR JUSTICE

13.   Our first pastoral concern is that justice be done in the future industrial development of the Canadian North. In various parts of the northern lands the Native Peoples' protests have drawn attention to a series of injustices.

(a) In several cases, governments and corporations have secretly planned and suddenly announced the construction of large industrial projects without prior consultation with the people who will be most directly affected.[8] As a result, the future lives of these Native Peoples and their communities tend to be planned for them by southern interests.

(b) The plans for these industrial projects are usually finalized and implemented before land claim settlements have been reached with the Native People of the region.[9] Yet, for people whose land is their life, and who wish to secure control over their future economic development, a just settlement of their land claims lies at the very heart of their struggle for justice.

(c) The construction of these industrial projects has sometimes proceeded without an adequate assessment of their environmental and social consequences. In several instances, the building of power plants and hydro dams will cause the flooding of vast areas of land, damage to the vegetation and wildlife, and the relocation of whole communities of people whose lives have traditionally depended on hunting, fishing and trapping.[10]

(d) The promise of jobs in the construction of these industrial projects has offered no real alternative way of life. For most of the Native Peoples, these jobs are temporary, paying relatively low wages for low-skilled labour.[11]

14.   As a result, more and more Native Peoples are being compelled to give up their land-based economy and move into urban centres where alcoholism and welfarism have become prevalent for many. While compensation may be offered, money can hardly replace the loss of land and what it means to the lives of the Native Peoples and their future economic development.

15. A sense of justice, coming from the living God, tells us there are better ways of developing the resources of the Canadian North. The Lord of Creation has given mankind the responsibility to develop the resources of nature, so as to make possible a fuller human life for all peoples.[12] This coincides with the beliefs of the Native Peoples who have traditionally called for a communal sharing of the land which belongs to the Creator.

16. To develop the resources of the Canadian North is a responsibility to be shared by all who live in this country, North and South. While Native Peoples in the North must be prepared to share in this responsibility, they rightly demand that their claims to justice be recognized. In the words of one northern native leader:

> We also want to participate in Canadian society but we want to participate as equals. It is impossible to be equal if our economic development is subordinated to the profit oriented priorities of the American multi-nationals... The Native People are saying we must have a large degree of control over our own economic development. Without control we will end up like our brothers and sisters on the reserves in the South: continually powerless, threatened and impoverished.[13]

17. Across the Canadian North Native Peoples' groups have begun to articulate a common program for justice.[14] Their goal is greater control over their own economic development. The key is a just settlement of their land claims. In recent years, native groups have been taking the land issue into the courtrooms to establish their traditional rights to these lands.

18. The living God calls on us to respond to these demands for justice. Christian love of neighbour and justice cannot be separated in the development of people. "For love implies an absolute demand for justice, namely a recognition of the dignity and rights of one's neighbour."[15]

IV — DEMANDS FOR STEWARDSHIP

19. A second pastoral concern is the demand for responsible stewardship of energy resources in the development of the Canadian North. Throughout this country, public interest groups are raising

serious questions about our highly industrialized society and the current exploitation of northern energy resources.

(a) The scramble for northern energy continues without adequate measures to regulate the patterns of relentless consumption in this country. In the last twenty-five years alone, Canada's consumption of oil, gas and electricity has multiplied three times over.[16] This extravagant consumption of energy generates increasing demands for the rapid development of northern resources.

(b) Northern development is also continuing without full public discussion of future energy needs. Governments and industries predict that Canada's energy needs will have to multiply by four by the end of this century, to maintain "a high quality of life".[17] But what is this "quality of life" and who determines what these future energy needs should be?

(c) The reasons for rapidly developing northern energy resources on such a massive scale at this time have also been seriously questioned.[18] While the sale of these resources will bring large profits for the energy industry now, it may also cause the rapid depletion of non-renewable supplies of oil and gas required for the future.

(d) In several cases, this energy is being rapidly developed now to feed the industrial centres of the United States.[19] Yet there are many other countries, especially poor nations of the Third World, that are suffering from acute shortages of energy required for basic survival.

20.   The United States and Canada are ranked as the highest users of energy in the world today. For these two countries, containing little more than 6.5% of the world's population, consume about 43% of the energy supplies of this planet.[20] All this energy goes to run the countless number of machines which have become "our energy slaves" in industries, businesses and homes. It is now estimated that, given the amount of muscular power required to do the work of these machines, each North American has the equivalent of four hundred "energy slaves" working for him.[21]

21.   We North Americans have created a highly industrialized society that places exorbitant demands on limited supplies of energy. The maximization of consumption, profit and power has become the operating principle of this society. These are the driving forces

behind the present continental struggle to gain control of northern energy resources.[22] These are the idols which turn many from service of man and the world and so from service of the living God.

22.   As a culture, we have not faced up to the fact that the world God created has its limits. Many voices now warn that mankind has reached a turning point in history: crucial decisions must be made now to stop plundering the Earth's non-renewable resources before it is too late.[23] Yet this industrialized society treats the resources of the earth as if they were limitless.

23.   In recent years, public interest groups have been calling for responsible stewardship of northern energy resources. They are calling for more effective measures to reduce levels of consumption and waste and preserve non-renewable resources. These groups contend that future resource development, which is largely controlled today by multinational corporations, must be made more accountable to the Canadian public.

24.   The living God calls us to a life of caring, sparing, sharing the limited resources of this planet.[24] This is no longer simply a moral imperative. It has also become a practical necessity for the survival of our common humanity.[25]

V — NORTHERN ALTERNATIVES

25.   We readily acknowledge that the Catholic Church must also take a critical look at itself. We now see that coming from another culture, the Church may have contributed to disruptive changes in Native culture while helping to bring Christianity to the North through the creative efforts of missionaries who have shared the hard lives of the people. At the same time, the Church has participated with others in the wealth and comfort of an industrial society which places enormous demands on energy resources at the expense of other people.

26.   We look to the past in order that we may learn to act more responsibly in the present. The present industrial development of the Canadian North poses new challenges for the Church. Some of our northern dioceses have been re-evaluating their missionary work

in the light of these challenges.[26] But the responsibility lies with all of us who comprise the Church in Canada.

27.   We believe that the Spirit is challenging the whole Church to fulfill its prophetic service in society today. As the Third Synod of Bishops asserted in 1971:

> Action on behalf of justice and participation in the transformation of the world fully appear to us as a constitutive dimension of the preaching of the Gospel, in other words, of the Church's mission for the redemption of the human race and its liberation from every oppressive situation.[27]

28.   We contend therefore, that there are better ways of developing the Canadian North. What is required today is a public search for alternative policies for northern development. This search is already under way through the activities of Native Peoples and public interest groups across the country.[28]

29.   We find ourselves in solidarity with many of these initiatives. based on the ethical principles of social justice and responsible stewardship, we believe that the following conditions must be met before any final decisions are made to proceed with specific projects for northern development:

(a) sufficient public discussion and debate about proposed industrial projects, based on independent studies of energy needs and social costs of the proposed developments;

(b) achievement of a just land settlement with the Native Peoples, including hunting, fishing and trapping rights and fair royalties in return for the extraction of valuable resources from their land claims;

(c) effective participation by the Native Peoples in shaping the kind of regional development, beginning with effective control over their own future economic development;

(d) adequate measures to protect the terrain, vegetation, wildlife and waters of northern areas, based on complete and independent studies of the regional environment to be affected by proposed developments;

(e) adequate controls to regulate the extraction of energy resources from the North, to prevent the rapid depletion of oil, gas and other resources which are non-renewable.

30. It remains to be seen whether Canada's "last frontier" will be developed according to the principles of justice and stewardship. The next two years will be a crucial testing period. In some cases, final and irreversible decisions have already been made. In other instances, there may still be a chance to alter the course of development. The Mackenzie Valley pipeline proposals presently being reviewed by the Berger Commission and the National Energy Board could provide the real test.

31. As Christians, as citizens, we have a responsibility to insist that the future development of the Canadian North be based on social justice and responsible stewardship. As responsible citizens are we prepared:

(a) to study one or more of the industrial projects in the northern parts of our provinces or the Territories?

(b) actively to support Native Peoples' organizations and public interest groups currently striving to change the policies of northern development?

(c) to engage policy makers, both federal and provincial, and local members of parliament in a public dialogue about the ethical issues of northern development?

(d) to raise ethical questions about corporations involved in northern development, especially those corporations in which Church institutions may have shares?

(e) to seek a just settlement regarding specific church landholdings that are subject to native claims?

(f) to design education programs, to examine personal life styles and to change the patterns of wasteful energy consumption in our homes, churches, schools and places of work?

(g) to collaborate with the other Canadian churches, in every way possible, in a common Christian effort to achieve the above objectives?

32. In the final analysis what is required is nothing less than fundamental social change. Until we as a society begin to change our

own lifestyles based on wealth and comfort, until we begin to change the profit oriented priorities of our industrial system, we will continue placing exorbitant demands on the limited supplies of energy in the North and end up exploiting the people of the North in order to get those resources.

VI — CONCLUSION

33. We wish to emphasize that this message is only one step in the continuing struggle for justice and stewardship in the Canadian North. For our part, we want to join with other members of the Catholic community, our fellow Christians, members of other faiths and our fellow citizens. Together we may be able to act in solidarity with the Native Peoples of the North, in a common search for more creative ways of developing the "last frontier" of this country.

34. Ultimately, the challenge before us is a test of our faithfulness to the living God. For we believe that the struggle for justice and responsible stewardship in the North today, like that in distant Third World countries, is the voice of the Lord among us. We are called to involve ourselves in these struggles, to become active at the very centre of human history where the great voice of God cries out for the fullness of life.

NOTES

1. These reflections and judgments are based on a variety of consultations and conversations with people concerned with the future development of the Canadian North. See in particular a recent work by Louis-Edmond Hamelin, *Nordicité Canadienne* (Montréal, H.M.H., 1975).
2. Cf. Éric Gourdeau, "The People of the Canadian North" and "Impressions of the Land", *Arctic Alternatives*, Ottawa, Canadian Arctic Resources Committee, 1973.
3. The particular phrase is the title of a documentary produced by the National Film Board and a direct quotation from the Cree Indian people of the Mistassini area of Northern Quebec. Variations of this theme are frequently expressed by Native Peoples throughout the North.
4. Cf. Lloyd Barber, "The Basis for Native Claims in Canada", address to the Rotary Club, Yellowknife, NWT, October, 1974. Mr. Barber is the Indian Claims Com-

missioner for Canada. See also René Fumoleau, OMI, *As Long as this Land Shall Last* (Toronto, McClelland and Stewart, 1975).

5. Cf. Wade Rowland, *Fueling Canada's Future* (Toronto, Macmillan of Canada, 1974), chap. 2.

6. This concern was expressed in a letter to Premier Bourrassa (July 11, 1973) by Maurice Cardinal Roy, President of the Assembly of the Bishops of Quebec, Cf. *La Justice Sociale,* édit. G. Rochais (Montréal, Éditions Bellarmin, 1984), p. 84.

7. Cf. two comparative articles, *Whose Development: the Impact of Development on the Native Peoples of Canada and Brazil,* and *What Price Development: Foreign Investment and Resources Extraction in British Columbia and Jamaica.* Both are available from the Inter-Church Committee for World Development Education, 85 St. Clair Ave. East, Toronto, M4T 1M8.

8. Cf. *L'Aménagement de la Baie James: progrès ou désastre?* (Montréal, Le Comité pour la défense de la Baie James); *The Churchill Diversion: Time Runs out for the Native People of the North* (Ottawa, Canadian Association in Support of Native Peoples); *Northwest Development: What and for Whom?* (Terrace, B.C., The Northwest British Columbia Conference Committee).

9. This has been the case with most of the major energy projects in the North to date. A land settlement is currently being negotiated with the Native People of the James Bay region, but these negotiations are taking place after the basic industrial plans have been established.

10. For example, the natives of Nelson House Reserve and South Indian Lake in northern Manitoba face serious problems of flooding. Cf. "Northern Manitoba: The Project and the People", *Bulletin,* Canadian Association in Support of Native Peoples, Ottawa, December, 1974.

11. For example, during the construction of the Pointed Mountain Pipeline in the Territories, only 30 native people were employed for a maximum of three months, while 320 workers were brought in from the south. In 1970, after the federal government has invested $9 million in Panarctic, it has employed only 6 natives at $1.75 an hour. Cf. Melvin Watkins, "Resources and Underdevelopment" in *Canada Ltd.,* ed. Robert M. Laxer (Toronto, McClelland & Stewart, 1973).

12. Second Vatican Council, *The Church in the Modern World,* 1965, n. 69; Paul VI, *The Development of Peoples,* 1967, *The Papal Encyclicals.* edit. Claudia Carlen, IHM (Wilmington, N.C., McGrath Publishing, 1981), V, 187, n. 22.

13. James Wash-shee, President, Indian Brotherhood of the Northwest Territories, cited in the Brotherhood's initial submission to the Berger Inquiry, 1975.

14. Cf. George Manuel and Michael Poslun, *The Fourth World* (Toronto, Collier Macmillan, 1974).

15. Third International Synod of Bishops, 1971, *Justice in the World,* P. II; cf. *The Pope Speaks,* Washington, 1971. XVI, 382.

16. Cf. *An Energy Policy for Canada: Phase I* (Ottawa, Department of Energy, Mines and Resources, 1973).

17. *Ibid.,* vol. 1, p. 11.

18. Cf. for example, Wade Rowland *op. cit.,* above note 5; *Gas from the Mackenzie Delta: Now or Later* (Ottawa, Canadian Arctic Resources Committee); James Laxer, *Canada's Energy Crisis: Background Statement on the Arctic,* Pollution Probe, University of Toronto, March 28, 1972, revised April 12, 1972.

19. Cf. Rowland, *op. cit.,* p. 44.

20. From statistics provided by Meadows *et. al.* in *The Limits to Growth,* Report for the Club of Rome's Project on the Predicament of Mankind (New York, New American Library, 1972).

21. Cf. Barbara Ward and René Dubois, *Only One Earth* (England, Penguin Books, 1972), p. 44.

22. Cf. Ivan Illich, *Energy and Equity*, (New York, Harper-Row, 1974).

23. Cf. Mihajlo Mesarovic and Eduard Pestel, *Mankind at the Turning Point*, the Second Report to the Club of Rome (New York, New American Library, 1976).

24. Cf. *Simplicity and Sharing*, Document 33 above, n. 5. Cf. also Thomas S. Derr, *Écologie et Libération Humaine* (Genève, Éditions Labor et Fides, 1974).

25. *Development Demands Justice*, Document 34 above.

26. *The Religious Situation of the Canadian Native People*, Canadian Oblate Conference, Nov. 1971, 153 Laurier Ave. East, Ottawa, K1N 6N8.

27. Third International Synod of Bishops, 1971, *Justice in the World*, Introduction; cf. *The Pope Speaks*, Washington, 1971, XVI, 377.

28. For detailed information cf. *Resource Kit on Northern Development*, Social Affairs Commission, the Canadian Conference of Catholic Bishops, 90 Parent Ave., Ottawa, K1N 7B1.

Document 41

ON IMMIGRATION POLICY
To the Special Joint Committee
of the Senate and of the House of Commons

Author — The Canadian Catholic Conference, September 15, 1975

I — INTRODUCTION

1. This brief is submitted as a contribution to the public opinion upon which you are to report to Parliament. As we understand your mandate, you are exploring what kind of society we want for the future. The Hon. R.K. Andras has pointed out that this far-reaching question underlies the Government's more specific inquiry into Canadian views about immigration and population policies. While there will be other stages in this public discussion, your report will have a central role in shaping subsequent discussion. For this reason we want to add our contribution to the other viewpoints that you are hearing and weighing.

2. Our brief will reflect the way we understand God's Word and the social teachings of the Church. From this starting point, we hold that migration is a right not merely a privilege. As Pope John XXIII said in his letter *Peace on Earth* (1963), every human being must have the right to freedom of movement and of residence at home, and for just reasons, the right to emigrate to other countries and take up residence there. For the fact that one is a citizen of a particular state does not detract in any way from membership in the human family, nor from citizenship in the world community and common ties with all persons.[1] Thus we see today that we are all called more and more to become a people without frontiers. Migrants therefore,

whether they move within Canada or come from beyond our shores, have a right to be received not as strangers but as sisters and brothers, with respect for their nationality and their own culture, and with no discrimination, whether based on race or social or economic condition.[2]

3. In particular our brief will further develop the basic principles outlined in the July *Statement on Immigration and Population Policies* of our Episcopal Commission for Social Affairs. As expressed there, one of our major concerns is that immigration policies for the future be approached as an aspect of overall planning for the redistribution of power and wealth, opportunities and amenities. For the essential motive of migration is the search for better life chances. People are prompted to migrate to Canada and within this country, largely because they experience socio-economic disparities. Thus the redistribution of wealth, not the control or exclusion of people, is the long range goal towards which we should aim in building the kind of future society we want.

4. In this spirit then, we shall offer our views as pastors and citizens. Much of our information about the current debate has come through our participation in the Inter-Church Project on Population. We also draw on what we have learned from the news media, the Minutes of your committee and other related sources.

II — REVIEW OF DEBATE

5. Potentially, the current discussion about immigration and population policies could occasion a great upsurge of creative thinking about the future. It seems from what they say that this is what people really want. People worry that the times are somehow out of joint. They express increasing concern that if creative new steps are not taken, the lot of future generations will be bleak indeed. But if there is this deep longing for fresh thinking, is it being satisfied in the current discussion? To date it does not seem so, and several explanations for this can be suggested.

6. During your cross-country hearings, members of your committee frequently emphasized that the government's Green Paper is only a discussion starter, not a policy statement. Yet the Green Paper

has become the predominant factor in defining the situation for this debate and so limiting it. People have tended to agree or disagree with the Green Paper, but hardly ever to go beyond it. Like the Green Paper itself, this debate has rarely looked beyond Canada's present or recent immigration laws and regulations, or those of some comparable nation. Those who have been identified and given special place as experts on immigration policies have discussed details of familiar concepts more frequently than they have explored new ones.[3] There has been a marked lack of critical analysis of popular assumptions and conventional opinions and a distinct scarcity of proposals for alternative perspectives. Past and present experience seems thus to stifle any imagination that might give rise to new approaches.

7.   This tendency, which in a general way characterizes both the briefs you heard and the questions your committee posed to witnesses, has been reinforced by the news media, which seem to have been less than industrious about seeking out views other than those immediately generated by the Green Paper.[4]

8.   For all its importance for the future, this then is a debate that so far has remained largely boxed into its initial framework. It is one of your responsibilities to try to take it beyond such limits. In particular, we hope you will see your task as more than just proposing details of a new Immigration Act that seems suited for today's conditions in Canada. These conditions themselves must be rigorously examined for the sake of the future that is to be built. As a contribution to this, our brief will have more to say about today's conditions than about details of a new Immigration Act.

9.   Such a new Act in turn, must not be written and administered as an instrument of Canadian self-interest and protectionism. Rather let us make it an expression of our increasing openness and generosity, especially towards those immigrants and refugees who are the most deprived and in need of our solidarity and assistance. To this end, we affirm many of the suggestions you have received in other briefs, from churches and other groups, especially to separate immigration and manpower issues, to develop a clear and open policy on refugees and to assure that there be no discrimination of any kind in practice as in principle.

III — RECOMMENDATIONS

10. Our recommendations have to do with the operating assumptions of your final report to Parliament. We are especially concerned that your report reach beyond the limited framework of the Green Paper to seek out fresh approaches to the issues of migration and the building of a future society. Towards the writing of your final report, we have three sets of recommendations to offer. It should (A) dispel some popular myths about migration; (B) clarify the basic causes of migration; (C) contribute to goals for building a new society.

A. *Migration: Popular Myths*

11. The current debate about immigration in Canada has given popularity to a number of myths. These myths foster the idea that migration, the movement of people, is a major cause of all our social problems. The immigrant therefore, tends to be made the scapegoat of our social ills. In part, these myths were fostered by the operating assumptions of the Green Paper. At the same time the news media have played a large role in popularizing them. Your Committee, in your report to parliament, has a major responsibility to dispel and reject the following myths about migration:

1) that migration of peoples can be singled out as a significant cause of such problems as urban crowding, housing shortages, traffic congestion, pollution, etc. The primary causes of these problems are to be found in industrial strategies, land-holding systems, the money market, planned obsolescence, the promotion of consumption, etc. They will never be solved by efforts to control movements of people;

2) that increasing immigration is turning Canada into a racist society. This is a myth in the sense that the roots of racism are far deeper than present patterns of immigration. The exclusion of strangers will not eliminate selfishness and hatred, nor put an end to covert racial discrimination that is an expression of these;

3) that immigration explains rising unemployment in Canada. Cyclical patterns of unemployment have to do with industrial planning in this country and our failure to establish and maintain a stable and equitable economy;

4) that future immigration will cause a rapid depletion of Canada's valuable resources. The major causes of resource depletion lie elsewhere: in our industrial policies, in corporate production and marketing practices, and in our affluent consumption habits.

B. *Migration: Basic Causes*

12. The current immigration debate has either confused or neglected the real causes of migration. There has been a pronounced tendency to look only at the impact of migration on other social factors. As a result of such one-direction analysis, much attention is directed to the "effects" of migration but almost none to its causes. Neither the Green Paper nor the media have done much to identify and clarify the primary causes of migration. The question of what motivates people to move is of central importance to the study of immigration policies. We believe that the Committee has a major responsibility to set forth the primary causes of immigration.

13. We therefore recommend that your Report to Parliament start from a study of migration within Canada in order to understand the primary causes of immigration into this country. Thus it will be seen:

1) that people move primarily because they see their situation as one of need, deprivation and poverty. That is, people migrate because they sense they can do better somewhere else. People move in search of greater access to the necessities and opportunities of life;

2) that migration within Canada primarily reflects regional disparities and rural underdevelopment. People move from the hinterland and rural areas of Canada to the metropolitan centres where wealth and opportunities have been overly concentrated by political and economic decision-makers;

3) that immigration to Canada is largely caused by persistence of poverty, underdevelopment and oppression elsewhere in the world. Refugees flee oppression and danger. Immigrants come to escape conditions of poverty and exploitation in search of their fair share of opportunities and wealth;

4) that domestic and global industrial strategies both plan and exploit the socio-economic imbalances and inequalities that induce

people to migrate. One example has been the promotion of immigration from depressed areas in order to make low-cost labour available in other areas;

5) that it is not particularly fruitful to take the view that immigration is primarily the result of overpopulation, surplus people, elsewhere in the world. Such a view is at odds with the position taken at the 1974 World Population Conference by many Third World delegations. They held that their social ills, which motivate migration, should be seen as stemming from the rich-poor gap, from deprivation and underdevelopment. This view is reinforced if the causes of migration within Canada are taken as a basis for understanding immigration into this country.

C. *Migration: New Approaches*

14.   The current immigration debate has given expression to various responses concerning the question of what kind of society we want to become. The debate has shown people to be frustrated over a host of societal problems. Underlying most of these problems is the sense of deprivation, poverty and powerlessness arising out of the inequitable distribution of resources within Canada and throughout the world.

15.   Immigration law reform will not really touch these problems. What is required is the creation of a new social order in Canada and the world, based on a redistribution of wealth and power for the sake of justice and peace. This implies among other things that, "wherever possible, the work to be done should be taken to the workers, not vice versa."[5] Your committee has a major responsibility to address these concerns.

16.   We therefore recommend that your report to Parliament emphasize the following objectives regarding the future of Canadian society:

1) that humanitarian values be given primacy over economic ones as a basis for future societal goals oriented toward the full development of peoples at home and in the world;

2) that immigration policies for the future be approached as an aspect of overall planning for the redistribution of wealth and power in Canada and the world at large;

3) that present patterns of urbanization, whereby two-thirds of Canada's population are concentrated in three or four metropolitan centres, be seen as neither inevitable nor irreversible;

4) that creative industrial strategies can and must be designed for the purpose of overcoming regional disparities and rural underdevelopment in Canada;

5) that this country's governments, corporations and all citizens undertake a greater responsibility for creating a New International Economic Order.

IV — CONCLUSION

17. We believe it possible to conclude that you can rightly reach beyond a narrow definition of the mandate you have from Parliament. Despite the fact that many witnesses discussed immigration only in a narrow and technical way, you heard ample testimony to conclude that what's wrong in this country is not an excess of immigrants. Conversely, you have heard considerable opinion that the management or restriction of immigration will have little to do with the difficulties we do have. Specifically, immigration curbs and controls will not solve unemployment, metropolitan congestion, housing shortages, loss of arable land, or damage to the environment. These conditions are signs of sinful greed and selfishness, of thoughtlessness, carelessness and mismanagement.

18. We urge you, instead of designing a legal stockade to keep Canada as it is, to aim at contributing to a global policy intended to help move all peoples to full realization of their capacities and worth as persons.

19. In this spririt, the content and application of a new Immigration Act for Canada should be based on generosity and openness, especially towards the most deprived and oppressed families and individuals who come to us as immigrants or refugees. This implies that you add your influential voices to a call for personal and collective change of heart and fundamental changes in structures and systems, so that human relations can be normalized in justice and fraternity.

20. As economist Barbara Ward has written: "To live simply, to love greatly, to give without stinting, to see a brother in all mankind — this is no longer a remote theory of ethical behaviour. It is the inescapable recipe of planetary survival".[6] To put such a challenge to the Parliament and people of this country is the only fitting conclusion to your summer's work.

NOTES

1. Cf. *The Papal Encyclicals,* edit. Claudia Carlen, IHM (Wilmington, N.C., McGrath Publishing, 1981), V, 109, n. 25.

2. Cf. Second Vatican Council, *The Church in the Modern World,* 1965, nn. 29; 60-66.

3. For example, we disagree with the view that the Green Paper contains "the full range of policy issues which need to be discussed". Cf. Freda Hawkins, "Review of the Green Paper on Immigration", *Social Sciences in Canada,* Ottawa, Vol. 3, 1975, n. 1-2, p. 30.

4. Cf. "There Was a Time When Strangers Were Welcome Here", Canadian Newssynthesis Project, Toronto, July, 1975.

5. John XXIII, *ibid.* in Carlen above, note 1, p. 118, n. 102.

6. *Our Sunday Visitor,* Huntington, IN., U.S.A., Dec. 3, 1972. For Canadian reactions to this statement, cf. *Public Consultation on Population Questions,* Canadian Institute of International Affairs, Toronto, (in cooperation with the Family Planning Federation of Canada and the Inter-Church Project on Population), May, 1974; "The Social Justice Approach", p. 16; "Population and Social Justice", pp. 19-21; "The Social Justice View", pp. 28 f.

Document 42

JUSTICE DEMANDS ACTION

Author — Canadian Church Leaders to the Prime Minister and
Federal Cabinet, March 2, 1976[1]

INTRODUCTION

1. We thank you for this opportunity to share with you our concern for justice on issues of pressing importance. This occasion has
special significance for us because it is the first time we have had
the opportunity to speak with the Prime Minister and a number of
Cabinet Ministers at the same time. Although we have a responsibility to minister to the personal needs of individuals, we are here
today to express our pastoral concerns for justice in Canada and
throughout the world.

2. We stand in the biblical tradition of the prophets where to know
God is to seek justice for the poor and the oppressed. (Jr 22:16) As
leaders of the Christian church in Canada we are conscious of our
responsibility to give witness to God's concern for justice. The
church cannot remain silent on the political and social issues of the
day if it is to claim obedience to Christ and His message of "good
news to the poor". (Lk 4:18)

BACKGROUND

3. This is not the first time that the Canadian churches have taken
a united stand on issues of social justice. Our recent history of common action can be traced from the 1968 National Poverty Conference
in Montreal. At that time the participants confirmed the view that

the causes of poverty are rooted in the economic order and the churches made a commitment to work together for a more just society. As an expression of this commitment, the Canadian churches sent a team of observers in 1972 to the third United Nations Conference on Trade and Development (UNCTAD) in Santiago, Chile. They raised serious questions about the efforts of the government of Canada at closing the gap between rich and poor nations. In March of 1973, in conjunction with Ten Days for World Development, the churches presented a brief to Cabinet entitled *Development Demands Justice* which said in part:

> The world's poor, including the poor in Canada, are outraged by the growing gap between themselves and the rich. They are demanding justice — not charity; the dignity of self-determination — not continuing dependency.[2]

4. Since 1973 the churches have developed a common programme of action on:

— issues concerning population and immigration through the Inter-Church Project on Population;

— issues about refugee policy through the Inter-Church Project on Chile;

— issues of Native Rights and Northern Development through Project North;

— issues concerning world hunger and the New International Economic Order through the GATT-Fly project;

— the issue of a Guaranteed Annual Income through the social action programmes of each of the denominations;

— issues concerning the social responsibility of corporations through the Taskforce on the Churches and Corporate Responsibility;

— public education concerning development through the Ten Days for World Development programme.

These projects have deepened our understanding of the issues, formulated alternative policy recommendations and implemented educational programmes among church members and the public at large.

5. Our experience has revealed many hopeful signs, especially

among the many diverse groups that are struggling against injustice and for a more just sharing of power and wealth. But our experience has also taught us that all too often the power of large corporations and governments is exercised in a way which, in practice, impedes the legitimate struggles of people for the changes necessary to bring about a more just economic and social order.

6.   The continuing existence and even the growth of disparities between the rich and the poor stands in judgment of the present economic order and those who control it for their own benefit. As Canadian churches we must confess our own participation in the fruits of injustice. We ask God's forgiveness. We must continue to see our responsibility as working at the side of the victims of injustice.

JUSTICE DEMANDS ACTION

7.   Social justice concerns the distribution of wealth and power. The basic question is, ''Who shall control and benefit from the earth's natural resources?'' Will they be used to enrich a minority as in the colonial model of development? Or will resources be used to meet the unfulfilled needs of the majority of mankind for adequate food, shelter, health care, education and employment necessary for a fully human life?

8.   The present economic order is characterized by the maldistribution of wealth and the control of resources by a small minority. In the Third World this order emerges from a history of colonialism. In Canada, in the words of the Senate Committee on Poverty, ''the economic system in which most Canadians prosper is the same system which creates poverty.''[3] In both Canada and the Third World powerful corporations are planning the use of natural resources without the participation of the people who are most directly affected. Governments in the First, Second and Third Worlds often do not exercise their responsibility to protect people from these abuses of power. The human consequences of the present order are dependency, loss of human dignity, poverty and even starvation.

9.   Today oppressed peoples are demanding an alternative to the present unjust order. The Third World is demanding a new international economic order which would enable them to pursue more

self-reliant modes of development where resource use is planned to meet basic human needs. Canada's native peoples are demanding that future development in the North not be determined by colonial patterns of development wherein a powerful few end up controlling both the people and the resources.

10.   In response to the demands of poor and oppressed peoples for justice we are proposing a series of policy recommendations for government action. At the outset, we stress that these recommendations in themselves will not bring about a new order based on social justice and human needs. The creation of such an order can only be achieved with the participation of the people themselves. Nevertheless we believe that these recommendations constitute politically feasible steps to remove obstacles to the achievement of a just distribution of wealth and power.

I — International Development

11.   The reforms of the international trade and payments system called for in the United Nations Declaration on the Establishment of a New International Economic Order are important not because in themselves they constitute a blueprint for self-reliant development, but because they provide a context in which countries with a will to do so can more easily re-orient their domestic economy to meeting the basic needs of their population.[4] At UNCTAD IV, we believe that Canada is in a position to take important initiatives in the area of commodity trade and the debt problems of the developing countries.

Commodity Trade

12.   Development planning continues to be hampered by the instability and decline of real export earnings of developing countries. In 1975 alone the industrial world gained $7.5 billion from the fall in the real value of the export earnings of developing countries which are not oil producers.

13.   At UNCTAD IV, we urge Canada to co-operate in establishing an integrated programme for commodity trade by:

a. offering to contribute to the common fund for establishing buffer stocks;

b. agreeing that the improvement of the real value of the export earnings of developing countries should be the aim of commodity agreements whatever the technical difficulties involved;

c. agreeing to establish more liberal and more automatic compensatory financing measures, as a supplement to commodity arrangements, especially for commodity-importing developing countries.

Debt Relief

14. For developing countries, the burden of making payments on their external debts now cancels out about half the value of new assistance they receive each year. Furthermore, creditor nations and institutions can too easily impose conditions on debtor nations that may prevent them from pursuing independent, self-reliant modes of development.

15. At UNCTAD IV we urge Canada:

a. to announce the cancellation of the official development debts of the poorest and "Most Seriously Affected" countries;

b. to accept a moratorium on the collection of debts from other developing countries;

c. to support the establishment of an International Bank for Debt Redemption to allow for the consolidation and automatic rescheduling of the debts of all developing countries, without the onerous conditions on refinancing imposed by the International Monetary Fund;

d. to participate in any United Nations Conference on debt requested by the developing countries.

II — Transnational Corporations

16. The federal government has a role to play in seeing that Canada-based transnational corporations or enterprises exercise social responsibility through their operations in other countries as well as in Canada. In particular we maintain that federal government should discourage investments by Canada-based corporations in countries which flagrantly violate human rights. For the partnership between Canada-based corporations and repressive govern-

ments of other countries means that natural resources are continually exploited without the participation of, and benefit to, the people most affected.

17.   As examples, we draw attention to the operations of Falconbridge Nickel Mines in Namibia and Noranda Mines Ltd. in Chile. When we recall the civil liberties and democratic freedoms that exist in Canada, we are greatly disturbed that the operations of these corporations in Namibia and Chile do not respect such fundamental rights as the freedom of workers to organize unions of their choice. Canada has supported United Nations resolutions condemning the denial of human rights in Chile. Canada has also condemned *apartheid* in South Africa and accepted the Security Council's ruling on the illegality of South Africa's occupation of Namibia. Yet the Canadian Government allows Falconbridge to deduct from its taxes, payments made to the South African government on its operations in Namibia.[5]

18.   We therefore urge the federal government:

a. to refuse export credits, investment insurance and assistance in obtaining international investment credits for such ventures as that of Noranda Mines Ltd. in Chile;

b. to implement the United Nations Decree on the Protection of the Natural Resources of Namibia which is designed to prevent the extraction of resources from Namibia by foreign corporations without the consent of the U.N. Council for Namibia;

c. to terminate the Canada-South Africa Treaty on the Avoidance of Double Taxation and the Canada-South Africa Preferential Trade Agreement.

III — Native Land Claims and Northern Development

19.   The Canadian North has become centre stage in a struggle to gain control of new sources of energy and minerals on this continent. Corporations and governments continue to plan the construction of power plants, pipelines, railways, highways and mining projects without the direct participation of native peoples in the North and before a just settlement has been reached on their land claims. For a people whose land is their life, and who wish to gain control

over their future economic development, a just settlement of their land claims lies at the very heart of their struggle for justice.[6]

20. We believe the federal government has a major responsibility to insist that colonial patterns of development not prevail in the Canadian North. The time pressures for northern resource development have become enormous, particularly in the Northwest Territories where the federal government retains complete jurisdiction. Steps must be taken now to achieve a just settlement of native land claims and responsible stewardship of northern resources to meet human needs and not simply the interests of transnational corporations.

21. We therefore urge the federal government:

a. to introduce a moratorium on major resource development projects in the Northwest Territories for the purpose of providing sufficient time to achieve the following objectives:

i) just settlement of native land claims;

ii) native peoples' programmes for regional economic development;

iii) adequate safeguards to deal with environmental problems like oil spills, well blow-outs, etc.;

iv) adequate programmes to regulate domestic consumption and export of energy resources. Independent studies now indicate that gas reserves south of the 60th parallel are sufficient to make such a moratorium feasible.

b. To re-examine current policy positions on the extinction of aboriginal title in view of the fact that the Nishga, the Dene and the Inuit of the Northwest Territories are, in various ways, asking for a formalization of their aboriginal rights. A more creative position might go a long way towards reducing tensions and assuring more constructive negotiations. Following the 1973 split decision in the Supreme Court (Calder vs. the Government of B.C.), the Prime Minister stated that the concept of aboriginal title was a valid one and that political settlements must ensue.

c. To provide assurances that:

i) no approval will be granted for the building of a Mackenzie Valley pipeline until the Berger Commission has submitted its final report and serious attention has been given to its findings and recommendations;

ii) no right of conveyance will be granted to any pipeline company or other resource companies in the Northwest Territories, at least until there has been a signed agreement in principle on all native land claims in the Northwest Territories;

iii) the proposed Polar Gas pipeline or any other major energy projects will not proceed until a public inquiry similar to that of the Berger Commission hearings is conducted.

IV — Income Distribution

22.   Although we recognize that some Canadians have achieved a degree of affluence that requires they be called upon to restrain consumption for the sake of the common good, we are acutely aware that many Canadians do not yet receive an adequate return for their labour nor a fair share of the wealth of this country. While recognizing the need to control inflation, we are concerned that the programme of wage and price controls and of cutbacks in expenditures, especially on social services, will accentuate the disparities that already exist.

23.   In recent months, there have been several shifts in the federal-provincial initiatives to establish a guaranteed income in Canada. Steps must be taken now to provide a more adequate income for families in the present welfare population and to close the gap between the working poor and the poverty line.[7] We fear however, that recent programme initiatives may result in inducting working people into a welfare psychology and leaving present welfare recipients in the same.

24.   We therefore urge the federal government in cooperation with the provinces:

a. to create cost-sharing formulae that will make it possible for the have-not provinces to be as generous with the poor as the rich provinces;

b. to create guidelines for minimum levels of income maintenance applicable to each province and territory;

c. to simplify all application procedures for whoever is in need of "support" or "supplement";

d. to devise a means whereby those citizens in need of income assistance can be a part of the decision-making and regulating of the system in which they are to be the beneficiaries. Groups of administrators, consultants and recipients need to come together in workshops designed to review and help eradicate all aspects of the present welfare system that are considered demeaning to human dignity;

e. to re-examine the present federal tax system and introduce tax reform measures to ensure a more effective distribution of income. Tax reform is directly linked to the whole problem of an adequate, non-inflationary programme that is responsive to the needs of poor people in this country.

V — Immigration – Population – Refugees

25. Our world and Canada itself are characterized by an uneven pattern of economic opportunities. This has forced people to migrate within countries and across national boundaries in search of a better life.[8] In recent years we have also witnessed the emergence of repressive regimes that do not respect even the most basic of human rights. This too has forced many people to flee their homelands in an effort to escape from the forces of repression.[9]

26. At the present time, the federal government is engaged in a process of formulating new policies regarding population, immigration and refugees. A new Immigration Act is being written, a National Demographic Policy Study has been initiated and a review of Canada's refugee policies is under way. In formulating these new policies, we urge the federal government to adopt the following proposals:

a. that the new Immigration Act:

i) be based on a policy framework which views immigration policies for the future as an integral part of planning for a new economic and social order in Canada and throughout the world;[10]

ii) incorporate the specific proposals for the new legislation which were outlined in Section 5.3 of the *Report on the Immigration Debate* by the Inter-Church Project on Population (ICPOP).[11]

b. That a review of immigration and refugee security criteria be initiated to ensure:

i) there is no political or social discrimination in the screening process;

ii) security procedures are not used as intelligence gathering instruments for Canadian or foreign intelligence agencies;

iii) Canada does not rely on information supplied by the police or intelligence agencies of repressive governments.

c. That fresh and immediate action towards refugees from Chile be undertaken:

i) by admitting several thousand Chileans from Argentina, where it is known that some 9,500 Chilean refugees registered with United Nations High Commission for Refugees (UNHCR) are presently living under conditions of harassment;

ii) by initiating a second programme to assist an additional 100 prisoners and their families to come to Canada. The churches in Canada, Argentina and Chile are prepared to assist in the implementation of these programmes.

d. That the National Demographic Policy Study:

i) follow the basic principles established in the World Population Plan of Action (for which Canada voted without reservation);

ii) assure that the federal-provincial discussions about population policy be open to public scrutiny and discussion;

iii) provide sufficient time and information for effective citizen participation in shaping population policies for Canada.

CONCLUSION

27.   These are not the only issues which constitute the churches' platform for social change. For example, we have recently expressed our concerns about capital punishment and the sale of CANDU reactors to repressive regimes. Through our projects however, we intend

to take the above issues to the members of our churches and to the Canadian people. We are aware that some among our church membership will resist some of the changes we have advocated, but we are prepared to inform them continually of the grounds for these positions.

28. Today however, resistance to social change for justice comes primarily from the relatively affluent and powerful sectors of our society. We must ask whether, as government leaders, you hear the voices of the poor as often and as effectively as you hear the voices of the rich.

29. We know that there are significant numbers of people engaged in working for social justice in this country, particularly among the poor themselves. We believe that these people have a fundamental role to play in building a new order based on justice. It is our hope that the church will come to act increasingly in solidarity with these people and assist others in becoming involved in political action for justice.

30. Ultimately, the challenge before us is a test of our faithfulness in the living God. For we believe that the Lord is present in the struggle for justice going on in the world today and His voice must be heard.

NOTES

1. This brief was presented by the Reverend N. Berner, President, Canadian Council of Churches; the Most Reverend G.E. Carter, President, Canadian Catholic Conference; Dr. D.C. MacDonald, General Secretary of the Administrative Council, Presbyterian Church in Canada; Dr. R. Nostbakken, President, Lutheran Council in Canada (represented by Dr. John M. Zimmerman, Past President); the Right Reverend Wilbur Howard, Moderator, United Church of Canada; the Most Reverend E.W. Scott, Primate, Anglican Church in Canada. The matter of the brief was the subject of an *in camera* discussion with government leaders. In addition to the Prime Minister, the Hon. Pierre E. Trudeau, members of the cabinet present included Judd Buchanan, Alistair Gillespie, Marc Lalonde, Allan MacEachen, Bryce Mackasey, John Munro and Mitchell Sharp.

2. Cf. Document 34 above, and note 1 in the same. Despite the quotation marks in n. 3 of the present document, I do not find this text in the brief to Government,

though a close paraphrase of the first part of the quotation is found in the ''presentation to the citizens of Canada'', Document 34, Section I.

3. *Poverty in Canada: a Report of the Special Senate Committee on Poverty* (Ottawa, Information Canada, 1971), p. xv.

4. Cf. *Reflections on the Seventh Special Session of the U.N. General Assembly*; also *What is the New International Economic Order?*, both by GATT-FLY Project, 11 Madison Ave., Toronto, 1975.

5. Cf. *Canadian Policy Towards South Africa*, an ecumenical consensus paper presented to the Hon. A.J. MacEachen and the Hon. D.C. Jamieson, Nov., 1975. Also, *Canadian Policy Towards Chile*, a brief presented to the Hon. A.J. MacEachen and the Hon. R.K. Andras by the Inter-Church Committee on Chile, Oct., 1974 (now the Inter-Church Committee on Human Rights in Latin America, 40 St. Clair Ave. E., Toronto, M4T 1M9).

6. Cf. Document 40 above.

7. Cf. *Response to the Working Paper on Social Security in Canada*, Feb. 1974, and *Brief to the Hon. M. Lalonde, Minister of National Health and Welfare, on Social Service and the Proposed Social Services Act*, Jan. 1976, both from Department of Church and Society, United Church of Canada, 85 St. Clair Ave. E., Toronto.

8. Cf. *Report on the Immigration Debate: to the Hon. R.K. Andras, Nov. 1975*, by the Inter-Church Project on Population (ICPOP), c/o Mr. Bernard Daly, Canadian Catholic Conference, 90 Parent Ave., Ottawa, K1N 7B1. Also found in *Canadian Churches and Social Justice*, edit. John R. Williams (Toronto, Anglican Book Centre and James Lorimer, 1984).

9. Cf. *Submission to the Special Joint Committee on Immigration Policy*, Inter-Church Committee on Chile (cf. note 4 above).

10. Cf. ICPOP *Report on the Immigration Debate*, Section 5.2, and cf. note 8 above.

11. *Ibid.*, Section 5.3.

Document 43

ON DECENT HOUSING FOR ALL

Author — The Episcopal Commission for Social Affairs,
May 21, 1976

INTRODUCTION

1 — Habitat '76: a World Policy on Human Settlements

Within a few days our country will be host to the United Nations.
Between May 27 and June 11, a few thousand delegates representing 145 countries will be meeting in Vancouver to study the problems of housing in the world. These problems are so important for
the future of mankind that they call for immediate and drastic action
on the part of all nations. That is why Habitat '76 has taken on a
clear and imperative purpose: that of getting people to share actively and promptly in developing and implementing a world policy
on human settlements.

2 — A Concern of the Canadian Bishops

To us Canadians this event has major importance, not only because
of our joint responsibility with all other peoples, but also because
many of our fellow contrymen are severely affected by the present
housing crisis. Frequently in the course of the last few years, this
country's Roman Catholic bishops have called attention to grave
problems that are dehumanizing over one fifth of the people of
Canada: conditions of poverty and of social injustice.[1] Basing their
convictions on the Gospel precept which proclaims that all men may
aspire to the Kingdom, they have urged their fellow citizens to con-

tend against social inequities and to establish a more humane and equitable society. In this same context we, members of the Episcopal Commission for Social Affairs, wish to share today with all fellow citizens our pastoral preoccupation with housing problems in the world and in this country.

HOUSING: A WORLD PROBLEM

3 — *The Poorly Housed*

Despite huge and unprecedented efforts in the last decade to improve conditions in the underprivileged countries, the map of the the world still shows widespread grey areas of undedevelopment, especially in equatorial Africa, Latin America and southern Asia. Housing problems are more acute there than elsewhere: the poor live in the disorder of overcrowded slums or squatter settlements on the outskirts of cities and towns, at times alongside the abodes of the wealthy who look down upon such neighbours as social inferiors.

4 — *Inadequate Essential Services*

And what about the scarcity of safe drinking water, a problem which in itself is a nearly unanswerable challenge in many lands? What must be done to safeguard and conserve the fast dwindling reserves of clean water, to purify polluted sources and ensure a more equitable distribution of this necessity of life? What about the shortage or lack of basic community services such as waterworks and sewers, which do not exist in thousands of ghettos and shantytowns? No wonder then that the highest rate of infant mortality and the lowest life expectancy are recorded among these people. If to these serious problems we add the almost complete lack of basic institutions such as schools and hospitals, we still have only an imperfect picture of an inhuman condition in which people are deprived of all but their own resourcefulness, or driven to utter despair.

5 — *Rapid Growth of World Population*

The seriousness of the present human settlement crisis allows us no respite. On the contrary, it is likely to grow worse as time goes on. In fact, if the present trend continues, world population will have nearly doubled by the end of the century. It will then be in excess of six and one-half billion people, more than half of them living in already crowded urban communities. In terms of the number of houses, factories, hospitals, cultural institutions, etc., that will have to be built, the challenge appears almost insurmountable. In this regard, we must heed the predictions of economist Barbara Ward:

> Within the next thirty years, the human race will have to erect more buildings than it has erected since the beginning of its history. In the underdeveloped countries, the immensity of the task is still more disconcerting: within twenty years, their cities and towns will have to equip themselves with as many houses and working plants as the industrial nations have erected during the last two centuries.[2]

6 — *Our Response to Poverty*

Conditions in developing countries contrast sharply with those in lands of plenty. While some people enjoy the amenities of life in cosy, sometimes sumptuous homes, many more live in hovels, even in tents or other makeshift shelters. This being so, how can we fail to react? As citizens of a land of plenty and as world citizens, what can we do, collectively, to enable the ill-sheltered to improve their situation so that they really enjoy the same rights as we do? What must we do together to come to grips with the wretchedness of the have-nots, of whom we are insistently reminded by Christ: ''For I was hungry and you gave me food; I was thirsty and you gave me drink; I was a stranger and you made me welcome.'' (Mt 25:35)

HOUSING: A CANADIAN PROBLEM

7 — *Canadian Aspirations*

The importance we attach to the Habitat Conference is based not solely on our concept of today's world scene but also, and more directly, on what we conceive our own country to be at this moment and what we want it to be in the future: what kind of life do we wish to lead? What sort of city, town or village do we want to live in, to preserve, develop or create? For whom do we want to build?

How should the manifold resources of our heritage be apportioned for the benefit of the entire community, so that all may be decently housed?

8 — Inadequacy of Canadian Housing

Canada, despite its abundant wealth, has not yet managed to provide all of its population with a decent shelter. Here and there we have our own grey areas of substandard dwellings that call to mind conditions in developing countries. Particularly in large cities, behind a screen of skyscrapers, wide avenues sometimes conceal blighted areas teeming with newcomers, unemployed workers, low wage earners or members of ethnic minorities. The development of suburbia has given rise to similar results. Alongside well appointed and serviced new residential areas are clusters of huts or shacks without essential services such as running water, adequate heating, transportation and sewers. In such marginal communities, the infant death rate is twice as high as the Canadian average. And that rate is higher still among Indians and the Inuit: strange contrasts between two worlds that face each other from afar and do not meet.

9 — City Centre Renovation and Displacement of Population

Again, referring to the centres of large cities, another fact commands attention. Under the pressure of urbanization, the structure of city centres is once more being completely changed to make it more functional for furtherance of commercial ends. Thus, whole streets are being torn up and low wage earners displaced. Then on those sites tall impressive buildings are going up, often symbolic of power and wealth, and broad air-polluting speedways are being provided. As a result, mainly for economic reasons, dwellings by the thousands have been expropriated and even more citizens uprooted and left to fend for themselves. Though public opinion has reproved this destructiveness, the "law of progress" keeps on adding new victims. All of this seems to us inconceivable, especially when the elderly or the helpless are involved.

10 — New Housing Requirements and Inflation

Between now and the year 1980, according to federal government estimates, a million new houses will have to be built, a minimum of 235,000 of them this very year. That is, right now our country must tackle the major problem of housing. To avoid swelling the ranks of the needy it will not be enough to build thousands and thousands of houses. We will first need to know where to build them, where to find the required capital and what types of dwellings are necessary for human community. That is why Canada must urgently adopt policies calculated to protect its citizens, especially its low wage earners, against galloping inflation of housing costs: rising mortgage rates, real estate speculation, increased costs of building materials, higher rents, etc.

A CALL FOR PARTICIPATION

11 — *Our Collective Dream: What is it?*

Of course, Canada in the year 2000 will be quite different from what it is now. What is really important is that it become the country Canadians want it to be. This all depends on our common dream and our collective ability to make that dream come true. Do we want a society whose overall priorities will be determined solely on the basis of economic principles? Do we want a society which perpetuates social differences, discrimination between the affluent and the destitute, between posh areas and slum dwellings? Or would we rather have a society in which people are foremost? Our task therefore, is to define clearly the links we wish between profit, consumption and the quality of life for us all. Housing for people or housing for profits? Food for the hungry or food as a market commodity? It is not that economic means are lacking: the problem is to find the will to restructure our society and reorder its priorities.

12 — *The Course of Events Can be Changed*

In recent years, significant experiences have shown that when citizens group together and decide to establish and carry out a plan, they can change existing conditions. We all know that here and there in Canada, groups have actively engaged in efforts to rejuvenate their run-down districts. Other groups have set up housing cooperatives enabling average or low-income people to build a decent home for themselves and yet avoid real estate speculation and excessive debts. We also know that farmers have devoted much energy to resource conservation, recuperation of arable land and soil improvement, and that ecology-conscious citizens have worked hard at preserving green belts and assuring environmental quality. Similarly the Native Peoples of northern Canada have established a common front to protect their rights and the quality of their natural habitat. Those examples show, as do a great many others, that direct participation by citizens in the organization of their area or city helps to improve the social and economic life of the community.

13 — *The Specific Commitment of Christians*

At the very core of these experiences Christians recognize the call that is contained in the Gospel and that can lead us to join in building "new heavens and a new earth where justice dwells" (2 P 3:13). Our commitment to social justice, particularly towards the humble and the weak, becomes the test of our fidelity to Jesus Christ and the Gospel. Thus the changes taking place in the world can be for us Christians occasions of collective sin or of commitment and solidarity which express the presence of the Kingdom.

14 — *A Sense of Social Responsibility*

As a result of the appeal being made to us by thousands of our fellow citizens deprived of their rightful share of housing facilities, we must develop a keen sense of our social responsibility. This requires us to live in close fellowship with the underprivileged, to help improve the quality of life in run-down districts and to share in the social and economic rehabilitation of marginal areas.

15 — *Paul VI's Appeal*

Such an engagement in temporal affairs, inspired by the Gospel, is at the heart of the Christian vocation. As Pope Paul VI wrote to Cardinal Roy, a Christian cannot be disassociated from what's going on in the world:

> To build up the city, the place where men and their expanded communities exist, to create new modes of neighbourliness and relationships, to perceive an original application of social justice and to undertake responsibility for this collective future,

which is foreseen as difficult, is a task in which Christians must share. To those who are heaped up in urban promiscuity which becomes intolerable, it is necessary to bring a message of hope. This can be done by brotherhood which is lived and by concrete justice.[3]

If all Christians in Canada thus resolved to commit themselves to their poorly housed and ill-provided neighbours, to rebuild today's society along the lines of equality and justice for all, in a few years the blight of Canadian underdevelopment would vanish. Is this possible? Of course! That is why today's pastoral concern can turn into genuine hope.

NOTES

1. Cf. *Development Demands Justice*, Document 34 above: *Sharing Daily Bread*, Document 36; *Sharing National Income*, Document 38; *On Immigration and Population Policies*, Document 39; *Northern Development: At What Cost?*, Document 40: *A New Commandment?*, *A Pastoral Exhortation for Lent*, 1976, Canadian Conference of Catholic Bishops, Ottawa, K1N 7B1; *Justice Demands Action*, Document 42.

2. *Human Settlements, Crisis and Opportunity* (Ottawa, Information Canada, 1974), p. 2.

3. *A Call to Action (Octogesima Adveniens)*, 1971, cf. *The Pope Speaks*, Washington, 1971, XVI, p. 143, n. 12.

Document 44

LABOUR DAY MESSAGE[1] — 1976
FROM WORDS TO ACTION
On Christian Political and Social Responsibility

Author — Administrative Board, the Canadian Catholic Conference

Urgent Signs of the Times

1. The signs of the times today compel us as Christians to think about our social responsibilities and to put our words into action. We live in a world that oppresses at least half the human race and this scandal threatens to get worse.[2] Right around us, human suffering of many kinds scars the face of Canada: poverty for many, inflating prices, housing crises, regional disparities, strikes and lockouts, cultural violations, native land claims, overcrowded cities and rural neglect. With all this comes a growing sense of loneliness, powerlessness and alienation in our society and institutions.[3] So we have cause for deep concern. But it is not enough to see injustice, disorder and violence at home and abroad and to worry about the future. These conditions will not improve on their own. We, the people, have the responsibility to change them.

What Gospel Response?

2. As Christians, we are faced with the question: what does faith in Jesus Christ tell us about our social and political responsibilities in these times? This is the basic question that we, as pastors of the Catholic Church in Canada, wish to address in this message to our brothers and sisters in the Catholic community. Some will say that

this is an old question and so it is. We have talked about some aspects of it in every one of our Labour Day statements and pastoral messages.[4] Now more than ever there is urgent need to bring the following questions to the center of our daily lives: what does the Gospel say about the creation of a new social order based on justice? What should a follower of Christ do in response to the many struggles for social justice going on around us?

A New Social Order

3.   Many people agree that there is something wrong with the present social and economic order. It fails to meet the human needs of the majority of people. The present economic order results in the very uneven distribution of wealth and the control of resources by a small minority. On the global scene, the poor peoples, especially the Third World, are calling for the creation of a new economic order based on a just distribution of wealth and power. And within this country, in its various regions and communities, there are similar signs that people want to find new approaches now, to make better use of human and material resources, to end waste and want and exploitation.[5]

The Gospel Message of Justice

4.   As disciples of Christ, all of us have a responsibility to play a role in the creation of a social order based on justice. For we stand in the biblical tradition of the prophets of Israel (Amos, Jeremiah, Isaiah) for whom to know God is to seek justice for the disinherited, the poor and the oppressed. The same Spirit of God that came upon the prophets filled Jesus of Nazareth. With the power of that Spirit, Jesus prayed and healed, all the while proclaiming that the Kingdom of God was at hand (Mt 4:17, 23; Lk 6:12, 11:1-4). In the light of the Spirit he announced he was the message of the prophets come true — "the good news to the poor" and "liberty to the oppressed" (Lk 4:18, 19).

True Liberation

5.   For the Christian community this struggle for justice is not an optional activity. It is integral to bringing the Gospel to the world.[6]

True, God's Kingdom and hence the mission of the Church reach far beyond this world (Jn 18:36). This mission goes further than mere liberation in the economic, political, social and cultural ordering of our lives. True liberation encompasses the whole person and makes men and women open to God.[7] This openness allows us to see the limits of our human activity and forces us to search for greater liberation. Yet this dimension of our religious life can be no excuse for retreating from the affairs of this world. Rather it calls us to work even harder for the creation of a just social order.

We Judge by the Gospel

6.   The Gospel, today as always, gives us a basis for judging the social order that is the product of human activity.[8] In that light we have focused our attention in recent years on the development of the earth's resources to meet the needs of people.[9] We have urged the heads of governments and corporations to assure that the earth's resources be developed not for the profit of a few but to serve the basic needs of the majority of people in this country and the world.[10] Who shall control, and who shall benefit from, the earth's natural resources? Will these resources be used to enrich a small minority? Or will they be developed to meet the unfulfilled needs of the majority of mankind for adequate food, shelter, health care, education and employment for a fuller human life?[11]

A Significant Minority

7.   Across Canada today, there are some encouraging signs among Christian people who are raising these and related ethical questions. Much of this activity for social justice and responsible stewardship of resources is occurring on an ecumenical basis. A variety of Christian groups have been working with the poor and oppressed peoples of their communities, organizing educational events on issues of injustice, and pressing leaders of governments and industry to change policies that cause human suffering. Unfortunately, those who are committed to this Christian way of life are presently a minority in the life of the Catholic community. Yet this minority is significant because it is challenging the whole Church to live the Gospel message by serving the needs of the people.

A Call to Conversion

8. As pastoral leaders, we have a responsibility to see that every member of the Church becomes fully alive in the service of God and neighbour. In this light, we would like to see more members of the Catholic community commit their lives to the task of creating a more just social order. But what does this really mean for us as persons? Clearly, the Gospel calls us to become new men and women in the service of others.[12] It also calls us to a conversion of attitudes leading to a change of those structures that cause human suffering. And this conversion requires all of us to see the reality of everyday life in a new light: from the perspective of Jesus Christ and his concern for the poor and the oppressed.

Guidelines

9. We propose the following six guidelines to help each of us — bishops, priests, religious and laity — commit ourselves more deeply to this new way of life as disciples of Christ.

(1) *Understanding the Gospel message of justice*

Clearly, some among us have never understood or have lost sight of this Gospel message of love and justice and of the social teachings of the Church. What is the relation between our personal and collective faith in Jesus Christ and the demands for social justice? Jesus taught that Christian love of neighbour means, first and foremost, identification with the plight of the poor and the oppressed. We must find relevant ways of probing the true meaning of this Gospel message. This calls for communities of people reflecting and acting on specific injustices in the light of the Gospel. Our community and religious education programs should give greater attention to these concerns.

(2) *Modifying our more affluent life styles*

We live in a society where people are encouraged to consume and waste extravagantly while others are left wanting. As Christians, we are called to turn away from material treasures and self-seeking (Lk 12:33-34). The teaching that "man does not live by bread alone" (Dt 8:3) is meant, among other things, to direct the more affluent away from this consumer way of life. Modifying luxurious living habits will not itself overcome the gross disparities and inequities among people today, but it can renew our spirit and open our hearts to the plight of the poor in our midst.

(3) *Hearing the victims of injustice in our communities*

Most of us have had little experience of the human suffering of poverty and oppression. Jesus taught that we can learn a great deal about justice from those who have suffered under these conditions (Mt 25:31-46). We can achieve a new vision of reality by becoming more present to the hungry, the homeless, the jobless, the native person, the poor immigrant and others who may be victims of injustices in our communities. By listening to their problems and sharing in their struggle we can learn much more about the attitudes, activities and structures that cause human suffering and what can be done about them.

(4) *Denouncing injustice in our communities*

Too often people see examples of exploitation around them but remain silent. Yet, silence amounts to a form of consent and approval of what is happening. In the tradition of the prophets, we are called to denounce injustice and speak the truth to those in power. As citizens we must exercise our freedom and responsibility to take positions on specific issues and speak out against the causes of injustice. Until the voices for justice are multiplied, they will continue to be ignored by those who hold power.

(5) *Collaborating to change the causes of injustice*

It is not enough to denounce social ills and talk about a new order. Social justice is the goal. We are called to participate in actions to change the policies of governments, corporations and other institutions that cause human suffering. People must come together to act for fundamental social change. This is our political responsibility as Christians and citizens in a democratic society.[13] We can exercise this responsibility by participating in religious and community groups acting today on specific examples of injustice.

(6) *Assisting the poor and oppressed*

The people experiencing poverty and oppression have a primary role to play in bringing about a more just social order, but many of them — and their groups — remain powerless. As Christians, we have a responsibility not simply to feed the hungry but to increase their power to change the causes of hunger. Some church groups are now providing funds, technical assistance and other forms of communal support to poverty groups involved in social change. This fraternal activity can help to increase effectiveness in action and offset frustrations which may lead to violence. But much more could be done.

Disturbing Experience

10.   The challenge of living the Gospel of justice in this way is a disturbing experience for all of us. Some who have committed themselves to this new way of life have been misunderstood and criticized, particularly by the more affluent and powerful sectors of their communities. But the message of Christ crucified is not a comforting message. We cannot take refuge in the position that as Christians our duty is simply to worship God and give alms to the poor (Mt 7:21-23). To do only this in our present situation would be to incur the wrath of Christ because, like the Pharisees, we would be neglecting "justice and the love of God" (Lk 11:42).

An Invitation to All

11.   We urge all our brothers and sisters to join us in a continuing process of action and reflection on these pastoral guidelines. It is in our local communities that we can best exercise these social and political responsibilities. This calls for our personal and collective participation in local struggles for justice with the jobless, exploited workers, poor or lonely immigrants, small producers, native people, the culturally oppressed and others. We therefore ask local Christian communities to stimulate and intensify this kind of activity through special study/action projects as well as by existing family and religious education programs. And we urge leaders in the political and economic spheres of Canada to increase their efforts towards building a more just social order. Such actions will say louder than any words: "I am in the midst of you as one who serves" (Lk 22:27).

A Sign of Hope

12. In a world being torn apart by injustice and conflict, this kind of active Christian witness will be a sign of hope. It both illustrates and contributes to the building of the Kingdom of God. For His Kingdom is an expression of the power of love, service and self-giving to all in need. This requires personal and collective prayer combined with vital public action. We must always remember that the credibility, authenticity and acceptance of our worship is conditioned by the exercise of justice (Mt 5:23-24). Only then will we be an authentic Christian community praising God through our actions as well as words.

NOTES

1. This is the last of the "Labour Day Messages", a series which ran from 1956-76. Thereafter, the bishops decided, statements would be issued as events occurred or occasion offered, rather than on a fixed date. Though the statement *A Society to be Transformed* (Document 46) had been projected as a Labour Day Message, it was not issued as such but in December of 1977.

2. At the Eucharistic Congress in Philadelphia, 1976, Archbishop Helder Camara called this the "scandal of the century": that rich countries and persons grow richer while poor nations and the poor in every nation become ever poorer.

3. For current examples of loneliness, alienation, etc., cf. Project Feedback, II. *Assessing Everyday Life;* V. *How People Feel about the 1980's,* Canadian Conference of Catholic Bishops, Ottawa, K1N 7B1.

4. Cf. the Documents of this Collection and *Messages des Évêques canadiens à l'occasion de la fête du travail,* édit. R. Arès, SJ (Montréal, Les Éditions Bellarmin, 1974).

5. For some examples cf. Project Feedback, I. *Peoples' Social Hopes,* cf. note 3 above.

6. Cf. Third International Synod of Bishops, 1971, *Justice in the World,* nn. 6, 34-35, *The Pope Speaks,* Washington, 1971, XVI, 377, 382; Paul VI, *Evangelization,* 1975, nn. 29 f., *ibid,* 1976, XXI, 17 f.

7. Paul VI, *op. cit.,* nn. 33, 34, 38, 70, *ibid.* pp. 19, 20, 40.

8. Cf. Paul VI, *The Development of Peoples, 1967,* in *The Papal Encyclicals,* edit. Claudia Carlen IHM (Wilmington, N.C., McGrath Publishing, 1981), V, p. 187.

9. Especially, Documents 36 and 40 above. These statements focused on the twin ethical themes of social justice and responsible stewardship of resources.

10. Through participation in action events around the world, in the World Population Conference in Bucharest, August, 1974; the World Food Conference in Rome, November, 1975; the Seventh Special Session of the U.N., N.Y., September, 1975; the U.N. Conference on Trade and Development, Nairobi, May, 1976, plus the annual shareholders' meetings of various transnational corporations and meetings with government leaders.

11. Cf. *Justice Demands Action,* n. 7, Document 42 above.

12. Cf. *A New Commandment?,* 1976; Canadian Conference of Catholic Bishops, Ottawa, K1N 7B1.

13. Cf. Paul VI, *A Call to Action (Octogesima Adveniens), 1971,* nn. 24, 46; *The Pope Speaks,* Washington, 1971, XVI, pp. 149, 159. See also *The Church and Human Rights* by the Pontifical Commission Justice and Peace, Vatican, 1974, nn. 52-80, in *Social Justice: Official Catholic Teachings,* edit. Vincent P. Mainelli (Wilmington, N.C., McGrath Publishing, 1978), pp. 366-377.

Document 45

TO THE CANADIAN CATHOLIC ORGANIZATION FOR DEVELOPMENT AND PEACE[1]

Author — Bishop G. Emmett Carter, President, the Canadian Conference of Catholic Bishops, February 23, 1977

1. This Lent we mark the tenth anniversary of two creative events in the life of the Roman Catholic Church, namely the launching of the Canadian Catholic Organization for Development and Peace (CCODP) and the publication of Pope Paul VI's social message *On the Development of Peoples*. We would like to commemorate these two events by sharing some brief reflections on the past ten years and the challenges which lie ahead.

2. In retrospect, CCODP was conceived in the experience of Vatican II. During the Council, the bishops of Africa, Asia and Latin America conveyed to the Canadian bishops the harsh realities of poverty and underdevelopment in the Third World. It became clear that the growing gap between the rich and the poor peoples on this planet is a great threat to mankind. The Council also made us aware of our responsibilities to work together, as a universal church, to erase these injustices. Responding to these realities and to the urging of concerned lay people in this country, the bishops of Canada founded Development and Peace. It was and is to assist the poor and the oppressed peoples of the world in their struggle for justice and to educate us in Canada about the problems of underdevelopment. Thus in the spirit of Vatican II, lay Catholics and their pastors came together in a programme designed to raise funds for development projects in the Third World and to inform, animate

and mobilize public opinion here in Canada on the problems of global poverty.

3.   In so doing, the Church in Canada took its inspiration from one of the major insights of the Council, namely that men have a dual commitment, to the salvation of the human person and to the renewal of the secular order. In the Christian view neither goal is sacrificed to the other, but the one which is the eternal salvation of mankind is inextricably bound up with the other which is the perfecting of the secular order by permeating it with the spirit of the Gospel. Thus the Church knows that "her contribution to liberation is incomplete if she neglects to proclaim salvation in Jesus Christ", and thus she "strives always to insert the struggle for liberation into the universal plan of salvation."[2]

4.   The founding purposes of CCODP were confirmed and strengthened by Pope Paul VI's 1967 encyclical. Referring to the times as an "hour of crisis," he challenged the affluent of the world to recognize that the "road to peace" lies in overcoming the problems of underdevelopment that afflict two-thirds of mankind. He constantly emphasized that the central purpose of development is man, and that our dignity as persons confers on us certain inalienable rights and duties. Of primary importance is the right to life and to all that renders life possible, such as food, clothing, shelter, education, employment and the right to participate in decisions affecting our lives. By the same token, every society possesses similar rights to self-determination and should be allowed to develop its own cultural, economic, political and social structures to meet the basic needs of its people.[3]

5.   In the course of the past ten years, CCODP has played a significant role in meeting the challenges posed by *The Development of Peoples*. Thousands of volunteers have become actively involved in the movement; the annual Share Lent campaign has funded hundreds of development projects in the Third World; and increasing numbers of Canadians have come to a deeper understanding of the causes of poverty and underdevelopment. But the realities of the Third World still exist and the gap between the rich and the poor is expanding. Moreover, these problems exist right here in Canada. If nothing else, it is becoming painfully clear that there are real obstacles to development which are deeply rooted in the economic and social structures that shape our times.

6. Indeed it is evident that the present world economic order fails to meet the basic needs of the majority of mankind. On the contrary, the present order is characterized by the maldistribution of wealth and power. In Third World countries, powerful corporations continue to plan the use of natural resources without the participation of the people most directly affected. And closer to home, unjust patterns of resource development occur in various regions of Canada. In effect, the earth's resources too often are developed to enrich a small minority rather than to meet the unfulfilled needs of the majority of people for food, shelter, clothing, health care and employment necessary for a fully human life.

7. Paul VI drew attention to some of the basic inadequacies of the present economic order. Following the tradition of his predecessors, he condemned the system of "liberal capitalism" which "considers profit as the key motive for economic progress, competition as the supreme law of economics, and private ownership of the means of production as an absolute right." For this is the same economic system which has been largely responsible for the history of colonialism in the Third World and the present realities of poverty and underdevelopment. In particular, Paul VI pointed to the mechanisms of international finance and trade which both maintain and extend the gap between the rich and poor nations of the world.[4]

8. Today the poor and the oppressed peoples are demanding an alternative to the present economic order. The nations of the Third World are calling for a New International Economic Order based on a just distribution of wealth and power. Greater emphasis is being placed on pursuing more self-reliant modes of development in which the resources of Third World countries are to be developed and used to meet basic human needs of their populations. Yet all too often, the legitimate struggles of peoples to bring about these necessary changes are impeded by local governmental and business elites, as well as by outside intervention of both governments and corporations.

9. In the decade ahead, CCODP could make a significant contribution towards the creation of a New International Economic Order based on justice. As Christians, we stand in the biblical tradition where to know God is to seek justice for the disinherited, the poor and the oppressed. The Gospel calls us to a new way of life, to a

transformation of personal attitudes and social structures that cause human suffering. Through CCODP therefore, we have a responsibility, first to challenge economic structures which cause poverty and underdevelopment and secondly to increase the capacity of the poor and the oppressed in their struggle for a just social order. Indeed these are among the "signs of the times" which we addressed in our 1976 Labour Day message, *From Words to Action.*[5]

10. In the Gospel story of the talents, the reward for wise use of human resources is an invitation to assume even greater responsibilities (Mt 25:23). In this spirit, our anniversary wish for CCODP is that their program of action and reflection be intensified and expanded to meet the even greater challenges of the next decade. To this end, we extend our fraternal support of and solidarity with these co-workers in the mission of the Church.

NOTES

1. For a brief exposition of the foundation and purposes of the Canadian Catholic Organization for Development and Peace, see Document 17 above, especially nn. 10-12.

2. Paul VI, *Evangelization*, 1975, nn. 34, 38, cf. *The Pope Speaks*, Washington, 1976, XXI, pp. 19 ff.

3. *The Development of Peoples, The Papal Encyclicals*, edit. Claudia Carlen, IHM (Wilmington, N.C., McGrath Publishing, 1981), V, p. 179 ff., nn. 1, 14-21, 22 ff., 40, 76.

4. *Op. cit.*, nn. 7 ff., 26, 56 ff.

5. Document 44 above.

Document 46

A SOCIETY TO BE TRANSFORMED

Author — The Canadian Conference of Catholic Bishops,
December 1, 1977

1. Even though our times are scarred by grave social ills, a number of Christians find reasons for hope. In many parts of the country, members of Christian communities are coming to know God more deeply by their efforts to overcome human suffering. As they join in struggles for justice, especially for the poor and oppressed, Christians find other groups striving to reach the same goal. All such social efforts against poverty and other forms of injustice and inequality are truly sources of hope.

2. We must not be misled however, if there are some good efforts and a few gains. We live in a world simmering with uncertainty, contradictions and conflicts. Everywhere people express their concern about the future. By comparison with many others, our own country seems particularly prosperous and peaceful. Nevertheless we are reminded every day that we too have imbalances and tensions, violence and fears of violence.

Signs of Underdevelopment

3. Although our country is called developed, it has many marks of underdevelopment. In 1971 one person in four had an income below the poverty line.[1] Since then inflation and high unemployment rates have worsened the situation. Powerful foreign-controlled companies exercise increasing power in society beyond the reach of effective public intervention. Their decisions directly influence housing, unemployment, increasing prices and the

declining value of earnings and savings. Economic and social disparities between regions of the country persist. Pollution and other forms of environmental damage show that natural resources are misused. Entire groups who are central to our country's future are uncertain of the survival of their very culture and customs. Workers, even those in unions, have little share in decisions affecting their livelihood and well-being. In turn, elected representatives at various levels of government seem to face insurmountable difficulties.

4.   It could be said that this situation is not new. Indeed in a series of statements extending back more than twenty years, we Roman Catholic bishops of Canada have spoken frequently about these and other ills of our society. However, people are more conscious today of the social malaise. Every day the news media report protests about actual conditions or new proposals for changing them. The diversity of these proposals shows that we face contradictory values and many views of mankind and of the world.

Two-fold Purpose

5.   We speak again about these matters to you, the Catholics of Canada, for two reasons. We invite you to get more involved in reshaping society and we urge a particular form of involvement. First, in the name of the Gospel, all Christians must involve themselves in transforming our ways of living and our social and economic structures. The Lord calls Christians to be present in every search for new or renewed ways — new or renewed techniques, plans, programmes, institutions or systems — to resolve today's difficulties. Secondly, we stress once again that Christians must be leaders in identifying and promoting the solutions that come only through new or renewed values, attitudes and relationships.

6.   At any period, ideas rule the world. People are guided by the values carried by current ideologies. For our part, we find in the Scriptures a concept of justice which lights the way for today. People will see their rights and needs respected and satisfied to the extent that men and women relate to one another in terms of justice and equality, and work together to shape institutions and structures according to these values.

Reasons for Hope

7. The difficulties we face are, for you and for us, a time and a place for making the incarnation and redemption of Christ ever more real in today's world:

> The Christian's hope comes primarily from the fact that he knows that the Lord is working with us in the world, continuing in His Body which is the Church — and, through the Church, in the whole of mankind — the redemption which was accomplished on the cross and which burst forth in victory on the morning of the resurrection. This hope springs also from the fact that the Christian knows that other men are at work, to undertake actions of justice and peace working for the same ends. [2]

The Christian Calling

8. The world in which we live recalls both Nineveh, the city of sin and pride, and Jerusalem, the Holy City, the place where God is encountered. [3] Work in such a world has special meaning for Christians. We have, as Pope Paul VI has said, "the mission of sharing in the creation of the supernatural world which remains incomplete until we all come to build up together that perfect Man of whom St. Paul speaks 'who realizes the fullness of Christ'." [4] Expectation of that new earth stimulates our concern for cultivating this one, "for here grows the body of a new human family, a body which even now is able to give some kind of foreshadowing of the new age". [5] God's Kingdom is still to come and yet has begun. [6]

9. All Christians, poor, rich and in between, are called to "put on a new self" and "be reconciled to God". [7] This two-fold call comes from God Who created the world and intervenes in human history as our Father, champion of love and justice. His love extends to all; in a special way He is the friend of the lowly, the outcast, those oppressed by any evil. By His word we are called to turn from self-seeking and greed, to respect and care for one another, to love our neighbours as ourselves.

10. A central theme running through the scriptures is that we come to know God, to experience Him truly, by loving and respecting

others, in seeking justice for the poor, the disinherited, the oppressed, the aged, sick and imprisoned.[8] This love requires that we fully respect the rights of others, renounce any will to dominate and establish the truest possible justice in all our relationships. The foundation of this true respect is the love that God has for everyone without exception. God is love. In Christ the Father loves all of us so that we may love one another, a love that is the new commandment (Jn 13:34-35; 1 Jn 4:7-12,16). Indeed, if we do not love other people whom we can see, we cannot love God Whom we cannot see (1 Jn 4:20). This kind of love leads on to a justice that seeks to promote greater equality among people.[9]

11. On Mount Sinai, God joined with his people in a Covenant that was renewed in the death and resurrection of Jesus Christ. Inheritors of that Covenant, Christians have received the mission to reunite all people with God by undertaking, as an ongoing challenge, the building of the kingdom based on justice and love. By the grace of baptism, we are remade in the image of God and plunged into a new life. Our participation in the Eucharist announces the glory that is to come and introduces us, even now, to the Kingdom that the Father has promised us. To these gifts of God we must reply by endless conversion, reconciliation and penance. Thus we place ourselves under the law of Christ (Gal 1:5; 6:2) and keep the Covenant with Him. The spirit of the beatitudes challenges Christians to transform the world in the name of Jesus. It inspires us to become peacemakers, merciful, pure in heart, poor in spirit, hungry and thirsty for justice, even when afflicted and persecuted (Mt 5:1-16).

Discerning the Gospel Message

12. God wills that the Gospel should transform not just our personal and private live but also all social and public behaviour, that is the attitudes, customs, laws and structures of the world in which we live.[10] He calls on us to build a more humane and fraternal world, in which injustice and violence no longer threaten, where no one person fears another, and where the resources of His creation are developed to supply what all people need for a decent life. It is up to Christian communities, Pope Paul VI has emphasized,

> ... to analyze with objectivity the situation which is proper to their own country, to shed on it the light of the Gospel's·

unalterable words and to draw principles of reflection, norms of judgment and directives for action from the social teachings of the Church.[11]

Applying the Gospel in this way to our own times, we are better able to identify and evaluate what is going on around us and make a positive contribution to human development.

The Heritage of Capitalism

13.   Some of the achievements of modern industrial society have been real factors in human progress. The secrets of nature are being gradually revealed through systematic research and much hard work. People have learned how to organize vast and daring ventures that could make the earth's riches available to all. However, despite the place given to individual freedoms, this potential remains largely unrealized. Instead, on the new conditions of society, a woeful system has been imposed, a system

"... which considers profit as the key motive for economic progress, competition as the supreme law of economics and private ownership of the means of production as an absolute right that has no limits and carries no corresponding social obligation.[12]

With no vision of an afterlife, this world is pictured solely as a place where people struggle for an ever more comfortable existence. The single-minded pursuit of self-interest is presented as a value. The theory of the survival of the fittest leads many to accept widespread poverty and the concentration of wealth and power in the hands of a few. Industrial strategies are designed specifically to produce maximum gratification and profit, so that wasteful consumption is systematically promoted. In the process, both human beings and natural resources are abused or destroyed.

14.   In many such ways, our country is still profoundly marked by the founders of liberal capitalism. We carry forward many of the consequences of their lives, for their ideas have become our institutions. Their values shape much of today's economic system which, in turn, gives rise to materialistic aspirations that are the idols that millions worship today. Those values constitute an economic religion that inhibits the development of an ethic of sharing. While

people have worked hard to plant the seeds of human solidarity and love, the dominant economic and social structures of our times have become the rocky ground of self-service and self-aggrandizement. The result is clear: many are kept from achieving certain basic necessities while others, trapped in their wealth, find great difficulty in meeting God, in knowing the person of Jesus and living His message. Succeeding generations are drawn into a culture, into ways of thinking and behaving, alien to God's purpose.

The Marxist Alternative

15. A growing number of our fellow citizens can no longer accept this established disorder. In a genuine search for a better world, some turn to Marxism as an alternative. Even some Christians, longing for justice and equality, trying to free present-day society from its idols and to change human relationships, seek to harmonize Marxism with the Gospel. There are however, grave dangers in this undertaking. There are some basic elements of Marxist ideology which Christians must reject. We cannot accept the denial of God's existence and intervention in history, the rejection of man's spiritual nature and destiny, the tendency to see in the person only an economic function, the dialectic of violence as the means of social change and the absorption of individual freedom in a collective social order.[13] As disciples of Christ, we cannot accept the idea that a paradise, an ideal city, can be fully created here on earth. The Kingdom promised by Christ reaches far beyond this world and calls people to renew themselves unendingly in the spirit of the risen Lord. You will therefore understand our concern that the Marxist ideology is spreading, especially among youth and activist groups.

16. Nevertheless some Christians engaged in struggles for justice use what is commonly called Marxist analysis. This approach can help to identify certain injustices and structures of exploitation. However there is a tendency in Marxist analysis to reduce every social struggle to two main actors — exploiters-exploited, dominators-oppressed, masters-slaves. We cannot deny that some class struggles have brought about important social changes in history. Grave consequences arise however, when such struggles are founded on a narrow vision of man, promote hatred and violence and give rise to new kinds of oppression. In proclaiming the Gospel message of justice and love, Christians speak of man as an image

of God with inalienable rights of which he must not be robbed in any social change. Christ's plan is that, even in the midst of real struggles, all people should undergo conversion of hearts and attitudes, so that they may "become new" (Ep 4:23 f.; Col 3:10)

Christian Pathways

17.   Amid the conflicts and contradictions that now separate and oppress people, we as Christians must strive to distinguish the promises of God's Kingdom from human utopias and ideologies, no matter how worthy. Many people see clearly that today's dominant ideologies, whether capitalism or Marxism, contradict Gospel values. Throughout the world these ideologies are expressed in many different social models all of which fail to meet human needs adequately. This is shown by the fact that a search for new social values, goals and structures is a mark of the times. In Canada and elsewhere, much human effort is going into study, debate and action to shape the future. In these events, God calls you to break out of inadequate patterns of thinking and acting, to live new lives, to join all men in building a new society in which there is a real freedom based on love and justice.

18.   In your neighbourhood you may be faced with a variety of options and strategies. Some people will choose to continue reforming our present capitalist system in the light of the Gospel. Others will choose to participate in socialist movements, trying to reconcile them with the teachings of Jesus. And still others, rejecting these options, will become involved in searching for some alternative socio-economic order based on Gospel principles. As people pursue these different strategies, there is bound to be within the Christian community tension and debate which can be a healthy process for change. But one thing is certain: no option is valid that does not unite people in efforts for the creation of a society based on justice.

Future Action

19.   We wish to express in the strongest possible way our continued support for the growing number of Christians engaged in struggles for justice. In the next two years, we intend to initiate a pastoral plan of action for the purpose of encouraging more members of the

Catholic community to become actively involved in creating a socio-economic order based on justice. We therefore urge people in Christian communities to become involved in the following steps:

(a) Review the six guidelines and study questions for Christian action outlined in the 1976 Labour Day Message, *From Words to Action*.[14] The guidelines contain practical suggestions whereby Christians can become actively involved in struggles for justice going on in local communities. The formation of local study/action groups on problems of injustice is essential.

(b) Participate in study/action projects which may be launched next year in each diocese and region. Next spring, a working document will be issued which is designed to stimulate greater Christian awareness and action in each region on the vital issues of injustice in Canada and the Third World.[15]

(c) Participate in regional conferences on social justice. During the next two years, there will be several opportunities for members of the Catholic community to come together on a regional basis for the purpose of sharing analyses and experiences on various problems of injustice and developing strategies for necessary social change in this country.

True Development

20. Ten years ago, describing true human progress in his encyclical *The Development of Peoples*, Paul VI appealed for universal solidarity among mankind. This solidarity must allow all peoples to develop their full personality as individuals and as groups. Such integral development calls for self-reliant peoples who will be the artisans of their own development, whose concern will be to build their solidarity, putting into it the best of themselves.[16] Different models of society can be built from Gospel values of love, justice and equality; but no social order built without these values can meet fully the legitimate aspirations of all mankind. Christians inspired by these values, who in the tradition of the prophets dedicate themselves to the cause of authentic social development, are witnesses to hope in the world today.

NOTES

1. Cf. *Poverty in Canada*, Report of the Special Senate Committee on Poverty (Ottawa, Information Canada, 1971), pp. 11 ff.

2. Paul VI, *A Call to Action (Octogesima Adveniens)*, 1971, n. 48, cf. *The Pope Speaks*, Washington, 1971, XVI, p. 162.

3. *Ibid.* 12, p. 143.

4. Paul VI, *The Development of Peoples*, 1967, n. 28; cf. *The Papal Encyclicals*, edit. Claudia Carlen IHM (Wilmington, N.C., McGrath Publishing, 1981), V, 188.

5. Second Vatican Council, *The Church in the Modern World*, 1965, n. 39.

6. Paul VI, *Evangelization*, 1975, n. 13; cf. *The Pope Speaks*, Washington, 1976, XXXI, p. 9.

7. *Ibid.* n. 2, p. 4.

8. Cf. Amos, Jeremiah, Isaiah, Hosea, in many places; Psalms 10 (9), 41 (40), 72 (71), 147 (146), unbracketed numbers are Revised Standard Version, bracketed from the Vulgate; Mt 25:31-46; Mk 10:42-45; Lk 4:18-20; Jm 2:1-13, 5:1-6.

9. Equality is difficult to attain but Christians must struggle towards such an ideal. They cannot accept present inequalities as the inevitable outcome of natural selection, as Social Darwinists would argue. Instead they should be guided by insights such as those found in the Acts of the Apostles (2:42-47; 4:32-35), and in St. Paul (2 Cor 8:13-15).

Pope Leo XIII in turn taught: "... when what necessity demands has been supplied, and one's standing fairly taken thought for, it becomes a duty to give to the indigent out of what remains over." (*The Condition of the Working Classes*, 1891, n. 22, in Carlen, note 4 above, II, p. 247) And Pius XI added: "A person's superfluous income, that is income which he does not need to sustain life fittingly and with dignity, is not left wholly to his own free determination." (*On Reconstructing the Social Order*, 1931, n. 50, in Carlen, note 4 above, III, p. 423).

10. Paul VI, *The Development of Peoples*, 1967, n. 81, in Carlen, note 4 above, V, p. 198.

11. *A Call to Action, (Octogesima Adveniens)*, 1981, n. 4, cf. *The Pope Speaks*, Washington, 1971, XVI, p. 139.

12. Paul VI, *The Development of Peoples*, 1967, n. 26, in Carlen, note 4 above, V, p. 187 f.

13. Paul VI, *A Call to Action (Octogesima Adveniens)*, 1981, n. 26, *The Pope Speaks*, Washington, 1971, XVI, p. 139.

14. *From Words to Action*, Document 44 above, n 9.

15. In the event, this appeared only in May, 1979, *Witness to Justice: a Society to be Transformed*. A substantial book of 135 large pages, it consists of three working papers: *Faith and Justice*, the scriptural and church teaching on Christian responsibility for social justice; *Justice in Canada*, a survey of social and economic ills and inequities at home; *Justice in the Third World*, to develop awareness of the same abroad and of Canada's relationship thereto. A very competent primer, with good bibliography and action projects, this was the most ambitious pastoral-education effort of the Conference's Commission for Social Affairs in the area of social justice. Still useful, it is available from CCCB Publications Service, 90 Parent Ave., Ottawa, K1N 7B1.

Document 47

ON RESPONSIBLE INVESTMENT
To Mr. Fred H. McNeil,
Chairman of the Board, Bank of Montreal

Author — Archbishop Gilles Ouellet, President, the Canadian
Conference of Catholic Bishops, May 11, 1978

Dear Mr. NcNeil

On behalf of the Canadian Conference of Catholic Bishops, I wish
to thank you for sending me and my brother bishops of Canada,
the minutes of the recent Annual General Meeting of shareholders
of the Bank of Montreal. This transcript, you will recall, records
the question period of your meeting in which representatives of
our bishops Conference, along with other official Church representatives, raised questions about the ethical implications of continuing loans by the Bank of Montreal to the governments of South
Africa and Chile. While this reply is rather lengthy, I feel it is
important to take the opportunity to explain the concerns of the
Canadian bishops, the nature of our involvement, and the difference
in our respective moral positions in this matter.

Initially I wish to clarify some of the reasons why the Catholic
Church has become actively engaged in raising questions about the
social responsibilities of corporations and banks. We recognize that
a number of businessmen in Canada today are objecting to the more
recent activities of Christian churches regarding the operations of
corporations. I would underline that these remarks are not intended
exclusively for your bank. Rather, the occasion of your statement
provides an opportunity to indicate in a specific instance how we
believe Gospel values must enter the economic market place to

influence financial policies affecting the lives of so many people. The Church's social action springs from the Gospel message of justice which calls us to have concern for the poor, the disinherited and the oppressed. Indeed the Gospel itself encompasses all realms of human life and for this reason the Church firmly believes that religious and ethical matters cannot be separated from the economic, political and social issues of our times. The Church's social teachings encourage Christians to become actively involved in changing the attitudes and structures that cause human suffering. What follows is intended in no way as a general indictment of officials or persons in the employ of banks, corporations or other financial institutions, but is rather an attempt to offer a critique according to Christian principles of some policies adopted in certain cases by financial and economic institutions in our country.

Since the Second Vatican Council (1962-65), the Catholic Church has become increasingly concerned about the problems of injustice experienced by peoples of the Third World. During the Council, the bishops of Latin America, Africa and Asia emphasized the urgent problems of poverty, underdevelopment, and the growing repression of human rights that afflict two thirds of humanity. In the decade that followed, it became increasingly clear to many pastoral leaders of the Church in the Third World that the resources of their countries were not being developed to meet the needs of their people for food, clothing, shelter, employment, education, health care and other necessities required for a more fully human life. Instead, the resources of these countries were being developed primarily to serve the interests of transnational corporations, the western industrialized countries, local elites and dictatorial regimes. In response to these demands for justice, a call for Christian action has been issued repeatedly in the social teaching of Pope Paul VI, of the 1971 World Synod of Bishops on *Justice in the World*, and of the Canadian Bishops.

In Canada, the Catholic Church has been working with other major Christian denominations in developing a common response to global demands for justice. Through our network of missionaries and contacts with pastoral leaders of the churches in the Third World, the churches in Canada are being informed constantly about the sufferings of people in these countries. The continued oppression of black people under the *apartheid* regime of South Africa and the repression of people under the military *junta* of Chile are but two examples of pastoral problems which we are addressing in the Third World today. In these and related situations, we believe that the churches in Canada have a pastoral responsibility to raise ethical questions about the operation of the Canadian government and Canadian-based corporations in these countries. Our primary pastoral concern is to see that these Canadian institutions do not serve to strengthen the structures of oppression and the underdevelopment of peoples in those countries.

As to our position on Canadian bank loans to the Government of South Africa, you are no doubt aware that the Catholic Church throughout the world has condemned *apartheid* in South Africa, as a cruel offense against humanity. Faced with the life and death struggle of black people, our Church in South Africa has increased its opposition to *apartheid* through various measures, including attempts to defy state laws by integrating Catholic schools. In solidarity with the churches in South Africa, the major Christian churches in Canada have made numerous interventions urging Canadian institutions doing business with the government of South Africa to use their economic as well as their moral influence to dismantle the *apartheid* system. These church interventions have focused on Canada's trade relations with South Africa, the operations of several Canadian-based corporations in that country, as well as Canadian bank loans to the government of South Africa and its agencies.

In questioning the ultimate effect of Canadian bank loans to South Africa, we have been concerned primarily about the impact of foreign investment on *apartheid* itself. For us, the record clearly shows that foreign investment has not (as some western business leaders initially predicted) had a liberalizing impact on the *apartheid* regime. After thirty years, in which the western industrialized countries have pumped billions of dollars into the central economy of South Africa, the basic structures of *apartheid*, namely, the subordination of the black majority and the separation of the races, remain firmly intact. While industrialization has brought more black people into the labour market, it is clear that they form a cheap labour pool for the country's industrial growth, being subjected to conditions of low wages, no trade union rights and poor living conditions along with a legally enforced destruction of family life. Although it is difficult to bring forward absolute judgments in these matters we believe that a significant number of Canadian bank loans to the government of South Africa serve to strengthen the structures of *apartheid* and postpone the day when justice will be realized for the black majority. While opinions to the contrary have been expressed, can doubt any longer be cast on the evidence indicating that western bank loans contribute to the military and defense purposes of the South African government?

In your remarks, Mr. McNeil, you indicate that some black leaders and church leaders in South Africa favour foreign investment. It is our understanding however, that the situation is much more subtle and nuanced than you indicate, and that black leaders like Chief Buthelezi have taken a critical stance on foreign investments. A recent report from the Division of Justice and Reconciliation presented to the South Africa Council of Churches points out quite accurately the ambiguities which they see in the matter of foreign investment. Because of these ambiguities the committee which prepared this report is recommending that the National Conference of South African Churches call upon all churches in South Africa and overseas to question loans and investments in South Africa until a code of ethics for investment there is accepted. In a similar vein, the leading black journalist of South Africa, Percy Qoboza, although seeing a role for foreign investment, says in a recent article in *Time*:

> Far too many of these corporations have spoken some very good words but continue to drag their feet when it comes to meeting their obligations, seemingly content to reap the profits extended by a system that exploits the majority of the country's people. (*Time*, April 17, 1978, p. 26)

Similar positions have been adopted by the Christian Institute of South Africa. We should not be surprised however, to find black leaders, church leaders and others living in South Africa who are opposed to *apartheid* but unwilling to take a critical stance towards foreign investments in the central economy. Under the Terrorism Act of South Africa, it is a criminal offense for people to meddle or interfere in the economic affairs of their country. The detention without trial and subsequent violent death of black leader Steven Biko, following his call for economic pressures against South Africa, is a disturbing illustration of what can happen to people who oppose the maintenance of *apartheid*.

Realizing that the situation in Chile is very different, I would also like to explain our position concerning Canadian bank loans to this government. Since the military coup in 1973, the Chilean churches have been the only institutions defending human rights in the face of widespread repression. Through various programmes, the church in Chile has helped families to search for the whereabouts of their arrested members; assisted with food, shelter and legal services for the poor and the persecuted; and provided the only places where community groups, workers' organizations and human rights associations can meet with some sense of freedom. The Catholic Church moreover, has taken an increasingly critical stance towards the *junta's* ideology of the "national security state" and against its alliance with a rich domestic elite and with foreign investors. Responding to appeals, the Canadian Church has been engaged in material aid programmes for our sister Church in Chile. We have also urged the Canadian Government to accept more Chilean refugees forced into exile by the *junta,* and have assisted in the settlement of Chileans in various parts of Canada. Our concern has been expressed as well, in representations made to the Chilean ambassador in an effort to ease the continued and relentless repressions. At the same time, the Church wishes to urge Canadian-based corporations and banks to require, as a condition of their investments in Chile, that there be a clear indication of a restoration of basic human rights and evidence that the planned investments will be of significant economic benefit to the poor of that country.

In our opposition to current bank loans, we are primarily concerned lest such investment serve largely to strengthen the military *junta* and legitimate its repression of human rights. Following the coup in 1973, most foreign investors refused to do business with the new military dictatorship, but renewed loans by institutions such as the Bank of Montreal are understood in the financial community as a vote of confidence for the *junta.* We could better understand the banks' position if they could provide some evidence that such loans will benefit the majority of Chileans, especially the poorest sectors of the population. Although additional jobs may result, as long as the work force is a captive one, deprived of most of the union rights it once enjoyed, the benefits will be minimal. Additional revenues may also result, yet serious questions continue to be raised about the *junta's* use of these revenues to purchase military equipment rather than to restore vital social services and development programmes desperately needed by one-third of the population. Under such circumstances there will be little social benefit for the people of Chile.

In the past year, the Catholic Church of Chile has become increasingly critical of the economic policies of the *junta.* The present economic policies favour a privileged minority at the expense of the huge majority which is being deprived of the essentials of life. Today, some three million people out of a population of ten million live in misery, spending two-thirds of their income on food alone. In their last major statement, *Living Together as a Nation* (March, 1977, Documentation Catholique, Paris, LXXIV, p. 427), the Chilean bishops pointed out that the peasants, the workers and the poor were being compelled to "bear an excessive and disproportionate burden" of the country's current economic reconstruction. Until there are substantial changes, we feel that in the balance, the major impact of foreign investment by Canadian banks and corporations will serve to support the *junta's* oppressive economic policies and legitimate its continued repression of human rights.

Finally, I would add some clarification concerning our continuing work in the field of corporate social responsibility. As you know, our Conference participates, along with various Catholic religious orders and other churches, in the Taskforce on the Churches and Corporate Responsibility. The Taskforce assists the churches to promote social responsibility in the operations of Canadian companies. The common pastoral concerns, social teachings and social policies of its member churches provide the guiding framework for the work of the Taskforce. In those cases where the churches are questioning whether the operations of certain Canadian-based corporations cause or perpetuate social injustices, the Taskforce assists the churches in coordinating background research, arranging meetings with management, making presentations at shareholders meetings, preparing educational materials and developing follow-up strategies.

In terms of the Canadian Conference of Catholic Bishops, the Taskforce is accountable to our Episcopal Commission for Social Affairs. Our Social Affairs staff participates actively in the monthly meetings and sub-committees of the Taskforce. The bishops of the Social Affairs Commission discuss and review the issues of corporate responsibility and evaluate the work of the Taskforce on a regular basis. Decisions regarding the representation of the Bishops Conference and annual shareholders meetings of various companies were made by our Executive Committee. Once a year the bishops of Canada have an opportunity to review the work of the Taskforce and the other major projects of our Social Affairs Commission at our General Assembly.

Thus the Taskforce and its work concerning the social responsibility of Canadian corporations is an integral part of the pastoral programme of the Canadian bishops. It should be noted however, that the work of the churches on matters of corporate social responsibility has not been limited to Chile and South Africa. The Taskforce is engaged in dialogue with Canadian companies about their operations in several other Latin American, African and Asian countries. More recently the involvement of the Taskforce has been extended to the Canadian north.

While acknowledging therefore the complexity of the issues, I must state that the moral position in your statement of January 16th differs significantly from that of the Canadian Conference of Catholic Bishops.

At a later date we will be releasing this letter for publication, as it relates not only to your public statement but indicates the position of the CCCB in the whole question of foreign loans and investment.

I would very much appreciate it, Mr. McNeil, if a few of us could meet sometime in the near future to pursue this issue with a view to better fulfilling the respective responsibilities we have to the people of this country.

Document 48

SOCIO-ETHICAL GUIDELINES FOR INVESTMENT

Author — The Episcopal Commission for Social Affairs,
April 10, 1979 [1]

I — PASTORAL CONCERNS

The teachings of the Church, rooted in the Gospel itself, emphasize a variety of pastoral concerns pertaining to the social responsibility of economic institutions in society. The following are some examples drawn from the social teachings of the Church.

The Purpose of Creation

The Church teaches that "God intended the earth and all that it contains for the use of every human being and people". [2] Indeed all persons are made in the image of God. Our dignity as persons confers on us certain inalienable rights, primarily the right to life and all that renders life possible such as food, shelter, clothing, employment, education and health care. [3] Thus, the earth's resources and created goods exist to support human life. The resources and goods of the earth are not to be manipulated but to be used responsibly for the benefit of people. Indeed, "as all men follow justice and are united in charity, created goods should abound for them on a reasonable basis". This is the "universal purpose for which created goods are meant". [4]

The Common Good

The teachings of the Church further emphasize that the basic purpose of economic systems and structures "must not be the mere multiplication of products... (nor) profit or domination"[5] but to serve the needs of people for a more fully human life. The resources and goods of the earth therefore are to be developed to serve the common good. This is the basic principle which should govern all economic and political systems. And "all other rights, whatever they are, including property rights and free commerce must be subordinated to this principle; they must not hinder it, but must rather expedite its application".[6]

New Economic Powers

The teaching of the Church, in recent years, has pointed out that modern corporations, particularly transnationals, represent a new form of economic power and domination. The increasing concentration of economic power and the means of production in the hands of a small number of large corporations, represents a serious threat to the common good of peoples and nations. Indeed, a relatively small number of large corporations today have an enormous impact in determining the conditions under which people live. As these continue to expand their operations throughout the world, they "can lead to a new and abusive form of economic domination on the social, cultural and even political level".[7]

A Prophetic Mission

In proclaiming the Gospel in the world today, the Church has an important role to play in defending the rights of people who are victims of unjust systems and institutions. As the World Synod of Bishops declared in 1971:

Listening to the cry of those who suffer violence and are oppressed by unjust systems and structures, and hearing the appeal of a world that by its perversity contradicts the plan of the Creator, we have shared our awareness of the Church's vocation to be present in the heart of the world, by proclaiming the Good News to the poor, freedom to the oppressed and joy to the afflicted''.[8]

The Church has an important role in cooperating with the poor and the oppressed to change the social, economic and political structures that cause human suffering.

The Social Responsibility of Corporations

As part of its prophetic mission, the Church has a role in promoting the social responsibility of business corporations and other economic institutions. Indeed the Church has the right and the duty to declare to those institutions involved in the economic sphere that the fundamental purpose of their productivity ''must not be the mere multiplication of products... profits or domination''.[9] In the words of Pope Paul VI:

> Every programme geared to increase production must have no other view than to serve mankind, namely to lessen inequalities, to remove discrimination, to free men from the bonds of servitude and to enable them to improve their condition in the temporal order, achieve moral development and perfect their spiritual endowments.[10]

Church Investments

As one institution among others in the world, the Church must examine its own activities and operations to see that it is using its resources to serve the needs of justice in society. As the 1971 Synod stated,

> While the Church is bound to give witness to justice, she recognizes that anyone who ventures to speak to people about justice must first be just in their eyes. Hence we must undertake an examination of the modes of acting and of the possessions and lifestyle found within the Church itself.[11]

In particular, this involves an examination of how the Church invests its money and exercises its role as a shareholder in companies.

II — ETHICAL GUIDELINES

To carry out its prophetic mission, the Church requires some ethical guidelines for evaluating the operations of corporations and related economic institutions. The following suggested headings are divided into five categories. Each category provides a series of questions to be raised regarding the social responsibilities of companies doing business in Canada or other countries in the world. This is certainly not meant to be a comprehensive set of ethical guidelines. These are some examples: others could be added.

Category 1: *Social Responsibility to Workers*

Wages: Does the company pay adequate wages and benefits required for a decent human life? How do the company's wage and fringe benefits compare with those of other companies, other regions? How do wage increases compare with increased profits?

Working conditions: Does the company provide safeguards for the health and safety of its workers? How do these compare with those of similar companies? Are there any provisions for job security for the company's workers?

Trade unions: Does the company recognize the rights of workers to organize through trade unions? What has been its record of relationship with unions?

Worker participation: Does the company involve workers effectively in its decision-making process? Is the company open to forms of worker-ownership or worker-control?

Category 2: *Social Responsibility to the Community and Country of Operation*

Underdeveloped regions: Does the company operate in relatively poor, underdeveloped communities or regions? What is its impact on such conditions?

Job creation: Does the company provide many or few permanent jobs for the community? Are operations primarily labour intensive or capital-intensive?

Resource extraction: Is the community or country involved in processing and manufacturing its own resources? Does the company effectively limit the community's or country's involvement to supplying raw materials?

Tax incentives: Does the company require tax incentives from governments as conditions for investment? With what impact on the long term economic development of the community or country?

Capital re-investment: Does the company re-invest its profits in the community to serve local development needs? Are profits exported for investment elsewhere?

Category 3: *Responsibility to Social and Environmental Conditions of the Community or Country of Operation*

Company towns: Does the company operate "company towns" or "one industry communities"? What control or influence does it exercise over credit, police, products, laws, trade unions, cultural and educational activities?

Land use: Does the company own or control large tracts of agricultural land? Is the land being adequately used for food production and local benefit?

Internal migration: Do the company's operations compel workers to leave the land or to migrate to urban centers? What impact does this have on family life?

Minority groups: Does company policy provide jobs for minority groups (racial, cultural, women, etc.)? Are the languages, customs and values of minority groups respected by the company?

Pollution problems: Does the company use technology that causes pollution of air, water, soil or other forms of environmental damage? Are adequate safeguards employed by the company?

Category 4: *Social Responsibility as to Civil and Religious Liberties in the Community or Country of Operation*

Repressive regimes: Does the company operate under repressive regimes guilty of torture, murder or widespread repression of civil liberties? Do the company's operations strengthen or legitimate these repressive regimes?

Apartheid: Does the company operate in countries where there is segregation and subordination of certain races? Do the company's operations effectively support or oppose *apartheid* or repression?

Religious freedom: Does the company operate in countries or regions where there are legal restrictions on religious freedoms? Does the company actively oppose or support these conditions?

Cheap labour: Does the company operate in countries or regions where trade unions are outlawed or restricted in their activities? Does the company take advantage of such conditions?

Category 5: *Social Responsibility as to Production and Marketing*

Consumer goods: Does the company produce and sell luxury goods or the basic necessities of people? Does the product meet consumer needs? Is it serviceable and durable?

Harmful products: Does the company produce and/or sell products which are harmful to or destructive of human life (e.g., abortifacients)?

Arms production: Does the company engage in any aspect of arms production (weapons, military equipment, military facilities, nuclear energy, etc.)?

Advertising practices: Does the company's advertising present a true rather than false or misleading description of products? Does the company's advertising avoid every form of discrimination against or exploitation of particular groups (e.g., racial minorities, women, etc.)? Is advertising used to create artificial needs?

Monopoly control: Does the company exercise monopoly control over its particular markets? Itself or as a subsidiary of another corporation? Has the company a record of unfair business practices, of trust or monopoly violations, of price fixing?

III — INVESTMENT OPTIONS

The pastoral concerns and ethical guidelines outlined above provide a basis for critique of the investment policies of the Church. In this context, there are several investment options open to Church institutions, subject to any restrictions existing in law.

Like other institutions, the Church tends to place its money in conventional investments where financial opportunities exist. The Church however, is not a profit-making institution. It is therefore important for Church institutions to consider other investment options. Options as intended here are options rather of the Church in general than of the Canadian Conference of Catholic Bishops in particular. The term "church institutions" refers to dioceses, religious orders, etc.

(a) *Public Investments*

As an option, the Church should consider the advisability of investing capital in institutions of the public sector. For example, Church institutions could purchase municipal or utility commission bonds when it is clear that the capital is designated for social needs such as community development projects, poverty programmes, urban renewal projects, pollution control, etc. Such investment can highlight the importance of these public sector institutions designed to serve the needs of people in the community.

(b) *Creative Investments*

Church institutions should consider the advisability of investing capital in alternative development projects of social change programmes. Thus revenue from conventional investments could be used as seed money, direct loans or lines of credit for various creative projects. Such projects might include co-op housing or food stores, worker-owned industries, native land claims programmes. While Church institutions may not have large amounts of capital for creative investment, a few examples of this type of investment can serve to illustrate the larger purposes of the Church and its mission.

(c) *Incentive Investments*

Church authorities should also consider using capital as an incentive to stimulate or promote social responsibility on the part of companies. For example, Church institutions might invest in companies that employ an adequately defined code of ethics or social audit to evaluate their business practices. Church institutions could invest in small employment-creating companies that need assistance and are producing necessary and useful goods required by people in the community. This type of investment helps to support and stimulate those companies that are effectively practicing social responsibility in their business operations.

(d) *Conventional Investments*

It may be necessary for Church institutions to continue placing a portion of their capital in conventional investments. Where Church institutions are dependent on such investments for their pastoral budget, total abandonment of such income would be damaging to its mission. Moreover, conventional investments often provide opportunities for the Church, as shareholder, to raise ethical questions about the operations of the enterprise.

(e) *Strategic Investments*

The Church should also consider investing capital for the specific purpose of promoting corporate responsibility. For example, Church institutions might invest in companies known to be insensitive to social injustices, in order to raise ethical questions and to promote policy changes. As shareholders, Church institutions are often in a better position to advocate policy changes in the operations of a specific company. This type of investment therefore, aims to redress the unjust practices of specific companies.

(f) *Disinvestment Option*

The Church should also consider the option of taking its money out of companies that repeatedly refuse to change unjust practices. This option should be used as a last resort when it is clear that no changes are to be hoped from a given company. Disinvestment should be adopted as a means of drawing public attention to the particular injustices in the situation.

NOTES

1. These guidelines were prepared for the Administrative Board of the Canadian Catholic Conference and approved by the same.

2. Second Vatican Council, *The Church in the Modern World*, n. 69.

3. *Ibid.* n. 26.

4. *Ibid.* n. 69.

5. *Ibid.* n. 64.

6. Paul VI, *The Development of Peoples*, 1967, in *The Papal Encyclicals*, edit. Claudia Carlen, IHM (Wilmington, N.C., McGrath Publishing, 1981), V, 187, n. 22.

7. Paul VI, *A Call to Action (Octogesima Adveniens)*, 1971, cf. *The Pope Speaks*, Washington, 1971, XVI, n. 44, p. 158 f.

8. Third International Synod of Bishops, 1971, *Justice in the World*, Introduction, cf. *The Pope Speaks*, Washington, 1971, XVI, p. 377.

9. Second Vatican Council, *ibid.*, n. 64.

10. Paul VI, *The Development of Peoples*, n. 34, in Carlen, note 5 above, p. 189.

11. Third International Synod of Bishops, cf. note 8 above, P. III.

Document 49

UNEMPLOYMENT: THE HUMAN COSTS

Author — Administrative Board, the Canadian Conference of Catholic Bishops, January 4, 1980

"I'm just no good. I can't pay the bills and take care of my family" (a father)

"How many times can you be told you are not wanted and still keep your self-respect?" (a single woman)

"No wonder my husband drinks. He sees the children going without good food and clothing while the bills keep piling up. He can't face that day in and day out." (a mother)

"They tell us to get an education but if the unemployment situation keeps up, we won't be able to get jobs anyway, so why try?" (a young student)

1. These statements illustrate the human suffering experienced by the unemployed in our country today. They add a sense of urgency to the battery of monthly statistics on unemployment. Out of a work force of over 10 million in Canada, close to 800,000 people are jobless. In spite of the creation of new employment, the problem has become more serious in recent years than at any other period since the 1930's.[1] The unemployment situation today illustrates one of the major social issues identified in our recent pastoral program, Witness to Justice.[2] It also reflects the need for fundamental social change which we stated in our message, A Society to be Transformed.[3]

2. In the context of our pastoral program, Witness to Justice, we intend once again to speak out against the realities of unemployment as a particular example of injustice. As pastoral leaders of the

Catholic Church in Canada, we invite our brothers and sisters of the Christian community to join us in raising questions about the human realities of unemployment, its underlying causes, the distortion of social values and the possibilities for community action. In recent years, the bishops of Quebec have made several pastoral statements on the problem of unemployment. Today, our concern is to address the phenomena of unemployment in the whole of Canada. We hope that our reflections will bring some clarity to the public debate about this crucial issue and make some contribution towards overcoming the situation of injustice faced by the unemployed today.[4]

UNEMPLOYMENT: HUMAN REALITIES

The Victims of Unemployment

3.   In moving beyond the maze of statistics and graphs, it becomes clear that the problem of rising unemployment is hurting certain people and certain regions more than others in Canada. For example, unemployment generally hits the working class (e.g., blue collar workers) more than the middle class (e.g., professional people).[5] It is more common today among women than men.[6] Young people, particularly those entering the work force for the first time, are experiencing a much higher jobless rate than adults.[7] At the same time, unemployment is more heavily concentrated in certain regions of the country than in others. The Atlantic provinces for example, experience a jobless rate which is two and three times that of Ontario and the prairies.[8] In every province moreover, there are regions and communities always at risk of high unemployment, because of boom and bust cycles of economic development.

The Human and Social Costs

4.   As emphasized in previous pastoral statements, the human and social costs of continuing unemployment are themselves staggering.[9] There is the economic strain on family life that comes with the sudden drop in purchasing power and the possibility of indebtedness. There is the psychological strain that comes from loss of feeling of self-worth coupled with anxiety, frustration and bitterness. As a result, unemployment has meant lower productivity in the economy,

reduction in public revenues and increasing social welfare costs. These problems in turn are intensified by cut-backs in social services (including unemployment insurance benefits). Today, as unemployment threatens to become a more or less permanent fact of life in our economy, a substantial portion of our population is in danger of becoming more marginalized and disillusioned.[10]

The Christian Meaning of Human Labour

5. For Christians, human labour has always had a special value and meaning. The activity of work calls upon the creative spirit of the person and his or her capacity to cooperate with other members of the community or society. In doing so, people realize their human dignity. It is through their work that men and women are able to support themselves and their families. By interacting with fellow workers in a common task, people have an opportunity to develop their personalities and sense of self-worth. In this way, people are able to participate in building up their society and to give meaning to their existence as human beings. It was Jesus Christ Himself, "who conferred an eminent dignity on labour when at Nazareth, He worked with His own hands."[11] And when men and women offer their labour to God, they are "associated with the redemptive work of Jesus Christ."[12] Thus, the human activity of work, to earn a living that provides the basic needs required for a decent human life, is already part of God's plan and will for mankind.[13]

The Resulting Forms of Alienation

6. This human vocation cannot be achieved without the right of each person to work and thereby to contribute to the development of society and its well-being. Today, the dignity of increasing numbers of people is being violated by the very fact that they are unable to exercise fully these basic human rights. As a result, diverse forms of alienation emerge. The many thousands of jobless people, unable to participate in the production and development of our society, find themselves alienated from their fellow citizens. At the same time, many workers find that new technologies and relationships in their industry have made their job virtually meaningless.[14] Some workers, engaged in the production of wasteful or destructive products in our consumer society, question the value and meaning of their work.[15] While technological advances and economic growth may

provide the material for human progress they cannot, in themselves, bring it about.[16]

UNEMPLOYMENT: UNDERLYING CAUSES

7.   It is not easy to come to grips with the causes of continuing unemploymnt. Who are responsible?[17] Some people tend to put the blame on the unemployed themselves. It is often said for example, that there are plenty of jobs to go round and that the unemployed are "too lazy" or "too choosy". Undoubtedly this is true in some individual cases. The fact remains however that in recent years there has been only one job available for every 20 people looking for work.[18] Moreover, most of the new jobs being created are for white collar workers in service industries, rather than for blue collar workers who are experiencing higher rates of unemployment.

8.   There is also a tendency to put the blame on the large number of women and immigrants entering the labour market. However, women and immigrants have the same right as other people to earn their living and to fulfill their human aspirations. The rising cost of living has compelled many women to seek jobs outside the home.[19] Indeed, many women have had to enter the job market out of economic necessity in order to provide support for their families.[20] There are of course some people caught up in our consumer way of life, who take on extra jobs simply to earn more money for luxury expenses. At the same time, many immigrants and refugees are allowed into Canada each year simply because they will accept low-paying jobs or have the skills for certain jobs that nobody else has in this country. For the most part however, the factors identified above are not the principal reasons for continuing unemployment. Thus we are compelled to search further for the real causes of this social disease.

Economic Strategies

9.   We recognize that the problems of continuing unemployment are complex, that they are related to the global economy and that there are no instant or magic solutions. As bishops, we do not claim to be technical experts in economic matters. It is our responsibility however, to invite fellow Christians to take part in identifying the

causes of unemployment and seeking solutions. To this end, it is important to examine critically various economic, political and social explanations for continuing unemployment. Among those often identified by specialists are the following basic causes:[21]

(a) the concentration of the country's economic power in the hands of a small number of corporations which has made it difficult to develop labour-intensive industrial strategies that generate thousands of new jobs;[22]

(b) the continued centralization of the majority of job-producing industries in our major metropolitan areas, which contributes to growing problems of unemployment and economic disparities in several other regions of the country;[23]

(c) the high levels of foreign ownership and control of Canada's principal industries which generally put Canadian workers in a vulnerable position during times of economic recession, subject to plant shut-downs and layoffs;[24]

(d) the orientation of our economy towards exporting natural resources (gas, timber, coal and other minerals) rather than to manufacturing finished products, thereby giving up new employment opportunities;[25]

(d) the large investments of capital in high-technology, industrial projects (e.g., pipelines, hydro-electric projects), which may increase our gross national product but produce relatively few permanent jobs;[26]

(f) the prolongation of lockouts and strikes which result in a loss of productivity and aggravate conditions of unemployment in some regions of the country.

UNEMPLOYMENT: SOCIAL DEVALUATION

A Moral Disorder

10. These and related causes of unemployment point to more fundamental crises that exist in the values and priorities of our society. Indeed, unemployment is not simply a political or economic or social problem. It is a profoundly moral and spiritual problem in our times. As Pope John Paul II reminds us, the ''plague of

unemployment'' is symptomatic of a basic ''moral disorder''.[27] We are called therefore, to examine the basic values and attitudes that motivate the economic and political activities which make our society what it is today.

The Common Good

11.　The primary purpose of any economic system, the Church has consistently taught, is to serve the basic needs of all people required for a more fully human life.[28] In Canada today, despite the many efforts to deal with the urgent needs of people, our society is still a long way from achieving this principal goal. As we have stated in previous messages, the persistence of poverty, unemployment, regional disparities, and a variety of related social problems demonstrates that there is something wrong with our social and economic order.[29] It fails to serve the basic needs of all the people. As a consequence, the poorest and the weakest members of our society are made to suffer most.

Values and Priorities

12.　The human realities of unemployment raise vital questions about the values and priorities of our social order. As a modern capitalist society, have we reached the point where greater priority is placed on the value of machines than on the value of human labour? Where maximizing profits and growth takes precedence over the goal of serving real human needs? Where the protection of private property operates to the detriment of the right to work for thousands of people? Indeed are we moving towards that point in our society where, as the Holy Father warns, mankind is in danger of becoming ''... the slave of things, the slave of his own products, the slave of economic systems, the slave of production''?[30]

Alternative Visions

13.　As Christians we have an alternative vision of mankind and society. The Gospel calls us to prepare for God's Kingdom by participating in the building of a society that is truly based on justice and love. In Canada today, this vision includes a more equitable redistribution of wealth and power among all the people and the development of this country's resources to serve basic human needs.[31] It entails the creation of authentic human communities in which people live and work together in a lifestyle of "caring, sparing and sharing".[32] And this in turn requires that greater priority be placed on the value of human labour in our economic life and on the creation of socially useful work so that people can truly contribute to the development of a just society.

UNEMPLOYMENT: COMMUNITY ACTION

Alternative Industrial Strategies

14. We Christians should not stand idly by while thousands of our brothers and sisters are being deprived of their human dignity through unemployment. While there are no instant or magic solutions, it is important that we join with all people of good will in a common search for strategies and actions to overcome this disease of unemployment that plagues our society. A major long-term task is the development of alternative industrial strategies designed to serve the human needs of all people in this country.[33] This would require effective measures to increase the self-sufficiency of Canada's industries, strengthen the manufacturing sector and other job-producing industries, redistribute capital for industrial development in underdeveloped regions and increase community ownership and control of local industries. In so doing, emphasis should be placed on recognizing the dignity of human labour through the creation of socially useful work.

Guidelines for Study and Action

15. The long-range task of developing alternative industrial strategies requires study and action by people of good will in local and regional communities throughout this country. As a step in this direction, we encourage more local Christian communities to become involved in a process of:

(a) becoming aware of the local realities and experiences of unemployment. This includes being present to unemployed workers, listening to their problems and identifying current and future job needs in your region.

(b) analyzing the basic causes of unemployment in your region.

This includes some reflection on the structural causes of unemployment in our economy, which were noted above.

(c) making ethical judgments about the realities and causes of unemployment. This includes some reflection and education (in parishes, families, schools and community groups) on the Christian meaning of human labour and the primary goal of an economic order as serving human needs.

(d) supporting the specific struggles of unemployed workers in your region. This includes moral and financial support for activities aimed at creating new jobs, obtaining job security for workers, planning shorter work weeks, and generating public awareness about the realities and causes of unemployment.

(e) participating in efforts to develop alternative industrial strategies in your region. This includes assessing the economic potential of your region, developing alternative plans for economic development, and pressing local governments and corporations to change their priorities and industrial strategies.

(f) increasing community ownership and control of industries where desirable. This includes the promotion of cooperatives, worker-controlled industries and other initiatives to develop more effective community participation and control of economic life in your region.

Community Action Models

16. In offering these suggestions, we recognize that in different parts of the country, Christian groups are already engaged in study and action on the complex problems of unemployment and industrial strategies. In several places, Christians are hard at work on these issues through participation in the activities of their local labour union, coalition for full employment or small producer association.[34] In other situations, Christian communities have initiated study-action projects, notably in Newfoundland, Quebec and Nova Scotia, on problems of regional unemployment.[35] In each of these cases, it is important to note that Christians are directly involved with the victims of injustice — the unemployed, the exploited workers, the small producer — and others who have been marginalized in our economy. Together, these and related models for study and action may provide further insights on how Christians can become

more directly engaged in the problems of unemployment and in developing alternative industrial strategies in local communites or regions.[36]

Labour Unions

17. Labour unions, in addition to government and business, clearly have a vital role to play in developing strategies for full employment in our society.[37] Today a major concern of many unions in labour-management negotiations is job security for their own workers. Major problems are evident however. On one hand, the prolonged strikes of some powerful labour unions have aggravated conditions of unemployment in certain regions of the country. On the other, the existence of large numbers of unemployed is frequently used by companies as an instrument to impose lower wage settlements and inferior working conditions on their workers. It must also be remembered that close to 60% of Canada's work force is unorganized and thus unable to protect their employment aspirations. We therefore urge labour unions not only to seek job security for their own workers, but to join ranks with the unemployed and non-unionized workers in a common strategy to overcome the basic structural causes of unemployment in our society.

CONCLUSIONS

18. In the final analysis, the complex problems of unemployment are deeply rooted in the economic order. Bold transformations in the values and priorities of our society will be necessary. As Pope John Paul II reminds us: ''This difficult road of the indispensable transformation of the structures of economic life is one on which it will not be easy to go forward without the intervention of a true conversion of mind, will and heart.''[38]

19. In this connection, the set of working instruments recently prepared by our Social Affairs Commission are aimed at helping Christian communities to become more committed to the struggle for social and economic justice.[39] These instruments are designed to provide local Christian animators with some of the tools and resources required to develop study-action projects for the transformation of our society. It is our hope that these initiatives will

encourage and assist more Christians to travel along the difficult road of building a new society based on justice and love. Finally, we pray the Lord that He instill in His people the courage and the strength to become true witnesses for justice in our times.

NOTES

1. It is difficult to obtain an accurate picture of the number of people who are unemployed. Official statistics do not include the "hidden unemployed", the countless numbers of people who have given up looking for work after numerous frustrations.

2. Cf. *Witness to Justice: A Society to be Transformed*, Commission for Social Affairs (Ottawa, K1N 7B1, CCCB Publications Service, 1979).

3. *A Society to be Transformed*, Document 46 above.

4. The Canadian bishops have often addressed the problem of unemployment, e.g., in the Labour Day Message of 1964, Document 12, above. More recently the Quebec bishops have issued three pastoral messages: *La dignité de l'homme n'a pas de prix* (1977); *Discovering the Unemployed as Brethren* (1978); *Les jeunes n'ont pas choisi d'être chômeurs* (1979), (Montréal, Assemblée des Evêques du Québec). A pastoral letter by Bishop A. Carter and Mgr A. Proulx, *Layoffs by Inco and Falconbridge*, 1977, addresses the problem of layoffs in the mining industry at Sudbury (Chancery Office, P.O. Box 510, North Bay, Ont., P1B 8J1).

5. In mid-1977 the *Financial Times of Canada* (Toronto) reported that there were 112,000 fewer manufacturing jobs than one year earlier. This had a particular impact on blue collar workers.

6. In September of 1979 the official statistics stated that 8.5% of women in the labour force were unemployed while the figure for men was just 6.2%.

7. In September of 1979 the jobless rate for those under 25 stood at 12.3% while it was 7.1% for the labour force as a whole, and 5.1% for those over 25.

8. In September of 1979, the national average stood at 7.4%. The regional breakdown was as follows: Newfoundland, 14.1%; P.E.I., 10.6%; New Brunswick, 10.7%; Nova Scotia, 10.2%; Quebec, 9.1%; Ontario, 6.1%; Manitoba, 5.0%; Saskatchewan, 3.9%; Alberta, 3.7%; and British Columbia, 7.7%. For some insights on the social and economic effects of uneven patterns of development, cf. *Une région où règne l'insécurité, le Nord-ouest québécois*, (Montréal, Dossier "Vie Ouvrière", n. 127, 1978).

9. In *Discovering the Unemployed as Brethren* (cf. note 4 above), the Quebec bishops describe the economic, psychological, moral and social ordeals which unemployed people suffer today.

10. For a popular discussion of these concerns, see *Quand ferment les usines* (Montréal, Dossier "Vie Ouvrière", n. 117, 1977 and a more recent publication of the same title, *Quand ferment les usines* (Montréal, Centre Saint-Pierre Apôtre, 1979).

11. Second Vatican Council, *The Church in the Modern World*, n. 67.

12. *Ibid.*

13. *Ibid.* nn. 35 f.

14. Cf. R. Blauner, *Alienation and Freedom: the Factory Worker and his Industry* (Chicago, U. of Chicago Press, 1964); *Work in America: Institute Studies in Productivity*,

(Cambridge, Mass., MIT Press); S. Turkel, edit., *Working People* (New York, 10019, Avon Press, 1975).

15. For a discussion of wasteful or destructive forms of production in our consumer society, cf. B. Commoner, *The Closing Circle* (New York, Bantam Books and Beekman Publishers, 1973).

16. Second Vatican Council, *op. cit.*, n. 35.

17. For discussions of popular misconceptions about unemployment see *Unemployment*, Issue, n. 18, Department of Church in Society, United Church of Canada, 85 St. Clair Ave. E., Toronto, 1978.

18. Cited in *Jobs and People*, (Ottawa, Economic Council of Canada, 1976). This study also concluded that four out of five drawing Unemployment Insurance benefits are unemployed for reasons beyond their control, because of layoffs or job termination.

19. It is now estimated that 57% of Canadian families are dependent on two salaries in order to meet rising costs. The number of working women or those looking for work, has tripled over the last thirty years. Yet the jobs that the vast majority of women are generally compelled to take in the labour market tend to offer relatively low wages, unstable employment, few benefits, and little opportunity for career development or advancement. In a recent study, *Women and Work: the Second Time Around, a Study of Women Returning to the Work Force* (Ottawa, Advisory Council on the Status of Women, 1979), Mary Pearson concludes that economic necessity is the primary motivating force behind women re-entering the job market. ''Inflation has made two incomes essential for many families in order to maintain economic stability and to provide for future financiel security''. (p. 9) In the case of poor families living under the poverty line, the study shows that ''many low-income families may be above the poverty line only because both husband and wife are paid workers. Clearly, these women are bread winners and the financial stability of their families depends in part on their salaries''. (pp. 9-10)

20. *Ibid.*: ''... almost 40% of all working women are single, divorced, separated, or widowed and therefore must work to support themselves and their families with the necessities of life; all too often 'frills' are out of the question''. (pp. 10-11)

21. In *Witness to Justice: A Society to be Transformed*, our Social Affairs Commission has provided a set of working instruments which may be useful in analyzing many of the economic and political strategies outlined below. See discussions on: ''Global Economy'' p. 35; ''Concentration of Corporate Power'' p. 38; ''Centralized Economy'' p. 39; ''Hinterland Regions'' p. 62; ''Foreign Ownership'' p. 37; ''Economic Dependency'' p. 37; ''Increasing Lay-Offs'' p. 50; ''Exploitation of Workers'' p. 51; ''Control of Workers'' p. 52; ''Southern Impact'' p. 70.

22. For a detailed study on the concentration of economic power in Canada, see Wallace Clement, *The Canadian Corporate Elite: An Analysis of Economic Power*, (Toronto, McClelland and Stewart, 1975). For a brief treatment of the subject, see *Who's in Control?*, Issue n. 14, cf. note 17 above. Cf. also Second Vatican Council, *The Church in the Modern World*, n. 65. For an analysis of economic concentration in Quebec, see Arnaud Sales, *La Bourgeoisie industrielle au Québec* (Montréal, Presses de l'Université de Montréal, 1979).

23. For an overview of the regional disparities that result from a centralized economy, see Paul Phillips, *Regional Disparities* (Toronto, Lorimer, 1978). See also *Atlantic Regional Disparities*, the Social Action Commission, Roman Catholic Diocese of Charlottetown, P.E.I.; *Now That We've Burned Our Boats* (St. John's, Nfld., People's Commission on Unemployment, 1979); A. Dubuc, ''Recul de Montréal ou socio-développement du Québec?'' in *L'Économie québécoise*, (Montréal, Presses de l'Université du Québec, 1976), pp. 439-49.

24. A recent study by the Science Council of Canada (Ottawa, K1A 0M5, 1972) shows that foreign investment has had a negative effect on Canada's present and future industrial performance. See J.H.N. Britton and J.M. Gilmour, *The Weakest Link* (Ottawa: Supply and Services Canada, 1978). There are many reports and studies illustrating the vulnerability of Canada's economy due to high levels of foreign ownership. The classic work is Kari Levitt's *Silent Surrender: The Multinational Corporation in Canada* (Toronto: Macmillan, 1979).

25. See the report of the Science Council of Canada (cf. note 24), *The Structure of Canadian Industry*, which pointed out that Canada's policies of exporting natural resources has resulted in a new loss of jobs. In this study, the Science Council also contends that the strengthening of Canada's manufacturing sector is essential to overcoming problems of continuing unemployment. Moreover, the Organization for Economic Cooperation and Development (OECD) reports that Canada now employs a smaller percentage of its labour force in manufacturing than all other industrialized countries except Turkey and Greece.

26. For a case study of the impact of capital-intensive resource development on workers in Canada, see *Paying the Piper*, prepared by GATT-Fly Project, Toronto.

27. *The Redeemer of Mankind*, 1979, n. 53 in *The Papal Encyclicals*, edit. Claudia Carlen, IHM (Wilmington, N.C., McGrath Publishing, 1981), V, p. 258.

28. Cf. Second Vatican Council, *The Church in the Modern World*, nn. 63 and 26; Paul VI, *The Development of Peoples*, n. 22, in Carlen (cf. note 27), V, 187.

29. Cf. Document 44, n. 3 and Document 46 above.

30. John Paul II, *The Redeemer of Mankind*, n. 50, in Carlen (note 27), V, 258.

31. The Canadian bishops, *From Words to Action*, nn. 3, 7, Document 44 above.

32. The Canadian bishops, *Simplicity and Sharing*, 1972, Document 33 above.

33. For some insights on alternative economic strategies, see E.F. Schumacher, *Small Is Beautiful* (New York, Harper and Row, 1976) and Hazel Henderson, *Creating Alternative Futures* (New York, Berkley Publishing, 1978). For an overview of industrial democracy and worker-controlled industries, see David Jenkins, *Job Power: Blue and White Collar Democracy* (New York, Penguin, 1974).

34. The ecumenical project, Ten Days for World Development, has recently launched a three-year education program on the rights and needs of working people, including the problems of unemployment, in Canada and the Third World. See *Making a Living* (Ten Days for World Development, 85 St. Clair Ave. E., Toronto, M4T 1M4). In Quebec, le Mouvement des Travailleurs chrétiens and la Jeunesse Ouvrière Catholique are two examples of direct involvement of Christians in the struggles of workers. For further information, contact Mouvement des Travailleurs chrétiens, 7559 boul. St-Laurent, Montréal, and la Jeunesse Ouvrière, 685 Décarie N., Montréal, P.Q.

35. See, for example, *Now That We've Burned Our Boats* (Newfoundland: People's Commission on Unemployment). This is the report of the People's Commission which was organized by labour unions and other regional groups to conduct a public inquiry into the human realities and causes of unemployment in Newfoundland. See also *Working Together: A Report by the National Council of Welfare on Creating New Job Opportunities* (Ottawa, K1A 0K9, 1978).

36. For an example of alternative industrial strategies in community development, see C. Banville, *Les Opérations dignité* (Québec: Le Fonds de recherches forestières de l'Université de Laval, 1977).

37. For previous statements by the Canadian bishops on the important role of labour unions, see Documents 18 and 19 above.

38. *The Redeemer of Mankind*, n. 55, in Carlen (note 27), V, p. 258.

39. *Witness to Justice: A Society to Be Transformed*, cf. note 2.

Document 50

ON OIL AND GAS LEGISLATION: BILL C-48
To the Prime Minister

Author — Bishop Remi De Roo, Chairman, the Episcopal
Commission for Social Affairs, March 25, 1981

We are deeply concerned by your government's recent proposals
for oil and gas legislation (Bill C-48) which is currently before this
session of Parliament. If enacted, this legislation would pose a
serious threat to the aboriginal peoples of the North and other
permanent residents of the territories. We believe this proposed
legislation also contradicts the basic spirit and values which you and
your government are striving to enshrine in the Constitution through
a Charter of Rights. More specifically, the new oil and gas bill:

1) Undermines the proposed guarantee of aboriginal rights in the
Constitution and prejudices native claims negotiations before they
have been successfully completed. Under Bill C-48, the native
peoples of the North would be unable to claim aboriginal rights
to lands designated for oil and gas development, let alone rights
over such resources in their own homeland.

2) Concentrates the decision-making powers over northern oil and
gas developments in one single federal ministry of Energy, Mines
and Resources. Under Bill C-48, the federal energy minister would
also have sweeping emergency powers over oil and gas activity
in the North with the result that rights of direct public participation in review and decision-making could be eliminated.

3) Seriously impairs the ability of the people of the territories to

develop economically viable forms of responsible government. Under Bill C-48, the Yukon and Northwest Territories, would be denied the right to develop their own fiscal base through control over oil and gas resources in their region, thereby perpetuating their economic dependency on the rest of Canada.

4) Increases the danger of uncontrolled environmental and social costs from major oil and gas developments. Under Bill C-48, proposed oil and gas developments would no longer have to be tested in the public eye through regulating agencies, to see if they are environmentally safe, socially fair, and economically sound.

In effect, this proposed legislation would further entrench the people of the North in a situation of colonialism in Canada. It not only threatens to violate the aboriginal rights of the native peoples but also to deny all the peoples of the North some of the basic democratic rights and freedoms which we have come to know and expect in other regions of Canada.

Along with church leaders in the North, we therefore join the major northern native and political organizations in opposing Bill C-48. We respectfully urge you, Mr. Prime Minister, to take now whatever steps are necessary to withdraw this proposed legislation from Parliament.

Document 51

TOWARDS A NEW INTERNATIONAL ECONOMIC ORDER

To the Prime Minister

Author — Bishop Remi De Roo, Chairman, the Episcopal Commission for Social Affairs, October 21, 1981

For several months, leaders of nation states and international organizations have underlined the urgent need to return to the North-South Dialogue. We recognize and affirm in particular, the role that you and your colleagues have played, Mr. Prime Minister, in attempting to renew these critical discussions between the developed and underdeveloped countries. On the eve of the Cancun meetings,[1] we would like to draw your attention to several of our concerns.

As you know, the socio-economic conditions experienced by peoples in the Third World, exposed by the Brandt Commission[2] are not new. For many years now, numerous observers, including the Canadian churches, have drawn public attention to the widening gap between the rich and poor countries and its underlying causes. The Brandt Report has simply launched another cry of alarm.

We believe it is imperative that the Cancun meetings go beyond the narrow limits of renewing this difficult dialogue simply to serve the interests of countries presently in economic crises. Seven years have gone by since the original call for the creation of a New International Economic Order. The time has come for action. It is essential that effective steps be taken now to break the systematic cycle of poverty, dependency and repression that conditions the lives of millions throughout the Third World. This requires models of development designed by and for the peoples of these countries.

To begin this process, we hope that the Canadian delegation at Cancun will question the very structures of the world's economic order which are the root causes of conditions of extreme poverty described in the Brandt Report:

a) the existing models of economic development which deny the right to work, ruin the environment, develop resources for the benefit of a few and exploit poorer sectors of the population in countries, both north and south;

b) the reluctance to recognize the political rights of Third World peoples to self-determination as masters of their own economic development and the refusal to support popular struggles for liberation from oppressive regimes;

c) the operations of transnational corporations which extract valuable resources and capital from Third World countries, thereby depriving those national governments of revenue sources required to serve the needs of their own populations;

d) the lack of progress in establishing adequate measures for stabilizing the price of raw materials and restraining speculation on international markets, which would allow Third World countries more effective utilization of their natural resources in the development of their societies;

e) the continuing repression of basic human rights by authoritarian or military regimes in many Third World countries and the ways in which governments and corporations of industrialized countries tend to strengthen these repressive regimes through their economic and political transactions with little regard for human rights;

f) the escalation of military expenditure and arms trade, which draws approximately $20 billion from Third World countries alone, that is, an average of one and a half times the total spent for health and education in these countries.

Finally, Mr. Prime Minister, as a symbol of renewed commitment to the advancement of North-South relations, we hope Canada will pledge its support for the development of new nations and societies in the Third World, such as Nicaragua and Zimbabwe, which have been born out of popular struggles against oppression.

We wish you well in your efforts to accomplish these important tasks at Cancun.

NOTES

1. Convened on the island of Cancun, Mexico, Oct. 24, 1981, the Conference was an effort, strongly sponsored by Prime Minister Trudeau and President Jose Lopez Portillo of Mexico, to renew the North-South dialogue of the Paris Conference of October, 1975.

2. The Independent Commission of International Development Issues, chaired by Willy Brandt, issued its report in 1980, *North-South: A Program for Survival* (Cambridge, Mass., The MIT Press).

Document 52

THE NEUTRON BOMB
ENOUGH IS ENOUGH!

Author — The Assembly, Canadian Conference of Catholic Bishops,
November 4, 1981

1. Humanity seems to be rushing at breakneck speed to nuclear self-destruction. There is a growing sense among people today that the arms race is out of control. A global holocaust within this generation looms as a distinct possibility. The superpowers appear insensitive to the stakes involved, namely the annihilation of life on this planet which the Lord of Creation called "good". (Gn 1:5)

2. Into this world, already overshadowed by nuclear overkill, comes the neutron bomb. It is the latest and the most devastating weapon to appear on the assembly line of death. In a tragic twist of irony, the United States government announced its decision to proceed with the development of the neutron bomb on August 9 of this year, the thirty-sixth anniversary of the atomic bomb attack on the people of Nagasaki.

3. The teachings of the Church have steadfastly resisted the arms race. "Any act of war", declared the Fathers of the Second Vatican Council, "aimed indiscriminately at the destruction of whole cities... and their inhabitants is a crime against God and humanity itself."[1] The Church has repeatedly declared that "the arms race is to be condemned unreservedly", "it is an injustice", "it is a form of theft", "it is completely incompatible with the spirit of humanity and still more with the spirit of Christianity."[2]

4. In Hiroshima this year, Pope John Paul II spoke of "a new

world-wide consciousness against war and a fresh determination to work for peace."[3] The Holy Father went on to say that "there is no justification for not raising the question of the responsibility of each nation and each individual in the face of the nuclear threat."[4] The development of the neutron bomb compels us to deal with some profound issues facing the future of our common humanity on this planet.

5. The American decision pushes the United States and the Soviet Union into a perilous cold war climate. Rather than making us more secure, it creates conditions that heighten international insecurities which could lead to the first nuclear strike. Indeed, "limited nuclear war" is a dangerous game which threatens to turn our planet into a giant crematorium.

6. The neutron bomb, with its "enhanced radiation warhead", particularly offends the deepest sensibilities of humanity. To describe a bomb as "clean" because it preserves property and destroys only people simply demonstrates how morally bankrupt our civilization has become. To exult in the destruction of humanity while saving inanimate property violates our most cherished ideals: namely, that people are made in the image of God and that human life has a sacred value. Indeed nothing else illustrates quite so clearly the perversion of values in our time.

7. We therefore join our fellow bishops of the United States and the growing number of American citizens in condemning the decision of their government on the neutron bomb. We also ask members of the Catholic community and the people of Canada to oppose vigorously the build-up of nuclear arms by all nations and especially the United States and the Soviet Union. At some point we must say: STOP. That time is now.

8. We believe, for the sake of its own citizens and the rest of the world, the Canadian government must take its responsibility to do everything possible to challenge the United States' initiatives on the neutron bomb. The proliferation of nuclear weapons, especially by one of the superpowers, is a critical problem of global proportions. As a member of NATO and a partner with the Americans in a military alliance, the time has come for Canada to insist that all governments face the moral and political responsibilities of nuclear armament.

9. In the Old Testament, the prophet Isaiah warned: "Woe to those... who build their hopes on cavalry, who rely on the number of chariots and on the strength of mounted men but never look to the Holy One of Israel." (Is 31:1) Moreover Jesus taught us not only to be good citizens but also to remember our creaturehood and to let God be God. "Give back to Caesar what belongs to Caesar and to God what belongs to God." (Lk 20:25).

10. Today we urge members of the Catholic community and all citizens to join in the struggle against nuclear arms. We call on you to make your opposition known to all government decision makers. We pledge ourselves to support creative initiatives seeking the conversion of warlike mentalities and social change for justice and peace. In this regard, we particularly emphasize the work of the Canadian Catholic Organization for Development and Peace.

11. Finally, we invite all families and Christian communities to pray to the Lord for guidance along the path of authentic peace based on "justice and social love."[5]

NOTES

1. Second Vatican Council, *The Church in the Modern World*, n. 80.

2. *The Holy See and Disarmament*, Document presented by Msgr. Giovanni Cheli, permanent observer of the Holy See at the United Nations, to Special Committee for Study of U.N. role in Disarmament, cf. *The Pope Speaks*, Washington, 1977, XXII, 243 ff. With the Additional Notes, pp. 255 ff., this is a useful summary and source of papal statements on disarmament, war, peace, etc.

3. John Paul II, Address at Peace Memorial Park, Hiroshima, Feb. 25, 1981, cf. *Catholic Mind*, N.Y., June, 1981, LXXIX, p. 55 ff.

4. *Ibid.*

5. John Paul II, *The Redeemer of Mankind*, 1979, in *The Papal Encyclicals*, edit. Claudia Carlen, IHM (Wilmington, N.C., McGrath Publishing, 1981), V, p. 258, n. 51.

Document 53

ON PREPARATION FOR THE SECOND SPECIAL SESSION OF THE UNITED NATIONS ON DISARMAMENT

To the Standing Committee on External Affairs and National Defence[1]

Author — The Canadian Conference of Catholic Bishops, February 16, 1982

INTRODUCTION

We want to thank you, Mr. Chairman, for the opportunity of appearing before the Standing Committee on External Affairs and National Defence. There is no question that today global disarmament constitutes the most pressing challenge facing political leaders in particular and humanity in general.

We want to assure you that the Catholic Church is deeply concerned about the urgent need to make significant progress in the field of global disarmament with respect to nuclear and conventional weapon systems. Indeed the present state of the arms race poses a profound challenge to the very foundations of the Church's teaching. The following excerpt from Pope John Paul II's message on the World Day of Peace, January 1 of this year, illustrates these concerns:

> (As Christians) strive to resist and prevent every form of warfare, we have no hesitation in recalling that, in the name of an elementary requirement of justice, peoples have a right and even a duty to protect their existence and freedom by

proportionate means against an unjust aggressor (cf. Second Vatican Council, *The Church in the Modern World*, n. 79). However, in view of the difference between classical warfare and nuclear or bacteriological war — a difference so to speak of nature — and in view of the scandal of the arms race seen against the background of the needs of the Third World, this right, which is very real in principle, only underlines the urgency for world society to equip itself with effective means of negotiation. In this way the nuclear terror that haunts our time can encourage us to enrich our common heritage with a very simple discovery that is within our reach, namely that war is the most barbarous and least effective way of resolving conflicts. More than ever before, human society is forced to provide itself with the means of consultation and dialogue which it needs in order to survive, and therefore with the institutions necessary for building up justice and peace.[2]

We understand that you will be hearing testimony from a variety of expert witnesses. We wish to emphasize that we do not consider ourselves to be technical experts on the subject of disarmament as such. What we can offer is a brief ethical and social analysis of some of the major issues of disarmament from the standpoint of the Church's teaching and its experience in acting on these concerns. In so doing, we will be speaking with the awareness that there is growing moral commitment to the struggle for global disarmament among Christians, both here in Canada and elsewhere in the world.

Unfortunately, the time you have given us to prepare and present a brief on such a serious topic has been, to say the least, incredibly short. Nevertheless we have chosen to address three major issues in anticipation of Canada's participation in the United Nations Second Special Session on Disarmament.[3] The first concerns nuclear weapons and the growing threat to human survival. The second has to do with militarism and the continuing underdevelopment of peoples in the world today. The third issue concerns the rise of military regimes and the increasing repression of human rights.

I — NUCLEAR WEAPONS: Threat to Human Survival

1.   Our first critical concern regarding the arms race has to do with the threat of nuclear war. The following recent quotations illustrate the urgent concerns of the Church today.

Humanity seems to be rushing at breakneck speed towards nuclear self-destruction. There is a growing sense among people today that the arms race is out of control. A global holocaust within this generation looms as a distinct possibility. The superpowers appear insensitive to the stakes involved, namely the annihilation of life on this planet which the Lord of Creation called "good" (Gn 1:5).[4]

I have in fact the deep conviction, that in the light of a nuclear war's effect, which can be scientifically foreseen as certain, the only choice that is morally and humanly valid, is the reduction of nuclear arms, while waiting for their future complete elimination, carried out simultaneously by all parties, with explicit agreements and with the commitment to accept effective controls.[5]

1.1 *Church Initiatives*

In the course of the past year alone, the Catholic Church has expressed increasing opposition to the continuing build-up of nuclear arms. Last February in Hiroshima, the Pope called for "a new world-wide consciousness against war... in the face of the nuclear threat".[6] Following this event, he commissioned a team of scientists from different countries to study the consequences of nuclear weapons. In December, the scientists' grim findings and their call for progressive reduction in nuclear weapons were communicated via special papal delegation to the President of the United States, the President of the Soviet Union, the Prime Minister of Britain, the President of France and the United Nations itself.[7] At the same time, Church leaders in the United States, Canada and Western Europe have taken a strong stance against the proliferation of nuclear weapons. In the United States for example, the Conference of Bishops launched a protest[8] against the nuclear weapon policies of the Reagan Administration and the Archbishop of Seattle went so far as to encourage people to consider withholding their taxes as an act of civil disobedience against U.S. policies on nuclear armament.[9]

1.2 *The Nuclear Arms Race*

The dramatic escalation of the nuclear arms race in recent years gives cause for considerable alarm. Since the last U.N. disarmament conference four years ago, the nuclear arms race has plunged the United States and the Soviet Union into a perilous cold war climate. In 1979 four nuclear weapon powers conducted 53 underground explosion tests, thereby stimulating an expansion in nuclear armaments. It is now estimated that the nuclear powers together have several thousand nuclear weapons in their arsenals. Today the destructive capacity of the more sophisticated nuclear weapon systems — the neutron bomb, the SS-18, the MX missile, the SS-20, the Cruise missile, the Trident submarine — presents a profound problem for mankind. They pose a severe threat to the survival of our common humanity on this planet.

1.3 *The Proliferation of Nuclear Weapons*

At the same time, international trade in nuclear know-how is resulting in the proliferation of nuclear weapon capacity among other countries. It is now estimated that another thirty to forty nations will join the nuclear arms club by the end of this century. Indeed nuclear technology and materials are now so available that any country with moderate industrial capacity will be able to acquire nuclear weapons if it so desires. In addition to the two superpowers an increasing number of countries are working to acquire nuclear weapons, largely to gain the advantage in conflicts with hostile neighbours (e.g., India, Pakistan, South Africa, Israel, etc.). The possession of nuclear weapons by such countries in volatile situations heightens the danger that these weapons may be activated through accident, miscalculation or plain folly.

1.4 *Global Insecurities*

The prospects of a global holocaust within a generation loom large. Rather than making countries more "secure", the build-up of nuclear weapons creates conditions which inevitably heighten international insecurities. These in turn enhance pressures for igniting the first nuclear strike. In this perilous cold war climate, the idea of a "limited nuclear war" is a dangerous game. It serves to erode whatever political and psychological barriers exist to the use of nuclear weapons. It opens a Pandora's box of unthinkable evils, threatening "to turn our planet into a giant crematorium".

1.5 *Basic Moral Issues*

Thus the nuclear arms spiral poses a deep and profound challenge to the moral principles and values of human civilization. The neutron bomb, with its "enhanced radiation warhead", "offends the deepest sensibilities of humanity". As the Canadian bishops recently declared: "To describe a bomb as 'clean' because it preserves property and destroys only people simply demonstrates how morally bankrupt our civilization has become". Indeed both the use and the threat of using such nuclear weapons must be considered morally wrong. As the Second Vatican Council put it: "Every act of war directed to the indiscriminate destruction of whole cities or vast areas with their inhabitants is a crime against God and humanity, which merits firm and unequivocal condemnation".[10] The possession of nuclear weapons for deterrence can be tolerated only as long as progress is being made in the reduction of nuclear stockpiles through continuing negotiations among the nuclear weapon states.[11] Our goal must be the eventual and complete elimination of nuclear weapon systems.

1.6 *The U.N. Program*

You will recall that in 1978 the U.N. Special Session launched a plan of action for nuclear disarmament. It called for the urgent negotiation of agreements aimed at the cessation of the qualitative improvement and development of nuclear weapon systems, of the production of all types of nuclear weapons and their means of delivery, of the production of fissionable materials for weapons purposes, along with a comprehensive program with agreed time-tables for the gradual reduction of nuclear stockpiles (para. 50). As significant steps in this direction, the plan of action proposed the establishment of a comprehensive test ban and nuclear weapon free zones (para. 60; 61; 62; 63). A number of proposals were advanced for encouraging negotiations among the nuclear weapon states and the non-nuclear weapon states regarding these issues and the non-proliferation of nuclear arms.

1.7 *Canada's Role*

We are aware that Canada made a significant contribution at the U.N. Special Session by advocating a "strategy of suffocation" for the nuclear arms race. That strategy, you will recall, was aimed at "depriving the (nuclear) arms race of the oxygen on which it feeds". It called for a comprehensive test ban on nuclear weapons, a moratorium on flight testing of new delivery systems and on production of fissionable materials for nuclear weapons, plus reduction of spending for new strategic nuclear weapon systems. Yet Canada's record in this "strategy of suffocation" in this country leaves something to be desired. Nuclear weapons are located on Canadian soil (e.g., Comox, British Columbia). U.S. and Soviet submarine nuclear weapons (e.g., the Trident submarine) are allowed to pass freely through Canadian waters. Canadian industries are engaged in manufacturing component parts for nuclear weapon systems (e.g., the Cruise missile system). And serious questions are being raised about the "safeguards" involved in the export of Canada's CANDU technology to certain countries (e.g., India, Argentina, S. Korea).

1.8 *Some Recommendations*

At the Second Special Session on Disarmament, we believe Canada should give more effective leadership in implementing the "strategy of suffocation". However, attention needs to be given to concrete proposals and actions to be taken over the next four years by the international community and Canada itself. Accordingly we urge the Canadian government to give serious consideration to the following suggestions in preparation for the Second Special Session on Disarmament:

a) specific measures for speeding up negotiated agreements for a comprehensive test ban on nuclear weapons, including appropriate incentives and time-tables;

b) specific proposals for progress on agreements to stop the flight testing of all new strategic delivery systems; to prohibit the production of fissionable materials for weapons; and for reductions in military spending on nuclear weapon systems;

c) specific plans for establishing Canada as a "nuclear weapon free zone", including proposals for the removal of all nuclear weapon systems from Canadian soil and a declaration that our boundary waters be nuclear free;

d) specific legislation to phase out the manufacture of component parts for nuclear weapon systems in Canada, along with an assistance program for Canadian industries to convert to non-nuclear production;

e) specific steps for a critical review of the "safeguards" for the export of Canada's nuclear technology, including proposed revisions to assure that our nuclear technology will not be sold to states seeking nuclear weapon capacity.

II — ARMAMENTS: Cause of Social Injustice

2. Our second critical concern has to do with the arms race as a continuing cause of social and economic underdevelopment in the world. The following quotations underscore the urgent concerns of the Church today:

> The arms race is a scandal; the prospect of disarmament is a great hope. The scandal relates to the crying disproportion between the resources in money and intelligence devoted to the service of death and the resources devoted to the service of life. The hope is that by cutting military expenditure, a substantial part of the immense resources that it now absorbs can be employed in a vast world-wide development project... we now repeat this appeal with still greater force and insistence, calling upon all countries to study and to put into operation an organic plan, within the framework of programmes for the fight against inequality, underdevelopment, hunger, disease and illiteracy. Justice demands it...[12]

> We urge the Canadian delegation at Cancun to question the very structures of the world's economic order which are the root causes of extreme poverty... the escalation of military expenditures and arms trade, which draws approximately $14 billion from Third World countries alone, an average of one and a half times the total required for health and education in these countries.[13]

2.1 Church Initiatives

In the teachings of John XXIII, Paul VI, and John Paul II, the Catholic Church has consistently emphasized the following themes: that the arms race is a scandal to humanity; that militarism is a cause of injustice; that injustice is a cause of war; that the true road to peace lies in the integral development and liberation of peoples. In the words of Paul VI, "development is the new name for peace".[14] This message has been stressed constantly in numerous Vatican submissions to the United Nations and in statements and programs initiated by episcopal conferences in countries all over the world. In order to pursue this message in our own country, the Canadian bishops established the Canadian Catholic Organization for Development and Peace. Its program has two main thrusts: funding social and economic development projects in Third World countries and generating public awareness here in Canada about the problems and causes of underdevelopment in the Third World. In the past two years, CCODP's education program has focused on the theme: "Militarism: Obstacle to Development".

2.2 *Military Expenditures*

In spite of these and countless other initiatives by institutions and people of good will all over the world, the arms race continues to escalate, mobilizing resources for the 'service of death' rather than the 'service of life'. The annual military expenditure in the world has now reached $500 billion: well over one billion a day. The training of military personnel in the U.S. alone costs twice as much a year as the education budget for some 300 million school aged children in South Asia today. In fact the industrialized nations spend an average of 20 times more of their national income on their own military forces than on development aid to the Third World. It is estimated that current military spending is double the Gross Domestic Product of the continent of Africa and equal to that of Latin America.

2.3 *Underdevelopment and Dependency*

The direct sale of military arms and equipment to Third World countries also contributes to underdevelopment and economic dependency. An estimated 70% of the international arms trade now involves Third World recipients. Despite severe food shortages, underdeveloped nations are using an average of five times as much of their foreign exchange for the import of arms as for agricultural machinery. These disproportionate military expenditures are often provoked by industrialized nations seeking to establish military alliances in certain regions and offering military assistance to poorer countries. As a result, substantial amounts of limited foreign currency in many developing countries are earmarked for the import of weapon systems and the construction of infrastructure (e.g., airships, airports, maintenance facilities, and domestic facilities for expatriate trainers and technicians). All this in turn, creates major pressures on poor countries to increase their foreign exchange earnings through the export of natural resources and cash crops and through policies designed to attract foreign capital. In effect, much of the resources and commodities produced by peasants and workers in many Third World countries end up paying for 70% of the world's arms trade rather than serving development needs at home.

2.4 *Militarism and Insecurity*

Worse still, the realities of militarism — its weaponry, its values, ideology, and behaviour — end up undermining the very "security" it was ostensibly created to ensure. In other words, militarism in the Third World has generated greater "insecurity". Since 1945, there have been more than 130 wars, most of which have involved Third World countries. In most cases, these wars have involved border and political conflicts that are, in large measure, the legacy of colonialism and neo-colonialism. These wars in turn have often been fueled and intensified by military support from the industrialized states. Thus the militarization of the Third World not only makes the outbreak of warfare more likely, it also frequently prolongs such warfare because of the ongoing supply of weapons from industrialized countries.

2.5 *The Roots of Injustice*

We do maintain that nations have a right to engage in just struggles to defend their national sovereignty. Similarly, repressed peoples have the right to struggle for the overthrow of tyrants when all democratic means are frustrated. The real scandal of militarism lies in the misallocation of such a massive amount of the world's resources to maintain and increase systems of injustice between and within nations. As the Brandt Commission Report[15] pointed out: the cost of a ten-year program which would meet essential food and health needs of all the poor in all underdeveloped countries would be less than half of one year's military spending. The roots of this injustice are found in the very structures of the world's economic order. For the present economic order perpetuates a systematic cycle of poverty, dependency and repression. These conditions in turn, breed insecurities which give rise to increasing militarization and the ongoing perpetuation of the cycle.

2.6 *Canada's Role in Military Armament*

As you know, Canada is now ranked among the largest arms exporters in the world. Last year Canadian military exports reached the $600 million mark. Since 1959, some 600 Canadian companies had sales in defence-related products totalling $6 billion. Due to the Canada/U.S. Defence Production Sharing Agreements, most of Canada's arms exports are sold to the United States and NATO countries, yet a disturbing number of Canada's arms exports are going to military regimes in the Third World. These include sales of artillery systems to South Africa and Thailand, plus aircraft sales to the air forces of Chile and the Cameroons. And Canadian-built armoured personnel vehicles have been promoted for sales to Indonesia and Malaysia. While these countries have the right to defend their population against aggression, our concern has to do with the vast amounts of money that are spent on military arms rather than serving the basic social and economic needs of people in those countries and Canada's role in perpetuating this problem. Moreover as new weapon systems are acquired for North American defence, Canadians are likely to see marked increases in the percentage of defence expenditures during the 1980's as Canada becomes locked into further NATO (North Atlantic Treaty Organization) and NORAD (North American Air Defence Agreement) commitments. Meanwhile the percentage of Canada's development aid is likely to remain frozen.

2.7 *Some Recommendations*

The first U.N. Special Session on Disarmament drew attention to what is called "the colossal waste of resources" exhibited by the global arms race. As the Final Document puts it: "the economic and social consequences of the arms race are so detrimental that its continuation is obviously incompatible with the implementation of the New International Economic Order based on justice, equity and cooperation". While recognizing that progress is painful, we firmly believe that every effort must be made to develop and implement a global security plan linking disarmament and development strategies. It is imperative however, that concrete measurable steps be taken in this direction over the next four years. Accordingly we urge the Canadian government to give serious consideration to the following suggestions in preparation for the Second Special U.N. Session on Disarmament:

a) specific proposals for advancing international negotiations and agreements on gradual reductions in military spending and the corresponding re-allocation of funds for social and economic development, particularly in the Third World;

b) specific measures for monitoring and controlling the arms trade with Third World countries, including incentives for transferring priorities from military armaments to economic and social development;

c) specific steps for public review of Canada's own defence and military spending policies; including a re-examination of Canada's role in NATO and NORAD;

d) specific proposals for alternative Canadian defence policies based on reduced military spending and production, restrictions in arms sales to Third World countries and increased funds for economic and social development of underdeveloped countries;

e) specific measures for assisting the workers in Canada's defence industries in the process of converting from the production of military goods.

III — MILITARY REGIMES: Increasing Repression

3.   Our third critical concern has to do with the build-up of military regimes and the corresponding repression of human rights in the countries concerned. The following quotation illustrates the serious concerns being raised in the Church today about these issues.

I am deeply disturbed over the news that the United States government is studying a way to accelerate El Salvador's arms race by sending military teams and advisors to ''instruct three of El Salvador's battalions in logistics, communications and intelligence techniques''. If this information is true, the contribution of your administration, instead of favouring greater justice and peace in El Salvador, will almost surely intensify the injustice and repression of the common people who are organized to struggle for respect for their most basic human rights.

Unfortunately the present government *junta,* and especially the armed forces and security forces, have not demonstrated any ability to solve structurally or in political practice our serious national problems. In general, they have only resorted to repressive violence and this has resulted in a much greater toll of dead and wounded than in previous military regimes whose systematic violation of human rights was denounced by the Inter-American Commission on Human Rights.[16]

3.1 *The Role of the Church*

In the past few years, the repression of human rights by military regimes has become a major pastoral concern for the Catholic Church. In a growing number of countries, the Church has become the major institutional recourse for human rights against the repressive measures of military states. The situation in Central America (e.g., El Salvador, Guatemala) and that in Poland are primary examples today. The repressive situations in Chile and South Africa also continue to illustrate these concerns. And Pope John Paul II's journeys to Brazil and the Philippines have highlighted other cases where the Church is engaged in a protracted struggle for human rights. For the Canadian Church too, these issues have become a major priority. The Canadian bishops, through their Human Rights Committee, have actively pressed the Canadian government and Canadian corporations to change those economic and/or political transactions with particular military regimes, which strengthen the hand of repression in those countries. These initiatives have been enhanced by the work of ecumenical action/research coalitions, notably the Inter-Church Committee on Human Rights in Latin America and the Task Force on the Churches and Corporate Responsibility, along with the public education program of Development and Peace in the Catholic Church.[17]

3.2 *Military States*

The build-up of military regimes, employing repressive

technology and weapons to control their own populations, constitutes one of the most recent and tragic consequences of the global arms race. The most recent example is the situation in Poland. While a critical analysis of repression in that country is just beginning, our attention in recent years has been focused on the rise of military states in the Third World. In the last decade, we witnessed a dramatic rise in the number of military states, particularly in Third World Countries. In Latin America some twenty countries are governed by military or authoritarian regimes. In such Third World situations, increasing economic disparities and social injustices give rise to greater unrest for social change which, in turn, leads to a military takeover of the government in order to protect the *status quo* from the people. The military *junta* concentrates political power in its own hands and assumes control over the legislative body — directly or indirectly. Constitutional guarantees — democracy, free speech, free assembly, trade union rights, and even religious freedom — are often suspended or curtailed. Arbitrary detentions, torture of political prisoners, along with murder and assassination of opposition groups become commonplace. The military *junta* rationalizes all this in the name of "national security". In most military states, one of the obvious effects is that the security of the rich and the powerful is protected, while the security of the vast majority, namely the poor, is subject to violation.

3.3 *Trade in Repression*

The major industrial powers for the most part are responsible for supplying the internal "security" hardware required by these military regimes. This hardware may include lethal weapons such as guns, hand grenades, ammunition and related explosives. It may also involve non-lethal weapons such as prison gear, surveillance systems, armoured cars, torture devices or riot control equipment. Often such military assistance includes training of security forces, technical advisors and intelligence exchanges. This is effectively an international repression trade system. In some countries (e.g., El Salvador, Guatemala, South Korea, etc.) it has resulted in the militarization of entire societies in order to wage an internal war against perceived threats from their populations. Moreover this trade in repression is growing. The Institute for Policy Studies in Washington reports the president of an arms exporting company as saying: "There are more riots and upheavals than ever before, and so we're doing more and more business every year."

3.4 *Spheres of Influence*

The build-up of military regimes and their internal security forces is also related to the strategies of the major industrial powers to maintain political and economic spheres of influence in different regions. For example, the Soviet Union (re Afghanistan, Poland) and the United States (re El Salvador, Guatemala) will provide substantial amounts of assistance to maintain military regimes in order to protect their "spheres of influence", those regions which are considered part of their "backyard" and must be guarded against external threats. Large amounts of military and economic aid are funnelled into these satellite countries in order to secure rights for military bases, develop military and political alliances and gain access to important sources of raw materials and markets. These are modern forms of "military colonialism" and the people of these colonies generally find themselves subjected to continuous rule by repression.

3.5 *Canada's Role*

Canada once again is not exactly an innocent bystander in the build-up of Third World military regimes. Canadian-based corporations, banks and crown corporations continue to do business with military regimes engaged in gross violations of human rights, thereby legitimating and strengthening the hands of the internal repression in such countries. The sale of Canadian manufactured artillery systems to South Africa also gives cause for real concern. The sales of Canada's CANDU nuclear energy technology to military regimes in South Korea and Argentina raises similar questions. While Canada may not be directly involved in supplying arms and technology to military states for purposes of internal repression, questions should be raised as to whether arms exports are being used for these ends. The Canadian government however claims that the aircraft will not be used for military purposes.

3.6 *Some Recommendations*

In the first U.N. Session on Disarmament, insufficient attention was given to the realities of militarization for internal repression. Yet this form of military armament has a greater and more direct impact on the daily lives of people than other forms of militarization.

We believe that these issues should be given serious attention at the forthcoming Session. Accordingly, we urge the Canadian government to give serious consideration to the following suggestions in preparation for the Second Special Session on Disarmament:

a) specific steps to assure that the problem of "military armament for the repression of human rights" be a major topic on the agenda;

b) specific proposals for monitoring and controlling the sale of repression technology to military states for use in repressing social unrest, internal dissent or waging war against large segments of the population;

c) specific legislation in Canada providing a set of human rights criteria which must be satisfactorily met by military states before Canadian crown corporations be permitted to do business;

d) specific proposals on how Canada will require government agencies, Canadian-based corporations and banks to apply human rights criteria in future transactions with military states.

NOTES

1. The brief was presented by Msgr. Dennis Murphy and M. André Vallée, p.m.e., General Secretaries of the Canadian Conference of Catholic Bishops, with Dr. Tony Clarke, Co-director of the Conference's Department for Social Affairs.
2. In *Origins*, Washington, 1982, XI, n. 30, p. 478 ff.
3. Convened June-July, 1982.
4. The Catholic bishops of Canada, Document 52 above.
5. John Paul II, Angelus Message, Dec. 13, 1981, *Osservatore Romano*, English edition, Vatican, Jan. 11, 1982.
6. John Paul II, Address at Peace Memorial Park, Hiroshima; cf. *Catholic Mind*, New York, 1981, LXXIX, June, p. 55.
7. Cf. *Catholic Mind*, New York, 1982, LXXX, March, p. 27 ff.
8. Cf. Report of the *ad hoc* Committee on War and Peace of the National Conference of Catholic Bishops, *Origins*, Washington, 1981, XI, p. 402.
9. Archbishop Raymond Hunthausen in an address to the Synod of the Lutheran Church in America, cf. *Origins*, Washington, 1981, XI, p. 110 ff.
10. Second Vatican Council, *The Church in the Modern World*, n. 80.
11. Cf. testimony of John Cardinal Krol before the U.S. Senate Foreign Relations Committee, 1979, *Origins*, Washington, 1979, IX, p. 195.

12. Paul VI, *Message to the First U.N. Special Session on Disarmament*, 1978, cf. *The Pope Speaks*, Washington, 1979, XXIII, p. 278.

13. *Towards a New Economic Order*, Document 51 above.

14. *The Development of Peoples* in *The Papal Encyclicals*, edit. Claudia Carlen, IHM (Wilmington, N.C., McGrath Publishing, 1981), V, 197, n. 76.

15. *North-South: A Program for Survival* (Cambridge, Mass., MIT Press, 1980).

16. Archbishop Oscar Romero (Managua, Nicaragua) to U.S. President Jimmy Carter, Feb. 17, 1980, cf. *Origins*, Washington, 1980, IX, p. 634.

17. Inter-Church Committee on Human Rights in Latin America, 40 St. Clair Ave. East, Toronto, M4T 1M9; Task Force on the Churches and Corporate Responsibility, 129 St. Clair Ave. West, Toronto, M4V 1N5; Development and Peace, 3028 Danforth Ave., Toronto, M4C 1N2.

Document 54

ON PEACE AND DISARMAMENT
To the Prime Minister

Author — Canadian Church Leaders,[1] December 14, 1982

INTRODUCTION

1. We are pleased to have the opportunity to address this petition to you and we do so on the basis of certain beliefs and principles which we hold to contain relevant norms for the behaviour of nations as well as of individuals. Our concern about the escalating nuclear arms race, as well as our views on ways to control it, grow out of our knowledge that the earth is God's and that all that is in it is under both His love and His judgment.

2. To be faithful stewards of God's creation we are called to participate in the work of reconciliation that was exemplified in the ministry of Jesus and thereby to stand against the forces of injustice and destruction. We are called to love our enemies and we know that this cannot be accomplished through the build-up of nuclear arsenals which seek, not to defend against attack, but to threaten and carry out retaliatory destruction. We are called to stand in solidarity with our oppressed neighbours and to pray for and sacrifice on behalf of the persecuted and even of those who persecute us.

3. We address this petition to you, knowing that you share these beliefs. We also know that the applications of these principles in the contemporary world, particularly in relation to questions of

national security, is not a simple matter and we wish to assure you of our prayers as you exercise your awesome responsibilities.

4.   From each of our denominations and institutions you have from time to time received various written representations and we are now grateful for the opportunity to address our concerns to you directly.

5.   As Canadians we are proud that Canada has in the past made significant and constructive contributions to the cause of international reconciliation and we believe that there will be major opportunities to do so again in the future. To that end, and because Canada has given us so much, we place great value on the preservation of the Canadian nation state but we must also remind you and ourselves, that the preservation of the ultimately transient institutions of nation states, even our beloved country, is not an ultimate value and that there are clear limits to the measures that can justifiably be taken for national defence.

6.   Indeed we wish to commend you and your government for providing leadership in placing prudent limits on Canada's military response to the problem of national security. We note with appreciation that you and your Government have taken major steps toward making Canada a nuclear weapon-free zone by eliminating nuclear weapons from Canada's Armed Forces in Europe and by initiating steps to remove all nuclear weapons from Canadian soil. We also note with approval that, as a proportion of gross national product, Canadian resources have quite properly been devoted more to the social well-being of Canadians than to military defence.

7.   We take these actions to be constructive initiatives within the international community, and in our petition we have some suggestions to make regarding further constructive measures.

8.   First, we wish to outline in very brief form our understanding of the current international situation regarding the nuclear arms race and of Canada's response to that situation.

9.   We have decided to confine ourselves on this occasion, to the problem of the nuclear arms race because we consider it to be an issue of special urgency. Our own constituencies, through resolutions taken at various levels and through personal representations,

have encouraged us to make these representations on their behalf, regarding the threat of nuclear war and Canada's response to that threat.

THE CURRENT SITUATION

10.   While nuclear weapons in any form and in any number cannot ultimately be accepted as legitimate components of national armed forces, the present build-up of nuclear weapons is of particular concern on two additional counts.

11.   In the first instance, the sheer numbers and explosive power (the equivalent of one million Hiroshima bombs) of present nuclear weapons are now sufficient to threaten the continuation of life as we know it on this planet. In the words of Jonathan Schell, nuclear war cannot now be considered as merely "the defeat of some purpose, but an abyss into which all human purposes would be drowned for all time". Again in the words of Schell, we believe that "we have no right to place the possibility of this limitless, eternal defeat on the same footing as risks that we run in the ordinary conduct of our affairs in our particular transient moment of human history".[2]

12.   While the threat to human survival is real, the second reason for our concern about the build-up of nuclear arsenals is not only survival itself, but the quality of survival. We oppose nuclear weapons, not only because they threaten us (though that they surely do), but because without ever being "used" (in the sense of being detonated) they obstruct and frustrate the attempt to build a world in which justice and equity count for more than coercion and domination. Former External Affairs Minister Mark MacGuigan said that in linking disarmament and development,

> ... we are pointing to a more positive motivation for disarmament than simple survival. If even a small fraction of the more than $500 billion spent annually on military purposes were to be added to the $20 billion now spent on aid, there would be a real possibility of making concrete, and even dramatic progress in solving existing development problems.

13.   Nuclear weapons further frustrate development in that they

join the conventional military arsenals of the major northern powers as means by which the present inequitable international economic order is entrenched. The present build-up of nuclear arsenals has come to focus on new generations of weapons that are designed to go beyond deterrence, to be available for the purpose of fighting prolonged nuclear war, of projecting force into the world beyond national borders and of influencing the behaviour of rival states in the Third World.

14.   Paul Warnke, former head of the U.S. Arms Control and Disarmament Agency has put it this way:

> There are disturbing signs of a growing reliance on nuclear weapons as an instrument of foreign policy — to gain political ends, not just to prevent nuclear attack. Some advisors to the (Reagan) Administration have stated categorically that we should "devise ways to employ strategic forces coercively" and "must possess the ability to wage nuclear war rationally". Other Administration officials have maintained that the goal of our nuclear arsenal should be to prevent others from using conventional military force against our interests while leaving us free to utilize our own conventional force as we see fit. And the argument that nuclear arms are useful only for deterrence now seems to be losing ground to the argument that we can and should shape our forces to fight, survive and win a nuclear war.

15.   The development of "usable" nuclear weapons expands the number of potential circumstances under which the use of nuclear weapons will be deemed to be advantageous, dramatically increasing the likelihood of nuclear war and the prospect of annihiliation.

16.   The development of nuclear weapons as instruments of diplomacy now means that they are already being "used" — not by detonation, but in the same way that a bank robber prefers to use a weapon, by brandishing it and intimidating his victim into compliance. In this way nuclear weapons are becoming part of the means by which northern industrial states compete for influence and domination in the Third World and by which they seek to keep in place a world economic order that bestows extraordinary benefits on the powerful and that exacts extraordinary costs from the power-less.

CANADIAN POLICY IN THE CURRENT SITUATION

17. We perceive Canadian policy to be responding to these developments in the nuclear arms race on two levels.

18. On the one hand, Canada has made and continues to make important contributions to international forums devoted to the search for ways to control and reverse the nuclear arms race. We have noted with appreciation Canada's participation in the Geneva-based Committee on Disarmament and that, among other things, Canadian officials have contributed important studies on technical means of verifying arms control agreements.

19. In 1978 we again noted with appreciation your own speech at the First U.N. Special Session on Disarmament (UNSSOD I) and the proposal to "suffocate" the arms race. The strategy of suffocation embodied Canada's long-standing efforts to achieve a comprehensive test ban on nuclear weapons and added a significant and innovative proposal to international discussions — the proposal to ban the flight-testing of new strategic delivery vehicles. We agreed with and supported your suggestion that the nuclear arms race, independent of political and military considerations, was being fueled by technological developments in weapons laboratories and test sites and that if the arms race was ever to be extinguished or suffocated, this source of oxygen would have to be cut off.

20. At the same time, we have noted that Canada actively supports the development of new nuclear weapons systems, including weapons systems that are designed to go beyond deterrence to intimidation, war-fighting and the threat of first-strike. Specifically, we note that Canadian industry is encouraged, through both the facilities and the funding of the federal government, to participate in the production of components for nuclear weapons systems such as the MX missile and the Trident missile systems. Neither of these systems can be described as simply deterrent or retaliatory weapons. They are designed as "hard target-killing" missiles and are intended to threaten Soviet land-based Intercontinental Ballistic Missiles (ICBMs) with a first-strike. We believe that such weapons, rather than enhancing deterrence, are destabilizing and actually create incentives for the Soviet Union itself to entertain first-strike options.

21.   We also understand Canadian policy is to support U.S. efforts to develop, in addition to first-strike weapons, nuclear weapons that are designed for conducting prolonged nuclear war. In particular, the Cruise missile, in its air-launched or strategic configuration, is designed to strike at secondary military and industrial targets in the Soviet Union and to enable the United States, in the words of Secretary of Defence Caspar Weinberger, "to prevail should deterrence fail". In order words, weapons such as the Cruise missile are deployed on the premise that if nuclear war should break out, the United States should have the capacity to prolong such a war until such time as Soviet society had sustained greater damage than American society and that the United States would thereby "win" the war. Again, the Canadian government has encouraged, with the aid of public funds, Canadian industrial participation in building a "war-fighting" nuclear weapon and now is in the process of agreeing to test it on Canadian soil and in Canadian air space.

22.   Finally, we also understand that Canadian policy supports the idea that a nuclear war could be fought and won in Europe and that, in particular circumstances, Western Europe could benefit from the use of nuclear weapons on its soil. We have drawn this conclusion from the fact that Canada has refused to support a policy of no-first-use of nuclear-weapons. Canada supports the North Atlantic Treaty Organization (NATO) policy of reserving the right to introduce nuclear weapons into a European conventional military conflict.

RESPONSE OF THE CHURCHES TO CANADIAN POLICY

23.   We have noted with appreciation the numerous occasions on which you and members of your Government have spoken publicly of the tragedy and danger of the nuclear arms race, representing as it does a threat to survival and a perverse misuse of human resources in the present world order. These words are appreciated, particularly since we are convinced that persons in positions of leadership and of influence have a special responsibility to make our people aware of the dangers of the path we are now walking.

24.   We must however, convey to you our very deep concern and the concern of the people whom we represent, that Canada is at the same time a willing participant on a path that we believe promises only destruction and defeat of the struggle for justice. The

policies of your Government suggest to us that, despite grave and, we believe, sincere concerns, Canada accepts the now prevailing view in the Reagan Administration that the West must mount a nuclear arsenal capable of threatening the Soviet Union with pre-emptive attack and of prolonged nuclear war. We assume that these policies are supported under the assumption that nuclear war is in fact winnable and that circumstances could occur in which Canadians could benefit from the use of nuclear weapons.

25.   We are more inclined to support the view of George Kennan:

There is no issue at stake in our political relations with the Soviet Union — no hope, no fear, nothing to which we aspire, nothing we would like to avoid — which could conceivably be worth a nuclear war. And... there is no way in which nuclear weapons could conceivably be employed in combat that would not involve the possibility — and indeed the prohibitively high probability — of escalation into a general nuclear disaster.

26.   The creation which God judged to be good cannot be enhanced by the development of "usable" nuclear weapons. Even to contemplate the use of nuclear weapons in support of political and economic interests is to choose death over life.

27.   Inasmuch as we are called to share in God's redemptive purpose and to restore the convenant of love and blessing between God and His creation, we are called also to pursue national policies which seek to reduce, and ultimately to eliminate, our reliance on the destructive power of nuclear weapons for advancing the national interest.

28.   We believe therefore that nuclear weapons must ultimately be eliminated from all military forces and immediate steps be taken, not only to move us toward that goal, but also to reduce the likelihood of war involving the nuclear arsenals that now exist. We wish to refer you in particular to measures designed to reverse the trend toward expanded roles for nuclear weapons — to halt the move to take nuclear weapons beyond the role of nuclear deterrence to first-strike, war-fighting and intimidation roles. The m present for your consideration would not undermine ' nuclear deterrence that now obtains. These measure' to work against the introduction of new and destabi'

systems and thereby work toward the creation of a more stable strategic environment in which mutual reductions of nuclear weapons, even their eventual elimination, would have a better chance for success.

ALTERNATIVE CANADIAN POLICIES

(a) *A Comprehensive Nuclear Test Ban*

29. We commend Canada's consistent and vigorous diplomatic efforts to achieve a comprehensive test ban and pledge our continued support for these efforts. We believe such a ban to be essential to prevent the introduction of large numbers of additional warheads, not to mention new warheads such as enhanced radiation weapons, into the arsenals of the major powers. Various "low-yield" warheads for example, serve to lower the nuclear threshold and to increase the likelihood of the introduction of nuclear weapons into conventionally fought disputes.

(b) *No-First-Use of Nuclear Weapons*

30. Canada should insist upon a no-first-use policy within NATO and urge all nuclear weapons states to undertake a similar pledge. In order to use nuclear weapons as extensions of diplomacy it is necessary to threaten and to be willing to use them first. A pledge by all nuclear weapons states renouncing first-use would go a long way toward undermining the political/military utility of nuclear weapons in limited conflicts. At the same time, a no-first-use pledge would not undermine the role of nuclear weapons as deterrents to nuclear war. A no-first-use agreement is not made redundant by the UN Charter's prohibition on the first use of any force. The UN Charter also reserves the right of all states to use force in response to aggression and the no-first-use pledge is aimed at averting the escalation of a conventional war into a nuclear war. The no-first-use pledge is the placement of limits on the right to respond to aggression; states that make the pledge are saying that even in the course of defending themselves against unlawful aggression, they will not resort to the use of nuclear weapons except in response to nuclear weapons used against them.

(c) *Support for the Suffocation Strategy and Nuclear Freeze*

31.   Canada   should,   in   compliance   with   the   "strategy   of suffocation", support international efforts to bring about a mutual freeze on the production, testing and deployment of new nuclear weapons systems. We regret therefore, that your Government did not support the draft resolutions for a nuclear freeze, brought to UNSSOD II by Mexico, Sweden and India, when they were sub-mitted to the current session of the UN General Assembly. The draft resolution of Mexico and Sweden for example, had close parallels to Canada's suffocation strategy, calling for a comprehensive test ban, a complete cessation of the manufacture of nuclear weapons and of their delivery vehicles, a ban on all further deployment of nuclear weapons and of their delivery vehicles and a complete cessation of the production of fissionable material for weapons purposes.

(d) *No Tests of Cruise or Nuclear Vehicles in Canada*

32.   Canadian refusal to test nuclear weapons delivery vehicles within Canadian territory would be consistent with your Govern-ment's moves toward a non-nuclear role for Canada within both the NATO and NORAD (North American Air Defence Agreement) alliances. We also believe that the strategy of suffocation correctly identifies the testing of delivery vehicles as part of the oxygen that fuels the arms race. Another way of stating the same thing is that the testing of nuclear weapons vehicles by one side provides incentives for the other side to develop similar new weapons vehicles as well. Consistent with Canadian efforts to play a constructive diplomatic role in the search for multilateral disarmament and arms control agreements, Canada should not be a participant in the development of new weapons vehicles by either side in the arms race. This is all the more important when such a new vehicle is itself destabilizing and promises to complicate the matter of arms control verification, a matter which has been of special interest to Canada.

(e) *No Production of Components of Nuclear Weapons*

33.   By virtue of Canada's role as a participant in multilateral arms control and disarmament negotiations, of our country's non-nuclear role within alliances and of Canada's long-standing interest in

making constructive contributions to the peaceful settlement of disputes, Canada should forego participation in the production of nuclear weapons systems. A minimum and immediate gesture by the Canadian government should be the curtailment of grants out of public funds (Defence Industry Productivity Programme) designed to assist Canadian firms in winning contracts for components for nuclear weapons systems.

(f) *Declare Canada a Nuclear Weapon-Free Zone*

34.   Canada should extend policies already adopted and declare itself a nuclear weapon-free zone. We recognize the initiatives already taken by your Government to place Canadian Armed Forces in exclusively non-nuclear roles in Europe and to remove tactical nuclear weapons from Canadian territory within the current decade. As a natural extension of those initiatives Canada should declare its intention to end all participation in nuclear weapons systems, this being consistent with Canada's support in principle at the UN for Nuclear Weapon-Free Zones as "confidence building measures".

(g) *Strengthen Peacekeeping*

35.   Canada has played an important role in developing and carrying out forms of third-party intervention in local disputes to create opportunities for the peaceful settlement of these disputes. In the decade before us there are two kinds of disputes in particular that will involve the major powers and which in turn lend themselves most clearly to neutral third party intervention. In both cases Canada is in a position to make constructive contributions.

36.   In the first instance, increased competition for resources and energy supplies (not to mention Third World markets) promises that in the 1980's the major powers will increasingly see direct threats to their interests in regional conflicts in the Third World, and the temptation to intervene directly will increase. The need for effective third-party intervention to monitor cease-fires and arms flows and to permit local interests the breathing space to deal with their conflicts without the threat of outside intervention, will have to be met if these conflicts are to be kept from escalating dangerously. Canada has already made significant contributions in this regard and we urge increased emphasis on building a peacekeeping capacity.

37. The second type of international conflict in need of third-party intervention is of course the nuclear arms race itself. Stability in the nuclear arms race and any hope of halting and then reversing the rate of nuclear weapons deployment depends, among other things, on a secure system of satellite surveillance. Canada should contribute to international efforts to provide an independent means of monitoring agreements and activities, on which both sides can rely — specifically, the proposed international Satellite Monitoring Agency.

FUNDING RESEARCH
FOR ALTERNATIVE SECURITY SYSTEMS

38. We urge the Canadian government to support the principle of the "Waldheim proposal" to fund peace research and disarmament education at home as well as internationally, through the World Disarmament Campaign. The urgency for establishing public funding for peace research and disarmament education stems from the fundamental distinction between strategic analysis and peace research. In the case of strategic analysis, the assumption is that war is a legitimate extension of national diplomacy and the objective is a more effective and efficient use, or threatened use, of armed force in the pursuit of the national interest. The assumption of peace research is that war is an unacceptable extension of national diplomacy and the objective is the development of alternatives to the use of armed force in the resolution of conflict and in the pursuit of the national interest.

39. Public funds currently support several chairs of strategic studies at Canadian universities. Additional public funds should be made available for institutes of peace research and public education concerning disarmament and the peaceful settlement of disputes.

THE TASK BEFORE US

40. As representatives of the Canadian churches we commit ourselves to the building of a world in which the foundation of our social and economic security is justice. We have proposed policies which we believe will move us toward that goal and which will turn us away from the attempt to build our security on the power to destroy.

41. Our churches have undertaken a variety of educational programmes and are planning additional means of bringing issues
related to the nuclear arms race to the attention of our people. In
this task we praise our Creator for the abundant life which He has
granted to us in this land, we pledge ourselves to support the pursuit
of justice and equity in all lands and we commit ourselves to work
toward the removal of the arsenals of destruction which frustrate
the search for justice and which threaten life itself, in our land and
throughout the world.

42. We look forward to your response to the proposals which we
have put forward and we wish to assure you of our eagerness to
discuss these and other proposals with you and to hear your
suggestions for the constructive participation of the churches in the
search for the peace which we all seek.

NOTES

1. This brief was presented to the Right Honourable Pierre Elliott Trudeau, Prime
Minister, by Dr. Robert Binhammer, President, Lutheran Church in America (Canada
Section); Most Reverend Henri Légaré, President, Canadian Conference of Catholic
Bishops; Dr. Russell Legge, President, Canadian Council of Churches; the Right
Reverend Clarke MacDonald, Moderator, the United Church of Canada; the Most
Reverend Edward W. Scott, Primate, the Anglican Church of Canada; The Most
Reverend Wayne A. Smith, Moderator, Presbyterian Church in Canada.

2. Jonathan Schell, *The Fate of the Earth* (New York, Avon Books, 1982), p. 95.

Document 55

ETHICAL REFLECTIONS ON THE ECONOMIC CRISIS[1]

Author — The Episcopal Commission for Social Affairs,
December 22, 1982

1 — INTRODUCTION

As the New Year begins, we wish to share some ethical reflections on the critical issues facing the Canadian economy.

In recent years, the Catholic Church has become increasingly concerned about the scourge of unemployment that plagues our society today and the corresponding struggles of workers in this country. A number of pastoral statements and social projects have been launched by church groups in national, regional and local communities as a response to various aspects of the emerging economic crisis.[2] On this occasion, we wish to make some brief comments on the immediate economic and social problems, followed by some brief observations on the deeper social and ethical issues at stake in developing future economic strategies.

As pastors, our concerns about the economy are not based on any specific political options. Instead, they are inspired by the gospel message of Jesus Christ. In particular, we cite two fundamental gospel principles that underlie our concerns.

The first principle has to do with the preferential option for the poor, the afflicted and the oppressed. In the tradition of the prophets, Jesus dedicated his ministry to bringing "good news to the poor" and "liberty to the oppressed".[3] As Christians, we are called to follow Jesus by identifying with the victims of injustice, by analysing the dominant attitudes and structures that cause human suffering and by actively supporting the poor and oppressed in their struggles to transform society. For, as Jesus declared, "when you did it unto these, the least of my brethren, you did it unto me."[4]

The second principle concerns the special value and dignity of human work in God's plan for Creation.[5] It is through the activity of work that people are able to exercise their creative spirit, realize their human dignity and share in Creation. By interacting with fellow workers in a common task, men and women have an opportunity to develop further their personalities and sense of self-worth. In so doing, people participate in the development of their society and give meaning to their existence as human beings.[6] Indeed, the importance of human labour is illustrated in the life of Jesus who was himself a worker, "a craftsman like Joseph of Nazareth."[7]

It is from the perspective of these basic gospel principles that we wish to share our reflections on the current economic crisis. Along with most people in Canada today, we realize that our economy is in serious trouble. In our own regions, we have seen the economic realities of plant shutdowns, massive layoffs of workers, wage-restraint programs, and suspension of collective-bargaining rights for public sector workers. At the same time, we have seen the social realities of abandoned one-industry towns, depleting unemployment insurance benefits, cut-backs in health and social services and lineups at local soup kitchens. And we have also witnessed first hand the results of a troubled economy: personal tragedies, emotional strain, loss of human dignity, family breakdown and even suicide.

Indeed we recognize that serious economic challenges lie ahead for this country. If our society is going to face up these challenges, people must meet and work together as a "true community" with vision and courage. In developing strategies for economic recovery, we firmly believe that first priority must be given to the real victims of the current recession — namely, the unemployed, the welfare poor, the working poor, pensioners, Native Peoples, women, young people, small farmers, fishermen, some factory workers and some small business men and women. This option calls for economic policies which realize that the needs of the poor have priority over the wants of the rich; that the rights of workers are more important than the maximization of profits; that the participation of marginalized groups has precedence over the preservation of a system which excludes them.

In response to current economic problems, we suggest that priority be given to the following short-term strategies by both government and business.

First, unemployment rather than inflation should be recognized as the number one problem to be tackled in overcoming the present crisis. The fact that some 1.5 million people are jobless constitutes a serious moral as well as economic crisis in this country. While efforts should continually be made to curb wasteful spending, it is imperative that primary emphasis be placed on combating unemployment.

Second, an industrial strategy should be developed to create permanent and meaningful jobs for people in local communities. To be effective, such a strategy should be designed at both national and regional levels. It should include emphasis on increased production, creation of new labour-intensive industries for basic needs and measures to ensure job security for workers.

Third, a more balanced and equitable program should be developed for reducing and stemming the rate of inflation. This requires shifting the burden for wage controls to upper income earners and introducing controls on prices and new forms of taxes on investment income (e.g., dividends, interest).

Fourth, greater emphasis should be given to the goal of social responsibility in the current recession. This means that every effort must be made to curtail cutbacks in social services, to maintain adequate health care and social security benefits, and above all, to guarantee special assistance for the unemployed, welfare recipients, the working poor and one-industry towns suffering from plant shutdowns.

Fifth, labour unions should be asked to play a more decisive and responsible role in developing strategies for economic recovery and unemployment. This requires the restoration of collective bargaining rights where they have been suspended, collaboration between unions and the unemployed and unorganized workers and assurances that labour unions will have an effective role in developing economic policies.

Furthermore, all people of good will in local and regional communities throughout the country must be encouraged to coordinate their efforts to develop and implement such strategies. As a step in this direction, we again call on local Christian communities to become actively involved in the six-point plan of action outlined in the message of the Canadian bishops on *Unemployment: The Human Costs.*[8]

We recognize that these proposals run counter to some current

policies or strategies advanced by both governments and corporations. We are also aware of the limited perspectives and excessive
demands of some labour unions. To be certain, the issues are
complex; there are no simple or magical solutions. Yet, from the
standpoint of the Church's social teachings,[9] we firmly believe that
present economic realities reveal a "moral disorder" in our society.
As pastors, we have a responsibility to raise some of the fundamental
social and ethical issues pertaining to the economic order. In so
doing, we expect that there will be considerable discussion and
debate within the Christian community itself on these issues. We
hope that the following reflections will help to explain our concerns
and contribute to the current public debate about the economy.

2 — THE ECONOMIC CRISIS

The present recession appears to be symptomatic of a much larger
structural crisis in the international system of capitalism. Observers
point out that profound changes are taking place in the structure
of both capital and technology which are bound to have serious social
impacts on labour.[10] We are now in an age when transnational
corporations and banks can move capital from one country to
another in order to take advantage of cheaper labour conditions,
lower taxes and reduced environmental restrictions. We are also in
an age of automation and computers, when human work is rapidly
being replaced by machines on the assembly line and in administrative centres. In effect, capital has become increasingly capital-
intensive. The consequences are likely to be permanent or structural
unemployment and increasing marginalization for a large segment
of the population in Canada and other countries.[11] In this context,
the increasing concentration of capital and technology in the
production of military armaments further intensifies this economic
crisis, rather than bringing about recovery.[12]

These structural changes largely explain the nature of the current
economic recession at home and throughout the world.[13] While there
does not appear to be global shortage of capital, large-scale banks
and corporations continue to wait for a more profitable investment
climate. Many companies are also experiencing a contemporary
shortage of investment funds required for the new technology, due
largely to an overextension of production and related factors. In
order to restore profit margins needed for new investment, companies are cutting back on production, laying off workers and

selling off their inventories. The result has been economic slow-down and soaring unemployment. To stimulate economic growth, governments are being called upon to provide a more favourable climate for private investments. Since capital tends to flow wherever the returns are greatest, reduced labour costs and lower taxes are required if countries are to remain competitive. As a result, most governments are introducing austerity measures, such as wage-restraint programs, cutbacks in social services and other reductions in social spending, in order to attract more private investment. And to enforce such economic policies, some countries have introduced repressive measures for restraining civil liberties and controlling social unrest.

3 — A MORAL CRISIS

The current structural changes in the global economy, in turn, reveal a deepening moral crisis. Through these structural changes, "capital" is reasserted as the dominant organizing principle of economic life. This orientation directly contradicts the ethical principle that labour, not capital, must be given priority in the development of an economy based on justice.[14] There is, in other words, an ethical order in which human labour, the subject of production, takes precedence over capital and technology. This is the *priority of labour* principle. By placing greater importance on the accumulation of profits and machines than on the people who work in a given economy, the value, meaning and dignity of human labour is violated. By creating conditions for permanent unemployment, an increasingly large segment of the population is threatened with the loss of human dignity. In effect, there is a tendency for people to be treated as an impersonal force having little or no significance beyond their economic purpose in the system.[15] As long as technology and capital are not harnessed by society to serve basic human needs, they are likely to become an enemy rather than an ally in the development of peoples.[16]

In addition, the renewed emphasis on the "survival of the fittest" as the supreme law of economics is likely to increase the domination of the weak by the strong, both at home and abroad. The "survival of the fittest" theory has often been used to rationalize the increasing concentration of wealth and power in the hands of a few.[17] The strong survive, the weak are eliminated. Under conditions of "tough competition" in international markets for capital and trade, the poor majority of the world is especially vulnerable. With three-quarters of the world's population, the poor nations of the South are already expected to survive on less than one-fifth of the world's income. Within Canada, the top 20% of the population receive 42.5% of total personal income, while the bottom 20% receive 4.1%.[18] These patterns of domination and inequality are likely to grow worse as the "survival of the fittest" doctrine is applied more rigorously to the economic order. While these Darwinian theories partly explain the rules that govern the animal world, they are in our view morally unacceptable as a "rule of life" for the human community.

4 — PRESENT STRATEGIES

There is a very real danger that these same structural and moral problems are present in Canada's strategies for economic recovery. As recent economic policy statements reveal, the primary objective is to restore profitability and competitiveness in certain Canadian industries and provide more favourable conditions for private investment in the country.[19] The private sector is to be the "engine" for economic recovery. To achieve these goals, inflation is put forth as the number one problem. The causes of inflation are seen as workers' wages, government spending and low productivity rather than monopoly control of prices. The means for curbing inflation are such austerity measures as the federal 6-and-5 wage-restraint program and cutbacks in social spending (e.g., hospitals, medicare, public services, education and foreign aid), rather than controls on profits and prices.[20] These measures in turn have been strengthened by a series of corporate tax reductions and direct investment incentives for such sectors as the petroleum industry. In effect, the survival of capital takes priority over labour in present strategies for economic recovery.

At the same time, working people, the unemployed, young people and those on fixed incomes are increasingly called upon to make the most sacrifice for economic recovery. For it is these people who suffer most from layoffs, wage restraints and cutbacks in social services. The recent tax changes, which have the effect of raising taxes for working people and lowering them for the wealthy, add to this burden. And these conditions are reinforced by the large-scale unemployment, which tends to generate a climate of social fear and passive acceptance. Moreover, the federal and provincial wage-control programs are inequitable, imposing the same control rate on lower incomes as on uppor incomes.[21] If successfully implemented, these programs could have the effect of transferring income from wages to profits.[22] Yet there are no clear reasons to believe that working people will ever really benefit from these and other sacrifices they are called to make. For even if companies recover and increase their profit margins, the additional revenues are likely to be reinvested in some labour-saving technology, exported to other countries or spent on market speculation or luxury goods.

5 — ALTERNATIVE APPROACHES

An alternative approach calls for a reordering of values and priorities in our economic life. What is required first is a basic shift in values: the goal of serving the human needs of all people in our society must take precedence over the maximization of profits and growth, and priority must be given to the dignity of human labour, not machines.[23] From this perspective, economic policies that focus primary attention on inflation and treat soaring unemployment as an inevitable problem, clearly violate these basic ethical values and priorities. There is nothing "normal" or "natural" about present unemployment rates. Massive unemployment which deprives people of the dignity of human work and of an adequate family income, constitutes a moral evil. It is also a major economic problem, since high unemployment rates are accompanied by lower productivity, lower consumption of products, reduced public revenues and increasing social welfare costs. So alternative strategies are required which place primary emphasis on the goals of combating unemployment by stimulating production and permanent job creation in basic industries; developing a more balanced and equitable program for curbing inflation; and maintaining health care, social security and special assistance programs.

An alternative approach also requires that serious attention be given to the development of new industrial strategies.[24] In recent years, people have begun to raise serious questions about the desirability of economic strategies based on megaprojects, wherein large amounts of capital are invested in high-technology resource developments (e.g., large-scale nuclear plants, pipelines, hydroelectric projects). Such megaprojects may increase economic growth and profits, but they generally end up producing relatively few permanent jobs while adding to a large national debt. In our view, it is important to increase the self-sufficiency of Canada's industries, to strengthen manufacturing and construction industries, to create new job-producing industries in local communities, to redistribute capital for industrial development in underdeveloped regions and to provide relevant job-training programs.[25] It is imperative that such strategies be developed wherever possible on a regional basis and that labour unions and community organizations be involved effectively in their design and implementation.

6 — NEW DIRECTIONS

In order to implement these alternatives there is a need for people to take a closer look at the industrial vision and economic model that govern our society.[26] It is becoming more evident that an industrial future is already planned by governments and corporations. According ot this industrial vision, we are now preparing to move into the high-technology computer age of the 1990's.[27] In order to become more competitive in world markets, the strategy for the eighties is to retool Canadian industries with new technologies, create new forms of high-tech industries (e.g., micro-electronic, petrochemical and nuclear) and phase out many labour-intensive industries (e.g., textile, clothing and footwear). This industrial vision in turn, is to be realized through an economic model of development that is primarily: capital-intensive (using less and less human labour); energy-intensive (requiring more non-renewable energy sources); foreign controlled (orienting development priorities to external interests); and export oriented (providing resources or products for markets elsewhere rather than serving basic needs of people in this country).

There are of course alternative ways of looking at our industrial future and organizing our economy. This does not imply a halt to technological progress but rather a fundamental reordering of the basic values and priorities of economic development. An alternative economic vision, for example, could place priority on serving the basic needs of all people in this country, on the value of human labour and on an equitable distribution of wealth and power among people and regions. What would it mean to develop an alternative economic model that would place emphasis on: socially useful forms of production; labour-intensive industries; the use of appropriate forms of technology; self-reliant models of economic development; community ownership and control of industries; new forms of worker management and ownership; and greater use of the renewable energy sources in industrial production? As a country, we have the resources, the capital, the technology and, above all else, the aspirations and skills of working men and women required to build an alternative economic future. Yet the people of this country have seldom been challenged to envision and develop alternatives to the dominant economic model that governs our society.

At the outset, we agreed that people must indeed meet and work together as a ''true community'' in the face of the current economic crisis.[28] Yet in order to forge a true community out of the present crisis, people must have a chance to choose their economic future rather than to have one forced upon them. What is required in our judgment, is a real public debate about economic visions and industrial strategies, involving choices about values and priorities for the future direction of this country. Across our society there are working and non-working people in communities — factory workers, farmers, forestry workers, miners, people on welfare, fishermen, native peoples, public service workers, and many others — who have a creative and dynamic contribution to make in shaping the economic future of our society. It is essential that serious attention be given to their concerns and proposals if the seeds of trust are to be sown for the development of a true community and a new economic order.

For our part, we will do whatever we can to stimulate public dialogue about alternative visions and strategies. More specifically, we urge local parishes or Christian communities, wherever possible, to organize public forums for discussion and debate on major issues of economic justice. Such events could provide a significant opportunity for people to discuss: (a) specific struggles of workers, the poor and the unemployed in local communities; (b) an analysis of local and regional economic problems and structures; (c) major ethical principles of economic life in the Church's recent social teachings; (d) suggestions for alternative economic visions; (e) new proposals for industrial strategies that reflect basic ethical principles. In some communities and regions, Christian groups in collaboration with other concerned bodies have already launched similar events or activities for economic justice. And we encourage them to continue doing so.

We hope and pray that more people will join in this search for alternative economic visions and strategies. For the present economic crisis, as we have seen, reveals a deepening moral disorder in the values and priorities of our society. We believe that the cries of the poor and powerless are the voice of Christ, the Lord of History, in our midst. As Christians we are called to become involved in struggles for economic justice and to participate in building a new society based on gospel principles. In so doing, we fulfill our vocation as a pilgrim people on earth, participating in Creation and preparing for the coming Kingdom.

NOTES

1. No message of the Canadian Catholic bishops speaking to an issue of social justice received greater publicity or excited more comment, favourable and critical, than this Document 55. For an excellent ethical and economic commentary see Gregory Baum and Duncan Cameron, *Ethics and Economics: Canada's Catholic Bishops on the Economic Crisis* (Toronto, Lorimer, 1984). The daily press as well as business and financial papers carried many articles and notices.

Comment of other church leaders was very widely favourable. Cf. also A.M.C. Waterman, "The Catholic Bishops and Canadian Public Policy" in *Canadian Public Policy — Analyse de Politiques*, IX:3, 372-382, 1983, and a reply of B.W. Wilkinson, *ibid.*, X:1, 88-91, 1984.

Also *Canada's Unemployed: The Crisis of Our Times, Report of the Hearing Panel on "Ethical Reflections on the Economic Crisis"* (Toronto, Archdiocese of Toronto, M5B 1Z8, 1983).

2. Among the more recent pastoral statements, see, Document, 54, above; *Les luttes des travailleurs en temps de crise*, 1982, and *Les jeunes face à la crise*, 1982, Comité des affaires sociales de l'Assemblée des Évêques du Québec, both in *La justice sociale comme bonne nouvelle*, édit. G. Rochais (Montréal, Éditions Bellarmin, 1984), pp. 184 and 190. For an ethical reflection on the economic crisis in France cf. "Pour des nouveaux modes de vie, Déclaration du Conseil permanent de l'Épiscopat", *Documentation Catholique*, Paris, 1982, LXXIX, 937.

3. Cf. Lk 4:16-19, 7:22; Mt 11:4-6.

4. Mt 25:40.

5. Cf. John Paul II, *On Human Work*, 1981, in *The Papal Encyclicals*, edit. Claudia Carlen, IHM (Wilmington, N.C., McGrath Publishing, 1981), V, p. 301 ff., sections 4, 6, 9, 24, 25, 26.

6. Cf. Document 49, above, n. 5.

7. John Paul II, *op. cit.*, in Carlen note 5, above, Section 26, n. 118, p. 323.

8. Document 49, above, n. 15.

9. Cf. John Paul II, *On HumanWork* and *The Redeemer of Mankind*; Paul VI, *The Development of Peoples*, in Carlen, note 5 above, vol. V; Paul VI, *A Call to Action (Octogesima Adveniens)*, 1971, *The Pope Speaks*, Washington, 1971, XVI, p. 136; Third International Synod of Bishops, *Justice in the World*, *ibid.*, p. 377.

10. See, A.G. Frank, *Crisis in the World Economy* (New York, Holmes and Meier, 1980); Samit Amin et al. *La Crise, quelle crise? Dynamique de la crise mondiale* (Paris, Maspero, 1982); S. Rousseau, *Capitalism and Catastrophe: A Critical Appraisal of the Limits to Capitalism* (Cambridge, Cambridge University Press, 1979); *Social Analysis: Linking Faith and Justice* (Washington, D.C., 20017, Centre of Concern, 1980); *La Crise économique*

et sa gestion (Montréal, Boréal Express, 1982); Cy Gonick, *Inflation or Depression: An Analysis of the Continuing Crisis in the Canadian Economy* (Toronto, Lorimer, 1975).

11. See the forecasts of the Conference Board of Canada (Ottawa, K1L 6R3), Nov. 1982. These predict moderate recovery with greater unemployment. With forecasts of economic recovery for 1983 and 1984, unemployment is forecast at 12.7% for 1983 and 11.4% for 1984.

12. Observers point out that the highly capital-intensive nature of modern weapons manufacture creates a more rapid rate of technological obsolescence of fixed capital and thus leads to greater inflationary pressures and higher unemployment. See M. Kaldor, *The Role of Military Technology in Industrial Development,* U.N. Group of Government Experts on the Relationship of Disarmament and Development, May 1980. For a more extensive analysis of this question, see A. Eide and M. Thee, eds., *Problems of Contemporary Militarism* (London, St. Martin's Press, 1980).

13. See, e.g., *La crise économique et sa gestion* (cf. note 9, above), P. I, "La crise actuelle des sociétés capitalistes".

14. John Paul II, *On Human Work,* Section 12, nn. 52-57, in Carlen (cf. note 5, above), p. 309.

For excellent commentary, cf. Gregory Baum, *The Priority of Labour,* (New York, Paulist Press, 1982), esp. pp. 22-40.

15. Cf. John Paul II, *op. cit.,* Section 13, nn. 58-62, in Carlen note 5, above, p. 311. The Pope comments particularly on the errors of "economism" and "materialism".

16. Cf. John Paul II, *op. cit.,* Section 5, nn. 16-21, in Carlen note 5, above, p. 302.

17. Cf. Document 46 above; Paul VI, *The Development of Peoples,* 1967, nn. 33, 57, in Carlen note 5, above, pp. 189 and 193.

18. For analysis of global disparities, cf. the Brandt Commission Report, *North-South: A Program for Survival* (Cambridge, Mass., MIT Press, 1980). For data on disparities in Canada, see *Income Distribution by Size in Canada, Statistics Canada,* 1980. For more extended analysis, see J. Harp and J.R. Hofley, eds., *Structured Inequality in Canada* (Scarborough, Prentice-Hall, 1980).

19. See the budget statements of the Hon. Allan MacEachen, November 1981 and 28 June 1982, plus the recent statement on the economy by the Hon. Marc Lalonde, 29 October 1982.

20. See budget statement of Hon. Allan MacEachen, 28 June 1982. Finance Department officials have stated that the 6 and 5 program will have the "unintended effect of transferring income from wages to profits" (see Toronto *Globe and Mail,* 28 August 1982).

21. It should be noted that: (1) people earning $18,000, who can least afford restriction of salary increase below the inflation rate, are subjected to the same rate of control as people earning $50,000 or more, who could afford an income freeze; (2) it is estimated that approximately 30% of the total Net National Income generated in Canada (1981) came in the form of dividends, interest and other investment income rather than in wages and salaries which are subject to controls.

22. Cf. concerns expressed by Canadian Labour Congress (Ottawa, K1V 8X7) in their *Statement on Economic Policy,* July 8, 1982. For a further perspective cf. "Wage Controls Won't Work", *Public Employee* (Ottawa, K2P 0W6, Fall, 1982). See also the report of the Confédération des syndicats nationaux (CSN, Montréal, H2K 4M5), "Du travail pour tout le monde", fév. 1982.

23. Cf. Document 49, above, n. 12.

24. Cf. *ibid.,* nn. 9, 14.

25. For examples of proposed industrial strategies, cf. Canadian Labour Congress

Document 55

(Ottawa, K1V 8X7), *Statement on Economic Policy,* May, 1982. Also the recent proposals of the Confédération des syndicats nationaux, *La Presse,* Montréal, 18 nov. 1982.

26. As an example of thinking about alternative directions, see J.P. Wogaman, *The Great Economic Debate* (London, SCM Press, 1977).

27. Cf. the following reports of The Science Council of Canada (Ottawa, K1P 5M1): *The Weakest Link: A Technological Perspective on Canadian Industrial Underdevelopment; Forging the Links: A Technological Policy for Canada; Hard Times/Hard Choices: Technology and the Balance of Payments.*

28. For references to "true community", cf. Rt. Hon. Pierre E. Trudeau, *Statements on the Economy,* Parts I and III.

Document 56

ETHICAL REFLECTIONS ON CANADA'S SOCIO-ECONOMIC ORDER

To the Royal Commission on the Economic Union and Development Prospects for Canada [1]

Author — The Canadian Conference of Catholic Bishops, December 13, 1983

Introduction

1. Mr. Chairman, members of the Royal Commission on the Economic Union and Development Prospects for Canada, we welcome this opportunity to present our concerns regarding the current realities and future prospects of Canada's economy. As representatives of the Canadian Conference of Catholic Bishops (CCCB), we believe that there are some important ethical priorities to be addressed with respect to Canada's social and economic order at this particular moment in history.

2. Your commission, as we understand it, has been given the mandate to study and make recommendations regarding the future of Canada's economic order in relation to changing world conditions. In your terms of reference, it is recognized "that significant changes are occurring in the world economy, particularly in the sphere of industrial activity, the utilization of natural resources, and the movement of capital within and among countries". These changes have resulted in new global economic conditons affecting the political economies of all countries. In this context, your commission has been charged with the responsibility of identifying the challenges,

prospects and implications of these new global conditions for Canada's own political economy. This entails an identification of national goals and policies that may, in turn, require changes in Canada's economic and political structures. Also implicit here is a recognition that basic decisions on goals and priorities involve value choices about the kind of society we want to build in the future.

3. In recent years, we have attempted to stimulate ethical reflections on these major concerns through a series of social teaching documents. Perhaps the best known example is the New Year (1983) statement of our Social Affairs Commission, *Ethical Reflections on the Economic Crisis*, which drew upon the insights developed in Pope John Paul II's encyclical, *On Human Work*, 1981. In addition, the CCCB has issued several related social teaching documents including: *From Words to Action* (1976); *A Society to be Transformed* (1977); *Witness to Justice: A Society to be Transformed* (1979); and *Unemployment: the Human Costs* (1980); plus a series of Labour Day Messages on questions of social and economic justice. Taken together, these documents constitute an ongoing process of ethical reflection on Canada's socio-economic order. At the same time, the CCCB participates in collaboration with other Canadian churches in a variety of research, education and action projects concerned with social and economic justice in this country.[2]

4. In addition, a particular pastoral methodology is generally used in the formulation of our ethical reflections, (WA, n. 9; ST, n. 19; JW; key below). This pastoral methodology involves a number of steps:

(a) being present with and listening to the experiences of the poor, the marginalized, the oppressed in our society (e.g., the unemployed, the working poor, the welfare poor, exploited workers, native peoples, the elderly, the handicapped, small producers, racial and cultural minorities, etc.);

(b) developing a critical analysis of the economic, political and social structures that cause human suffering;

(c) making judgments in the light of Gospel principles and the social teachings of the Church concerning social values and priorities;

(d) stimulating creative thought and action regarding alternative visions and models for social and economic development; and

(e) acting in solidarity with popular groups in their struggles to transform economic, political and social structures that cause social and economic injustices.

5. Our purpose here is to continue this process of ethical reflection in terms of several themes and topics that relate to the mandate of your commission and the nature of your inquiry. In accordance with the first phase of your inquiry, we have divided our submission into

A Table of Social Documents Frequently Cited

GS *(Gaudium et Spes) The Church in the Modern World,* 1965, Second Vatican Council

LE *(Laborem Exercens) On Human Work,* 1981, John Paul II, cf. *The Papal Encyclicals,* edit. Claudia Carlen, IHM (McGrath Publishing, Wilmington, N.C., 1981), vol. V, p. 299

PP *(Populorum Progressio) The Development of Peoples,* 1967, Paul VI, in Carlen above, p. 185

PT *(Pacem in Terris) Peace on Earth,* 1963, John XXIII, in Carlen above, p. 107

OA *(Octogesima Adveniens) A Call to Action,* 1971, Paul VI, cf. *The Pope Speaks,* Washington, 1971, XVI, p. 137

JE *Justice in the World,* Third International Synod of Bishops, 1971, cf. *The Pope Speaks,* Washington, 1971, XVI, p. 377

ER *Ethical Reflections on the Economic Crisis,* 1982, CCCB, Document 55 above

ND *Northern Development,* 1975, CCCB, Document 40 above

ST *A Society to be Transformed,* 1977, CCCB, Document 46 above

UC *Unemployment: The Human Costs,* 1980, CCCB, Document 49 above

WA *From Words to Action,* 1976, CCCB, Document 44 above

WJ *Witness to Justice: A Society to be Transformed,* 1979, CCCB Publications Service, Ottawa, K1N 7B1 three parts. In part one, we will attempt to clarify the *perspective* from which we speak about our socio-economic order. In part two, we will identify some of the major *problems* of our socio-economic order from the standpoint of our ethical perspective. In part three, we will attempt to outline some of the basic *challenges* to be faced regarding the future of Canada's economy. In the final analysis, the fundamental question before us is what kind of society and people do we want to become.

6. It should be noted that it is not our intention here to make moral judgments in a dogmatic or authoritarian fashion. Moral principles are themselves universally valid. But their application to concrete situations allows for a diversity of options. Our primary concern here is to stimulate serious public discussion about some major ethical issues regarding the future development of our economy and society.

I — PERSPECTIVE

7. Our first task is to clarify the perspective from which we speak about the economic order of our society. As bishops, we do not claim to be technical experts in economic matters. Our primary role is to be moral teachers in society. In this capacity, we attempt to view economic and social realities primarily from the perspective of the Gospel message of Jesus Christ and his concern for the poor, the marginalized and the oppressed (WA, n. 9). From this perspective, we believe there are fundamental ethical questions to be raised about the values and priorities that govern any socio-economic order. Thus, we have a responsibility to stimulate ethical reflections on the values, priorities and structures of this country's socio-economic order.

8. In recent years, we have tried to stimulate some critical ethical reflections on Canada's economy through various social statements, working instruments and education projects. Our experience to date however, indicates that this is not always an easy endeavour. Ethics and economics have become separate disciplines in the historic evolution of liberal capitalism itself. The emphasis on economistic and mechanistic approaches has managed to drain the moral content out of economics as a discipline over the past century or more (ST, n. 13; LE, Sec. 7, nn. 28-31). As a result, serious ethical discourse about the Canadian economy rarely occurs in our culture and society.

9. The Roman Catholic Church, through almost a century of social teaching, has consistently maintained that there is an ethical order to be followed in the organization of an economy. This is evident, for example, in the writings of Pope John Paul II. In Catholic social teaching, the value and dignity of the human person lies at the centre of an economy based on justice. This means, in turn, that all persons in a given society should have the right of common access to, and use of, the goods produced by the economy (LE, Sec. 14, nn. 63-71). In this context, peoples are meant to be the agents of their own history. Through their labour, workers are to be the subject not the object of production. In turn capital and technology are seen as the instruments of production (LE, Sec. 12, 13, nn. 52-62). It follows therefore that people in general and human labour in particular, take priority over both capital and technology in an economic order based on justice.

10. In general, this is the perspective from which we have attempted to stimulate some ethical reflections on the Canadian economy. This ethical perspective in turn, is rooted in several major themes and principles developed in the scriptures and in the social teachings of the Church.

Subjects of Creation

11. According to the scriptures, all persons are made in the image of God. Thus the human person is meant to be the subject of creation and the subject of a given economy. As subjects of creation, all persons have certain inalienable rights. Of primary importance is the right to life and all that makes for a more fully human life such as adequate food, clothing, shelter, employment, health care, education and effective participation in decisions affecting their lives (GS, n. 26; PT, nn. 8-26). As subjects of creation, all persons are entrusted also with the responsibility of being co-creators of the Earth and stewards for the sake of present and future generations (Gn 1 and 2). This means in turn, that the human person is meant to be the co-creator of an economy and the subject of production.

Primary Purpose

12. Throughout the scriptures, the Earth is understood to be God's gift for present and future generations of humanity (Gn 1 and 2;

Ps 8, 9, 104). The resources of the Earth are to be developed for God's intended purpose, namely to serve equitably the needs of all people for a more fully human life. This is the "universal purpose of created things" (GS, n. 69). It follows therefore, that the primary purpose of a socio-economic order should be to develop its resources to serve the common good, the basic life needs of all its people for food, clothing, shelter, education, employment, health care. And "all other rights whatsoever, including those of property and free commerce, are to be subordinated to this principle." (PP, n. 22; LE, Sec. 14, nn. 63-69)

Integral Development

13. The primary purpose of an economy should be reflected in its models of development. From this perspective, models of development cannot be limited to mere economic growth (PP, n. 14). To be authentic, development must be integral, encompassing the social, economic, cultural and spiritual needs of the whole person. Integral development therefore encompasses both the personal and the communal dimensions of human living. To be sure, economic growth can be an important dimension of economic development of a society or community. However, economic strategies aimed at maximizing private profits and consumption, and technological growth designed to maintain power and domination, constitute distorted models of "development" and must be resisted.

Priority of Labour

14. The value and dignity of human work have special significance in God's Plan for Creation. It is through the activity of work that people are able to exercise their creative spirit, realize their human dignity and participate in the development of their society (UC, n. 5). In this context, working people are to be viewed as the subjects not the objects of production in a given economy. Human labour therefore should not be treated as a commodity to be bought and sold in the market place (LE, sec. 7, nn. 28-31). On the contrary, human labour must be the subject of production, taking precedence over both capital and technology in the production process (LE, sec. 12, nn. 52-57). In effect, the basic rights of working people take priority over the maximization of profits and the accumulation of

machines in an economic order (ER). This is the priority of labour principle.

Priority of the Poor

15. The needs and rights of the poor, the afflicted, the marginalized and the oppressed are given special attention in God's Plan for Creation (WA, n. 4). Throughout his ministry Jesus repeatedly identified with the plight of the poor and the outcasts of society (e.g., Ph 2:6-8; Lk 6:20-21). He also took a critical attitude towards the accumulation of wealth and power that comes through the exploitation of others (e.g., Lk 16:13-15; 12:16-21; Mk 4:19). This has become known as "the preferential option for the poor" in the scriptures. In a given economic order, the needs of the poor take priority over the wants of the rich (ER). This does not mean simply more handouts for the poor. It calls instead for an equitable re-distribution of wealth and power among peoples and regions (WA, n. 3; ST; UC, n. 13).

Means of Production

16. In the Church's social teaching, capital and technology are understood to be the means or instruments of production (LE, Sec. 12, nn. 52-57). In any economy therefore, capital and technology should be used for humanly constructive purposes, namely the integral development of peoples. At the same time, the means of production should not be owned in opposition to human labour or owned for the sake of owning them (LE, Sec. 14, nn. 63-69). Legal title does not confer absolute ownership. The only title to their ownership is that they serve the basic needs of all people, especially human labour and needs of the poor. There is, in other words, a "social mortgage" on the means of production.[3] Capital and technology must be used for constructive rather than destructive purposes in the development of peoples.

Effective Participation

17. As subjects of creation, all peoples have rights to self-determination, to define their own future and to participate effectively in decisions affecting their lives (PP; JW, nn. 16, 17). This is essential if working people, the poor and the marginalized are

going to exercise their rights to be subjects of their own history. This means for example, that working people as subjects of production should have an effective and meaningful role to play in social and economic planning regarding the use of capital and technology. Effective participation in these kinds of decision-making processes is a basic part of being human. It is essential for an integral model of development (JW, nn. 1, 13-19). In effect, the participation of the marginalized takes precedence over an order which excludes them (ER).

Self-Reliance

18.   Integral development also requires an emphasis on more self-reliant models of development. An economy that is organized largely to provide for external interests and dependent on externally controlled means of production, cannot serve the basic needs of its own population (PP, n. 58). Through self-reliance, peoples' energies are directed towards developing local resources to serve the basic human needs (JW, nn. 1, nn. 13-19). This requires in turn that local communities identify their basic needs, assess their human and material resources and acquire communal control over the necessary means of production. In this way, people can be empowered to organize their economy to serve their own basic needs. Moreover, self-reliant development is rooted in the socio-cultural heritage of the people themselves.

Responsible Stewardship

19.   As subjects of creation, people are also called to be responsible stewards of natural resources in a socio-economic order (ND. nn, 19-24; WA, n. 6). The resources of planet Earth are not limitless. The abuse and waste of finite resources affect the health and well-being of present and future generations. Nature should not be treated coldly and calculatingly as a mere storehouse of commodities (Ps 104). In our times, humanity must learn to organize socio-economic systems in such a way that nature remains sufficiently balanced and human needs are adequately satisfied (i.e., eco-development). This means finding ways of using capital and technology in partnership and harmony with nature. In this context, consideration needs to be given to sustainable models of development based on renewable as well as non-renewable resources.

Global Solidarity

20. The global realities of interdependence in the modern world call for new forms of solidarity between peoples throughout the world (LE; PP, nn. 43 ff). The structural causes of poverty and oppression in the Third World for example, are linked to the international economic order dominated by affluent and powerful nation states of the First World. The fact that four-fifths of the earth's population is expected to survive on one-fifth of the world's resources can no longer be ignored or tolerated. What is required is the cultivation of new forms of solidarity — with and among working and non-working peoples — with and among the poor and oppressed peoples of the world — in the building of a new international economic order. This is the principle of universal solidarity. As such, it guards against any narrow nationalistic chauvinism in developing the economies of nation states.

21. These then are some of the major principles involved in the ethical ordering of an economy and society. Taken together, these moral themes and principles provide an ongoing challenge to all institutions in our society — governments, businesses, labour unions, community organizations, religious institutions and others. The state however, has a particularly important role to play in assuring that this ethical order is achieved in the organization and operations of an economy. Indeed, the state has a major responsibility to ensure that the whole economy itself lives up to the criteria of this ethical order (LE, Sec. 18, nn. 82-87). This means that the state has the responsibility to intervene in the operations of an economy to ensure that basic human rights and moral principles are realized (LE, *ibid.*). In order to do so, the state must be able to stand aside from the particular interests of power elites and act on behalf of the common good (OA, n. 46), with special concern for the poor and powerless groups of society.

22. The problems being raised today — and is it really only today? — about human labour do not, in fact, come down in the last analysis — I say this with respect for all the specialists — either to technology or even to economics but to a fundamental category: *the category of the dignity of work,* that is to say, of the *dignity of man.* Economics, technology and the many other specializations and disciplines have their justification for existing in that single essential category. If they fail to draw

from that category and are shaped without reference to the dignity of human labour, they are in error, they are harmful, they are against man. This fundamental category is *humanistic*. I make bold to say that this fundamental category, the category of work as a measure of the dignity of man, is *Christian*. We find it in its highest degree of intensity in Christ.[4]

II — PROBLEM

23.   Our second task is to identify some of the major problems to be faced concerning the future of Canada's socio-economic order. In our most recent social statements, we have emphasized that the current economic recession is symptomatic of a deeper structural crisis that is taking place in the international system of industrial capitalism itself (ER). As Pope John Paul II has noted, industrial societies are moving from a relatively benevolent to a more rigid stage of capitalism that holds forth the prospect of a grim future (LE, Sec. 1, nn. 2-5). These changes, as we shall see, reveal a deepening moral crisis which deserves serious attention regarding the future of our socio-economic order.

24.   As many observers have noted, basic changes are taking place in the structure of both capital and technology that will have profound social consequences. Today transnational corporations and banks can move capital from one country or region to another, taking advantage of cheaper labour conditions, lower corporate taxes and reduced environmental standards. As a result, transnationals can shift their operations anywhere in the world on almost a momentary basis, thereby outflanking both workers' demands and labour unions. At the same time, the introduction of automation and computers to the production process has meant that human work is being replaced rapidly by machines on the assembly line and in administrative centres. As a result, the workerless factory and the automated office may well be among the chief characteristics of this new industrial age. All of this points to a continuing social crisis of permanent or structural unemployment.

25.   In effect, capital has become fully transnationalized while technology has become capital-intensive. And both have become increasingly concentrated in fewer centres of power. At the same time, these structural changes have created a new global economic

environment. The international movement of capital has restored *laissez-faire* competition on a global basis as nation states compete with one another for investment by transnational corporations and banks. The new technological rationalization of production has altered dramatically the division of labour between countries and within countries. These new economic conditions in turn have served to heighten global tensions — East and West, North and South — thereby contributing to the escalating nuclear arms race and the increasing militarization of national economies (especially in the Third World).

26. In this new global environment, it appears that nation states like Canada (and its provinces) are being compelled to restructure their economies for the "tough new world of competition". Indeed Canada finds itself in a somewhat vulnerable position, given such structural problems as high levels of foreign ownership and economic dependency on the United States. In the short term, federal and provincial governments are attempting to restore the profitability and competitiveness of certain industries and to provide a much more favourable climate for private investment of capital and technology. In the long term, both sets of governments are attempting to restructure Canada's economy for the high-tech computer age of the 1990's, with the private sector being designated as the engine for economic development. And in order to become more competitive in world markets, the strategy for the eighties appears to be that of re-tooling Canadian industries with new technologies, creating new forms of high-tech industries, initiating new mega-projects of resource development, and phasing out many labour-intensive industries.

27. Under these new conditions, capital and technology are being re-asserted as the dominant organizing principles of our socio-economic order. These structural changes in turn will have profound social consequences. From the perspective discussed above (Part I), our society seems to be faced with a deepening moral crisis. The following are some of the signs of this moral disorder in our economy today.

Massive Unemployment

28. The current structural crisis has generated the highest levels of unemployment in this country since the Great Depression of the

1930's. The official unemployment statistics, combined with the numbers of discouraged workers (those who have given up looking for work) and the numbers of underemployed workers (part-time workers seeking full-time employment) mean that well over two million people are being deprived of an adequate family or personal income. Moreover, long range forecasts indicate that this pattern will not change substantially for the remainder of this decade. Indeed, the rapid introduction of labour-saving technologies has intensified the crisis. As a result, there seems to be a growing cynical resignation to the continuing realities of high unemployment in our society.[5]

29. It would be false and deceptive to consider the distressing problem (of unemployment) — which has become endemic throughout the world — as the product of passing circumstances or as a purely economic and socio-cultural problem. It is really an *ethical* problem, a spiritual problem, because it is a symptom of a *moral disorder* existing in society when the hierarchy of values is broken.

   ... The state must not resign itself to having to tolerate chronic high unemployment. The creation of new jobs must constitute for it a priority as much economic as political.[6]

Social Deprivation

30. The adoption of monetarist policies has resulted in a series of major cut-backs in social spending at both federal and provincial levels. This includes reductions in revenue for hospitals, public services, education, social agencies, environmental protection and foreign aid. The introduction of extra-billing and user-fees for medicare in several provinces further magnifies the problem. If this trend continues, it likely will result in the dismantling of the social welfare apparatus that gradually was put in place following the second World War. Despite safety net provisions, the main victims of these social cut-backs are still the poorest sectors of the population including the elderly, people on welfare, the working poor and the unemployed. Moreover, the current trends towards privatization indicate the possibility of reverting to a system where basic social services are made available to people on the basis of their ability to pay.[7]

Labour Devaluation

31. The structural crisis has had a major impact on most working people. Wage restraint programmes, suspension of collective bargaining rights and withdrawal of job security provisions have taken their toll, largely on public sector workers. In the private sector, plant shut-downs and lay-offs, the de-skilling of workers in certain industries and the general streamlining of the labour force for a high-tech future have had major social consequences. Under conditions of high unemployment, non-working people have little choice but to price themselves back into the labour market by accepting lower wages and working conditions. As a result, human labour is being further reduced to a commodity, having little or no significance beyond its economic function in the system.[8]

Increasing Marginalization

32. The introduction of computers and robots into industries and offices has begun to create what may become a new class of people, namely the so-called "techno-peasants". These are the men and women who are being shut out or marginalized by their functional illiteracy in the new technologies. The most affected are expected to be workers in manufacturing, agriculture and resource industries. Indeed it is the middle classes which are most vulnerable to increasing marginalization due to the new technologies. The upward social mobility of the post-war years is rapidly giving way to the new trend of downward social mobility for many people. This is likely to contribute to an enlargment of the sectors of poverty and powerlessness in our society.[9]

Economic Disparities

33. There are also signs that economic disparities between classes and regions are growing. In recent years personal income taxes have been steadily rising while corporate income taxes have been declining as part of economic strategies to attract more private investment. Since lower income Canadians pay a proportionately larger percentage of their income in taxes than wealthier Canadians, the inequalities between social classes are likely to widen further. At the same time, the continuing centralization of job producing industries in the major metropolitan centres has further aggravated

economic disparities between regions. Indeed the highest rates of unemployment and plant closures, plus some of the sharpest cutbacks in social services, are occurring in the poorest regions of the country. Moreover renewed reliance on the "trickle-down" mechanism for income distribution through the private sector will likely accentuate these disparities.[10]

Economic Dislocation

34. The structural crisis has also intensified the concentration of economic power in the hands of a small number of large corporations exercising monopoly control over key sectors of the economy. As a result, many small businesses and small producers (e.g., farmers and fisherpeople) have been forced out of the market. This is evident by the large number of farm bankruptcies, plant shut-downs, small business closures and the disruption of one industry towns. In this kind of economic climate, capital and technology tend to become further concentrated in the hands of few transnational enterprises. Under these conditions of excessive competition, only the strong are able to survive while the weak are eliminated from the market and from participation in society.[11]

Export Orientation

35. A major part of the restructuring of Canada's economy is the retooling of Canadian industries and the streamlining of both resource and industrial sectors for competition in world markets. This trend serves to intensify the export orientation of our economy. As a result, greater emphasis is placed on organizing our economy to serve external market interests rather than on producing for the basic needs of our own population. Thus even though a major food producing nation, Canada is importing an increasing amount of basic food products. In other words, our country is becoming more and more dependent on other countries for the basic food needs of our population. Moreover increased emphasis on export orientation serves to perpetuate the economic dependency of Third World countries on global markets.[12]

Militarization Trends

36. Canada's economy has certainly not been immune to the escalating arms race. In recent years, military spending on the part of the federal government has increased significantly to maintain North Atlantic Treaty Organization (NATO) commitments while social spending has steadily declined. The testing of the Cruise Missile in Canada is a further symbol of this trend toward militarization. Even more disturbing is the retooling of Canadian industries for military production. While a number of Canadian companies are already engaged in nuclear and conventional arms production under the U.S./Canada Defense Sharing Agreement, more industries are being lured into military production due to weak market conditions elsewhere. As a result, the Canadian economy becomes more closely linked to the arms race.[13]

Ecological Damage

37. In order to attract private investment, some governments have lowered environmental standards or decreased their monitoring activities regarding pollution control. In some regions of the country, renewable resources like forests and fish are directly affected by the lack of environmental regulation. In others the storage of radio-active wastes from uranium mines and nuclear plants poses a serious environmental threat to communities and a potential health hazard for workers. At the same time, new industrial technologies continue to generate pollution-causing materials which have a damaging effect on the air, lakes, rivers and waters. The acid rain issue is the most obvious example. The apparent unwillingness of governments and agencies in the United States to enter into agreements with Canada on effective acid rain control is a disturbing sign of the times.[14]

Social Breakdown

38. Finally, there are growing signs of social breakdown. Underneath the continuing unemployment crisis lies a deepening human and social tragedy. The experience of unemployment generates a sense of alienation and powerlessness that comes from a loss of personal identity and self-worth. These personal traumas tend to translate into social crises such as increasing alcoholism, suicides, family breakdown, vandalism, crime, racism and street

violence. A dramatic illustration is the number of suicide pacts over the past year among young people who see no hope for the future. The personal insecurities associated with unemployment are creating a climate of social fear and passive acceptance of these new realities. Taken together these are some of the disturbing signs of the times emerging in this new industrial age. To us, they indicate a deepening moral disorder in our society.[15]

39. In the midst of the present structural crisis, capital and technology are being re-asserted as the dominant organizing principles of our socio-economic order. Under these new conditions, governments and other institutions are being called upon to reorganize their economic strategies and social programs. The social consequences, as we have seen, appear to be a series of assaults on the human dignity of a substantial number of people in this country. The primary victims of this assault are workers, the unemployed, the poor and the growing number of marginalized people. Today these trends are evident in Canada as a whole and in each of the provinces.

40. It should be understood clearly that we are not taking a stand against progress and technology as such. On the contrary, modern advances in the development of capital and technology could be used to enhance greatly the development of peoples here in Canada and throughout the world. The critical question however, is who controls these instruments and how they will be used. Unless communities and working people have effective control over both capital and technology, these tend to become destructive forces rather than constructive instruments in economic development. Under these conditions the human person becomes more and more redundant and a victim of impersonal economic forces. This is the central problem of our times. It is first and foremost a moral or ethical problem in the structural order of our economy and society.

III — CHALLENGE

41. Our third task is to identify the basic challenge which we see emerging with respect to the future of Canada's socio-economic order. Given our perspective (Part I) and our analysis of the problem (Part II), we believe the fundamental challenge involves a

combination of moral vision and political will. The primary task, in our view, is not simply a question of how governments can better manage the economy in the new high-tech industrial age. It is not a question of how to make people adjust, accommodate, adapt, retrain, relocate and lower their expectations. What we are facing are some basic structural problems in our economy that reveal a moral disorder in our society.

42. The challenge before us therefore is to search for alternative visions and models for the future development of our socio-economic order in the new industrial age. As emphasized above, the basic social contradiction of our times is the structural domination of capital and technology over people, over labour, over communities. What is required is a radical inversion of these structural relationships. In other words, ways must be found for people to exercise more effective control over both capital and technology so that they may become constructive instruments of creation by serving the basic needs of people and communities. This requires in turn that efforts be made to stimulate social imagination concerning alternative economic visions and models.

43. There are of course some built-in problems in our culture and society which limit our capacities for social imagination. For example, the restricted ideological choice between two systems, either capitalism or communism, tends to stifle social imagination (ST, nn. 14-20). At the same time, the dominant forces of transnational capital and technology largely dictate what is desirable and feasible, thereby limiting the capacities of nations and peoples to develop viable options. In addition, social imagination is further hampered by the kind of technological rationality that prevails in our culture today. This is the kind of reasoning that avoids fundamental questions by reducing everything to factual and quantifiable knowledge through a technical means-ends process. Finally, the continued problems of personal selfishness, possessive individualism, pursuit of narrow self-interest and collective greed prevent some people from developing a capacity for creative social imagination.

44. It is essential that people find ways of breaking out of these dominant modes of thought and develop new ways of thinking about social and economic alternatives (ST, nn. 17-18). We believe that the moral principles outlined above (Part I), provide some guide posts for thinking about alternative visions and models. At this point

we do not intend to put forward detailed proposals or strategies. Our primary concern is to stimulate more creative thinking about social and economic alternatives. We have however, several questions, comments and suggestions to share with you regarding alternative directions.

Moral Purpose

45. *First,* what can be done to develop a clear statement of purpose regarding Canada's socio-economic order that reflects basic moral principles? From our perspective, the primary purpose of our socio-economic order should be to develop our resources to serve the basic needs of all people for a more fully human life in this country. This includes such basic life needs as adequate food, clothing, housing, education, employment, health care, energy. It also means putting an emphasis on the integral development of peoples, the value and dignity of human work, the preferential option for the poor and the marginalized, and the priority of labour. What can be done to develop a process that leads towards a consensus on these and related principles as the foundation stone of our economy?

46.   Through its authoritative social teaching the Church recalls that the ways to a just solution of this grave problem (of unemployment) demand a revision of the economic order as a whole. Comprehensive planning of economic production, not simply planning by sectors, is needed. The correct and rational organization or work is necessary, not only on the national level but also on the international level. The solidarity of all working people is needed for this.[16]

Social Goals

47. *Second,* what can be done to develop a new set of social goals that adequately reflect these basic purposes and principles? From our perspective, this involves a renewed national commitment to full employment with an emphasis on permanent and meaningful jobs, new patterns of work, with adequate personal or family income. It also entails a fresh commitment to the development of more meaningful and effective forms of providing basic social services (e.g., education, health care, social security benefits, etc.). These social objectives in turn require a commitment to finding new

and more effective ways of redistributing wealth and power among both people and regions in this country. What can be done to develop a consensus around these and related social goals for the future development of this country?

Empower the Powerless

48. *Third,* what can be done to empower the poor and the marginalized to play a more meaningful and effective role in shaping the future development of our socio-economic order? Across this country, there are working and non-working people, men and women, in communities — small farmers, fisherpeople, factory workers, forestry workers, miners, native people, office workers, people on welfare, public services workers, small business people and many others — who have a creative and dynamic contribution to make in shaping the social and economic future of this country. A clear social commitment is required to enable these people truly to become subjects of production and subjects of their own history. What steps can be taken to develop or redistribute resources and means for production in order to achieve this objective?

Economic Planning

49. *Fourth,* what can be done to develop more participatory and effective forms of economic planning for the future development of our society? From our perspective, a new approach to both centralized and decentralized planning may be required. The new economic forces of transnational capital/technology mean that nation states must engage in centralized planning in order to ensure the realization of the common good and respect for basic moral principles (LE, Sec. 17, 18, nn. 77-87). This may require the nationalization of key sectors of Canada's economy. Yet experience has also shown that nationalization does not, in and of itself, guarantee popular participation in economic planning. Thus decentralized forms of economic planning and decision-making are also required to ensure the participation of workers, the poor and the marginalized. What steps can be taken to develop this kind of approach to economic planning in this country?

Economic Strategies

50. *Fifth,* what can be done to develop new economic strategies based on integral, self-reliant models of development? As a country, we are blessed with an abundance of resources required to serve the basic needs of all our people for food, clothing, housing, employment, education, health care, energy and related needs. A new commitment however is needed to break the bonds of dependency and to develop new economic strategies based on self-reliance. At one level, this means increasing the self-sufficiency of our industries to manufacture our natural resources as finished products for markets. At another level, it means increasing the capacities of local communities and regions to design models of economic development to serve the basic needs of their communities. What steps can be taken to make these kinds of self-reliant economic strategies a priority in this country?

Social Ownership

51. *Sixth,* what can be done to promote new forms of social ownership and control by communities and workers in our society? Indeed the road to self-reliance itself requires new forms of ownership and control over the means of production. If communities are going to develop their resources to serve basic human and social needs, it is essential that they have effective control over the capital and technology required to achieve these objectives. If working people are going to exercise their right to become subjects of production, then new forms of worker controlled industries need to be developed. Across the country, there are a few significant experiments in community and worker controlled enterprises that may offer some insights into the problems and possibilities to be faced. What steps can be taken to put a priority on stimulating new forms of social ownership and control by communities and workers?

Social Production

52. *Seventh,* what can be done to design more sustainable and socially useful forms of production and development? This means giving serious attention to developing forms of industrial production that make greater use of renewable energy sources (e.g., electricity, sun, wind, methane, tidal power, etc.) rather than main-

taining sole dependence on non-renewable energy (e.g., oil, gas, coal, etc.). It also means developing strategies to assist workers and industries involved in military production to re-direct their energies into more socially useful forms of production. These social objectives, along with corresponding conversion strategies, need to be given serious attention in future economic planning. What steps can be taken now to design and implement more sustainable and socially useful forms of production for the future?

Global Solidarity

53. *Eight*, what can be done to develop economic strategies in the context of global solidarity, Given the international realities of economic interdependence today, any significant changes in Canada's economic strategies are bound to have an effect on working people in other countries. This is especially critical for the poor countries of the Third World. It is important therefore to establish new forms of consultation, not only with the countries affected but especially with the workers in related industries. If, for example, specific strategies were proposed to strengthen the textile and clothing sectors of our economy, then direct consultations should take place with the workers in related South East Asian industries that would be affected by such changes. What steps therefore could be taken to ensure that this kind of global solidarity is actualized in the process of developing new economic strategies?

54. These are some of the fundamental challenges, Mr. Chairman, facing the future of Canada's socio-economic order. Taken together, these challenges involve basic value choices about what kind of nation and people we want to become. As a country, we have the resources, the capital, the technology and above all else, the aspirations and skills of working men and women required to build an alternative economic future. Yet the people of this country have seldom been challenged to envision and develop alternatives to the dominant economic model that governs our society. What is required, in the long run, is a dynamic public process designed to stimulate social imagination, to develop alternative models and to forge a new cultural vision in this country.

55. We hope and pray that your commission will be able to play a significant role in initiating this kind of dynamic public process.

For our part, we will continue to do whatever we can to generate critical awareness in local Christian communities. For the present structural crisis constitutes a crucial turning point in our history. It is imperative that conscious decisions be taken now to forge a human economy and a true community for the sake of future generations.

56. Work has a power in itself that can give life to a community, to solidarity: the *solidarity of work,* which spontaneously develops among those sharing the same kind of work or profession, so as to embrace, through the interests of all individuals and groups, the common good of all society; *solidarity with work,* that is to say, with each person who works, which... makes its own the drama of the unemployed and those in hard working conditions; finally, *solidarity in work,* a solidarity without boundaries because it is based on the naturalness of human work, that is to say, on the priority of the human person over things... Brothers and sisters, may your sensitivity as believers, your faith as Christians, help you to live the "good news", the gospel of work.[17]

NOTES

1. At the request of the President and Executive Committee of the Canadian Conference of Catholic Bishops, the brief was presented to the Commission by Bishop Remi De Roo (Victoria, B.C.) and Mgr Gérard Drainville (Amos, Qué.). It is the most complete single exposition of the ethical principles of the Canadian Catholic hierarchy relative to the goals of a just socio-economic order and the means to achieve them. It has been published, together with discussion starters, graphics and a resource list for group study and action, by Publications Service, CCCB, Ottawa, K1N 7B1.

2. These ecumenical projects include Project North, GATT-Fly, Taskforce on the Churches and Corporate Responsibility, Inter-Church Committee on Human Rights in Latin America, Ten Days for World Development, PLURA, and Inter-Church Committee on Refugees.

3. John Paul II, to an Indian audience in Mexico, Jan. 29, 1979, *The Pope Speaks,* Washington, 1979, XXIV, 207.

4. John Paul II, *Work and Man's Dignity in a Christian Perspective,* a homily to workers, Nowa Huta, Cracow, 1979, cf. *Origins,* Washington, 1979, IX, 76.

5. Concerning the official unemployment statistics, observers have pointed out the rate calculated by Statistics Canada understates the real extent of unemployment in the country. The methodology used arbitrarily excludes hundreds of thousands

of Canadians from the "labour force" category. A study by the Social Planning Council of Metropolitan Toronto for example, estimates that in May, 1983, there were 470,000 discouraged workers plus another 427,000 part-time workers seeking full employment who simply do not appear in the official unemployment statistics. In effect, there are over two and a half million unemployed or underemployed people in this country, representing 20 percent of Canada's "labour force". For an examination of the methodology used by governments to understate the dimensions of labour supply and hence the quantity of unemployment, see Stanley Moses, "Labour Supply Concepts: the Political Economy of Conceptual Change", in *The Annals, American Academy of Political and Social Science*, Philadelphia, March, 1975.

6. John Paul II, *The Gospel of Work*, an address in Barcelona, 1982, cf. *Origins*, Washington, 1983, XII, 375, n. 5.

7. For data on poverty in Canada, see David P. Ross, *The Canadian Fact Book on Poverty* (Ottawa, K1Y 4G1, Canadian Council on Social Development, 1983); David P. Ross, *The Working Poor: Wage Earners and the Failure of Income Securities Policies* (Toronto, Lorimer, 1981).

For an analysis of the erosion of social security programs see Allan Moscovitch, "The Rise and Decline of the Canadian Welfare State", in *Perception* (Canadian Council of Social Development, Ottawa), Vol. 6, n. 2, 1982; Angelo Djao, *Inequality and Social Policy*, (Toronto, Wiley, 1983). See also Randy Sykes, "Privatization" in *C.U.P.E. Facts*, (Canadian Union of Public Employees, Ottawa, K2P 0W6), Vol. 5, n. 3, 1983; Tony Wohlfarth, "Cutbacks — Provincial Style", *ibid.*, n. 8, 1983.

8. For an examination and analysis of the phenomenon of labour devaluation see: John Paul II, *On Human Work*, in *The Papal Encyclicals*, edit. Claudia Carlen, IHM (Wilmington, N.C., McGrath Publishing, 1981), V, 299, sec. 7, nn. 28-31; sec. 11-15, nn. 46-71; also Address to Business People and Economic Managers, *Man and His Values: the Principle and Aim of Economics*, in *The Pope Speaks*, Washington, 1983, XXVIII, 264; Gregory Baum, *The Priority of Labour* (New York, Paulist Press, 1982); *Unemployment: The Human Costs*, CCCB, 1980, Document 49 above; Harry Braverman, *Labour and Monopoly Capital: The Degradation of Work in the Twentieth Century* (New York, Monthly Review Press, 1974); Walter Johnson, edit., *Working in Canada* (Montreal, Black Rose Books, 1975). See also John Paul II to Members of the Trilateral Commission, *Technology and Ethics are Inseparable*, Osservatore Romano (English edition), April 25, 1983; also Address at Toronto Airport, Sept. 15, 1984, *Technology at the Service of Man, Canadian Catholic Review*, Saskatoon, Vol. 2, 1984, Oct., 55-56.

Also D.F. Noble, "Present Tense Technology", Parts I and II, in *Democracy*, Vol. 3, nn. 2 and 3, 1983; Patricia McDermott, "The New Demeaning of Work" in *Canadian Dimension*, Winnipeg, Dec. 1981.

9. See Ed Finn, "Decline of the Middle Class" in *C.U.P.E. Facts* (Canadian Union of Public Employees, Ottawa, K2P 0W6), Vol. 5, n. 9, 1983; and Bob Kittner, "The Declining Middle", in *The Atlantic Monthly* (Boston), July, 1983.

10. For information on current tax measures see Marc Lalonde, *Budget Papers*, Ottawa, April 19, 1983, p. 25 ff. Observers have pointed out that while business will receive an estimated $905 million in tax reductions in 1983 and $955 million in 1984, an increasing proportion of the tax burden will be transferred to working families. The inequitable tax system maintains a lower top marginal tax rate. The effect is to elevate more Canadians living below the poverty line to the status of tax payers. At the same time, affluent Canadians are now able to avoid paying taxes on the inflation portion of capital gains made from shares in Canadian corporations.

See also the study prepared for the National Anti-Poverty Organization by Ernie S. Lightman, *Canada's Tax System and the Poor*, Ottawa, 1984.

See also Duncan Cameron, "Wage Earners, The Liberals and the Canadian Economy", in *Our Generation*, Montreal, Vol. 15, n. 4, 1983.

11. For documentation on corporate concentration see Peter C. Newman, *The Canadian Establishment*, Vol. II, *The Acquisitors*, Appendix, "The Take Over Record, 1975-1981", (Toronto, McClelland and Stewart, 1981). For an example of concentration in the agricultural sector, see GATT-Fly (Toronto), "Canada's Agricultural Marketing Board: A Clearer View", Part II, June 1983.

12. For a general discussion of this problem see GATT-Fly, Toronto, "The Limitations of the Trade Issue", July 1973. For an analysis of the food trade issue, *ibid.*, "Canada's Food Trade — By Bread Alone?", August, 1978; "Canada's Food: The Road to Self-Reliance", September 1979.

13. For an analysis of the politics and economics of the arms race in Canada see Ernie Reigehr and Simon Rosenblum, eds., *Canada and the Nuclear Arms Race* (Toronto, Lorimer, 1983); Carole Giangrande, *The Nuclear North: The People, the Regions and the Arms Race* (Toronto, Anansi, 1983). For an example of a detailed proposal for "boosting" the economy through increased production of armaments by Canadian industry see the report prepared for Bob Runciman, M.P.P. (Ontario), "The Armaments Industry". (Legislative Service, Toronto, M7A 1A2), 1983.

For an analysis of the arms race and the factors sustaining it, see Johan Galtung, "The War System", in *Essays in Peace Research*, Vol. IV (Copenhagen: C. Ejlers, 1975).

For an ethical perspective on these issues, see the submissions by the CCCB (Document 53 above) and by the Canadian Council of Churches to House of Commons Standing Committee on External Affairs and National Defense, *Minutes of Proceedings and Evidence, Issue* No. 57, 1982, Division of Mission, United Church of Canada, Toronto; also two briefs of Canadian Church Leaders, *On Peace and Disarmament*, Documents 54 above and 57 below. See as well the statement of the U.S. National Conference of Catholic Bishops, *The Challenge of Peace: A Pastoral Letter on War and Peace*, May 1983 (Boston, St. Paul Editions, 1983).

14. For an assessment of geological disposal of high-level radioactive waste see *Policy Formation on Aspects of Canada's Nuclear Wastes*, Brief to the Atomic Energy Control Board, June 1982, Taskforce on the Churches and Corporate Responsibility, 129 St. Clair Ave. E., Toronto, M4V 1N5. For an introduction to the acid rain problem see *Acid Rain Primer* (Toronto, Pollution Probe Foundation, 1982).

For a theological reflection on the ecological crisis see the special issues on "Écologie et théologie" in *Foi et Vie*, Paris, 1974, nn. 5 and 6; Rosemary Ruether, "The Biblical Vision of the Ecological Crisis", in *Christian Century*, Chicago, 22 Nov. 1978; also Douglas Hall, *The Steward: A Biblical Symbol Come of Age* (New York, Friendship Press, 1982).

15. See Harry MacKay, "Social Impact of Unemployment", in *Perception* (Ottawa), Vol. 6, n. 5, 1983. For a systematic study on the set of relationships between unemployment and social pathologies (disease, mental illness, suicide and crime) see, Harvey Brenner, *Estimating the Social Costs of National Economic Policy*, A Study Prepared for the Joint Economic Committee, U.S. Congress (Washington, D.C., Government Printing Office, 1976). For a recent Canadian study see Sharon Kirsh, *Unemployment: Its Impact on Body and Soul*, Canadian Mental Health Association, Toronto, November, 1983.

16. John Paul II, *op. cit.* above, note 6, p. 375, n. 6.

17. John Paul II, *ibid.* p. 376, n. 10.

Document 57

ON PEACE AND DISARMAMENT
To the Prime Minister

Author — Canadian Church Leaders[1], December 14, 1983

1. A year has passed since we last had the opportunity to speak directly with you about the deteriorating international political/ military environment, the growing incidence and destructiveness of conventional war and the increasing threat of nuclear war. While the international situation has continued to deteriorate during the past year, we are greatly encouraged that your own personal concern and that of your government have led you to undertake a special peace initiative.

2. In this brief we want, above all, to encourage you in your peace efforts. We attach great significance to your initiative, we are convinced that Canada has a long-term constructive role to play, and we assure you of our continuing prayers and support. We can also report with confidence that the millions of Canadians whom we represent are following your undertakings with eagerness and with renewed hope that the world will yet learn to turn away from the study of war and to turn instead, with renewed energy and commitment, to the pursuit of equity and justice.

3. In the following paragraphs we wish to reiterate briefly the faith and commitment that are the basis of our petition to you, to elaborate on our support for bold Canadian undertakings in the pursuit of peace, and to set out a number of additional specific proposals for Canadian action which we believe would contribute to an international environment of peace with justice.

A — THEREFORE CHOOSE LIFE

4. As leaders of major Canadian Christian communities, we base our comments and proposals related to issues of peace and justice on the knowledge that God continues to place before all people the choice between life and death. We speak out of the knowledge that God desires for all people the abundant life of peace with justice, and are moved first to repent of our too easy acquiscence to the powers of injustice and death. Too often the churches have remained silent and have not understood, as the South African theologian Allan Boesak told the World Council of Churches last summer:

> ... every act of inhumanity, every unjust law, every untimely death, every utterance of faith in weapons of mass destruction, every justification of violence and oppression is a sacrifice on the altar of the false gods of death; it is a denial of the Lord of life.''

5. To choose life is to acknowledge that we are called to be not so much rulers as stewards of God's earth. And because we have regard for the security of the earth not only for this but also for succeeding generations, we cannot accept as ''defence'' any measures which threaten the planet itself.

6. While we honour, and seek to preserve and strengthen, national and international institutions that serve justice, we acknowledge the transitory character of all human institutions. This knowledge leads us to place clear limits on measures that may justifiably be taken in defence of human institutions. Ultimately, human loyalty is owed only to God and when defence of human institutions undermines the abundant life of God's people and threatens His earth, then we must regard it as contrary to the will of God.

7. This has particular implications for our attitude towards nuclear weapons, and we must say without reservation that nuclear weapons are ultimately unacceptable as agents of national security. We can conceive of no circumstances under which the use of nuclear weapons could be justified and consistent with the will of God, and we must therefore conclude that nuclear weapons must also be rejected as means of threat and deterrence.

8. We acknowledge however that nuclear weapons have never-

theless become central to the national security systems of the major powers, including those states which Canadians describe as allies. The common and uncompromised objective of all states must be the elimination of nuclear weapons from national security systems, but we also acknowledge that the process of disarming can itself be destabilizing and fraught with danger. We therefore also reiterate our support for a carefully planned, multilateral process for the reduction (and eventual elimination) of nuclear weapons. The proposals contained in this brief acknowledge (but do not condone) the presence of nuclear weapons and are designed to contribute to national and international initiatives which will lead to stabilizing reductions in nuclear arsenals. For this reason we have not called for unilateral, unreciprocated disarmament — we do however support and call for limited, independent actions (unilateral initiatives) which we believe will contribute to the process of broadly-based and mutual arms reductions.

9. Above all, our attention to questions of war and peace are informed by the reconciliation that is promised us in the ministry, death and resurrection of Jesus Christ. In Him there is no East and West, no North and South — under His reign all are one. Therefore we do not accept the division of the world into allies and enemies — and those who have been defined by others as our enemies, we regard as brothers and sisters whose welfare must remain our paramount concern.

10. The abundant life which God desires for us and the liberation that is promised us in His Son impel us to strive, not so much for security, but for justice; for it is only within the context of justice that true social and political peace can reside.

B — THE ROLE OF CANADA

11. Before commenting directly on appropriate policies for Canada to pursue, we wish to comment briefly on the role of Canada and the nature and extent of Canadian influence in the international community.

12. It has long been accepted in Canada that this country's credibility within alliances, and particularly with the United States, depends upon the extent of our contribution to that alliance. Canada

will be listened to by the United States, it is assumed, only to the extent that Canada pays its "fair share" of the common defence and only if it is supportive of the main thrusts of American policy and policy objectives.

13. We accept the assumption that direct influence upon the United States is related to Canada's stature as an important ally of the United States and that Canada must be sensitive to the legitimate and widely accepted security interests of the United States. We also acknowledge that, while there may be frequent disagreements between Canada and the United States on the matter of what actually constitutes legitimate security interests at any particular time, in most cases such disagreements are the subject of normal diplomacy between allies and involve compromises and giving each other the benefit of the doubt.

14. There are also times however, when doubt is not present — times when differences between allies involve fundamentally conflicting interpretations of international events and differing conclusions as to the best solutions to international concerns. We believe that Canada has reached such a moment with regard to the current military policies of the United States. The Administration of President Ronald Reagan, we believe, is sharply out of step with North American and Western national security traditions. It has rejected the principle of parity with the Soviet Union and has embarked upon a dangerous, even suicidal, quest for military superiority. While we believe the overwhelming majority of Canadians respect American cultural and political traditions, we do not believe that Canada should remain silent in the face of changing U.S. military policies and strategies.

15. In a climate in which U.S. and Soviet administrations seem intent on abandoning the conventions of diplomacy in favour of invective and self-indulgent rhetoric, it is all the more important that countries such as Canada become voices of clarity and restraint. We are pleased to say that Canada did indeed assume that role in response to the Soviet downing of the Korean Airlines aircraft and in response to the U.S. invasion of Grenada. We feel strongly that Canada must continue to perform this role, particularly in the context of the escalating arms race and of deteriorating international relations.

16. In the following sections of this brief, we wish to associate ourselves with elements of your peace initiative, and to propose additional measures which we think would strengthen this initiative and contribute to the long-term effectiveness of Canadian diplomacy and foreign policy relative to issues of peace and justice.

C — THE NUCLEAR CRISIS

a. Current Trends

17. In reviewing events of the past year, we unfortunately are drawn to the conclusion that the dangers posed by global militarization and the nuclear arms race have not abated with the passage of time. As you pointed out in your speech at the University of Guelph, East-West relations continue to be dominated by policies that are "dangerously confrontational", by an "intellectual climate of acrimony and uncertainty", and by a "widening gap between military strategy and political purpose".

18. The concerns which we expressed a year ago are now accentuated by a sense of even greater urgency. Even as we prepare this statement, trucks and aircraft are delivering Cruise and Pershing II missiles for deployment in the United Kingdom, the Federal Republic of Germany and Italy. In the Soviet Union the deployment of SS-20 missiles continues apace and plans are now being made to deploy new missiles in the territories of several of its East European allies.

19. Both the United States and the Soviet Union continue to develop and deploy nuclear weapons systems whose main function is not confined to threatening retaliation to nuclear attack, but is to demonstrate to the other that it has the technical capacity and the political will actually to engage in nuclear battle. In the United States, nuclear war-fighting strategies have been made explicit in public documents which record American defence planning (similar Soviet documents are not available, but Soviet deployments carry the same message), and in both countries these strategies are reflected in deployments of tactical and intermediate-range nuclear missiles in Europe and in new strategic systems. The preparation for nuclear war surely represents the logical, horrific extension of what you in Montreal called "the brutalization of political life".

20. Both the Soviet Union and the United States have continued to develop nuclear weapons designed to threaten pre-emptive attack on the weapons of the other side, as well as to conduct what military planners seem to think could be a prolonged nuclear war. The Department of Defence in the United States has in the past year stated explicitly that the role of nuclear weapons cannot be confined to deterring nuclear attack and that nuclear weapons are being integrated into all levels of American military planning. Admiral Powell Carter told the Senate Armed Services Committee that "we have revamped the training command in order to teach our people how to think nuclear. We are extending it to the point that all our war exercises are into a nuclear phase." And in defence of the MX missile system, the chairman of the Joint Chiefs of Staff, General Vessey, said this: "We have to look at the prospect of deterrence failing and of actually having to fight a nuclear war. We want to tell you (Congress) that the hard-target kill capability of the MX has a usefulness there."

21. It is in rejection of such policies that we have opposed the deployment of Cruise and Pershing II missiles, seek reductions in SS-20 missiles in Europe and oppose the deployment of the MX missile and strategic Cruise missile by the U.S. and the USSR. While we oppose the escalation of the nuclear arms race by both East and West, as citizens of the West we call upon our governments to take special initiatives in rejecting destabilizing nuclear policies. The first-strike and war fighting scenarios of the Soviet Union are not neutralized or deterred by American first-strike and war-fighting strategies. In both instances, the danger and likelihood of nuclear war are increased.

22. There is no justification for American deployment of such weapons — regardless of Soviet deployment. In the face of Soviet first-strike forces, only American second-strike forces (of which the U.S. has many thousands) can be considered stabilizing. Yet Canada's principal ally (with this country's apparent approval) continues to deploy destabilizing first-strike and war-fighting weapons.

23. While the MX is intended to threaten a first-strike against Soviet land based weapons, Cruise and Pershing II weapons are to be deployed in support of the idea that, in the event of setbacks in a conventional war, Cruise and Pershing II weapons could be engaged

to reach behind Soviet lines to destroy secondary military and industrial targets — in other words, the idea that nuclear weapons can be used to gain military advantage.

b. Canadian Policies

i) *Rejection of Nuclear War Strategies*

24. While Canadian policy has supported nuclear deterrence, there have been no statements of support of nuclear war-fighting doctrines as such. The time has come for Canada to declare clearly that the development of first-strike and war-fighting nuclear weapons is not consistent with its understanding of the requirements of nuclear deterrence.

ii) *The No-First-Use Pledge*

25. A concrete expression of Canada's rejection of nuclear war-fighting strategies would be a call for a U.S./NATO pledge never to be the first to use nuclear weapons. This would support a fundamental principle, both moral and military. The moral principle of course is the acknowledgement that nuclear weapons are fundamentally different from other weapons and that the legitimate rights of states to arrange for their national defence do not include the right to initiate nuclear war. The military principle involves the recognition that nuclear weapons are not military weapons in the normal sense of that term. They are means of extermination, not means of defending or holding territory. Any first-use scenario (and we do not here confuse this with a first-strike scenario) for nuclear weapons is premised on the assumption that military advantage can be derived from their use. We reject categorically such notions of limited and successful uses of nuclear weapons and urge Canada to call on all nuclear weapons states to declare that they will never be the first to use them.

iii) *Missile Deployment in Europe*

26. In the context of strong support for your peace initiative, we were disappointed that the broad elements of your programme, which you announced in Montreal, do not address directly the immediate crisis in Europe. NATO is now in the process of

introducing still more intermediate weapons onto a continent that is ultimately not defensible by nuclear weapons. While we welcome the announcement that NATO is unilaterally withdrawing 1,400 tactical nuclear warheads from Europe, we do not believe that this action should be cited as a rationale for introducing Cruise and Pershing II missiles. As we noted last year during our conversation with you, deployment of NATO intermediate range nuclear missiles will not result in any reduction of the Soviet threat emanating from SS-20 missiles.

27.   As a minimum response to this crisis, Canada should call for a halt in the deployments now underway and seek a resumption of negotiations — the first order of which should be the offer to accept as an interim step the Soviet offer to dismantle SS-20 missiles down to the level of French and British missiles.

iv) *Canadian Production of Nuclear Weapons*

28.   While Canada should be sensitive to the security interests of the United States, this should not include participation in the development and production of nuclear weapons systems which are not essential for nuclear deterrence but are intended to demonstrate American capacity to conduct prolonged nuclear war and even to threaten the Soviet Union with pre-emptive first-strike. Cruise and MX missiles fall into these categories, and in compliance with Canada's international efforts to halt the nuclear arms race and to steer the superpowers away from the deployment of destabilizing systems, Canada should end immediately its involvement with both missiles. In the case of the Cruise missile this would mean non-participation in either the production of components or in the testing of the missile's guidance system on Canadian territory. In the case of the MX missile, this would mean non-participation in the production of its components.

29.   We view these proposals as fully in line with your own Government's decision at the beginning of the 1970's to end Canada's nuclear role in NATO and with your proposal for a strategy to suffocate the arms race. We believe, as does your Government, that Canada can make a more constructive contribution to international security as a non-nuclear country, and we also believe that the particular weapons which Canada is helping to build and test are

destabilizing and increase, rather than decrease, the likelihood of nuclear war.

v) *Support for a Nuclear Freeze*

30. Few arms control proposals have captured the public imagination as has the proposal to freeze the testing, production and deployment of nuclear weapons and their delivery systems. The freeze proposal is in fundamental accord with your own "strategy of suffocation" in that it is bilateral, it is directed toward halting the technological momentum of the arms race and it is verifiable. We would therefore like to register our grave disappointment at Canada's active opposition to freeze resolutions in the United Nations. Despite the fact that one NATO country supported the recent freeze vote in the First Committee and four others abstained, Canada voted against the resolution. Such a vote cannot be justified on grounds of alliance solidarity nor on grounds that it is contrary to Canadian proposals to halt the arms race.

31. We therefore urge Canada to alter its attitude toward the nuclear freeze proposal, to announce its support of the same and to seek opportunities in international forums such as the UN to mobilize further international support.

vi) *Rejection of Space Weapons*

32. Another welcome first step in the rejection of nuclear war weapons is your own proposal to ban all antisatellite systems designed to operate at high altitudes. The spectre of space-based systems represents, as you have pointed out, a dangerously destabilizing development. We urge you and your officials to persist in your pursuit of this measure and to extend it to encompass all missile defence systems. In the present environment, ballistic missile defence systems, whether operating from high altitudes or ground-based, are destabilizing inasmuch as they can be perceived to be in support of pre-emptive, first-strike scenarios.

vii) *Horizontal Nuclear Proliferation*

33. We applaud your emphasis on the fact that the problem of proliferating nuclear weapons is both vertical and horizontal. Indeed, it is the abandonment of all restraint in the vertical proliferations

of the two superpowers that has threatened most directly the present non-proliferation regime. Canada, as a nation with nuclear weapons capability that has exercised the choice in favour of non-nuclear status, could be a leader in diplomatic efforts to persuade other middle power and Third World states not to acquire nuclear weapons, and in maintaining public focus on the threat of horizontal proliferation that derives from current vertical proliferation.

viii) *Five-Nation Forum on Nuclear Weapons*

34. In the present climate of East-West animosity, and particularly in the context of disarmament negotiations which are stalled on the issue of nuclear weapons possessed by countries not party to the negotiations (e.g., the Intermediate-Range Nuclear Forces (INF) and France and Britain), Canada's proposal for a forum of all current nuclear weapons states represents an important initiative through which suspicions may be mitigated and negotiations advanced. It is of course important that such a forum not become simply another occasion for stalemate. The meeting should not be seen as replacing current stalemated talks (e.g., INF, Strategic Arms Reduction Talks (START), Mutual Balanced Force Reductions in Europe (MBFR), etc.), but as a means of shifting talks in other forums off-centre and of setting the stage for greater progress in each.

D — LINKING DISARMAMENT AND DEVELOPMENT

35. The links between disarmament and development are perhaps most clearly understood when the proposition is turned around to show the ways in which armaments are linked to underdevelopment. The growing expenditures on military forces in the Third World significantly inhibit and distort economic development. One of the most prominent ways in which the militarism of the northern hemisphere is transferred to the south is by means of the transfer of weapons systems from north to south. Weapons imports reinforce links of political and economic dependence on the supplier, lead to distortions in domestic development and contribute ultimately to the erosion of political and human rights. Our churches, all of which have had a long-standing involvement in the struggle to preserve and restore human rights both at home and in the Third World, are particularly aware of the relationship between the militarization of national institutions and the distortion of political

life. Stated another way, we have seen firsthand the relationship between militarization and the undermining of the institutions of popular participation in decision-making and the violation of civil and basic human rights.

a. An International Arms Trade Registry

36. A key way therefore in which development can be the beneficiary of disarmament, is to remove the debilitating effects of armaments by the development of multilateral measures to restrict the international trade in arms. We recognize the many impediments to such an agreement but we are dismayed that the attempt to reach an agreement is currently absent from the international political agenda. We urge you, as part of the follow-up to your call for strengthening the relationship between disarmament and development, to initiate, in the appropriate international forums, measures that will serve to resume discussions of ways to control the arms trade. We think particularly of the proposal for an international registry of arms transfers, an idea that has surfaced from time in international talks. Such a registry could be an important first step in creating an accepted system for monitoring and reporting the arms trade, upon which the verification of subsequent agreements could be based.

b. Canadian Military Exports

37. Canada participates directly in the militarization process in two ways: by the direct sale of military commodities to the Third World and by the sale of components to other industrialized countries, where they are incorporated into weapons systems for export to the Third World. We believe that Canadian policy must be changed in two particular ways in order to bring Canada more fully in support of potential international efforts to control the arms trade.

i) *Full Disclosure of Military Exports*

38. In the first instance, Canada should declare its intention to monitor more closely the export of Canadian military commodities and, as a first step, to require full disclosure of all military export permits and of subsequent sales under such permits. As Julius Nyerere has stated:

The selling of arms is something which a country does only when it wants to support or strengthen the regime or the group to whom the sale is made. Whatever restrictions or limits are placed on that sale, the sale of any arms is a declaration of support... You can trade with people you dislike; you can have diplomatic relations with a government you disapprove of... But you do not sell arms without saying, in effect: "In light of the receiving country's known policies, friends and enemies, we anticipate that... we will be on their side in the case of any conflict. We shall want them to defeat their enemies."

39. In other words, military commodities are not ordinary goods. They communicate specific political messages and have direct military and political implications in the recipient countries and regions. And while Canada prides itself on having very restrictive guidelines for the export of military commodities, our experience is that these guidelines are subject to widely divergent interpretations and that they are in our view regularly violated. All military sales should be subjected to public scrutiny, with the Government's current declared guidelines being the measure of the acceptability of sales.

ii) *No Subsidy of Armament Production for Export*

40. Secondly, public funds should no longer be available for the purpose of promoting and subsidizing Canadian industrial involvement in the arms trade. We are thinking in particular of the Defence Industry Productivity Programme and other public supports for increased military production for export.

E — THIRD PARTY INITIATIVES

41. Finally, we would like to reiterate our confidence that Canada does have an important role to play in the search for greater international equity and peace. Your efforts to develop a "third rail of political energy" represent an important example of the kind of contribution that Canada can make. In the past and at present, there have been, and are, other examples.

a) Peacekeeping and the Settlement of Disputes

42.   As we noted in our brief to you a year ago, Canada has an honourable record of contributions to international peacekeeping operations. We urge Canada to restore this as a top priority of the Canadian Armed Forces and that peacekeeping roles receive prominent attention in the acquisition of new equipment for the forces. We also urge active Canadian participation in institutions such as the International Peace Academy for the purpose of developing international systems for the peaceful settlement of disputes.

b) Non-Nuclear Security in Europe

43.   Perhaps the most significant contribution which Canada could make to the long-term security of Europe would be in the development of greater technical understanding of, and political support for, a European defence strategy that would not rely upon nuclear weapons. Your proposals for revitalized negotiations on Mutual Balanced Force Reductions (MBFR) in Europe speak to this same point. A specific Canadian initiative could include a rational and independent assessment of the nature of the military threat facing Western Europe, an independent assessment of the real capacities of the relevant military force structures now existing in East and West Europe and the exploration of possible means of establishing a more stable military environment, at significantly lower levels of arms.

44.   We are concerned that the present climate of fear regarding nuclear weapons may be exploited to create public support for significant escalations in conventional weapons. Conventional weapons are themselves in many instances weapons of mass destruction and threatening conventional force structures are no less destabilizing than threatening nuclear force structures. There is therefore an urgent need in Europe for the development of purely defensive, non-threatening force structures and for the decoupling of European security needs from the global competition of the two superpowers.

F — CONCLUSION

45.   We reaffirm our continuing support for constructive Canadian efforts to reduce the likelihood of nuclear war, to combat the trends toward global militarization and to strengthen the institutions of justice upon which political and social peace must ultimately rely. Our respective churches are committed to long-term educational programmes designed to help our communities better understand the threats to peace and the means by which it may be restored. In this task, as we noted a year ago:

> We praise our Creator for the abundant life which He has granted to us in this land, we pledge ourselves to support the pursuit of justice and equity in all lands and we commit ourselves to work toward the removal of the arsenals of destruction which frustrate the search for justice and which threaten life itself, in our land and throughout the world.[2]

NOTES

1.   This brief was presented to the Right Honourable Pierre Elliott Trudeau, Prime Minister, by Dr. Robert Binhammer, President, Lutheran Church in America (Canada Section); Dr. Russell Legge, President, Canadian Council of Churches; Dr. Clarke MacDonald, Moderator, United Church of Canada; Dr. Donald MacDonald, Moderator, Presbyterian Church in Canada; the Most Reverend Edward W. Scott, Primate, Anglican Church of Canada; Rev. Dr. Ronald Watts, General Secretary, Baptist Convention of Ontario and Quebec; Most Reverend John M. Sherlock, President, Canadian Conference of Catholic Bishops; Msgr. Dennis J. Murphy, General Secretary, Canadian Conference of Catholic Bishops; Mr. E. Regehr, Researcher and Education Office, Ploughshares (Project Ploughshares, University of Waterloo, Ont. N2L 3G6).
2.   Cf. Document 54 above, n. 41.

Document 58

DEFENDING WORKERS' RIGHTS
A NEW FRONTIER

Author — The Episcopal Commission for Social Affairs, May 1, 1985

Today, the first of May, International Workers Day is being celebrated in many countries throughout the world. The first of May is also a Christian feast dedicated to St. Joseph the Worker. It is an occasion for celebrating the value of human work and defending the dignity of working people.

The Feast of St. Joseph the Worker provides an occasion for Christians to become a living witness to the Church's teachings on the rights of working people in a technological age. It reminds us that Jesus himself was a worker and that His Gospel message has a great deal to say about the dignity of human work and the rights and responsibilities of working people. The Church must proclaim this message, particularly in these times of high unemployment and economic insecurity.

The feast of the first of May is opportune for deepening the awareness of the irreplaceable role which work plays in the growth of the human person and in building a society. This fundamental truth of the value of work and of the dignity of those who work is today under threat. Current trends point to a society of "winners" and "losers" unfolding in Canada. As our society moves into the high-tech age, significant forms of work are being eliminated.

Canada appears to be heading towards a deeply stratified society in which there is, on the one hand, a substantial group of people who are completely and permanently unemployed, and on the other, a more secure group of workers who are permanently employed. Between these two solitudes, there lie a growing number of workers who depend on part-time jobs for their livelihood. These people are generally left with no job security nor protection for their basic rights as workers.

On this feast of work, we wish to draw particular attention to the plight of unorganized and vulnerable workers, especially of women, employed in the retail industry, for we see this as a new frontier for workers' rights emerging in our society. Here workers, mainly women, are engaged in efforts to organize themselves into unions for the purpose of securing their rights to collective bargaining and fair employment practices. These concerns for justice are evident in the current dispute at Eaton's.[1]

We believe that these struggles for justice should be supported for the following reasons:

1. As the Church has consistently taught,[2] all working people have the right to organize their own association or union for the purpose of defending their rights, securing just wages and benefits and promoting healthy working conditions.

2. The increasing trend in our economy today towards the expansion of low-wage, part-time or insecure forms of employment threatens the value and dignity of human work, especially for poor and single-parent families.

3. These jobs are generally filled by women who have no union protection and therefore find themselves vulnerable with respect to inadequate working conditions, low wages or paternalistic and arbitrary employment practices.

Workers in retail chain stores are generally very loyal to their employers. This good will however, should not be abused in an attempt to wait out disputes and to prevent workers from organizing their own unions. Indeed the Church's social teaching maintains that any attempt to deny workers the right to organize and to bargain collectively or to prevent them from organizing by intimidation or threats is an attack on human dignity itself.

We believe that this is a time for affirming the value and dignity of human work. Recently, people in the labour movement, in women's organizations and other community groups have been demonstrating their support for workers' rights in the major retail stores. On this feast day we encourage members of the Catholic community and all people of good will to join them in publicly expressing their support for this pressing issue of justice.

On this feast day, may all working and unemployed people in Canada become conscious of their dignity and of the contribution they are called to make in building a society based on justice.

NOTES

1. The dispute affected several of the Eaton's of Canada stores in Toronto and southern Ontario.

2. For close to a century, Catholic social teaching has maintained that working people have the right to organize labour unions. This traditional teaching has been strongly re-emphasized by Pope John Paul II in his encyclical *On Human Work (Laborem Exercens)*, 1981. Trade unions manifest the human need for solidarity. "The experience of history teaches that organizations of this type are an indispensable element of social life, especially in modern industrialized societies... They are indeed a mouthpiece for the struggle for social justice." *op. cit.,* in *The Papal Encyclicals,* edit. Claudia Carlen, IHM (Wilmington, N.C., McGrath Publishing, 1981), V, 319, section 20, nn. 95 f.

Document 59

SUPPORTING LABOUR UNIONS A CHRISTIAN RESPONSIBILITY

Author — The Episcopal Commission for Social Affairs, May 1, 1986

1. Today, the first of May, the one hundredth anniversary of International Workers Day is being celebrated in many countries throughout the world. In the Catholic community, the first of May is also recognized as a feast day dedicated to St. Joseph the Worker. It is an occasion for Christians to recall that Jesus, guided by Joseph and Mary, became a worker Himself and identified with the working world (cf. Mk 6:2-3; Mt 13:55). On this feast we recognize the value of human work, defend the dignity of human labour and celebrate the irreplaceable role that human work has in God's plan for creation and the building of society (cf. Gn cc. 1 and 2). Indeed, this is part of the Church's recent call for a new "civilization of work" aimed at the "socio-economic liberation" of peoples.[1]

LABOUR UNIONS

2. On this year's Feast of St. Joseph the Worker, we wish to share some brief reflections on some of the critical problems facing labour unions, the vital role they have to play in building a society based on justice and the involvement of Christians in new forms of solidarity with labour unions in Canada. Our reflections on labour unions are based on the Church's consistent social teaching concerning the value of human work, the priority of human labour and the basic rights of workers.[2]

3. We believe that this is a critical moment for labour unions and

the labour movement in our society. Despite the public image of labour unions as powerful institutions, many find themselves in a vulnerable situation today. During these times of high unemployment there is a greater tendency for some employers to turn their backs on organized labour and take advantage of pools of "cheap labour" composed of jobless people and the working poor. This trend is further reinforced by the disturbing phenomena of "contracting out" work to non-unionized labour, increased efforts to reduce rights of collective bargaining, recent court challenges to labour unions, and renewed calls for the adoption of numerous anti-union legislative measures in this country. Indeed, an anti-union bias has begun to surface once again, along with a renewed emphasis on individualism in our society.

ETHICAL VALUE

4. In its social teachings, the Catholic Church firmly maintains that labour unions have an essential role to play in preventing the violation of the dignity of human work and serving as a "mouthpiece for the struggle for social justice".[3] Without unions, working people have no collective voice in our industrialized society. Through labour unions, workers are able to strive for just wages, decent working conditions, appropriate social benefits and a democratic voice in the workplace. Through labour unions, workers are also able to press for changes in public policy and to participate in a broader social movement to build a just society. In effect, the Church maintains that labour unions are an "indispensable element of social life". For these reasons, Church teaching encourages Catholic workers to become actively involved in their own unions and urges the Catholic community as a whole to support the essential role that labour unions have to play in society.

5. It is important to remind ourselves of the history of the labour movement in Canada and its contribution to building a more just society. While workers in Canada have generally had the freedom to organize their own unions, the struggle has been prolonged and sometimes bitter. For its part, the Church has actively supported the formation of unions, although it must be admitted, there have been notable exceptions. In any case, the persistent organizing efforts of workers has led to the formation of an active labour movement in both private and public sectors of the economy. Along

with other community organizations, labour unions have been a major factor in promoting some of the most progressive social legislation in this country, including medicare, social housing, unemployment insurance, health and safety regulations and consumer protection measures. In so doing, they have played an important role in enhancing the social and economic rights of workers and of the poor and defenceless in our society.

CRITICAL MOMENT

6.   Today however, unions appear to be one of the scapegoats of the present economic crisis. Profound structural changes are taking place in our economy which, in turn, are having a serious impact on the nature of human work and the role of labour unions. New technologies in the workplace pose a serious threat to job security. In many industries and services, there is a clear trend towards low-wage, part-time or insecure forms of employment. This is favoured by high levels of unemployment, cut-backs in social services, the privatization of public services and enterprises, and the deregulation of certain sectors of the economy. Taken together, these trends weaken labour unions and undermine their basic role in our society. As a result, the percentage of unionized workers in Canada has declined in recent years.

7.   Indeed, there seems to be a growing tendency to view labour unions as some sort of anachronism, perhaps needed in the past but having outgrown their purpose in our modern technological society. Instead of appreciating their essential role in a democratic society, certain sectors tend to perceive unions as somewhat illegitimate entities, having little legal or moral right to exist. We might well ask what part the media play in fostering such an anti-union bias in public opinion and what effect this has had on attitudes and perceptions in our own church institutions. These negative attitudes have all too often been reinforced when workers have been compelled to defend their rights through strike activity. While the right to strike must be firmly upheld,[4] people of good will are sometimes embarrassed when they witness hasty or excessive use of this form of action. This has been particularly true when vital community services affecting the sick and the elderly have been disrupted.

SOCIAL CHALLENGES

8. Notwithstanding the influences which try to distort the true ethical value of labour unions, we firmly believe that they have an essential role to play in defending the dignity and rights of working people in a high-tech market economy. To perform this role however, unions need to be revitalized and strengthened. Clearly, unions have a major responsibility to continue striving for just wages, benefits and working conditions for their own members and all working people. In so doing, it is imperative that basic principles of justice be respected. It is also important that unions develop new strategies in relation to changes in the workplace and the realities of a high-tech age. At the same time, the contributions of the labour movement and its unionizing process need to be extended to unorganized workers.

9. We also believe that the labour movement has a major role to play — along with the churches, women's organizations, farmers' associations, native groups, social agencies, plus other popular organizations and related professional groups — in forming a broader social movement for building a new society based on social and economic justice. This includes active support for the rights of the poor, the defenceless and future generations. In particular, concerted efforts must be made to support the cause of the unemployed and underemployed, many of whom are women and young people. Moreover, collective efforts to develop and promote alternative economic and social policies for Canada need to be intensified. Wherever possible, these various initiatives should be pursued in solidarity with working people, not only in this country, but elsewhere in the world.[5]

SOLIDARITY INITIATIVES

10. For our part, we encourage all members of the Catholic community to follow the Church's social teachings on human work by becoming actively involved in supporting, strengthening and revitalizing the contributions of the labour movement along these lines. This calls for new forms of solidarity. In particular, we propose:

a) that Catholic workers become more actively involved in their own unions by participating in union meetings, volunteering their time for committee work on social justice concerns and running for office;

b) that parish councils and communities become more aware of local union concerns and activities, by inviting union representatives to discuss common issues and by constructively challenging any anti-union bias that may exist;

c) that local parish and Christian groups join with other community organizations and labour unions in actively supporting the struggles of workers and the unemployed in their own communities and regions;

d) that church institutions and agencies undertake positive initiatives to reexamine their own employment policies and practices in the light of the Gospel and the Church's social teaching on workers' rights and labour unions.

11. Finally, on this feast day, we encourage all people of good will to join with us in actively supporting the cause of working people and labour unions in this country. Together we can act in solidarity to build a new society that truly affirms the values of human work and the dignity of working people.

NOTES

1. Cf. the Congregation for the Doctrine of the Faith, Vatican City, *Instruction on Christian Freedom and Liberation*, March 22, 1986, chap. 5, nn. 81-90, in *Origins*, National Catholic Documentary Service, Washington, vol. 15, n. 44, April, 1986, p. 725.

2. For recent social teaching on the value of human work, see John Paul II, *On Human Work (Laborem Exercens)*, 1981, in *The Papal Encyclicals*, edit. Claudia Carlen, IHM (Wilmington, N.C., McGrath Publishing, 1981), V, 301, sections 4-6, 9, 12, 16, 18 f.; also corresponding statements of the Canadian bishops, Documents 55 and 56 above.

3. Quotations in this paragraph are from John Paul II's encyclical *On Human Work*, 1981, section 20, in Carlen, note 2 above, p. 319. The Church's teaching on labour unions has developed over the past century, from Leo XIII's *The Condition of the Working Classes (Rerum Novarum)*, 1891, to Pius XI's *On Reconstructing the Social Order (Quadragesimo Anno)*, 1931, to John XXIII's *Peace on Earth (Pacem in Terris)*, 1963, all in Carlen note 2 above, respectively, II, p. 241; III, p. 415; V, p. 101.

4. John Paul II, *op. cit.*, section 20, n. 100.

5. Further to these concerns of the Canadian Conference of Catholic Bishops, see Documents 49, 55, 56, 59, above.

Appendix

SOME CANADIAN CHURCH AND INTER-CHURCH AGENCIES FOR SOCIAL JUSTICE

1. Anglican Church of Canada,
   Unit on Public Social Responsibility,
   600 Jarvis St., Toronto, Ont., M4Y 2J6

2. Baptist Convention of Ontario and Quebec,
   Social Action Committee,
   217 St. George St., Toronto, Ont., M5R 2M2

3. Canada Asia Working Group,
   11 Madison Ave., Toronto, Ont., M5R 2S2

4. Canadian Catholic Organization for Development and Peace
   3028 Danforth Ave., Toronto, Ont., M4C 1N2

5. Canadian Conference of Catholic Bishops,
   Episcopal Commission for Social Affairs,
   90 Parent Ave., Ottawa, Ont., K1N 7B1

6. Canadian Council of Churches,
   40 St. Clair Ave., East, Toronto, Ont., M4T 1M9

7. Evangelical Lutheran Church in Canada,
   Division for Church and Society,
   1512 St. James St., Winnipeg, Man. R3H 0L2

8. GATT-Fly,
   11 Madison Ave., Toronto, Ont., M5R 2S2

9. Inter-Church Coalition on Africa,
   129 St. Clair Ave., West, Toronto, Ont., M4V 1N5

10. Inter-Church Commission on the Social Impact
    of Resource Development,
    P.O. Box 2097, St. John's, Nfld. A1C 6E6

11. Inter-Church Committee for Refugees,
    Suite 201, 40 St. Clair Ave., East, Toronto, Ont. M4T 1M9

12. Inter-Church Committee on Human Rights in Latin America,
    Suite 201, 40 St. Clair Ave., East, Toronto, Ont. M4T 1M9

13. Inter-Church Fund for International Development,
    Suite 204, 85 St. Clair Ave. East, Toronto, Ont. M4T 1M8

14. Inter-Church Project on Population,
    c/o Bernard Daly
    90 Parent Ave., Ottawa, Ont. K1N 7B1

15. Jesuit Centre for Social Faith and Justice,
    947 Queen St. East, Toronto, Ont. M4M 1J9

16. National Inter-Faith Immigration Committee,
    67 Bond St., Toronto, Ont. M5B 1X5

17. PLURA
    c/o Mr. Roy Shepherd,
    11 Byron, New Hamburg, Ont. N0B 2G0

18. Presbyterian Church in Canada,
    Board of Congregational Life,
    50 Wynford Drive, Don Mills, Ont. M3C 3E5

19. Project North,
    80 Sackville St., Toronto, Ont. M5A 3E5

20. Project Ploughshares,
    Institute for Peace and Conflict Studies,
    Conrad Grebel College,
    University of Waterloo, Waterloo, Ont. N2L 3G6

21. Salvation Army,
    Commission on Moral and Social Standards and Issues,
    20 Albert St., Toronto, Ont. M5G 1A6

22. Taskforce on the Churches and Corporate Responsibility,
    129 St. Clair Ave., West, Toronto, Ont. M4V 1N5

23. Ten Days for World Development,
    Room 315, 85 St. Clair Ave., West, Toronto, Ont. M4T 1M8

24. United Church of Canada,
    Department of Church in Society,
    Division of Mission in Canada,
    85 St. Clair Ave., East, Toronto, Ont. M4T 1M8

INDEX OF SUBJECTS

(Documents only)

Imprimerie des Éditions Paulines
250, boul. St-François nord
Sherbrooke, Qc, J1E 2B9

Imprimé au Canada — Printed in Canada

54030

Sheridan, E. F., ed.

AUTHOR
Do justice!

TITLE